The Bundesbank

David Marsh has been writing on European political and economic affairs since 1973, when he started his career with Reuters. He joined the *Financial Times* in 1978. For four years he was the *FT*'s correspondent in Paris and then for five years the newspaper's chief correspondent in Germany, based in Bonn. He is presently the *FT*'s European Editor. He is the author of the highly acclaimed *The New Germany: At the Crossroads*.

DAVID MARSH

The Bundesbank

The Bank that Rules Europe

Mandarin

For Veronika

A Mandarin Paperback
THE BUNDESBANK

First published in Great Britain 1992
by William Heinemann Ltd
This edition published 1993
by Mandarin Paperbacks
an imprint of Reed Consumer Books Ltd
Michelin House, 81 Fulham Road, London SW3 6RB
and Auckland, Melbourne, Singapore and Toronto

A CIP catalogue record for this title
is available from the British Library
ISBN 0 7493 1138 X

Printed and bound in Great Britain
by Cox & Wyman Ltd, Reading, Berks

Contents

Photo credits:

1, 2, 3, 4, 7, 11, 12, 15, 17, 18, 19: Bundesbank
5, 8: Ullstein
6: Würsching
9: König
13: Kleinhans
14: DPA
18: Wessel

Note for the Paperback Edition

This study on the Bundesbank has been given additional topicality by the tumultuous events of September 1992: the end of Britain's 23-month-old policy of pegging sterling to the D-Mark within the European Monetary System (EMS). Britain's humiliating departure from the exchange rate mechanism was accompanied by a burst of British government flak directed at the German central bank. When the German ambassador, Hermann von Richthofen, was summoned to the Foreign Office on 1 October 1992 to explain how a Bundesbank memorandum on the crisis had been leaked to the press, Anglo-German relations appeared at a nadir. Even in the post-war period, there has been, however, a precedent. On 20 November 1968, West Germany's ambassador Herbert Blankenhorn was called in to see Prime Minister Harold Wilson in the early hours of the morning. The storm had broken over Germany's unwillingness to revalue the D-Mark – obstinacy which was feeding speculation that the pound would have to be floated. 'Wilson spoke very roughly to him. He said that the attitude of the German government was "irresponsible" and "intolerable".'*

Unlike the events of autumn 1992, that meeting never made headlines. The latest monetary upheaval reverberates across a much wider radius than a quarter of a century ago, and with correspondingly greater effect. Yet there is room for hope – as in 1968 – that both Britain and Germany will not only survive the latest bruising encounter, but also learn from it.

David Marsh, Wimbledon, November 1992

* The tale is told by Roy Jenkins, who was present during the exchange as Chancellor of the Exchequer, in *A Life at the Centre*, published in 1991.

Preface

As a target for investigation, the Bundesbank fulfils a great many supremely appropriate criteria. The German central bank is clearly of eminent importance, for the Germans and for the rest of Europe. As the lynchpin of European monetary arrangements, the Bundesbank now effectively runs British monetary policies. The central bank's name is illuminated every day in the headlines chronicling economic affairs around the continent. Little light however normally falls on the way the Bundesbank works, or on the nature of the people who run it. The Bundesbank is a national institution; and of this genre of organisation, those involved in affairs of money are often the most fascinating, and the least well understood. Without, I hope, making the Bundesbank any less intriguing, this book aims to pierce the veil which surrounds this most eminently German of institutions, and to make good that gap in understanding.

For a variety of other reasons, the Bundesbank is an enticing subject. Its links with the pre-1945 Reichsbank have seldom been exposed to rigorous analysis. Men who acquiesced in the totalitarianism of the Third Reich were absorbed with surprising ease into the Bank deutscher Länder and Bundesbank after the Second World War, and carried out their part in Germany's renewal. Although it represented, in a certain manner, an instrument of historical continuity, the Bundesbank's main importance was, indeed, as a symbol of the country's new start. The Bundesbank played a central role in West Germany's post-war economic recovery – and in its political rebirth. Without sound money, the westwards-turning 1949 republic might have been barely happier than the one whose constitution was proclaimed in Weimar.

Forty years later, the Bundesbank occupied a central, and often controversial, place in the saga of German reunification, a process set in train with the entry of the Deutsche Mark into East Germany on 1 July 1990. Political unification took place on 3 October 1990, but 'growing together' will take a generation fully to accomplish. Out of two states which – though they never lost their 'Germanness' – had grown apart, one nation is being reforged: an operation bringing stimulus, but also pain. This is not simply a question of politics and economics, but also of people; and here the Bundesbank's own history is instructive. There are certainly parallels between the experiences of the men of the Reichsbank, integrated into the republic after the war, and the saga of the functionaries of the East German communist regime now entering the life of united, democratic Germany. Like the ex-Nazi officials in the period after 1945, the ex-communists in the early 1990s are not proud of their pasts. In both cases, the natural instinct of the persons involved is to try to cover up what they did (or what they did not do) under the *ancien régime*.

Events in Germany send out ripples across the whole of the continent. German unification has speeded up the momentum behind the drive towards European political and monetary union. Yet it has also increased the obstacles on the way to that goal. Again, the Bundesbank is at the centre of the debate. The Bundesbank controls the D-Mark. But, if Europe moved – as foreseen by the Maastricht treaty – to a single currency before the end of the twentieth century, then the D-Mark would disappear. Will the institution which helped bring about German unification be sacrificed for the good of greater unity? Or will it live on regardless? This book tries to provide some answers.

This undertaking would not have been possible without the assistance of many people, inside and outside Germany. I am grateful to my colleagues on the *Financial Times*, above all its present and past editors, Richard Lambert and Sir Geoffrey Owen, for encouraging my curiosity, and giving me time to write this book.

My main helpers, of course, have been the many people on whom this book is focused: the men (only very few women have ever reached senior positions at the central bank) of the Bundesbank itself. The central bank has undoubtedly played a part in creating its own sometimes exaggerated institutional mythology. Yet it is an extremely open organisation, greatly aware of the need to present itself and its policies before the eyes of public opinion. The Bundesbank is a place where received wisdom can continually be put to the test in the cut-and-thrust of debate. During my period of contact with the Bundesbank, which started in 1974, I have virtually unfailingly been received with patience, courtesy, understanding and humour.

I am indebted above all to Karl Otto Pöhl, president between 1980 and 1991, who has given me many hours of his time over the years. It is to him that I owe my principal insights into the psychology and the politics of central banking; for the profession is as much (or more) an art involving people as a science dealing with numbers. I am grateful, too, to Helmut Schlesinger, the present president, and Hans Tietmeyer, his deputy, for their invaluable assistance during lengthy interviews, both in specific preparation for this book and as part of my normal reporting for the *Financial Times*.

I thank Manfred Körber, the head of the Bundesbank's public information department, for his unstinting help in the general preparation of this book. Dieter Lindenlaub, the head of the Bundesbank's archives department, went considerably beyond the call of duty in aiding my comprehension of Bundesbank matters, organising the collection of archival material, and commenting critically and cogently on drafts of my manuscript. My hours of conversation with him, always good humoured, always fair, on abstruse aspects of the Bundesbank's history were among the most enriching components of my research. It is to Dr Lindenlaub that I owe my frequent experiences of the Bundesbank's staff canteen.

Responsibility for the views expressed in this book – as well as for any errors – of course rests with the author.

Among past and present members of the Bundesbank council, I profited from long conversations, sometimes on several occasions over a period of years, with Leonhard Gleske, Johann Wilhelm Gaddum, Wendelin Hartmann, Hans Hermsdorf, Helmut Hesse, Dieter Hiss, Otmar Issing, Reimut Jochimsen, Norbert Kloten, Claus Köhler, Werner Lucht, Lothar Müller, Kurt Nemitz, Wilhelm Nölling, Friedrich-Wilhelm von Schelling, Johann Baptist Schöllhorn, Werner Schulz, Günter Storch and Karl Thomas. Other Bundesbank staff members to whom I extend my thanks for their comments and insights are Jürgen Becker, Thomas Buch, Bernhard Gaude, Thomas Gierenstein, Siegfried Guterman, Gerd Häusler, Klaus Hanau, Jürgen Matthiessen, Heinz-Dieter Maurer, Detlev Rahmsdorf, Wolfgang Rieke, Franz Scholl, Peter-Wilhelm Schlüter and Peter Walter.

I owe a particular debt of gratitude to former chancellor Helmut Schmidt for a number of conversations touching on the Bundesbank and its policies. I would also like to thank the following people who gave me their time and assistance appertaining to various aspects of this book: Hermann Josef Abs, Ulrich Barth, Kurt Biedenkopf, Wilfried Guth, Hellmut Hartmann, Horst Köhler, Manfred Lahnstein, Hans Matthöfer, Lothar de Maizière, Bernhard Molitor, Karl Schiller, Otto Schlecht, Horst Teltschik.

Special thanks are due to David Marwell at the Berlin Document Centre for his tireless assistance. Klaus Oldenhage and Kurt Metschies at the former East German state archives at Potsdam, now part of the Bundesarchiv, were supremely helpful, as were the staff of the main Bundesarchiv at Koblenz. I would also like to express my gratitude to Elmar Brandt and his staff at the Goethe Institute in London; Ottfried Dascher and Wilfried Reininghaus at the Westfälisches Wirtschaftsarchiv in Dortmund; and to the Bundestag library in Bonn.

I benefited from conversations with officials from the former East German Staatsbank: Horst Kaminsky, Eberhardt Geißler and Bruno Meier. My special thanks go to Walter Krüger and Wolfrid Stoll. At the Bank of England I was grateful for conversations with Robin Leigh-Pemberton and Andrew Crockett, and for the help of John Footman, Elizabeth Ogborn and Henry Gillett. At the Banque de France I enjoyed several spirited discussions with Jacques de Larosière. At the Nederlandsche Bank, I was helped by Wim Duisenberg and André Szasz. Alexandre Lamfalussy, Horst Bockelmann, Rickie Hall and Manfred Weber were of great assistance at the Bank for International Settlements. I must record my thanks to Dr Lindenlaub's colleagues in the archive department – Harald Pohl, Rolf Herget, Gerd-Christian Wannovius, Karin Fitzner and Cornelia Richter – for their support and forbearance.

I much appreciated the essential suggestions and advice of colleagues and friends who read parts of the manuscript: Hans-Peter Fröhlich, Anthony Loehnis and Holger Schmieding. Harold James supplied valuable insights into the life of Hjalmar Schacht. Johannes Puhl and Paula Muhlke helped with details of the Reichsbank. My thanks, too, to Arthur Goodhart, my agent, and Tom Weldon and Emma Rhind-Tutt at William Heinemann. Once again, my old friend Rudolf Lauer was a pillar of strength. Without my wife and daughters, this would have been neither possible nor worthwhile.

Glossary

1 **billion** 1,000 million
1 **trillion** 1,000 billion

Bank deutscher Länder. Forerunner of the Bundesbank, set up by the Allies in 1948 as the federally organised, provisional central banking institution in the western occupied zones.

Bank for International Settlements. International bank set up in 1930 to handle German reparations payments, owned by the world's most important central banks and based in Basle, Switzerland.

Bundesbank. Established to replace the Bank deutscher Länder with the passing of the Bundesbank Law in July 1957.

Central bank council (Zentralbankrat). Principal organ of Bundesbank decision-making. Consists of the seven members of the Bundesbank's Frankfurt-based directorate together with the 9 heads of the *Land* central banks in united Germany. A reorganisation which came into effect in November 1992 cut the number of *Land* central banks. The nine *Land* bankers have their headquarters in the following *Länder*: Baden-Württemberg, Bavaria, Berlin, Hamburg, Hesse, Lower Saxony, North Rhine-Westphalia, Rhineland-Palatinate, Saxony.

Deutsche Mark (DM). West German currency, set up in June 1948. Became the currency of East and West Germany (then two separate states) on 1 July 1990.

Directorate (Direktorium). Frankfurt-based executive board of Bank deutscher Länder and Bundesbank. Members have sat on Zentralbankrat since 1958.

Discount rate. Interest rate at which Bundesbank lends to banks through 'rediscounting' trade bills and Treasury bills falling due within three months.

East Mark (EM). Inconvertible East German currency. Came to an end on 1 July 1990.

5

European Monetary System (EMS). Exchange rate stabilisation scheme started in March 1979, under which most European Community currencies move within fixed fluctuation bands against each other.

European economic and monetary union (Emu). Plan to fix irrevocably European exchange rates, in a system run by a European central bank. First proposed 1962, with goal reiterated in 1970, and then abandoned. Proposed again in Maastricht treaty.

Land central bank (*Landeszentralbank*). Central bank in German federal state (*Land*). The *Land* central banks were established after the Second World War, based on the old Reichsbank network, as the basic components of the central banking system in western Germany.

Lombard rate. Interest rate at which the Bundesbank extends credit to commercial banks to bridge temporary financing gaps. Banks deposit securities with the Bundesbank as collateral.

Maastricht treaty. Agreed by EC leaders in December 1991. Foresaw European monetary union by 1999 at the latest. Ratification held up in 1992.

Minimum reserves. Specific proportion of commercial banks' liabilities, maintained in interest-free deposits at the Bundesbank as a way of controlling banking liquidity.

Open market policies. Purchases and sales of securities by the Bundesbank in trading with banks. Used to 'fine tune' interest rate policies.

Rediscount quotas. Total amount of credit which can be granted to commercial banks through rediscounting of bills. Volume set by central bank council.

Reichsbank. Established under the Banking Act of March 1875. Started operating on 1 January 1876 to run the Mark, the currency of the united German state established in 1871.

Reichsmark (RM). Currency established at the end of 1923 and beginning of 1924 to replace the Mark after the great German inflation.

Securities repurchases. Transactions under which Bundesbank grants short-term loans to banking system. Commercial banks sell to Bundesbank fixed interest securities, and simultaneously buy them back for forward settlement.

Staatsbank. East German central bank. Central banking functions ceased with German reunification.

Dramatis personae

Adenauer, Konrad. West German chancellor, 1949–63.

Bernard, Karl. President, Bank deutscher Länder council, 1948–57.

Blessing, Karl. Reichsbank directorate member 1937–39. Bundesbank president 1958–69.

Emminger, Otmar. Bundesbank vice-president 1970–77, president 1977–79.

Erhard, Ludwig. West German economics minister 1949–63, chancellor 1963–66.

Funk, Walther. Reichsbank president 1939–45.

Havenstein, Rudolf. Reichsbank president 1908–23.

Hitler, Adolf. German chancellor 1933–45.

Honecker, Erich. East German communist party first secretary 1971–89.

Klasen, Karl. Bundesbank president 1970–77.

Kohl, Helmut. West German chancellor 1982–90. German chancellor 1990–.

Luther, Hans. German finance minister 1923–25. German chancellor 1925–26. Reichsbank president 1930–33.

Pöhl, Karl Otto. Bundesbank vice-president 1977–79, president 1980–91.

Schacht, Hjalmar. Reichsbank president 1923–30, 1933–39.

Schlesinger, Helmut. Bundesbank vice-president 1980–91, president 1991–93 (foreseen).

Schmidt, Helmut. West German chancellor 1974–82.

Tietmeyer, Hans. Bundesbank vice-president 1991–93, president 1993– (foreseen).

Vocke, Wilhelm. Reichsbank directorate member 1919–39. President, Bank deutscher Länder directorate, 1948–57.

Waigel, Theo. West German finance minister 1989–90. German finance minister 1990– .

7

1

The Hub of Europe

> If many people today have a bad memory and forget the
> terrible distress of 1923, then I must assure you that my
> memory is not so short . . . A stable currency is the condition
> for our daily bread.
> *Hans Luther, Reichsbank president, 1931*[1]

> There can be no hard currency without hard measures.
> *Karl Blessing, Bundesbank president, 1966*[2]

> Since German unification, our role and our weight in Europe
> have changed. Germany is the model at which our
> neighbours in East and West are looking . . . Our currency,
> and the central bank which is responsible for it, are
> becoming, if anything, still more important.
> *Karl Otto Pöhl, Bundesbank president, 1991*[3]

In the autumn of 1960, a tongue-in-cheek article in Britain's pink-coloured business newspaper produced red faces at the Bundesbank's Frankfurt headquarters – and sent a burst of amusement down the austere corridors of the Bank of England. Willy Tomberg, an official in the Bundesbank's foreign department, mistook an ironic passage in the often eccentric Lombard column of the *Financial Times* for something of altogether deeper significance. The Deutsche Bundesbank ('German Federal Bank') had been created in 1957, only three years previously. It was the successor to the Bank deutscher Länder, the institution set up by the US and Britain* in 1948 to serve as the provisional central bank in the western occupied zones of ruined, defeated and humiliated Germany. Though the post-war 'economic miracle' was in full swing, Germany was still a divided country, and the Bundesbank was only a junior player in the international financial league. For a representative of this humble monetary newcomer, puzzled by a

---

* The Bank deutscher Länder ('Bank of German States') was extended later to the French zone. See chapter 6.

British financial riddle, what more natural reaction than to seek advice from the titans of Threadneedle Street?

Tomberg wrote a meekly inquisitive letter to Donald Thomson at the Bank of England's Overseas Department: 'I read an article in the *Financial Times* about an "Academy for Central Bankers" at Hetheringstoke, the head of which is Mr Gressing Vocham. Could you please give me some detailed informations [sic] about this institute, in particular whether it is of public or private character.' Tomberg added politely: 'I would further like to know whether regular lectures are given and – if that is the case – whether these lectures are arranged in certain terms, say four weeks or three months. I would also like to hear your opinion whether it would be of some use if people of our bank take part in these lectures.'[4]

When Tomberg's inquiry crossed the Bank of England's portals, the revelation that the Bundesbank had fallen for a schoolboyish hoax in the City's parish newspaper brought a rare outbreak of mirth to the Old Lady's pursed lips. Thomson was told by one of his colleagues: 'I don't know if Tomberg has a sense of humour but you may have fun in putting to him that the "Academy of Central Bankers" is not quite what he thinks it is!' The Tomberg letter was sent to the deputy governor, with the remark, 'I think you may care to see this letter from Tomberg of the Bundesbank, with its terrifying implications. I have told Thomson that this is a letter which cannot be answered in writing and that he must do his best to save Tomberg's face on the telephone.'

Lord Cobbold, the governor of the Bank of England, was quickly alerted to the Bundesbank's communication. It clearly provided a pleasant diversion from worrying about sterling. Cobbold, who had been a key figure on the British side when the Bank deutscher Länder was set up in 1948,* penned a dry gubernatorial missive to Lord Drogheda, chief executive of the *Financial Times*:

My dear Drogheda,
I thought I must pass on to you this morning's joke (not of course for any form of publication or reference in print!). One of our people has had the attached letter from a friend in a Central Bank abroad. When it was sent in to me I thought

* See chapter 6.

somebody was having fun, but I am assured that it is a perfectly
serious enquiry! Bless me.
Yours sincerely
C. F. Cobbold

Drogheda, too, could not resist the opportunity for a little aristo-
cratic jocularity at the Bundesbank's expense. 'The puckish Lombard will be tickled pink to know that he is taken so seriously,' the
F.T. chief executive replied to the governor. 'I am sure that he
would be delighted to arrange a private course for the central
banker concerned!'

Everyone enjoyed the *Schadenfreude*. The confusion, small as it
was, did nobody any harm. The episode gave comforting support
to the Bank of England's quiet sense of moral superiority over
foreigners in general – and Germans in particular. In 1960, Britain
could still relish the taste of hard-won victory in the Second World
War. No one in London realised that the next battle for Europe
was already under way; and that it would be decided not by force
of arms, but by the power of German money.

i. Wider than the Reich

Three decades later, the Bundesbank is no longer a laughing
matter. Of its prestige and professionalism, its pride and potency,
there is no doubt. The Bundesbank has replaced the Wehrmacht
as Germany's best-known and best-feared institution. From Tokyo
to Toronto, from Bogota to Budapest, the bank's very name is a
watchword for anti-inflationary rectitude. Its counsels find grave
and attentive listeners at the tables of the mighty; and its writ runs
wide. As the guardian of the Deutsche Mark, the quintessential
strong currency which became the symbol of Germany's post-war
recovery, the Bundesbank holds sway across a larger area of Europe
than any German Reich in history.

Statutorily independent from government, the Bundesbank is no
ordinary central bank. Its field of action is politics as much as
economics. The bank is embroiled in a lengthy tussle with the Bonn
government over the economic consequences of German unification.
One of the larger questions is whether the Bundesbank – eventually,
with East Germans sitting on its governing council (Zentralbankrat) –
will prove as successful in running monetary policies for the whole of

Germany as it has been for the western part of the nation. Germany's post-unification financial strains have been the main cause of high Bundesbank interest rates at the beginning of the 1990s – the main factor behind Britain's ignominious departure from the European exchange rate mechanism in September 1992. The Bundesbank is also at the centre of extraordinary political turbulence over the European Community's project for European monetary union (Emu). This is the plan to introduce a single European currency by the end of the century – a proposal which would go further than the gold standard and the post-war Bretton Woods system in irrevocably fixing exchange rates. Everywhere, the message is clear: those who trifle with the Bundesbank do so at their peril. For the Bank of England, the Bundesbank has long ceased to be the butt of gentlemanly jokes.

The Bundesbank's direct monetary command spreads across reunified Germany, the world's third most important economy, and the home of one-quarter of the European Community's gross national product. Its sphere of influence, however, stretches far beyond Germany's enlarged borders. The Bundesbank has taken over from national governments as the driving force behind monetary policy across Europe, a region accounting for roughly one-third of world economic output. This is a consequence both of Germany's economic muscle and of the D-Mark's pivotal role within Europe's exchange rate stabilisation scheme, the European Monetary System (EMS). By joining the exchange rate mechanism (ERM) of the EMS in 1990, the British constrained sterling to follow the fluctuations of the D-Mark, set by the guiding hand of the Bundesbank.*

As chancellor of the exchequer in October 1990, the last month of Margaret Thatcher's eleven and a half years in office, John Major powerfully contributed to breaking down Thatcher's long-standing resistance to forging the D-Mark link. The Conservative government finally abandoned years of discredited home-grown efforts to curb price rises through domestic monetarism. Instead, it handed over to the Bundesbank the task of bringing down British inflation to German levels. Major was aware that submission to Germanic discipline would be painful. The inventor of the phrase, 'If it's not hurting, it's not working,' Major once described the ERM as 'a modern-day gold standard with the D-Mark as the anchor.'[5]

---

* See chapters 7, 9.

Major had little idea, however, just how painful the experience would be. The Bundesbank's interest rate increases in 1991 and 1992 considerably handicapped Britain's efforts to ease the cost of credit, adding to the severity of the UK's longest recession since the 1930s. Eventually, the pound buckled. Less than two years after entry, sterling left the ERM on 'Black Wednesday' – 16 September 1992 – following a catastrophic day on the foreign exchanges in which Britain's official foreign exchange reserves fell by an estimated £10 billion. On the evening of 16 September, after the announcement that the pound's membership of the ERM was being 'suspended', Downing Street officials lambasted the Bundesbank for having 'talked down' the pound. Norman Lamont, Major's chancellor of the exchequer, had dutifully geared monetary policy towards maintaining sterling's central DM2.95 parity. After being forced into what amounted to a large devaluation, Lamont now broadcast a different line. 'We are floating and we will set monetary policy in this country to meet our objectives and it will be a British economic policy and a British monetary policy.'[6] One of the most notable U-turns in British economic history was complete. And, on one point, there was no quarrel. The 16 members* of the Bundesbank's Zentralbankrat who discuss German interest rates every fortnight in Frankfurt clearly had more economic clout than all Her Majesty's ministers and mandarins put together.

The D-Mark's function as the lynchpin of the EMS plainly increased in importance as a result of West Germany's greatly improved economic performance in the second half of the 1980s. The Federal Republic's economic dynamism was, in turn, an important factor behind the momentum towards German unification which built up in 1989 and, in 1990, became unstoppable. Abruptly leaving the economic doldrums of the early 1980s, between 1986 and 1990 West Germany registered an annual average growth rate of 3.1 per cent, with inflation kept down to only 1.4 per cent – and chalked up a current account surplus averaging 4 per cent of gross national product.† Easily outstripping most of its European partners, this was the country's best overall economic showing since the 1960s.

If the Bundesbank finds itself at the centre of attention, events

* Lowered from 18 to 16 in November 1992
† See Appendix.

within Germany provide just part of the explanation. A series of far-reaching international developments has thrust the Bundesbank into the world spotlight:

- The European Community has decreed that the mooted European central bank which will operate European monetary union should be set up on the same lines as the independent Bundesbank. Germany has persuaded the rest of the Community to base the plan for a single European currency on strict anti-inflation principles. But since the proposed Euro-bank would supersede the Bundesbank as the institution in control of European money, the project is the object of intense Bundesbank distaste. The Emu scheme will attract renewed controversy during the 1990s. It looks set to provide the sternest test of the Community's cohesion since the signing of the Treaty of Rome in 1957.

- The liberation of formerly communist eastern Europe, culminating in the break-up of the Soviet Union, has heightened the Bundesbank's standing in the struggling eastern half of the continent. This is expressed by the growing use of the D-Mark as a 'parallel' transaction and investment currency in eastern Europe. The Bundesbank's commitment to sound money played a vital part in Germany's post-war metamorphosis from totalitarianism to a prosperous free market democracy. Hoping to accomplish the same result, a range of countries in eastern Europe, as well as in the Third World, have been remodelling their central banks on Bundesbank lines as part of efforts to implement a German-style 'social market economy'.[7]

- West Germany's industrial efficiency and strong foreign trade performance turned it during the 1980s into the world's second most important creditor nation after Japan. At the same time, reflecting the international attractiveness of the D-Mark, foreign investors greatly increased their holdings of the currency. Both developments considerably buttressed the Bundesbank's position on the world monetary stage. Although the Bundesbank for a long time resisted the use of the D-Mark in official foreign exchange reserves, the D-Mark during the 1970s took over sterling's traditional role as the world's Number 2 reserve currency after the US dollar. During the subsequent decade, the Germans bowed to the inevitable, and accepted the desire of foreign central banks to build up D-Mark assets. At the end of 1991, reserve holdings of D-Marks totalled DM229 billion, 18 per cent of world currency reserves. Overall D-Mark assets held by foreigners amounted to more than DM1 trillion – three times the level of 1980.[8]

• The internationalisation of the D-Mark symbolises Germany's financial virility; but it also greatly complicates the running of monetary policy. The weight of foreign holdings of D-Marks on world banking and bond markets makes the Bundesbank's task of controlling the D-Mark much less straightforward than if it were in charge of a purely 'domestic' currency. During a period of uncertainty about the direction of economic policy, the Bundesbank has to redouble efforts to keep money tight – as happened in 1991–92 – in order to maintain the confidence of foreign investors.

• The failure of US and British attempts to provide radical free-market routes to non-inflationary growth has furnished a further important reason for world-wide interest in the German model of economic management. At the beginning of the 1990s, the Bundesbank faces massive problems caused by sharp economic imbalances between the two highly disparate parts of the united German economy. However, compared with the setbacks faced by policy-makers in other industrialised nations, the Bundesbank's achievements during the 1980s look like a convincing record of success.

ii. Ensconced on the throne

All this has clearly boosted the Bundesbank's renown – and its role as an international yardstick for economic management. When an institution as powerful as the Japanese finance ministry trumpets the case of fiscal conservatism, it describes itself not by reference to Reaganomics or Thatcherism, but in terms of its aspiration to become 'the Bundesbank of Japan'.[9] Yet there has been no parallel increase in understanding of how the Bundesbank works. No other monetary institution is the focus of so much mythology and mystification.

In the eyes of the outside world, the Bundesbank embodies a unique mix of characteristics. Venerated for its attachment to financial orthodoxy, yet vilified for its obstinate penchant for standing up to governments at home and abroad, it is deity and demon combined. The US Federal Reserve may be mightier, and the Bank of Japan more inscrutable. But neither matches the Bundesbank's independence, nor its pride in taking unpopular decisions which can send financial tremors around the globe. Only the International

Monetary Fund, alternatively revered as a worker of miracles and berated as the scourge of Third World debtors, comes close to rivalling the Bundesbank's chill international image.

Of European central banks, most of the larger ones – including the Bank of England – are under direct government control. Several smaller central banks, in the Netherlands, Switzerland and Sweden, for instance, are, like the Bundesbank, independent from their governments. As a result of differences in their legal statutes and traditions, in few of them does the determination to operate *Stabilitätspolitik* ('stability policy') run quite so deep. And, in framing their monetary strategies, the other central banks are almost universally constrained to follow policies made in Frankfurt.

Although ensconced on the throne of European money, the bank is not without rivals who resent its supremacy – and seek to pull it down. An important motive behind the campaign for Emu is the desire of other European countries – particularly France – to weaken the Bundesbank's monetary predominance. French enthusiasm for a single European currency and a European central bank is founded on the desire to shackle the D-Mark – and, eventually, to bring about its demise.

The question of uniting Europe's currencies is emerging as a potent force for European division. France's tactics confront Chancellor Helmut Kohl with a serious dilemma. On the one hand, he wants to maintain the goal of European political and monetary union to assuage his neighbours' fears that a strong unified Germany will threaten European stability. On the other hand, for both political and economic reasons, Kohl does not want to take away the stable pillar of the D-Mark at a time when the German economy is already facing great post-unity strains.

At the Maastricht summit in December 1991, Kohl was forced to agree to a plan promoted by the French and Italian governments to introduce a single European currency by 1999. The Bundesbank's unease over seeing the D-Mark replaced by a new, untried European currency is shared by a large majority of the German electorate. The central bank has served notice that it will not be dislodged from its pedestal without a fight. Just over a week after the summit, in a defiant gesture to show that it was redoubling its anti-inflation efforts, the bank raised Germany's official interest rates to their highest levels since the 1930s. This increase was necessary to curb the inflationary impact of high German budget deficits. But it helped prolong a period of high unemployment and slow growth across the whole of the continent – a contributory factor behind political turbulence in several important countries. The stern monetary message was repeated in July 1992 when the Bundesbank again raised its discount rate – a move which added to growing economic weakness in Germany itself, as the economy slowed dramatically after the 1989–90 unification boom. The central bank does not want to – and cannot – sabotage European monetary union directly. But Emu will be practicable only if it commands a Europe-wide political consensus. If, as a result of the Bundesbank's stern guiding hand, the route map for the journey to Emu starts to look increasingly like a charter for deflation, political opposition may ensure that the destination will never be reached.

iii. 'We are arrogant because we are good'

The Bundesbank spreads its doctrine of monetary probity not only through its decision-making rigour, but also through the compulsion of logic and argument. The past two decades have yielded remarkable success. Insistence on Bundesbank-style *Stabilitätspolitik* now forms the core of international economic policy. Since the late 1970s, the conviction has been enshrined in a thousand summit communiqués and ministerial declarations. Bundesbank officials are the evangelists of world finance. As they sometimes admit, arrogance is not far below the surface. One Bundesbank representative once put it, with commendable straightforwardness: 'We are arrogant because we are good.' At international monetary conferences, Bundesbank functionaries never look crumpled, like the French, or harassed, like the British, or out of their depth, like the Americans. The Bundesbankers are secure in the knowledge that, by defying inflation, they are pursuing the brightest and most meaningful lodestar in the sky. Their devout wish is that others, too, will follow.

Whenever the Bundesbank irritates other countries by increasing interest rates at an inopportune moment, it has a standard response: beating inflation serves the interests not just of Germany, but of the whole of Europe. The proximate cause for the post-Maastricht increase in interest rates was the rise in German inflation to beyond 4 per cent: but the Bundesbank had Europe at the forefront of its mind. Helmut Schlesinger, the long-serving Bavarian economist who has been Bundesbank president since August 1991, put forward the following all-encompassing justification for the action: 'The D-Mark is currently the leading currency in Europe, and it would not be in the interest [of our neighbours] if the Mark became a currency of inflation.'[10]

The December 1991 and July 1992 interest rate increases marked a watershed. Most countries in the rest of Europe – above all, Britain and France – had been seeking to lower the cost of credit to ease their way out of recession. Never had the Bundesbank flexed its monetary muscles at quite so inconvenient a time. The central bank was however acting true to a pattern established two decades earlier. The Bundesbank came of age in March 1973, when the post-war Bretton Woods system of fixed world exchange rates finally collapsed. The arrival of floating exchange rates freed the bank from absorbing disruptive currency inflows through obligatory dollar purchases to maintain the rate between the dollar and the D-Mark. This allowed the Bundesbank, for the first time, to concentrate fully on the objective of holding down price rises. In 1974, the Bundesbank was the first central bank to tighten credit to counter the inflationary impact of the sharp rise in the price of oil after the Yom Kippur war in October 1973. Ever since, it has maintained its reputation for decisive action to nip inflation in the bud.

Foreshadowing the anti-inflation rationale subsequently propagated by governments throughout the world, the Bundesbank invented the slogan 'There is no alternative' early in the 1970s. A 1975 statement from the central bank contains the phrase which became one of the prime tenets of Thatcherism:

> In its monetary policy for 1974 the Bundesbank primarily pursued the aim of reversing the price trend by limiting monetary expansion . . . This stabilisation process did not take place without exacting a price from the economy as a whole and without sacrifices for individuals. The only justification for these sacrifices was that there was no real alternative to the stabilisation policy.[11]

If western leaders now universally recognise that inflation 'does not cure unemployment, but rather is one of its causes', they are faithfully repeating the Bundesbank's creed. This phrase became part of the litany of international policy-making as long ago as 1977. It was inserted into the communiqué after the London economic summit of the world's top seven industrialised countries, at the behest of Karl Otto Pöhl, the Bundesbank's mercurial president between 1980 and 1991, who was then one of Chancellor Helmut Schmidt's senior summit advisers.[12]

Price stability, in a precise sense, has seldom, if ever, been reached. For all the Bundesbank's relative success in minimising German inflation, the D-Mark has lost two-thirds of its value since 1948. The Bundesbank's long-term aim is to maintain average inflation at about 2 per cent a year – the same level as in the 1950s and 1960s. Since the breakdown of Bretton Woods, the average West German inflation rate fell from 6 per cent in the first half of the 1970s to 4 per cent at the beginning of the 1980s, and only 1 per cent towards the end of the 1980s. The renewed rise in inflation to 4 per cent in the early 1990s thus confronted the Bundesbank with its greatest challenge for a generation.

iv. A product of history

Like all national institutions, the Bundesbank is a product of history: in Germany's case, a singularly tortuous tale. The bank's abiding nightmare – exaggerated though it might often seem – remains the hyper-inflation of 1923. 'Never again!' is the Bundesbank's rallying cry. It knows that the one sure way to lose its reputation is to err on the side of pecuniary laxity. One of the most fascinating of the Bundesbank's accomplishments has been its ability to remind the German public continually of the cautionary lessons of the great inflation seventy years ago, yet to cover up the awkward or embarrassing traces of more recent central banking history.

The Bundesbank was born in 1957. It is not, however, a completely new institution. Its roots stretch back to before the Second World War. The Bank deutscher Länder, set up by the Allies during the post-war occupation, was transformed into the Bundesbank in July 1957. This was the result of the passage of the Bundesbank Law, which refashioned the central bank's legal status to meet the requirements of a country allowed again to run its own affairs.[13] The legislation, brought on to the statute book after years of political deliberations, maintained the bank as a federally organised body. It also confirmed its independence from government. But the Law increased the powers of the executive board – the directorate (Direktorium) – compared with the representatives on the governing

council of the German provinces, the federal states or *Länder*.*
Henceforth, the members of the directorate as well as the chiefs
of the *Land* central banks sat on the governing council – a crucial
change strengthening the trend for the bank to be run more from
the centre in Frankfurt than from the regions.

In spite of the bank's statutory independence, the Bonn government saw its role strengthened. Whereas the Bank deutscher Länder
had been owned by the central banks of the *Länder*, ownership of the
Bundesbank passed to the central government, which henceforth
had the power to appoint the president and the other members of
the directorate. The *Land* central banks, which previously had the
right to choose the president of the governing Zentralbankrat and
his deputy, became subsumed into the overall Bundesbank organisation. As the years went by, rivalry between the *Länder* banks and
the central directorate spurted occasionally into the headlines; it
came to a head in 1990–92, during the dramatic events connected
with German unification and European monetary union.

The statutory autonomy of the post-war central bank represented
a far-reaching change. But in some other key areas, characteristics
of the Bundesbank and the Bank deutscher Länder were inherited
from the pre-1945 Reichsbank. So were a large proportion of the
leading personnel. Above all because of the prescripts of the western
Allies, several prominent non-Nazis from outside the Reichsbank
were appointed immediately after the war to the top echelons of
the Bank deutscher Länder. Later, however, the followers of the
ancien régime made their way back. Thirty-nine per cent of the
officials who sat on the executive and governing boards of the Bank
deutscher Länder, the *Land* central banks and the Bundesbank
between 1948 and 1980[14] were former members of the Nazi party.
Their decisions to join the party had been prompted, on the whole,
more by opportunism than by conviction. None the less, these men
– like the ex-communist functionaries still holding positions of
influence in today's eastern Germany – could hardly claim to be
standard-bearers for the new democracy.

The Bundesbank's independence adds palpably to its self-confidence – one of the chief differences compared with the deferential
Reichsbank. The anti-inflation rhetoric used by successive generations at the Bank deutscher Länder and the Bundesbank shows

* See chapter 6.

Nazi party membership of leading officials

	Total number	*of whom, ex-Nazis*	
1948			
Bank deutscher Länder			
council	13	1	(8%)
council & directorate	18	3	(17%)
1958			
Bundesbank			
council	19	5	(26%)
council & *Land* boards	34	13	(38%)
1968			
Bundesbank			
council	20	8	(40%)
council & *Land* boards	34	18	(53%)
1978			
Bundesbank			
council	19	2	(11%)
council & *Land* boards	34	6	(18%)
1948–1980 (cumulative)			
Bank deutscher Länder			
& Bundesbank			
council, directorate & Land			
boards	126	49	(39%)

however intriguing similarities with the conventional economic wisdom of the 1930s and 1940s: a sign of how *Stabilitätspolitik* transcends the boundaries between dictatorship and democracy. In spite of an increasingly reckless course of reflation and rearmament, Nazi Germany – with spectacular inconsistency – sought to maintain monetary stability of the type formerly associated with the gold standard. Adolf Hitler came to power promising greater devotion to the cause of currency stability than any other government leader in world history. His insistence, like his failure, was overwhelming.

The aim of *Stabilität* was first propounded under the empire of the Kaisers. To emphasise that the Third Reich would not be treading the disastrous 1923 route to hyper-inflation, after Hitler took over in 1933 the cause of 'stability' was perpetually propounded on the German airwaves and in the columns of the Nazi-controlled press. It was even advanced by the Reichsbank to justify marching into foreign countries and taking over their central banks. The phrase 'no experiments' – much used after the war to describe West Germany's commitment to financial orthodoxy – was first employed in the 1930s.* In popular parlance, following a tradition initiated at the beginning of the century, the Reichsbank was termed the *Hüterin* of the Mark.[15] The same word – whose meaning in English is a combination of 'defender', 'guardian' and 'shepherd' – is used today to describe the Bundesbank.

Most of the former Nazis who afterwards found employment at the Bank deutscher Länder wanted to forget as quickly as possible the service they had rendered to totalitarianism. They succeeded. Most managed to bury their past beneath the detritus of the Third Reich. They co-existed in surprising harmony with another batch of Bundesbankers – those who had suffered moderate oppression from the Nazi regime. In this latter category were a number of early members of the Bank deutscher Länder council and directorate who had Jewish wives, as well as a few who had stood up to the more obvious inanities of Hitlerian economics.

The sheer task of surviving Germany's vicissitudes before and after 1945 left scars even on the most astute and adaptable of central banking functionaries. The men who crossed to the Bank deutscher Länder had been forced to adjust to the deprivations of depression, dictatorship and defeat; immediately after the war, several of them suffered periods of imprisonment at the hands of the victors. It was not simply the Russians who acquired a reputation for brutality. Karl Blessing,† the ambitious Nazi technocrat who became the first president of the Bundesbank, was beaten up in an American post-war detention camp.[16]

In the new democratic West Germany, officials like Blessing won the same plaudits for promoting sound money as they had received while proclaiming the same goal during the Third Reich. The difference was that they were a great deal more successful.

* See chapter 4.
† See chapters 2 and 4.

Functionaries who had formerly acquiesced in totalitarianism, like those who had fallen foul of it, found in the Bundesbank a welcome haven; gratefully, they closed ranks and concentrated on the new job in hand.

v. The end of the cadres

The men of the Reichsbank formed a technocratic cadre which persisted – above all at the directorate level – in the early years of post-war central banking, but now no longer exists. The present structure of Bundesbank officialdom is much more heterogeneous. Unlike the élite groups who traditionally sit at the levers of corporate or government power in Britain, France or the US, today's Bundes-bankers do not stem from a common background. The men of the governing council, on the whole, have been given no special advantages by education, privilege, class or family connections. Germany is a more obvious meritocracy than many of its competitors: there is no equivalent to the Oxford and Cambridge network, nor to the US Ivy League, nor to the ubiquitous French circuit of Polytechnique and Ecole Nationale d'Administration graduates.

Three officials who have occupied the helm of the Bundesbank since the 1980s – Schlesinger, his predecessor Pöhl, and the dour Westphalian vice-president Hans Tietmeyer – all come from remarkably humble families. Pöhl, for instance, spent his boyhood in poverty. The trio are men of vastly different character and tem-perament; but they share the experience of having made their own way to the top in an uncertain world. If there is one characteristic linking those who have ascended the Bundesbank heights, it is, indeed, a curious clannishness: of disparate men who have often been united by different forms of adversity.

This factor has certainly strengthened the bank's independent-mindedness over the years, and its belief in its own righteousness. To describe this curious phenomenon of stubborn institutional independence, Bundesbank insiders, with grim historical relish, draw on the saga of Henry II's chancellor Thomas à Becket, who opposed the King after he was made Archbishop of Canterbury – and was murdered for his pains. The process under which outsiders brought into the bank often end up conforming far more than expected to the straight-and-narrow principles of *Stabilitätspolitik* is known within the Bundesbank as 'the Becket effect'.[17] Like the erstwhile archbishop, the Bundesbank normally expects to win its tussles with the government; and, like Becket, too, its self-confidence can sometimes be over-stretched.*

vi. Pragmatism and survival

Many believe that Germany is the repository of rigid thinking; yet one of the Bundesbank's most important characteristics is pragmatism. In steering its way through the monetary shoals of the 1990s, the Bundesbank will draw upon flexibility and resilience in equal measure.

The Bundesbank shows its adaptability to outside events in its approach to monetarism. Whatever their reputation for orthodoxy, the men of the Bundesbank are far from being unbending monetarists – even though they played a pioneering role during the 1970s in setting annual targets for controlling the growth of the money supply. The central bank adopted the practice at the end of 1974, as a new control mechanism to guide the economy following the collapse of fixed exchange rates. This was several years before similar moves by central banks in Britain, the US and France. The Bundesbank establishes the target for the M3 definition of the money supply every December on the basis of forecast economic performance during the following twelve months. Normally, it has been able to predict a fairly accurate relationship between the extra amount of money flowing into the economy, and the increase in prices and output produced as a result. From the political point of view, the Bundesbank can justify the exercise as an additional tool to help the country come near to achieving the economic ideals set down in the 1967 Stability and Growth law. Under this legislation, introduced in the hope of providing a panoply of macroeconomic instruments to deal with future downturns similar to the 1966–67 recession, the government attempts to achieve price stability, a high level of employment, balance of payments equilibrium and 'appropriate' economic growth. On the whole, the Bundesbank regards the money supply as simply one of a series of economic variables it attempts to keep under control, along with the exchange rate and inflation figures.

* See chapter 7.

The Bundesbank is well used to handling one particular dilemma arising out of its anti-inflation doctrine: the need to balance the sometimes conflicting objectives of price and exchange rate stability. A stable exchange rate may be of great benefit to the exporters on which Germany's wealth ultimately depends; in order to meet its prime goal of keeping down domestic price rises, the Bundesbank however much prefers permanent gentle upwards pressure on the D-Mark. By reducing import prices, this offers a classic defence against inflation 'imported' from abroad. During periods of sharp fluctuations in exchange rates, the Bundesbank has often had to find a mid-course between the competing requirements of 'external' and 'internal' monetary stability. The bank would never be so foolish as to constrain itself by fixing firm money supply targets over a period of several years, as the Thatcher government tried to do after 1979 with its ill-thought-out and ultimately abandoned Medium Term Financial Strategy. As long ago as 1980, a senior Bundesbank official bluntly told a House of Commons select committee that setting targets for more than one year ahead was 'unrealistic'.[18]

If deemed necessary – for instance, if inflation is falling fast, or the exchange rate is strong – the Bundesbank simply overrides the money supply target set the previous December. During the seventeen years between 1975 and 1991, the Bundesbank achieved its annual monetary goal nine times and exceeded it (sometimes only very slightly) on eight occasions.* The tendency towards over-shooting gathered pace in 1992, when, for the first time, the Bundesbank recorded a very sharp rise in money supply for reasons which it could not properly explain.[19] The Bundesbank regards combating inflation not as an exact science, but as an art, where judgment always has to take precedence over monetary technicalities. At several points in its history, the Bundesbank erred by putting its foot on the monetary brakes too late, exacerbating the size of the economic slowdown it subsequently produced. It is unlikely, however, that pursuit of slavish monetarism would have produced better results.

Karl Otto Pöhl used to quip that the central bank only took its monetary targets seriously when it was seeking an additional excuse for a decision to put up interest rates. Around the time of the

* See Appendix.

December 1991 interest rate increase, the central bank indeed put unusual emphasis on the surging German money supply as a means of justifying the unpopular decision to tighten credit. In 1992, however, money supply growth continued to soar well beyond the Bundesbank's target range. The central bank was forced to concede that it had no chance of meeting its target for the twelve months under review – a serious setback to its monetary credibility.

Flexibility and pragmatism have also been necessary over the question of the Bundesbank's independence from government. The Bundesbank has always known that its statutes neither give the bank full protection from government interference, nor provide the country with a complete guarantee of monetary stability. 'The regulations of the Bank Law alone are not sufficient to assure a successful monetary policy. The most decisive factor is the way they are deployed by the men responsible for the German currency,' declared Karl Blessing in 1960.[20] Somewhat more pithily, when asked about the Bundesbank's power, Pöhl quoted Stalin's ironic remark, 'How many divisions has the Pope?' He meant that the Bundesbank's greatest support came not from the statute book, but from the reputation it enjoyed in public opinion, together with the competence of the men in charge. The experience of the Reichsbank – which presided over ruinous inflation in 1923 when it was nominally autonomous – provided ample evidence that independence alone is not enough to assure stability.

In a strict sense, the field in which the central bank can unambiguously apply its independence is rather narrow. Its competence is massively concentrated on monetary policy. Its ambit extends neither to fiscal matters nor to social or wage policies; the government even sets the level of salaries paid to the Bundesbank's own staff. The Bundesbank is not directly involved in either banking supervision or affairs of industrial policy. Its massive annual profits, DM14.4 billion in 1991, stemming from its net interest receipts,[21] are channelled automatically to the government, and the Bundesbank has no influence on how the money is spent. The government, not the central bank, has the final say over decisions on the exchange rate. Whenever the D-Mark has been revalued, both under the Bretton Woods system and under the European Monetary System, the finance minister, not the Bundesbank, makes the ultimate decision. Tussles over the exchange rate have frequently been a source of discord with Bonn – and were of particular significance in the 1990 dispute over German monetary union.*

The Bundesbank Law's celebrated commitment to monetary stability, too, is capable of differing interpretations. In its early years, the central bank's task of fighting inflation was occasionally overshadowed by its commitment to maintain the external stability of the D-Mark. This was an instinct partly inherited from the period of the gold standard and the 1930s dogma of the Reichsbank. The shift towards a policy giving unambiguous priority to maximising price stability came only towards the end of the Bretton Woods system, when the commitment to steady exchange rates was necessarily downgraded.

Despite the sporadic disagreements with Bonn, there is substantial logic to dividing up economic responsibilities between the government and the Bundesbank. German politicians have a strong interest in seeing that unpopular monetary measures are carried out by a body responding not to the exigencies of the electoral timetable, but to the overall objective of monetary stability. The finance ministry knows that the threat of higher Bundesbank interest rate action can have a helpful impact on budget policy, by forcing discipline on high-spending government departments. When the Bundesbank increases interest rates, the action seldom draws public criticism from Bonn; the finance minister realises that, in the eyes of the electorate, this would be a sign of weakness. Politically, the most appropriate reaction is nearly always to compliment the Bundesbank on its firmness.

This has been a successful and enduringly Germanic system of handling monetary affairs. Under European monetary union, everything would change. The prospect confronts the Bundesbank with a fundamental challenge – not just to its ethos and its viability, but to its existence. The basic questions in the Emu debate concern power and virtue. Who will control European money in the 1990s and beyond? And can Germany's moral attachment to sound money be transferred without upsets to other countries?

During four successful decades, the Federal Republic discovered for itself the self-fuelling benefits of a stable currency. Not the least of the prizes was the achievement of German unification. If it gave up its monetary sovereignty in favour of a pan-European central

* See chapter 8.

bank, Germany would surrender part of its birthright as a reforged nation. Since the Second World War, the Germans have longed to be 'good Europeans'. Never before, however, have they been asked to make such a fundamental sacrifice to live up to that ideal. This time, do the Germans intend to place the nation before Europe? The Bundesbank will provide the answer. During its first three and a half decades, the Bundesbank battled for stability. During the 1990s, it will be fighting for survival. It is a fight the Bundesbank means to win.

2

Safeguarding the Currency

It will be your task to secure the absolute stability of wages
and prices and thus continue to uphold the value of the
Mark.
*Adolf Hitler to Walther Funk, president of the Reichsbank,
1939*[1]

States and governments perish for two reasons: war and bad
finances.
*Hjalmar Schacht, looking back at his two pre-war periods as
president of the Reichsbank, 1968*[2]

We are now one country; we share a common economic
destiny. There is no longer a border for prices and costs.
Instability in the east will influence the west of Germany,
and vice versa.
Helmut Schlesinger, Bundesbank president, 1991[3]

The Germans lead the world in preaching and practising the doctrine of sound money. Endorsed with zeal and propagated with
persuasion, it has become many things: the hallmark of post-war
rebirth, the purveyor of order, the provider of security at home and
respect abroad.

Without monetary stability, prosperity can be neither created nor
sustained. It is the guarantor of holidays in the sun, of glossy
abundance in the mail order catalogues, of peace in the high streets
and goodwill in the factories: the Germans' endowment to their
children, and to the world. Other nations may live off memories of
past empires, of the glory of their landscapes, of prowess in sport,
in political leadership or in the manufacture of electronic chips.
Germany vaults the D-Mark, the backbone of the nation.

i. A fixed point in the ocean

Attachment to monetary stability is by no means simply a product of the period after 1945. Nor is it founded completely on the searing experience of the 1923 inflation. The tale was handed down to subsequent generations as a particularly outlandish form of twentieth-century folklore: when a postage stamp cost as much as a villa had done a few years earlier, the wheelbarrow replaced the counting scales as the instrument for measuring the money supply, and, with true German precision, the Mark ended up at exactly one-trillionth of its 1913 level against the dollar.*

The roots of the Germanic attention to stability, indeed, go deeper, to the concept of order as the foundation of state power. For a land with shifting boundaries and a contorted history, the stable Mark allows an escape from past traumas; it establishes one fixed point in an ocean of flux and change. The yearning for sound money was as strong in the 1930s as it is today. The Reichsbank carried out the will of a totalitarian state, the Bundesbank serves a democracy. But both were allotted the same statutory objective. Taken fully under Hitler's control in 1939, the Reichsbank was placed, for the first time, under the legal obligation to 'safeguard the currency'.†[4] When the Bundesbank was set up in 1957 as the successor to the Bank deutscher Länder, it was legally enjoined to pursue 'the aim of safeguarding the currency'.[5]

The Reichsbank in 1939 was a subservient appendage of the Hitlerian state. But when the Bundesbank Law was drawn up eighteen years later, the debauchment of the currency under the Third Reich had made parliamentarians wiser. The politicians assigned the conduct of monetary affairs to a body beyond their direct control, believing that this was the best way to guarantee monetary rectitude. Although required 'to support the general economic policy of the federal government', the Bundesbank was given the legal status of independence from government 'instructions'.[6]

Central banking independence could never be absolute, as some of the policy-making controversies between the central bank and the government were to illustrate during the next three and a half decades; nor was it a panacea against inflation. Independence did however give the Bundesbank a supremely powerful means of

* See chapter 4.
† See chapter 5.

guiding public opinion in its favour whenever there was doubt over Germany's economic priorities. The all-encompassing change in the political landscape brought a sizeable upgrading of the role of monetary policy. In pre-1945 Germany, it was the task of the state to stabilise money. Afterwards, the Germans learnt that stable money would stabilise the state; for without faith in money, faith in all else was likely to falter. According to Walther Funk, the dissolute Nazi technocrat who served as Reichsbank president between 1939 and 1945, strong money would flow automatically from strong government:

> The monetary question is always a question of trust. The security of a currency is determined not by gold and foreign currency, not by a portfolio of securities, but by the internal and external strength of the state. No one in Germany needs to have the slightest doubt. The Reichsmark has remained stable, the Reichsmark will remain stable – and after the war ends in victory, it will be more stable than ever![7]

After 1945, stable money became an anchor for the new system based on democracy and law. In a declaration accompanying the promulgation of the Bundesbank Law in 1957, the government of Konrad Adenauer, West Germany's first chancellor, declared: 'Safeguarding the currency forms the prime condition for maintaining a market economy and, ultimately, a free constitution for society and the state.' For Ludwig Erhard, Adenauer's economics minister and the architect of the economic 'miracle' of the 1950s and 1960s, monetary stability deserved a place as one of the 'basic human rights'.[8] Karl Schiller, the Social Democrat economics minister between 1966 and 1972, made the point with greater pithiness: 'Stability is not everything, but without stability, everything is nothing.'[9]

The desire for a stable currency was shared, too, by the communist state which grew up east of the Elbe. 'Monetary stability,' declared a confidential report from the Staatsbank, the East German central bank, in early 1989, 'is a fundamental condition for confidence in state policies.'[10] A primary reason why East Germany collapsed so quickly in 1989–90 was its evident failure to put this condition in place.

The Bundesbank's role clearly extends well beyond mere matters of money. In Germany, more than any other nation, monetary and political history have marched in tandem – with consequences which have changed the map of Europe. The three great monetary reforms this century – the creation of the Reichsmark after the 1923 hyper-inflation, the birth of the D-Mark in 1948, and the 1990 demise of the East Mark which accompanied the Bundesbank's expansion into East Germany – represented turning points along the winding route of Germany's national saga. Each time, near worthless, incon-vertible currencies, ravaged by political and social upheaval, were replaced by new units of value, promising a better and longer lasting order.

Each time, stable money was both the goal and the instrument of political change. The Reichsmark born out of the wreckage of 1923 was, for a time, the saviour of the Weimar Republic. In 1940, at the height of Hitler's sway, the Reichsmark was the pivot in the Nazis' plans for a new pan-European financial system.* If the drive for monetary stability was a dominant theme during the Third Reich, it fulfilled two eminently political objectives: to express the discipline inherent in dictatorial control and to provide reassurance that Nazi economics would prove effective in a hostile world environment. Defeat in 1945 changed all that. Like the Mark in 1923, the Reichsmark was consumed by grotesquely excessive defi-cit financing. The currency which the Führer declared must be made 'the most stable in the world'[11] was itself eclipsed in 1948 by the D-Mark, brought in under the aegis of the western victor powers who took on the role of midwife and sponsor to the new West German state.

Under the stewardship of the Bank deutscher Länder and the Bundesbank, the D-Mark proved a greatly more durable and effec-tive symbol of the new Germany than the Reichsmark had ever been. Four and a half decades after the collapse of the Third Reich, both East and West Germans have learned the benefits of solid monetary policies. East of the Elbe, they have seen for themselves how states can topple when undermined by economic and monetary decay.

The entry of the D-Mark into East Germany was the prelude to full political reunification on 3 October 1990. The currency which after the Second World War prised the Germans away from the

* See chapter 5.

cycle of defeat and destitution itself became the tool which ended dictatorship. This time, in sharp contrast to the currency reform of June 1948, Germany was in full control of its monetary destiny, on the way to regaining its status as a sovereign nation. It was to prove a process rich in contradictions and conflict, as well as reward.

ii. Metamorphosis in Berlin

If the D-Mark provided the hinge to German unity, the Bundesbank held open the door. At the stroke of midnight on Sunday 1 July 1990, the central bank extended its sovereignty 200 miles eastwards into the heart of central Europe, across a territory previously in the thrall of communism. German monetary union was a process of utmost economic as well as political significance, but the Bundesbank was only ostensibly in control. At several important stages, the central bank raised objections with the Bonn government over the economic risks involved – but was over-ruled. In particular, the Bundesbank pointed out that an artificially high conversion rate chosen for the East Mark would bankrupt much of East German industry.* It was concerned that excessive public borrowing to bolster living standards in East Germany would have inflationary consequences. The paradox was elegant in its piquancy. The events of July 1990 gave the Bundesbank unparalleled extension of its might. But it also revealed, more publicly than ever before, the limits of its celebrated independence.

Perhaps the most unlikely politician caught up in the drama was Lothar de Maizière, the first and last democratically elected prime minister of East Germany. A viola-playing lawyer hiding terrier-like intensity beneath a permanent look of quizzical bemusement, this authentic German anti-hero owes his Gallic name to Huguenot ancestors who fled to Brandenburg 300 years ago. De Maizière grew up in Thuringia close to the underground factory where slave workers built V-2 rockets during the Second World War; when hostilities stopped, he remembers, his father was among the gangs of German workers called upon to dismantle the works. De Maizière witnessed the implantation of communism on German soil; and then, during the 1989–90 revolution, he saw it crumble, almost literally overnight.

* See chapter 8.

After long years of coexisting with the communists, men like de Maizière suddenly learnt how to displace them. He was a member of the East German Christian Democrat Union (CDU) which before the breaching of the Berlin Wall in November 1989 had worked together in a nominal coalition government with the Socialist Unity Party (SED), the ruling communist party.[12] During the months leading up to monetary union, de Maizière's slender figure was seldom out of the TV cameras' spotlight, his sharp wits increasingly gaining the upper hand over his shyness. The words on everybody's lips were freedom and democracy. But the real issue was the desire for sound money – as much of it, and as quickly, as possible.

As the economic and moral bankruptcy of this last bastion of Stalinism became increasingly apparent, de Maizière was a prime advocate of rapid introduction of the D-Mark to reduce the fast growing migration to the west. He masterminded the campaign for a basic 1 to 1 conversion rate between the old and new currencies.[13] This was highly beneficial for East German consumers, but – together with the sharp increases in wages put into effect during 1990–91 – proved to be poison for East German manufacturing industry. On monetary union day, 1 July, de Maizière himself was on hand to watch the monumental Reichsbank building brooding over the Werdersche Wiese in East Berlin undergo a metamorphosis. For years, the vast block had been the headquarters of the state Socialist Unity Party, the repository of communist omnipotence. On the day of monetary union, the building formally took up its new role serving as the Bundesbank's chief administrative office for the eastern half of the nation. As the D-Mark took East Germany by storm, the temple of the *ancien régime* was transformed into the headquarters of the Bundesbank's assault brigade.

The Reichsbank block on the Werdersche Wiese was built from 1934 onwards as an extension to the existing nineteenth-century Reichsbank building on the adjacent Jägerstrasse. The new block became the home of 5500 Reichsbank functionaries. Marble-cladded, encrusted with leviathan murals and studded with tastelessly grandiose sculpture (including the inevitable busts of Frederick the Great and Adolf Hitler),[14] the place was described by the Nazis as 'the most modern bank building in the world'.[15] During the Second World War, the heavy-set Reichsbank extension and the neo-classical façade of the adjacent main central bank building stood defiantly like a pair of muscular ugly twins.

After the 1945 collapse, the new building was left to fare alone. The heavily bombed Reichsbank at its side was demolished, and the plot left eerily vacant. In the barren early years of the German Democratic Republic, as the new communist state struggled through an uneasy and sometimes violent pubescence, the Reichsbank extension was used for a while as the home of the finance ministry.[16] It became the permanent home of the central committee of the Socialist Unity Party after the 1961 building of the Wall.

As preparations for monetary union got under way in 1990, the stern colonnaded pile was the obvious choice for the Bundesbank's eastern outpost. It was one of the few places in East Germany offering large and secure vaults (8000 square metres of space, against only 6000 square metres at the Bundesbank in Frankfurt). The communists had made good use of the strongrooms. The Staatsbank, the East German central bank operated from the old nineteenth-century building of the Berliner Handelsgesellschaft in the nearby Charlottenstrasse, but continued to use the Reichsbank building's massive storage facilities for banknotes and coinage. Other material was deposited there too. When the first Bundesbank officials arrived to inspect the building earlier in 1990, they found the shredded remains of innumerable communist party personnel files previously stored in the strongrooms. Communist officials destroyed the archives in a desperate attempt to wipe out traces of a past they wanted to pretend had never happened.

On the afternoon of 1 July, de Maizière arrived for a tour of the monumental block. He was guided round by Johann Wilhelm Gaddum, the Bundesbank's scholarly directorate member in charge of East Berlin operations.[17] De Maizière said later the visit brought back memories of musical interludes in his boyhood, when he had attended post-war Bach and Brückner concerts in the building's cavernous ground floor banking hall.[18] Together Gaddum and de Maizière toured the vaults, piled high with stacks of D-Marks brought in across the Elbe in an operation of military efficiency. The hard money which had been circulating for years as East Germany's semi-official alternative currency suddenly became available to all. From Sunday onwards, a fortune in D-Marks was handed out as the conversion of East German savings started in 10,000 exchange centres around the country, including thousands of temporarily-converted schools and public buildings.* The day was not however totally free of technical hitches. De Maizière told Gaddum – half in jest, half seriously – that the Bundesbank had failed to make available enough DM20 notes for the everyday needs of the East German population.

Today, the Reichsbank building is once again the property of the unified German state, and proudly flies the federal German flag. All around, a new capital city is growing up from the ruins of totalitarianism. Above the three-pillared front portico, the offices overlooking the Werdersche Wiese once occupied by SED leaders Walter Ulbricht, Erich Honecker and Egon Krenz – who took over briefly when Honecker was ejected in October 1989 – have been freshly whitewashed. Those who used to give the orders have vanished into thin air. Interviewed here in November 1989, a fortnight after the opening of the Wall, Krenz boasted that reunification was 'not on the agenda'.[19] Gaddum and his Bundesbank colleagues now sit at plush desks in his former headquarters, and discuss the East German money supply. Outside, high up on the Reichsbank wall, where the hammer and compass insignia of the SED used to adorn the building's façade, there is nothing but a large faded patch. One of the few signs of the past, it appears to be retreating a little further into the stonework every day, a tribute to German skill in fashioning new structures from old.

iii. Breaking free

For Karl Otto Pöhl, Thursday 16 May 1991 was a day of emotion and pathos. During almost eleven and a half years as president of the Bundesbank, Pöhl, a former journalist seldom at a loss for a wry, well-honed phrase, had won a world-wide reputation for adept dealings with the press. As the chairman of the European Community's committee of central bank governors, and a key interlocutor in monetary dealing with the US, Pöhl's responsibilities extended well beyond Germany's borders. Perpetually tanned, with a tendency to paunchiness held in check by regular golfing (handicap 21) and skiing, Pöhl looked younger than his sixty-one years. Pöhl's evident mastery of his brief, combined with his whimsical irreverence, Levantine good looks and young, intellectual wife,

* See chapter 8.

Ulrike, from his second marriage, turned him into a virtual show-business personality. Running German monetary policy was a high-wire act. The ever-present attention of the media assured that the show was always well publicised.

On this Thursday in May, Pöhl was walking his ultimate tight-rope. Speaking to a packed news conference at the Bundesbank's headquarters after the regular fortnightly meeting of its policy-making council, Pöhl had to explain why he was resigning four and a half years before the expiry of his second eight-year term of office. But he had to avoid saying anything which would exacerbate the impression of serious differences with Chancellor Kohl over economic policy, above all over the consequences of German unification.

Kohl and Pöhl had both lived through the 1948 currency reform as eighteen-year-olds. For both men, the birth of the D-Mark allowed them to put the trials of the Second World War behind them. Yet their views about the second post-war monetary reform – that in East Germany in July 1990 – were diametrically opposed. Whereas Pöhl was highly sceptical about the economic challenges in East Germany, Kohl insisted on seeing the 1990 events in the most optimistic light. Their differences had intensified to the extent that some of Pöhl's letters to the chancellor (including those on the key issue of European monetary union) lately were not even being acknowledged, let alone answered. All this Pöhl could not divulge to the public; if he admitted the full extent of the strains, the news might weaken the D-Mark. He had to remain true to the Bundesbank Law. 'The aim of safeguarding the currency' had to be upheld – even (and especially) when the president was about to quit.

In charge of the D-Mark at a time of great challenge for Germany, Pöhl was caught in a spiral of conflict. His position as one of the world's best-known economic power-brokers, nurtured and enjoyed for so long, was starting to become an irksome burden. Pöhl was an unconventional Bundesbank president, a complex man who combines sometimes infuriating streaks of rebelliousness, high-handedness and vulnerability with a well-developed taste for good living. Now, his air of expertise and exuberance, displayed with brio at society parties and International Monetary Fund meetings alike, was looking distinctly ruffled.

Pöhl's nonchalant hedonism was partly an attempt to cast a veil over the humble circumstances of his youth. Born in 1929 in Hanover in north Germany, he had a miserable childhood. During the depression in Germany following the 1929 Wall Street crash, Pöhl's office-worker father suffered a long spell of unemployment. When the war came and the RAF bombs hailed down on Hanover, Pöhl spent much of his time shunted between bunkers and evacuation homes. After his mother died in 1945, Pöhl's father quickly remarried. The fifteen-year-old Pöhl helped the family make ends meet working for the occupation forces, sorting mail sacks during night-shifts at the British military post office in the nearby town of Herrenhausen.[20] His schooling incomplete, he left home at seventeen to fend for himself. After the economy started to recover following the 1948 birth of the D-Mark, Pöhl went to work as a trainee journalist in regional offices of the *Hannoversche Presse*, the local newspaper. The publishers gave him a DM150 a month grant to help him continue his studies and pass his high-school exam (*Abitur*) at a college in Wilhelmshaven.[21] The newspaper, owned by the Social Democratic Party (SPD), brought Pöhl into contact for the first time with the party. Although he was never particularly left-wing, he joined the SPD in 1948, partly because of his admiration for Social Democrats like Kurt Schumacher, the post-war party leader, who had spent much of the Nazi period in imprisonment.

Although one central banking colleague describes Pöhl as possessing 'the laziness of the intelligent man', Pöhl is no stranger to hard work; at the beginning of his career, he had no choice. In the early 1950s he financed his economic studies at Göttingen university by working as a freelance sports reporter for the local *Göttinger Presse*. Since he spent most Sundays covering local football matches, he seldom took holidays. After a short spell in economic research at the Ifo institute in Munich, he worked as journalist and lobbyist for the German Banking Association in Bonn during the 1960s before joining the government bureaucracy in 1970 as an official in the economics ministry. Pöhl always placed great emphasis on discharging his duties with a certain effortless ease.[22] Now, in May 1991, as the pressures crowded in from all sides, the ambience was growing increasingly tense. It was time to break free.

To assuage several different currents of sceptical opinion at once, Pöhl had become a virtuoso performer of the art practised by all central bankers, but mastered only by a few: delivering a series of different monetary policy messages all aimed equally convincingly at separate audiences. Among German central bank presidents, only Hjalmar Schacht, the Reichsbank president during two periods in the 1920s and 1930s, had shown similar deftness at juggling the nuances of the German language.* Schacht, like Pöhl, had started his career in journalism before switching to economics and banking. Pöhl not only was a master of Schachtian verbal acrobatics; he also practised the art under the challenging conditions of instant electronic communication.

Pöhl had to weave a delicate monetary pattern. Everything depended on keeping apart the diverse threads. While the Bonn government could be sporadically lectured about the need for fiscal soundness in financing Germany's economic unification, Pöhl had to take care to avoid over-censorious tones which could unsettle the exchange markets. The Bundesbank could rebuke the Americans over spendthrift budget policies – but had also to keep alive the delicate flame of trans-Atlantic monetary cooperation which early in the 1980s had been threatened with extinction. In speeches aimed at inflation-conscious members of the German business and banking communities, Pöhl needed to stress that any move towards European monetary union (Emu) would be conditional upon the toughest of anti-inflationary conditions.† But when it came to directing remarks towards the French government or the European Community, Pöhl was required to counter the feeling that the Bundesbank was single-mindedly blocking the path to Emu.

Pöhl's flexible nature, projected with intellect and aplomb, earned him high standing as an international financial diplomat. But it also brought him the occasional reproach of inconsistency or even unsoundness. For some of his critics, Pöhl was too pragmatic by half, too much of a chameleon. 'He sees things from so many sides that sometimes you wonder if he has an opinion,' said one close Pöhl-watcher on the Bundesbank council. 'Let me tell you something about Karl Otto,' former British prime minister Margaret Thatcher – whom Pöhl admired precisely for her straightforwardness – once declared to an interviewer. 'At some time or another, you will find, he has said everything.'[23]

By the beginning of 1991 Pöhl's complicated messages exuding

* See chapter 4.
† See chapter 9.

tones of warning and reassurance, concern and confidence had become increasingly tangled. He was growing tired of delivering them. His second term at the central bank ran until the end of 1995. But he had received several lucrative job offers in private banking. The desire to start a new career which would bring both a higher salary and a more placid, lower profile life-style for his youthful family had intensified during the drama of German unification. The passion for dominating the headlines was starting to be eclipsed by the yearning to leave them far behind.

Pöhl opened the 16 May press conference by confirming the rumours of his resignation which had been unsettling the financial markets since the beginning of the week. He declared that he was leaving the central bank 'for personal reasons' – a shorthand phrase encapsulating a dozen or more factors. He spelled out straight away the crucial statement aimed at underpinning the D-Mark on the currency exchanges: 'Nothing about the Bundesbank's policy of stability, which it has maintained for decades, will change as a result of my departure.'[24] Pöhl's message that stability would be maintained was startlingly similar to that issued by another central bank chief who left office sixty years earlier at another portentous moment in German history. Hans Luther, the hapless Reichsbank president during the years of the early 1930s Depression, who was forced to resign when Hitler took power in 1933,* wrote in his resignation letter of the overriding need 'to protect the currency, as the basis of Germany's economic life, from dangers and reverberations'.[25]

The journalists at the press conference were assembled in the Bundesbank's squat guest-house next to the main driveway across the central bank's park-like grounds. With plenty of room for TV cameras, the place is used for ceremonies and special meetings with the press, as well as for accommodating visitors; it is also the venue for regular Monday afternoon rehearsals of the Bundesbank orchestra. The media representatives had known for months that the Bundesbank president's job was growing steadily more difficult. Only very few however realised the full scale of the complexities. Pöhl's disenchantment reflected not simply difficulties in his relationship with the Bonn government, but also strains within the Bundesbank council. Since decisions are taken on the basis of

* See chapter 4.

majority voting, the president has just one vote – the same as everyone else on the council. He holds the chair; but, to push through decisions, the president has to rely on persuasion and argument, rather than decree.*

Pöhl had been a member of the council since 1977, when he joined the Bundesbank as vice-president. For five years before that, he had served, mainly in the government of Chancellor Helmut Schmidt, as the finance ministry's senior state secretary. From this long experience on the economic policy circuit, Pöhl knew that occasional disagreements with the government were not only inevitable, but also healthy – a sign that the Bundesbank really did have a separate point of view. Persistent discord was however something to be avoided, or at least to be kept out of the newspapers. Serious disputes with Bonn had a habit of damaging the D-Mark.

The tensions had been building up for a long time. Pöhl, along with the rest of the Bundesbank council, had been incensed by the Bonn government's decision in November 1987 (under pressure from Jacques Chirac, the then French prime minister, and Edouard Balladur, the finance minister) to set up a Franco-German Finance and Economic Council as part of a bilateral treaty to 'harmonise' economic policies between the two countries.[26] Another source of strain stemmed from the world stock market crash in October 1987. Kohl himself telephoned Pöhl to encourage him to cut interest rates in December 1987, as part of an internationally coordinated plan for economic stimulus which also included action to brake the fall of the dollar. Pöhl had little option but to comply. The German discount rate was reduced to a record low of 2.5 per cent. Later, as the German economy picked up steam unexpectedly quickly in 1988 and 1989, Pöhl swung round to the view that the central bank had over-relaxed monetary policy, and was subsequently paying the price in terms of higher inflation.[27]

The differences between Pöhl and Kohl stemmed less from deep-seated divergences on policy than from matters of style, presentation and personality. The chancellor and the Bundesbank president, both possessing remarkably thin skins, had never succeeded in establishing a common wavelength. Pöhl had found Kohl's verbosity and inability to come to the point increasingly wearying. The

* See chapter 3.

chancellery, for its part, believed that Pöhl was simply taking himself too seriously.

Mindful of past difficulties, at the 16 May press conference Pöhl sought refuge in the protective mantle of diplomacy. He conceded there had been 'occasional tensions and differences of opinion' between the government and the central bank. 'In a country which can count itself lucky to have an independent central bank, this is normal. It is not a sign of weakness of our system, but a sign of strength.' Beneath the functional politeness, Pöhl's misgivings about the economics of German unity were easily discernible. German monetary union had been a political decision which the Bundesbank had 'loyally supported, in spite of various doubts', he declared. The central bank's backing for government policy was a matter of 'duty', Pöhl told the press conference – leaving ostentatiously open the question of whether or not he agreed with it.

For more than a year, Pöhl had regularly warned that the hasty drive to reunification would seriously weaken the government's budgetary position. He perennially emphasised the need to cut public spending and subsidies in the prosperous western part of Germany to free extra resources for the east. The government had taken virtually no notice of his pleadings. In August 1991, Pöhl confessed: 'I had been talking myself blue in the face for eighteen months ... Everything I said was ignored ... If I had had the feeling that I could have prevented it [the deterioration of the budgetary position], I would not have quit.'[28] In the policy tussle with Bonn, Pöhl's exalted international stature ultimately counted for little. Even if you are one of the world's best-known central bankers, independence is not much help if the government is not listening.

iv. A sense of detachment

The unknowing outside world identified Pöhl with the Bundesbank; it is a matter of psychological as well as political interest that the president himself never did so. For all the professionalism and élan with which he carried out his functions, Pöhl remained curiously distant from Germany's monetary bureaucracy. Unlike most of his predecessors, Pöhl, a loner by nature, never felt completely at home in the Bundesbank. While public opinion frequently showed excessive reverence for the central bank, all too few – including most policy-makers in Bonn – realised the constraints under which the Bundesbank and its president were operating. During the 1989–90 wrangling over German unity, this lack of understanding became a serious gulf. The geographical distance between the government in Bonn and the central bank in Frankfurt is generally viewed as an advantage, buttressing the central bank's independent turn of mind. In Pöhl's case, distance turned into estrangement. With the energies of the Kohl government focused on East Germany, Bonn and Frankfurt suddenly seemed much further than a mere eighty miles apart.

In the end, Pöhl's departure from the institution in which he had played a pivotal role – as president and vice-president – for nearly a quarter of his life turned out to be curiously painless: a clinical break from high office. The man who took over at the age of sixty-six was his deputy, Helmut Schlesinger, a man who had spent practically the whole of his career in central banking. Schlesinger joined the Bank deutscher Länder in 1952. When Pöhl arrived at the Bundesbank in 1977, Schlesinger, long renowned as the central bank's most able economic technocrat, had already been there for a quarter of a century. An adept mountain climber, Schlesinger has no shortage of staying power. He maintains a daily keep-fit routine by scaling the twelve flights of stairs to his office. Climbing from the shadows into the limelight of the Number 1 job, Schlesinger brought with him the painstaking abilities of a well-respected monetary economist. He was not however equipped with the political capacity to confront and master the extraordinary challenge suddenly confronting the institution which he had made his life.

Along with stamina, Schlesinger possesses prodigious quantities of loyalty. He is the Boy Scout of German central banking. In speeches, he uses phrases such as 'We, the Bundesbank': words which Pöhl would find comical. In other ways, too, Schlesinger is everything Pöhl is not: orthodox, academic (he once told a Bundesbank colleague: 'The markets do not interest me'), ascetic, stubborn, wooden and a convinced believer in a united Germany. Although Schlesinger's sense of humour can be heavy-handed, it definitely exists. When a London banker paid a brief call on him in 1988, Schlesinger jocularly told his visitor, as he escorted him through the building: 'Take a good look at the place. We will be running things from here in about six years' time.' When he became president, Schlesinger's opposite numbers abroad found he purveyed unexpected courtliness and emollience during international financial meetings; he can be much less impatient than Pöhl. Although he is not a party member, Schlesinger is close to the Bavarian Christian Social Union.[29] His roots stretch back in a straight line to the Alpine town of Penzberg where he was born, deep in conservative Bavaria. One of Schlesinger's daughters and her husband still maintain there his father's glass and porcelain business.

Although possessing sufficient skill to be diplomatic when necessary, Schlesinger has established the keenest credentials as a hawkish propagator of the Bundesbank's monetary lore. Pöhl, on the other hand, habitually took a rather cynical view of the Bundesbank's status and the limits of its independence. Although he could hardly say so in public, he believed the institution was often overrated. Rather than as an independent organisation, Pöhl preferred to think of the Bundesbank as an arm of government to which the administration had delegated one key aspect of power: the ability to raise and lower interest rates.[30]

Once he had made his announcement, Pöhl was clearly relieved to leave. He advanced his departure date from the originally planned end of October to the end of July. His predecessors had departed from the central bank as old men: Wilhelm Vocke at seventy-one, Karl Blessing at sixty-nine, Karl Klasen and Otmar Emminger both at sixty-eight. By leaving before retirement age, and taking up a partnership with a prestigious private banking firm – the Cologne-based Oppenheim group[31] – Pöhl wanted to emphasise that there could, after all, be life after the Bundesbank. The Bundesbank council gave Pöhl the faintly quixotic present of a mountain bike as a departure gift; Pöhl himself took a small part of the Bundesbank's apparatus with him. When he moved later into Oppenheim's plush branch office in Frankfurt's West End, his Bundesbank secretary and chauffeur came along too.

By giving up one of Germany's most prestigious jobs, Pöhl left many observers perplexed, including most of his colleagues within the Bundesbank. He succeeded in throwing a smoke-screen over his reasons for leaving.[32] In his last public appearance in office, at a ceremony in Bonn in July 1991, Pöhl tried to explain that his early departure was not really so exceptional.[33] In the international arena, he pointed out, there had been two prominent precedents: at the same age, his friends Paul Volcker and Fritz Leutwiler had both left their jobs early (as chairman of the US Federal Reserve

Board and president of the Swiss National Bank, respectively) to take up posts in the private sector. Pöhl omitted adding a third name to the list, which would have put his resignation into a historical setting – albeit a somewhat uncomfortable one. Half a century earlier, in January 1939, Hjalmar Schacht departed from office at the same age of sixty-one, after a total of twelve years at the top of the Reichsbank – the consequence of the Reichsbank's memorandum to Hitler warning that 'unrestrained public spending' was posing inflationary risks.*[34] Schacht and Pöhl, at different turning points in German history, attempted to force the government of the day to change its policy priorities. Both men ended up realising the limits of their power.

v. A stable tradition

The primacy of the German central bankers' task of protecting the currency is beyond dispute. It is sustained by the force of principle, and by the unswerving tide of tradition. The six post-war German central bank presidents – Vocke, Blessing, Klasen, Emminger, Pöhl and Schlesinger – showed great diversity of character; yet they all succeeded in fostering the near-universal respect in which their institution is held. One factor unites them: they have been guided and bound by the Bundesbank's own peculiar institutional force. One well-informed Bundesbank observer is Manfred Lahnstein, the long-time finance ministry state secretary, who took over briefly as finance minister in 1982 during the closing months of Schmidt's government. 'Much more important than strengths and weaknesses of the individuals,' says Lahnstein – now a board member at the Bertelsmann media group – 'is that the institution is strong enough to bring these figures under its power. The institution moulds the president.'[35]

The incantation of ritual anti-inflation language plays an important part. In finding the right words for his utterances, a Bundesbank president cannot rely simply on dry formulae from the manual of monetary economics. To shield the D-Mark from ill-fortune, he must unsheathe his sword, and adopt the Nibelungen-like language of an epic struggle against adversity. Hans Matthöfer, the Social Democrat finance minister between 1978 and 1982, who formally

* See chapter 4.

decided Pöhl's appointment as central bank president in 1979, believes that the Bundesbank's power is partly a function of its predictability. 'When I inaugurated Pöhl into office, I told him: "I envy you for the simplicity of your decisions," ' Matthöfer says. 'At the end of my four years in office, I could predict all the Bundesbank's statements.'[36]

Bundesbank tradition deems that no president can leave office without a fulsome outpouring of public oratory. A grandiloquent ceremony in August 1991 in Frankfurt's rebuilt St Paul's church provided the occasion for Pöhl's formal departure and Schlesinger's official inauguration.[37] The church had been the venue for the convening of Germany's National Assembly after the short-lived democratic revolution of 1848. In 1991 the event was an appropriate moment to heap praise on the gospel of *Stabilitätspolitik*; but it also gave rise to words of warning. A fortnight earlier, the Bundesbank's council, meeting for the first time under Schlesinger's stewardship, had announced a one percentage point increase in the discount rate to signal unease about rising inflation. Monetary storm clouds were on the horizon.

Speaking to an audience grouping the élite of Germany's financial establishment, Helmut Kohl delivered an address mixing appropriately mellow phrases on Pöhl's leadership with pointed references to the disagreements over German monetary union. The chancellor restated his belief that the 1 July economic merger was 'politically necessary and economically viable'. And he took care to remind his audience that Pöhl himself, when he took office eleven and a half years earlier, had acknowledged that the Bundesbank, for all its independence, was legally required to support the government's overall economic policies.

In his own speech, Pöhl commented with satisfaction that 'price stability' was now accepted as the 'highest objective of monetary policy in Europe and elsewhere'. But his remarks on the economic consequences of unification were far less complimentary. Germany was suffering a 'home-made' acceleration in price rises resulting from the failure to tighten belts to finance German unity. 'This is the result of a development about which the Bundesbank and I, as its spokesman, have repeatedly warned – unfortunately without success.'[38] Pöhl spelled out his fears that 'monetary policy could be put under too much strain' – an oblique warning that the Bundesbank might have little choice but to tighten credit so severely that it would engineer a recession. When Schlesinger took the podium for the final speech of the ceremony, he turned to Kohl and put the message another way: 'Financial and monetary stability are decisive values for our country; they must be maintained. The Bundesbank is ready to play its part fully, not simply because the law consigns us to do this, but because stability is the soil which nurtures our prosperity.'

The St Paul's mixture of warning from the retiring Bundesbank president and firmness from the man taking over his office was intriguingly similar to the rhetoric served up twelve years earlier when Pöhl's predecessor Otmar Emminger was ceremonially dispatched into retirement at the end of 1979. The venue was a great deal less glittering. Emminger, a peppery economist who had been vice-president under Karl Klasen for seven and a half years before moving to the top job in 1977, had less sense of show than Pöhl; he chose for his send-off the downbeat surroundings of the Bundesbank's gymnasium.

Like Schlesinger, Emminger had spent a large part of his working life at the central bank, joining the Bank deutscher Länder in 1950. Before and during the Second World War Emminger worked at economic research institutes in Berlin and Vienna. He joined the Nazi party in 1937[39] – possibly to improve his chances of joining the civil service in 1938.[40] During the post-war decades he became the Bundesbank's 'foreign minister', well-known and highly regarded on the international circuit. By 1979, Emminger was disappointed that he had been able to remain at the Bundesbank helm for only seven months more than the minimum two-year span – and was now bowing out (as Pöhl was due to do twelve years later) at a time of accelerating inflation. Pointing to the spurt in the oil price stemming from revolution in Iran, Emminger had no compunction about stressing the uncomfortable legacy he was leaving; he was careful to underline, however, that it was not his fault. 'Monetary stability, whose maintenance is our prime objective,' said Emminger, 'is threatened by forces lying outside our control.'[41]

At the same Emminger ceremony in 1979, Pöhl had been inaugurated into office at the age of fifty – a decade younger than any other post-war central bank president. Pöhl was an owlish, slightly more awkward figure in his younger days, but he still showed plenty of self-confidence as he prepared to take on the mantle of the presidency. Pöhl sensed that, if he uttered the right words, his audience would know that he possessed the necessary gravitas:

> The world is being inundated by a new wave of inflation . . . There can be only one answer to the evident signs of danger to stability – to keep money tight . . . The experience of the last few years has shown quite clearly that stability policy is the best growth policy . . . Stability is the basis of our economic position in the world, and of our country's prosperity.[42]

Emminger himself had broadcast the same message at his own inauguration ceremony in 1977: 'The fight for monetary stability is more than simply a fight to bring down a price index. Monetary stability is linked up with general social stability – and with political stability.'[43]

Karl Klasen, the autocratic Social Democrat who was Emminger's predecessor as president between 1970 and 1977, used his investiture at the beginning of 1970 to outline a somewhat different theme. Klasen, probably the most political of all Bundesbank presidents, stressed that the central bank was 'autonomous' rather than 'independent' – an indication of the closeness of his links to the government of Chancellor Willy Brandt which had just taken power in Bonn.[44] Unusually for a Bundesbank president, Klasen placed equal weight on the need for adequate economic growth as on the need for monetary stability. Not just inflation, but also unemployment, had been 'traumas' for the German people, he reminded his audience. He made sure however to wind up his speech with the traditional rhetorical flourish: 'One thing I can tell you today: There will be no inflation in the Federal Republic of Germany.' The audience of a Bundesbank president is not looking for undue perspicacity. They simply want to be assured that their money is in safe hands.

vi. 'An asset more important than gold'

In the early years after the birth of West Germany in 1949, safeguarding the currency was of paramount importance. If tight money became a centrepiece of the crusade to shore up the new state's foundations, the commander was Wilhelm Vocke. The first president of the directorate of the Bank deutscher Länder, Vocke was a *Geheimrat* (privy councillor) of austere manner and impeccable Prussian bearing, possessed of an unshakeable belief in his own infallibility. For two decades before the war, he had been a member of the directorate of the Reichsbank.[45] He departed – on full pay – in the wave of dismissals which followed the drawing up of the Reichsbank's January 1939 anti-inflation memorandum. The document, signed by all eight members of the directorate, was partly based on a draft produced by Vocke – a fact which came to light only years afterwards.*[46]

The son of a pastor, Vocke was no Nazi – but neither did he show excessive evidence of resistance. One of his main character-istics during his Reichsbank days was indolence; a habit which Vocke claimed he cultivated during the 1930s as a necessary conse-quence of his increasing lack of influence.[47] During his twenty years on the Reichsbank directorate from 1919 onwards, Vocke's main feat was to avoid even the most remote responsibility for the Reichs-bank's numerous mistakes.[48] Although Vocke showed scorn and antipathy towards Hitler's cruder supporters, during most of the 1930s he played the not untypical role of a cautious, long-serving *Beamter* (functionary). Like many who were distressed at the dire effects of the Depression in the early 1930s, Vocke was an early supporter of the strategy of employment creation put into effect with such success in the early years of the Third Reich.[49] But he later claimed to have been aware all along of the 'unspeakable disaster' which Hitler would bring to the German people.[50]

After he left the Reichsbank, Vocke led a simple but peaceable enough existence in war-time Berlin. His only apparent activity was as a member of the committee of a branch of the Kaiser Wilhelm Society dealing with international law.[51] However, once he took up his new post at the Bank deutscher Länder in 1948† – at the age of sixty-two – Vocke was fired by the sanctimonious relish of a man who had at last found his life's mission. He possessed an indepen-dent turn of mind – with characteristic lack of sentimentality, Vocke ascribed this to the death of his father when he was only fifteen[52] – and he became the fiercest defender of the autonomous position of the Bank deutscher Länder.

Vocke took a censorious view about others' prowess in the monet-

* See chapter 4.
† See chapter 6.

ary field. Hans Luther, the Reichsbank president in 1930–33, 'understood really nothing about money and credit'.[53] Chancellor Konrad Adenauer, he scoffed, was 'a layman'.[54] Fritz Schäffer, Adenauer's finance minister, 'had little idea of credit and money'.[55] Vocke quickly gained the upper hand over a man who was, in nominal terms, his superior: Karl Bernard, the first post-war president of the central bank council, who was the formal head of the bank, ranking above the president of the directorate.[56]

Vocke used his first address to the Bank deutscher Länder on 1 June 1948 to underline the new spirit of self-reliance:

> The independence of the Bank and its leadership is an absolute necessity. Only when independence is guaranteed on all sides will the central bank be able to earn that asset which is more important than popularity and applause, yes, even more important than gold and foreign exchange – trust at home and abroad.[57]

The birth of the D-Mark under the currency reform on 20 June 1948 gave Vocke an unparalleled opportunity to show his steadfastness and foresight. Schacht, his former boss, superciliously told him that the new D-Mark – backed by neither gold nor foreign exchange reserves – would collapse within six weeks.[58] The prediction proved as accurate as Schacht's forecast nine years previously, shortly after the outbreak of war, that the German army would 'collapse' three weeks after invading Poland.[59] Profiting from foreign exchange controls and an undervalued D-Mark (which became convertible only in 1958), the Bank deutscher Länder in fact ended up amassing foreign exchange reserves well beyond Vocke's most optimistic expectations.[60]

Vocke correctly saw that confidence in the new currency was of more than simply economic benefit. It was the passport for establishing West Germany's political standing in the world. A stable currency would eventually 'open doors for German policies which are today closed'.[61] The door of German unity indeed remained shut for four decades; but in 1990, under conditions which Vocke might have foreseen, it swung open. Intriguingly, when Vocke referred in 1950 to 'the stable D-Mark' as one of the country's 'most valuable foreign policy assets',[62] he used almost exactly the same form of words as those employed by Kohl forty years later in announcing the arrival of the D-Mark into East Germany.*

vii. 'Experience has shown that we were right'

If there was one overriding theme of the Bank deutscher Länder and Bundesbank during the post-war period, it was this: West Germany had successfully insulated itself from the international trend towards devaluation and was leading the world in the fight for economic stability. During the Third Reich, under very different circumstances, the Reichsbank projected a similar message. Although the Reichsmark was still formally pegged to its pre-1914 value against gold, an ever-thickening forest of foreign exchange controls made the currency for all practical purposes inconvertible. Schacht's rigorous system of foreign trade planning – introduced under the so-called New Plan of 1934 to counterbalance protection-ism abroad and sparse currency reserves at home – ensured that Germany imported only from countries which bought its own goods in sufficient quantities. But Germany resolutely refused to follow the devaluation bandwagon set in train when Britain went off the gold standard in 1931.

The principle of maintaining the value of the currency became self-feeding faith and all-encompassing propaganda.[63] 'We have brought our economy into motion without participating in dubious experiments carried out abroad,' declared Schacht in 1935.[64] In June 1938 – only seven months before he departed from the Reichs-bank – Schacht was still proclaiming Germany's devotion to monet-ary virtue: 'Obviously it was not expected [abroad] that we would stick unshakeably to the old goal of every honest central bank policy: the internal and external defence of our currency. We may register with satisfaction that we have achieved this goal, while others have abandoned it.'[65]

One of Schacht's directorate colleagues at this time was Karl Blessing. A stocky thirty-eight-year-old from the southern German region of Swabia, Blessing was a man of intelligence, wit and prodigious opportunism. After a Third Reich career in which he scaled the peaks of the Nazi economic establishment, Blessing was destined to become, in 1958, the president of the Bundesbank.

* See chapter 8.

Already during the 1930s, his economic pronouncements carried weight. In a speech in February 1938, Blessing set out a ringing statement of Germany's 1930s monetary credo. His overriding desire to buttress the authority of the economic policies of the Third Reich produced an inevitable outpouring of self-righteousness:

> We in Germany during the last seven years have refrained from going along with the monetary experiments of the rest of the world. Experience has shown that we were right.[66]

Under the Third Reich, Blessing led a double existence of complexity and intrigue. During the later war years, mindful both of the growing excesses of the Nazi state, and of the vanishing chances of German victory, Blessing intensified his contacts with some of the conspirators who participated in the failed assassination attempt against Hitler on 20 July 1944. This was one of the more salutary facts about his past which, after the war, he succeeded in highlighting; other, more uncomfortable, aspects were simply written out of the story. During the 1960s, Blessing fought successfully to give the independent Bundesbank the strength and authority sought in vain by the Reichsbank. When he retired in December 1969 after twelve years at the Bundesbank helm, Blessing's admirers threw a celebratory gala dinner in Frankfurt. Blessing told the assembled members of Germany's financial élite that 'monetary discipline' had been the 'alpha and omega' of his career. He looked back briefly to the 1930s. His memory was, necessarily, highly selective. In contrast to his speech in 1938, Blessing – with the advantage of hindsight – could only find words of distaste:

> Formally, the Reichsmark remained linked to gold, but in practice this was worthless, since there were no free exchange rates any more. The Reichsmark became a domestic currency with every conceivable kind of special Marks, with bilateral clearing accounts, Aski accounts,* compensation deals and similar assistance measures. We lived until 1945, or, rather,

* *Ausländer Konten für Inlandszahlungen.* Special accounts established for the benefit of foreign companies doing large amounts of export/import business with Germany.

until 1948, with this many-headed, never-loved monster of
the Reichsmark, going downhill all the time.[67]

In fact, for a long period under the Hitlerian state, Blessing's career
path definitely headed up rather than down. During Schacht's
1930s term as Germany's monetary overseer, Blessing had been
the Reichsbank chief's brightest protégé. He joined the Nazi party
in May 1937,[68] a move which in 1947 he justified in the witness
stand at Nuremberg on the grounds 'that one should not leave the
government machinery entirely in the hands of radical elements'.[69]
One month later he secured his promotion to the eight-man Reichsbank directorate. He quit the Reichsbank board in February 1939[70]
in the second wave of dismissals after the memorandum affair.
Unlike Vocke, Blessing however did not retire from public life
during the Second World War. He transferred his allegiance to the
new Reichsbank president, Walther Funk. Soon after his dismissal
from the directorate Blessing joined the Reichsbank advisory board
and took part in regular meetings of the *Freundeskreis* group of
industrialists, associated with the most feared man in the Third
Reich, Hitler's police chief Heinrich Himmler.[71]

Blessing may not have been a whole-hearted Nazi; but he
appeared to enjoy the company of those who were. Blessing's outstanding talent was, indeed, his ability to get on well with nearly
everyone. According to the ever-censorious Vocke, 'He found it
difficult to say no.'[72] In one opposition list uncovered after the 20
July plot, Blessing was named as a potential economics minister in
a post-Hitler government.[73] After the conspiracy collapsed, Funk
successfully shielded Blessing from the attentions of the Gestapo;
the Reichsbank president told secret police investigators that Blessing had been unaware that his name was on the list.[74]

While he played out this shadowy double game, Blessing
remained a pivotal figure in the management of three areas vital
for Germany's war economy – money, raw materials and oil. He also
contributed to spreading German economic interests throughout
Europe. Germany's satellites in south-east Europe – Romania,
Hungary, Croatia and Bulgaria – were of particular importance;
Hitler believed that the Danube was 'the river of the future – the
petroleum and grain will come flowing to us'.[75] Blessing made a
two-week trip to Romania in autumn 1941 to advise the central

bank there on the best way of curbing inflation. This was 'the most unjust form of tax', he told the Romanian central bank governor. Blessing also put forward proposals for reducing the flight of capital which was sapping Romania's war-time reserves. This undesirable phenomenon, he suggested, was caused by 'Jews'.[76]

For work like this, the Nazi leadership held Blessing in the highest regard. In a letter to Joachim von Ribbentrop, the foreign minister, Funk in June 1944 praised Blessing as 'one of the few remaining German economic leaders who enjoy high international esteem'.[77] At the time, this was a description of which Blessing could be proud. Afterwards, he had a strong interest in ensuring that remarks like these passed into the realm of forgetfulness.

viii. Adjusting to circumstances

Blessing's ambition was backed by classic qualifications. He had joined the Reichsbank in 1920, leaving for a four-year spell at the Bank for International Settlements in the early 1930s, before moving back to Berlin in 1934 to posts at the Reichsbank and, soon afterwards, at the Reich economics ministry. During his 1930s work in the vital spheres of raw materials and foreign exchange, Blessing voiced his 'pride' in Germany's 'extensive system of currency controls'.[78] He maintained that foreign criticism of Hitlerian economics was based on 'complete ignorance of the German situation'.[79] Blessing denounced the Versailles treaty as 'the source of Germany's currency shortages' and declared that the days of free trade had passed away.[80] At the beginning of 1936 – the year when Hitler finally turned his back on Versailles with the reoccupation of the Rhineland – Blessing declared that export efforts would have to be redoubled 'if we are to succeed in buying foreign raw materials needed for the domestic economy and for armaments'.[81]

By November 1937, Blessing proclaimed that the policy of 'only buying abroad what can be paid for' and gearing imports to goods 'necessary for national economic and national political goals' had enabled the 'rearmament' of the German economy and the banishment of the *Diktat* of the Versailles treaty without 'in any way reducing the stability of the German currency'.[82]

Blessing's loyal service was rewarded in March 1938 when he was put in charge of organising the takeover of the Austrian

National Bank after the *Anschluss* with Austria.*[83] In a speech in Berlin in June 1938, Blessing summed up the success of the Austrian operation in epic terms:

> Just three months separate us from the memorable day, which will remain unforgettable for us. And yet in this short period, all the measures have been put into place with the goal of forging together the two economies into an unbreakable whole.[84]

After his departure from the Reichsbank directorate in February 1939, Blessing took his talents to industry, becoming a board member in April 1939 of the Berlin-based German subsidiary of Unilever, the Anglo-Dutch fats and oils company. Largely cut off from connections with the UK, Unilever – with which Blessing had already built up extensive contacts during his time in the Reich economics ministry[85] – occupied a vital strategic place in the German economy.[86] With responsibility above all for Unilever's margarine business, Blessing remained in the job between April 1939 and September 1941.[87] This period was punctuated by Germany's invasion of the Netherlands in May 1940. One of the many objectives of the Nazi occupation was to bring Unilever's considerable Dutch resources under German control.[88]

After the occupation of Holland, Blessing became one of the three administrators[89] of Unilever's interests in the expanded economic area of the German Reich.[90] He relinquished his post after a Reich commissioner was named to supervise directly the Unilever concern in June 1941[91] – and moved to the oil industry. While he was still at Unilever, Blessing had been voted on to the supervisory board of a new state-controlled oil holding company, Kontinentale Öl.[92] This was formally set up by Reich Marshal Hermann Göring in March 1941 – three months before the Wehrmacht's march into the Soviet Union – to manage and exploit the oil reserves of the widespread parts of central and south-eastern Europe now falling under German control.[93] Blessing was immediately made a member of the Kontinentale Öl administrative board. He stepped up to the three-man management board (*Vorstand*) at the beginning of October 1941.[94]

* See chapter 5.

Built up around oil holdings taken over from defeated Belgium and France, Kontinentale Öl's aim was to extend Germany's energy grip ever further eastwards. Although in some aspects of its work, Kontinentale Öl never progressed beyond the planning stage, Galicia in western Poland and Romania were a particular focus of activities.[95] Like many other German companies, Kontinentale Öl subsidiaries used concentration camp prisoners to enlarge the oil industry infrastructure in the east. Just before the area was captured by the advancing Soviet army, one of Blessing's managers complained in early March 1945 that extension of a refinery in Trzebinia in Upper Silesia was being held up by 'use of concentration camp prisoners of low performance'.[96]

When the fighting was over, Blessing was taken into custody in southern Germany while the Americans weighed up – and eventually rejected – the idea of bringing war crimes charges against him. He returned to a *Vorstand* post at Unilever in July 1948, and was soon back at his old task of exerting his influence throughout the world of business.* Blessing's war record remained a source of irritation to the UK government, which discreetly rejected his nomination to the board of the Bank for International Settlements in the early 1950s.[97]

After he took over from Vocke as Bundesbank president in 1958, Blessing showed that, whatever other vicissitudes Germany had to face, the goal of monetary stability would be pursued as zealously as ever. 'I have no intention of making the D-Mark soft, for I consider a sound monetary system to be the backbone of any orderly state,' he declared in January 1958.[98] 'I will never lend my hand to a thoughtless monetary policy,' he promised Bundesbank employees.[99] Blessing was, in fact, anything but a dogmatist: he showed considerable flexibility in steering the central bank through the D-Mark revaluation squalls in 1961 and 1969. As an amiable participant on the international central bankers' circuit, he won the confidence of the US government – above all because, during the 1960s, the Bundesbank (unlike the French authorities) loyally refrained from exchanging excess dollars for gold from the US reserves. The Americans even coined the phrase: 'What a blessing we have a Blessing.' British civil servants during the 1960s were less favourably disposed to him, baptising Blessing 'Mixed'.[100] Blessing was at

---

* See chapter 6.

his most persuasive when regaling visitors from the US Federal Reserve with his reminiscences of the bad old times under the Nazis: 'his anguished memories of those days as he watched the breakdown of international financial cooperation in the early 1930s,' as one unwitting US central banker put it.[101]

When Blessing died in 1971, only just over a year after retirement, Karl Schiller, the economics minister, delivered the funeral oration, summing up his life's work as 'the daily struggle for stability'.[102] The former Reichsbanker, oilman and Nazi go-between showed remarkable adaptability to circumstances. During the Third Reich and under the new democracy, Blessing never deserted the cause of 'safeguarding the currency': a sign of the steadfastness of German central banking tradition – in bad times, and in good.

3

Inside the Bundesbank

The central bank is fully sovereign in its relationship with the government; it is responsible only to itself. We have a body which is responsible to no one, neither to a parliament, nor to a government.
    Konrad Adenauer, West German chancellor, 1956[1]

Do you need to have a president of a Land central bank in the Saarland or in Kiel? What is his job? He has to discount one bill and travel to Frankfurt every other week and raise his finger and say no.
    Helmut Schmidt, former West German chancellor, 1991[2]

The president has to be careful. He cannot afford to lose against us.
    Karl Thomas, president of the Hesse central bank, 1991[3]

The road to the Bundesbank is paved with blandness, yet shimmers with the muted reflections of power. The thirteen-storey many-windowed block stares out imperturbably from a coil of *Autobahn* in the north-west suburbs of Frankfurt, erected on a green swathe of land wrested away in the 1960s from the local allotment gardeners. There is nothing extravagant about this three-winged colossus silhouetted against the Taunus hills, flanked, sentinel-like, by Frankfurt's city television tower and surrounded by a collection of football pitches and pastel-coloured American military housing. A nine-foot concrete wall set back from the chrysanthemum beds at the front gate bears the no-nonsense emblem Deutsche Bundesbank etched in two-foot-tall letters. Tens of thousands of motorists teem past the wall daily. They could be forgiven for mistaking the building for a high-rise Holiday Inn or a long-stay sanatorium.

i. The Gobelins are gone

The Bundesbank is a powerhouse; but it is a highly functional one. During the quarter of a century between the abandonment of the Reichsbank's bomb-torn imperial headquarters on the Spree and the inauguration of the new Bundesbank building in 1972, German central banking changed its image – from the pretentious to the pastoral, from the overwhelming to the unassuming. There was a time, before 1945, when German central bankers inhabited rooms festooned with gilded armchairs and heavy carpets, their walls hung with Gobelins, their meals brought to them by liveried footmen.[4] These days are gone, almost certainly for ever. The Bundesbank's offices are rectangular boxes carpeted in discreetly nondescript colours, dotted with department store furniture and adorned with twentieth-century paintings. The Reichsbank's art collection was lost in 1945, so the Bundesbank, in contrast to its sister European central banks, inherited nothing from the age of the Old Masters.

If Germany's history has made its citizens suspicious about grandiose government, it has also driven out flamboyance from civic architecture. Unlike other international central banks, there are no outer emblems of hauteur; the Bundesbank's pride is kept under wraps. In Washington, an American eagle in white marble perches over the bronze doors of the Federal Reserve building, gazing disdainfully up the green of the Mall and towards Lincoln's Memorial. The main façade of the Banque de France in the stockbroking quartier of Paris faces a commanding equestrian statue of Louis XIV erected in the centre of the seventeenth-century Place des Victoires. As if sensing the pull of money, the horse's elegantly flared nostrils point directly towards the Banque's grand *tricolore*-topped portal. Another horse-mounted statue stands in Threadneedle Street outside the Bank of England: the Duke of Wellington in bronze, cast from French cannon melted down after the Battle of Waterloo, and unveiled in 1844 in the presence of the King of Saxony. On the street outside the Bundesbank, the Wilhelm-Epstein-Strasse – named after a Frankfurt councillor who pioneered the city's evening classes – there is, by contrast, a distinct absence of historical depth. The closest approximation to a monument is the Number 34 bus-stop.

The Bundesbank is well away from the gloss, the vice and the skyscrapers of the Frankfurt city centre; there is a curious sense of other-worldliness about the place. The Bundesbank's headquarters has very few direct dealings with German commercial banks, whose accounts are held with the *Landeszentralbanken* in the regions. As a deliberate part of Allied policy towards Germany when the Bank deutscher Länder was set up in 1948, the post-war central bank was not allowed (in contrast to the Reichsbank) to lend directly to the industrial sector.* Unlike the Bank of England, the Bundesbank has never been called upon to play a role in restructuring or bail-outs for crisis-ridden manufacturing companies.

Additionally, the Bundesbank has no direct supervisory responsibility for the banking system, a role carried out by the federal banking supervisory office, the Bundesaufsichtsamt für das Kreditwesen, in Berlin. The arm's-length approach to banking regulation has on the whole been successful – helped, crucially, by the general soundness and distaste for excessive innovation of German banks. With some justification, the Bundesbank believes that a central bank will be better able to concentrate on its task of assuring monetary stability if it is as little distracted as possible by supervisory duties. It is wary of the possible conflict of interest which might arise from a statutory obligation both to safeguard the currency and to assure the soundness of the banking system. The only really serious post-war German banking crisis came in 1974 with the spectacular closure of the Herstatt bank in Cologne, caused by enormous ill-advised speculation on the currency markets. The Bundesbank blundered by allowing the Berlin banking supervisory office to close down the bank in late afternoon, when it was still morning in New York. Shutting a bank during a business day, when all its business and financial dealings are in a state of flux, is virtually unprecedented. The action caused large losses at a cluster of big American banks. The Herstatt débâcle has remained an exception. The Bundesbank not only takes pride in the prudent and well-run nature of German banks, but regards it as an important consequence of its own *Stabilitätspolitik*: further proof of the benefits of a sound D-Mark.

Although the central bank's main concern is for the welfare of the currency, it encourages employees to look after their own health as well as that of the nation's money. The Bundesbank guesthouse off the entry driveway boasts a bowling lane, gymnasium and

* See chapter 6.

swimming pool for staff and their children. Rabbits scamper in the park-like grounds, where Bundesbankers can take lunch-time walks around an ornamental lake. The reverie is broken only by the occasional rumble of Daimler-Benz and MAN money transporters, painted in garishly ecological green. Escorted by motor-cycle out-riders, the juggernauts head to and from the vaults ferrying consignments of D-Marks.

Guarding the citadel day and night is a 120-strong Bundesbank security force. This includes policewomen with soft eyes, long flowing hair and hard automatic guns. Several kennelfuls of guard dogs – the Bundesbank owns ten Alsatians, two Rottweilers and a Malinois – are on display, particularly when Bonn government ministers are in town for consultations on the money supply. With tired regularity, the show of force is stepped up whenever the Red Army Faction launches another terrorist assault on a member of the German establishment.

Belying the stern appearance, when a Bundesbank visitor arrives, security precautions normally turn out to be quite relaxed. A young and nervous green-coated policeman directs the guest up the drive towards the main building, where a sleek phalanx of directorate members' S-class Mercedes await their masters' bidding. Bundesbank guards have a distinct sense of status. 'A guest for Dr Pöhl,' the policeman would normally intone during the years when Karl Otto Pöhl held the job. The appellation was an honorary one. During his eleven and a half years in the post, Pöhl did not need a formal doctorate to become Europe's best-respected central banker, but Bundesbank watchmen cannot bear the idea that the person at the head of their institution should not carry the title *Herr Doktor*.[5]

The more traditional keepers of the Bundesbank's gates are happier with Pöhl's successor, Helmut Schlesinger. He corresponds more closely to the time-honoured image of a German central bank chief. Schlesinger carries the title of professor. What is more, with bald head and spectacles and the features of Doktor Allwissend, the all-knowing figure from the Grimms' fairy-tale, he looks like one too.

ii. The room at the top

A central bank's most precious commodity is normally its gold: buried in the vaults, hidden from the eyes of the nefarious, the devious and the merely inquisitive. The Bundesbank is an exception. The source of the central bank's sway over the world's money markets is on the top floor – in a high-ceilinged wood-panelled meeting room flanked by two coloured wall-tapestries of well-meaning abstraction created by Max Ernst, the surrealist painter from Cologne. Here assemble the eighteen men of the Bundesbank's council, venerated for their independence of mind and devotion to financial stability. The custodians of the currency are modern Germany's Knights of the Holy Grail. The council's weapons are gravitas and the trust invested in them by the German public; the dragon they must keep at bay, the evil of inflation.

Fifty metres below this room, a great number of banknotes, but very little gold, is stored in the Bundesbank's subterranean strong-rooms. Thanks to West Germany's export surpluses in the 1950s and 1960s, when gold was available for purchase at the bargain price of $35 and $42 an ounce, the Bundesbank has acquired one of the world's largest stocks of the yellow metal – 3701 tonnes, or just under 300,000 12.5 kg ingots, worth around DM60 billion at market prices. The Bundesbank is unique among the world's principal gold-holding central banks in that it keeps only a tiny proportion of the bullion on its own premises. Merely about 80 tonnes – just over 2 per cent – lies in the vaults in Frankfurt. The rest of the treasure trove is in the vaults of other central banks – the Federal Reserve Bank of New York, the Bank of England and (to a much smaller extent) the Banque de France.

As part of the operation of the European Payments Union and the London Gold Pool during the 1950s and 1960s, the bullion was acquired abroad, as a result of book-keeping operations with other central banks; the gold reserve (conservatively valued in the Bundesbank's accounts at well below the market price) has remained virtually unchanged since the mid-1960s. The bullion was never physically moved to Germany. During the years of the Cold War, the Bundesbank considered it a great deal safer to keep the gold abroad rather than in Frankfurt, just a few hours' Soviet tank drive from the fortified East–West German border. Now that Germany has been unified, the Bundesbank could probably make out a good case for repatriating at least part of the gold to Frankfurt. In the interests of international financial diplomacy, however, the vast store of bullion seems likely to be left undisturbed.

Very few of the Bundesbank's council ever have cause to go near the vaults. Their natural habitat is the room on the thirteenth floor. Here, every second Thursday, the seven-strong directorate, together with the presidents of the nine regional *Landeszentralbanken*,* cluster in their brown leather-upholstered chairs around an oval table of veneered oak to deliberate the Bundesbank's next monetary policy moves. This solid item of furniture is normally decorated simply with two rows of solid glass ashtrays (mainly used as paper weights, since few members now smoke). But on meeting days it is studded with bottles of soft drinks and piles of document folders. Around it, the fortunes of the D-Mark are weighed and moulded.

The Thursday meetings provide a forum to discuss the state of the domestic economy, international developments, and relations with the government. Members' most heated remarks often concern ostensibly banal matters affecting staffing and organisation – although these are frequently delegated to separate subcommittees. The centrepiece of the council's deliberations concerns the setting of its discount and Lombard rates.[6] These are the pivotal interest rates at which the Bundesbank lends out money to the banks; they represent the main instrument for influencing credit in Germany – and throughout Europe. As another means of carrying out monetary policy, the council has the power to alter the volume of funds in the banking system by changing banks' minimum reserves. These are deposits made by commercial banks around the country, held interest-free at the *Land* central banks as a 'buffer' against financial volatility. The system – established when the Allies set up the Bank deutscher Länder in 1948† – freezes a proportion of bank deposits and so increases the costs of their lending operations.

More important than adjustments to minimum reserves (these days, highly infrequent) are the Bundesbank's open market policies. Here, it regulates liquidity in the banking system through short-term purchases and sales of government bonds and other securities. The operational decisions on the volume of such transactions are made by the Bundesbank's directorate. The council however keeps

---

* Reduced in November 1992 from 11 *Land* central bank chiefs.
† See chapter 6.

the directorate on a relatively tight rein by setting overall interest rate guidelines for open market transactions at its fortnightly meetings. The Bundesbank has become much more innovative and flexible in its open market activities during the 1980s. In particular, it has had to deal with very large daily swings in the volume of funds circulating on money markets caused by the effect of greatly increased budget deficits on government finances.

Below the thirteenth-floor meeting room, the Bundesbank president and the rest of the directorate maintain their offices off a twelfth-storey corridor clad with well-trodden off-white carpet. To reach the floor above for their regular deliberations, the senior members of the Bundesbank ascend in stately fashion a spiral staircase. Sometimes, a respectful posse of TV cameramen is on hand to record the key figures in Germany's monetary theocracy smiling and shaking hands as they file in to the meeting chamber. On their way up the stairs, the council members wander past two eloquent examples of modern German art: a swirling mural display of large iron nails, and a gleaming white aluminium and glass collage, rotating like a piece of operating theatre equipment, and powered by a small motor. The nailed board – *Weisser Wind* ('white wind') – cost DM120,000, while the rotating oeuvre was acquired for DM70,000. Spendthrift tendencies are however firmly under control. The motor is turned off between 8 o'clock at night and 8 o'clock in the morning to save electricity.

The thirteenth floor is studded with colourful paintings from the Bundesbank's contemporary collection, but the council chamber makes no obvious concessions to luxury. It is a place for doing business; in the interests of efficiency and improved communication, the meeting table has actually shrunk over the years. The 1957 Bundesbank Law lays down that the directorate can contain up to ten members. Together with the *Land* central bank chiefs, the council would then comprise more than twenty members; the first Bundesbank meeting table was thus crafted to provide room for a corresponding number of chairs around it. The directorate has normally, however, been a great deal smaller. When he became president in 1980, Karl Otto Pöhl took over a directorate of only six. Together with the eleven *Land* central bank presidents, Pöhl therefore needed only seventeen seats; he reduced the size of the table in 1983 in an effort to increase the council's dynamism. The distance between seats was decreased further when the Bundesbank acquired a new and even smaller table in 1987; the current dimensions measure 17 feet by 8 feet. As part of attempts to improve spontaneity, and cut down the length of individual speakers' contributions, the fixed microphones around the table were removed during the 1980s. These days, the only amplification device is a sensitive high-tech microphone embedded in the centre of the table. This is for the benefit of the official note-taker, a Bundesbank official who sits hunched on a small podium in the right-hand corner of the room.

The Thursday deliberations start at 9.30 in the mornings, and normally last until lunch, which normally takes place from around 1 o'clock onwards. On especially fraught occasions – there were several in 1990 during the run-up to German monetary union – the gatherings can last all day. Early council sessions of the Bank deutscher Länder, when West Germany's own monetary system was being uprooted and replanted, sometimes spilled over into a second day. Participants admit that the quality of the lunch served in the council's top floor dining room often surpasses that of the conversations which precede it. After Pöhl took over in 1980, he inaugurated an important gastronomic change by markedly upgrading the Bundesbank's wine cellars compared with the niggardly stocks bequeathed by his predecessor, Otmar Emminger – a man with little interest in food and drink. One of the fixed items on the Bundesbank's internal calendar is a special festive lunch held to commemorate members' sixtieth birthdays. The central bankers relax and talk about the past, accompanied by speeches and toasts of sparkling wine. Given that the average age of the members is sixty-one or sixty-two, members can look forward to these occasions taking place at least once or twice a year.

Even though the German financial press is normally less inquisitive and sophisticated than in the US and the UK, the Bundesbank council during the 1980s became increasingly worried about leaks. The council has always ruled out any question of tape recording its deliberations, fearing that illicit transcripts would find their way to the press. A typewritten summary of the discussions is drawn up after every meeting, with copies sent to all council members as well as to senior officials in Bonn. These accounts of the Bundesbank's discussions are open for external perusal after thirty years.[7]

Intriguing changes in the Bundesbank's internal procedures have indirectly reduced its public accountability over the last decade.

During the early years of the Bundesbank, conscientious officials produced both a summary and a complete verbatim transcript of the council's fortnightly proceedings. Under the thirty-year rule, in 1991 full records of all meetings up to 1961 could be examined in the Bundesbank's own well-run archive department. Around the end of the 1970s, however, the Bundesbank stopped the custom of regularly writing up a verbatim account of the meetings.[8] In 1990, the council even dispensed with the services of the official stenographer who previously sat next to the note-taker. Accounts of the frequently controversial exchanges at the council's gatherings during the 1980s and 1990s will become eligible for publication from 2010 onwards. But future generations of monetary historians should not expect any revelations: only a highly selective version of the council's debates will ever be laid before their eyes.

iii. 'When we toss in a stone . . .'

Few of the *Landeszentralbank* chiefs are known to the general public. Individually, none of these financial bureaucrats would stand out in a crowd. Their intelligence, salaries, age and vanity are all above average. Some have weak eyes, and make special arrangements to sit on the darker side of the thirteenth-floor table, away from the glare of the south-facing window and the view of the Frankfurt skyline. Remarkably for a country which loves acts of symbolic reverence, no German street has ever been named after a member of the central bank council. Yet the collective importance of this improbable bevy of civil servants, professors and ex-politicians greatly exceeds the sum of its parts. The council's decisions on interest rates, communicated within seconds of their announcement via electronic blips on computer screens, surge through the foreign exchange markets, and thud into the consciousness of government chancelleries around the world. 'When we toss in a stone,' observes one of the council's more outspoken members, Reimut Jochimsen, the Social Democrat central bank president from North Rhine-Westphalia, 'back comes a great wave.'[9]

Every other Thursday morning, the large parking space in front of the Bundesbank's front door becomes an open-air Mercedes display. From all corners of Germany – Hamburg and Munich, Berlin and Bremen – the *Land* central bank chiefs arrive in their metallic-finish limousines (a few, exceptionally, have voted themselves high-powered BMWs), either driven direct from their regional headquarters or chauffeured in from the airport. The fortnightly council meetings form the high points of the *Landeszentralbank* chiefs' working lives. Their jobs are not particularly stressful. 'Well-paid sinecures,' scoffs former economics minister Karl Schiller.[10] In 1991, the presidents of the *Landeszentralbanken* earned roughly DM370,000 a year, the same as the ordinary members of the directorate. The only two on the council to earn more are the president, whose salary is more than DM600,000 (supplemented by additional emoluments as a director of the central bankers' bank in Basle, the Bank for International Settlements, total pay can approach DM700,000), and the vice-president, who earns around DM470,000. Compared with boardroom pay in the Frankfurt commercial banking community – where a senior banker earns well over DM1 million a year – the earnings of the Bundesbank's highest echelons look relatively low. Set against general civil servants' salaries, their wages are, however, embarrassingly high: this is one reason why the exact figures are not made public.

The *Land* presidents' plush offices in the banking centres of their respective states bear witness to their sense of self-importance. Most of the buildings have been rebuilt or extended during the last decade to add status and bearing to the cityscapes of *Land* capitals. The *Landeszentralbank* in Hesse – built next to the original Frankfurt Reichsbank office, which between 1948 and 1972 served as the home of the Bank deutscher Länder and the Bundesbank – is a splendid modern building erected at a cost of DM300 million, studded with fine art. The Saar central bank is a much more modest affair constructed in 1964 as part of sweeping modernisation of Saarbrücken city centre. Hamburg's central bank sits in an unseemly new city centre building created in 1981 to replace the post-First World War Reichsbank next to the city hall.

The Baden-Württemberg and Lower Saxony central banks have their headquarters in elegantly modernised former Reichsbank offices. The Bavarian bank occupies the site in Munich's Ludwigstrasse of a nineteenth-century palace built by the Grand Duke Maximilian, the nephew of the Bavarian King Ludwig I. A source of particular Bavarian pride, this is the place where the Empress 'Sissy' of Austria was born. The granite-clad *Landeszentralbank* in Rhineland-Palatinate – newly built on a green-field site outside Mainz at a cost of DM208 million – offers a different historical perspective. The building boasts not only a startling collection of futuristic sculpture but also the highest-quality and most secure vaults in Germany. The Bundesbank uses the Mainz strongrooms for some of its more delicate monetary transactions. Large quantities of the D-Marks introduced into East Germany in July 1990 were stored in Mainz. Additionally, stacks of new German-printed zloty notes were stored here in summer 1991, waiting to be introduced into Poland in the country's long-expected and much-delayed currency reform.

To make nominations independent of electoral cycles, council members are appointed for eight years – the regional central bank presidents by their respective *Land* government,[11] and the Frankfurt-based Bundesbank directorate members (including the president and vice-president) by the federal government in Bonn.[12] A candidate's political background is crucial: a *Land* central bank president is frequently a card-carrying member of the party in power in the region. Unless the government changes in the meantime, *Land* central bank chiefs are often re-elected for a second eight-year term, until they retire at sixty-six, sixty-seven or sixty-eight. Almost invariably, the top stratum of the Bundesbank is all male. Of the 75 people who have sat on the council since 1948, only one has been a woman, Julia Dingwort-Nusseck, a headstrong and obdurate TV journalist specialising in economic affairs, who served as head of the *Landeszentralbank* in Lower Saxony between 1976 and 1988. The Bundesbank made an extra effort to make her feel at home: a ladies' toilet was specially built for her on the thirteenth floor.

The *Landeszentralbank* chiefs come from a variety of backgrounds. Kurt Nemitz, the Social Democrat president of the Bremen central bank, and the longest-serving member of the council apart from Schlesinger, worked – like several other council members – as a journalist after the war. Nemitz, a man with strong trade union links, was once termed by Pöhl the Bundesbank's 'social conscience'.[13] He retired in March 1992, aged sixty-seven. Nemitz's aversion to interest rate increases was legendary; his family background is less well known. His father was the renowned Jewish doctor and parliamentarian of the Weimar Republic, Julius Moses. A leading figure in Berlin during the 1920s, Moses declined to seek safety abroad after the Nazi takeover in 1933, and met his death in the

Theresienstadt concentration camp in 1942 at the age of seventy-four. As a half-Jew, who took his mother's name, Nemitz himself suffered persecution during the Third Reich.

Lothar Müller, sixty-six, the bucolic president of the Bavarian central bank, and a former confidant of Franz Josef Strauss, the late Bavarian prime minister, is marked by a different form of war experience. As an eighteen-year-old parachutist in 1945, he lost his left arm as the result of splinter injuries received while holding out against the Russian advance on the River Oder. Müller found his way on to a hospital train en route to Denmark, and ended up as a British prisoner of war. Müller makes light of his disability, but when he invites visitors for a breakfast of beer and white Bavarian sausage at his Munich headquarters, a retainer has first to peel the sausage skin for him.

Although few would want to take over British living standards, many council members – like Müller – profess admiration for the English way of life. Another Anglophile is Wilhelm Nölling, the president of the Hamburg central bank, a literary Social Democrat who brings sizeable helpings of emotion and intellect to the council table. Whereas Müller's penchant is for visiting English cathedrals, the former Hamburg finance minister is a Shakespeare *aficionado* who likes to weave quotes from the Bard into his speeches on monetary policy. Nölling, a fierce critic of the Bonn government's economic policies over unification, resigned at the end of October 1992 at the age of fifty-eight – concluding his valedictory speech in Hamburg with a line from *Henry IV part ii*: 'Out of this nettle, danger, we pluck this flower, safety.' Dieter Hiss, sixty-two, the intellectual Berlin central bank boss, also has strong links with the Social Democrats, although he is not a party member. For four years in the 1970s he was Chancellor Helmut Schmidt's key economic policy assistant in the Bonn chancellery.

The most accomplished monetary technocrat among the *Land* chiefs was Karl Thomas, sixty-three, the Frankfurt-based president of the Hesse central bank, who was appointed after a long career in the Bundesbank's monetary department. Thomas, a member of the liberal Free Democratic Party (FDP), gained a considerable reputation as a thoughtful, softly spoken and humorous monetary hawk.* The most diffident member of the board is Heinrich

* Thomas died unexpectedly in August 1992. He was replaced by Horst Schulmann, a former senior adviser to Chancellor Helmut Schmidt.

Schreiner, sixty-five, a Christian Democrat state government official who heads the Rhineland-Palatinate bank in Mainz. With somewhat painful haplessness, Schreiner has been known to telephone economist colleagues from the private sector before meetings to ask their advice about important monetary matters on the agenda. The most controversial is Hans-Jürgen Koebnick, fifty-four, the mayor of Saarbrücken appointed in 1991 as head of the Saar central bank – against the opposition of the Bundesbank directorate. Pöhl wanted to phase out the Saar central bank under the Bundesbank's reorganisation plans – but the majority of the *Länder* resisted. Under the November 1992 reorganisation, the Saar *Landeszentralbank* merged with Rhineland-Palatinate. Koebnick was promoted to head the joint central bank, sending Schreiner into earlier-than-expected retirement.

Just to underline its seriousness, at the beginning of 1992 the line-up of *Land* central bankers included three professors.† The one with the greatest reputation for long-windedness is Norbert Kloten, sixty-six, a former chairman of Bonn's economic advisory council, who held the job in Baden-Württemberg between 1976 and his retirement in April 1992.** At the ceremony to commemorate Kloten's departure, Schlesinger remarked with feeling that one of Kloten's greatest strengths was to weigh up 'the pros and cons' of each argument:[14] an exercise which Kloten often carried out on the thirteenth floor with copious thoroughness. The two newer professors are both fifty-eight: Reimut Jochimsen, a former state economics minister for North Rhine-Westphalia, and Helmut Hesse, an international economics expert who now represents Lower Saxony.

The only council member with mainstream private sector experience is Werner Schulz, fifty-six, the head of the Schleswig-Holstein central bank, who was given the job after ten years as board chairman of Volksfürsorge, the trade-union-owned insurance company. A man of refreshingly open views, he took a 50 per cent salary cut when he came to the Bundesbank. But the job of a *Land* central banker is clearly much more relaxed; Schulz says he enjoys the new life twice as much.[15]

During the course of a year, in addition to the fortnightly council meetings, participants will see each other on numerous social

* See chapter 8.
† In addition, Schlesinger and Nemitz held honorary professorships.
** Kloten was replaced by Guntram Palm.

occasions – inauguration festivities for new *Landeszentralbank* presidents, ritualistic opening of buildings, retirement ceremonies and funerals. Once a year, the council decamps to hold a meeting in one of the *Länder*. On such occasions, monetary policy comes fairly low down the list of priorities. The host central bank likes to show off the delights of its home city by organising receptions and cultural attractions such as concerts and museum visits, including special 'spouse' programmes for wives and widows of former council members.

Sometimes, the *Land* central banks lay on festivities of baroque lavishness, In 1985, it was the turn of the *Landeszentralbank* in Bavaria to lay on the 'outside' visit. The result was three days of ceremonial events, culminating in an opera performance. The Bundesrechnungshof, the federal auditing agency, which regularly runs an eye over the Bundesbank's operating expenses, strongly criticised the expense of this get-together. It pointed out that one of the Bavarian *Landeszentralbank*'s receptions alone cost DM180,000 – of which DM13,000 was spent on 'small gifts' for the participants.[16] Lothar Müller, the gregarious Munich central bank chief, regarded the outlay as money well spent. He even had a special silver commemorative medal struck to mark the occasion.

For all their relative anonymity, the age and status of the council members assure them a high degree of prestige whenever they mount a public rostrum in Germany. These characteristics add palpably to their independence – as well as, sometimes, to their stubbornness. The most unlikely council members can turn out to be the strongest monetarist hawks. Several past SPD *Land* central bank presidents, for instance, astounded colleagues by the fervour with which they embraced the campaign against inflation. Hans Wertz, the prickly Social Democrat representing North Rhine-Westphalia, gained an extreme reputation for monetary conservatism. Hans Hermsdorf from Hamburg – a Social Democrat since 1932, who was incarcerated for two years by the Nazis – also became one of the Bundesbank's most orthodox monetarists. With a few exceptions, the occupant of a seat on the thirteenth floor will depart from the Bundesbank only when he retires. He is guaranteed a pension which will ensure him and his dependants a supremely comfortable existence. He will never again have to worry about finding another job. So if he votes for an increase in the discount rate, he is unlikely to lose much sleep about offending the government – or anyone else.

iv. Defiance at court

The Bundesbank president may be the ruler at court, but he is surrounded by defiant princes. Monetary decisions around the thirteenth-floor table are made on a show of hands; and the president has just one vote. Pöhl liked sometimes to create the impression that he alone dictated Bundesbank policies. In fact, Pöhl was the council's hostage as well as its leader. In more sombre moments, he would admit that he could not so much as buy a postage stamp without the approval of the other members. Both Pöhl and Schlesinger, his successor after August 1991, discovered that the council's *esprit de corps* can be remarkably brittle.

The Bundesbank directorate forms a smaller and more cohesive body than the overall council. The seven members of the directorate hold their own regular weekly meetings every Wednesday, and are far better able than the *Land* presidents to coordinate their positions before the alternate Thursday sessions of the full council.[17] Following Pöhl's departure in August 1991 the directorate was temporarily reduced to only five members, but it was back to the complement of seven by May 1992. Apart from Schlesinger, the key personality is Hans Tietmeyer, the vice-president, who joined the Bundesbank in 1990 after seven years as state secretary at the finance ministry. Tietmeyer, a member of the Christian Democratic Union, took an active part in the negotiations on German monetary union during 1990.* Like Otmar Emminger, the former Bundesbank president, Tietmeyer was once a keen table tennis player. He is being groomed to take over the Bundesbank presidency when Schlesinger retires in 1993. Tietmeyer combines missionary enthusiasm and formidable negotiating skills with the charm of a blunderbuss. 'I wouldn't like to have him as an enemy,' is the comment of one Bonn official who knows him well.

A man of somewhat lighter touch is Otmar Issing, a breezy professor from Würzburg. Responsible for macroeconomics, he has held the job since October 1990. Günter Storch, a former journalist and public sector banker from Chancellor Kohl's home state of Rhineland-Palatinate,[18] has been since 1987 responsible for coins and note issue, as well as personnel matters. Storch owes his post to his membership of the Free Democratic Party; to add balance to the political line-up of the directorate, it was necessary to find

* See chapter 8.

a candidate from the coalition partner in the Bonn government. Johann Wilhelm Gaddum, a former Christian Democrat finance minister from Chancellor Kohl's home state of Rhineland-Palatinate, has been in charge of banking and credit since 1986. In 1990, he moved to take responsibility for the Bundesbank's operations in East Germany as well.* The other two directorate members are both long-serving Bundesbank technocrats, appointed in May 1992: Wendelin Hartmann, who looks after the central bank's organisational and administrative affairs, and Helmut Schieber, formerly from the Baden-Württemberg *Land* central bank.

During the early post-war years, the personal bonds at the Bundesbank owed a great deal to the Reichsbank heritage. Compared with the earlier period under Vocke, Blessing or even Klasen, *Land* central bank chiefs are now less willing to accept the natural authority of the president. The entry of a significant number of Social Democrats during the past twenty years, too, has brought an extra dash of political pluralism into a body previously dominated by the Christian Democratic Union. Like Germany itself, the central bank council has become more heterogeneous, more argumentative, less disciplinarian – and more democratic.

To the general public abroad as well as at home, Pöhl was the all-powerful Mr D-Mark – a role he cultivated, but also came to dislike. In Germany, the guardian of the currency is automatically the recipient of the sort of respect shown in other countries towards monarchs or bishops. In his later years in office, Pöhl became increasingly irritated by some aspects of his celebrity status. He turned down invitations to go to balls, and refused endless requests from Germany's lurid popular newspapers for family photo sessions with his young daughter and son. Pöhl's colleagues on the international central banking circuit knew very well that his aura of monetary omnipotence was partly a façade. Pointing to the delicacy of Pöhl's position on the one-man-one-vote council, a prominent central banker who knows Pöhl well once commented: 'It is absurd to say that he is the most powerful central banker in the world. He is not taken that seriously.' Robin Leigh-Pemberton, the governor of the Bank of England, with whom Pöhl built up a close relationship during their monthly meetings at the Bank for International Settle-

* See chapter 2.

ments, said of him: 'To some extent, he is at the mercy of the Bundesbank council. This causes him to think carefully.'[19]

By the time of his resignation, Pöhl had grown progressively weary of the relentless fortnightly task of winning a consensus from this fractious coterie of elderly central bankers. They needed to be consulted not only on monetary policy decisions but also on seemingly routine organisational matters such as streamlining the Bundesbank's over-manned bureaucracy. Pöhl had entered office in 1980 with the hope of cutting sharp growth of staff levels at the Bundesbank's country-wide network of roughly 210 branches run by the regional central banks. He soon realised however that he could not embark on a collision course with individual *Land* central bank chiefs: this would jeopardise their support for his interest rate proposals. Between the start of Pöhl's presidency in 1980 and the beginning of 1990, the Bundesbank's total staff increased from 14,400 to 15,600; most of the increase represented extra employees taken on in the *Länder*. By the beginning of 1991, with personnel inflated by the network of fifteen branches in eastern Germany, total staff numbers increased to just over 17,500. In January 1992, the numbers were up further to 18,240.

Though council members may be opinionated, even the most assertive newcomer is put firmly in his place. Long-standing ritual decrees that the council's seating order depends on seniority. Newly arrived members start off at the foot of the table. The seniority seating system was introduced after the war in the spartan Taunusanlage quarters of the Bank deutscher Länder, by Karl Bernard, the first president of the council.* It can take a decade or more for a freshly appointed Zentralbankrat member painstakingly to work his way towards the president and his deputy seated at the far end. Occasional guests from the government – normally the finance or economics ministers, a state secretary or, exceptionally, the chancellor himself – sit on the right hand side of the president.[20] Under Article 13 of the Bundesbank's law, government representatives – either ministers or officials – have the right to attend meetings, but not to vote. If the Bundesbank decides a measure with which the government disagrees, the government has the legal power to hold up decisions for two weeks. This temporary veto has never been formally deployed, although the Bundesbank has sometimes

* See chapter 6.

acceded in advance to government wishes by postponing for two weeks an interest rate decision which it knows will be unpopular.*

Council sessions follow a set-piece pattern. The meetings start with an introduction of variable length from the president, followed by surveys on macroeconomic developments, the credit markets and international affairs (in that order) from the directorate members responsible for these areas. For the more timid members of the council, the monologues can constrain their own readiness to speak up. The more seasoned *Land* central bank chiefs often react differently: they find the long exposés an irksome reminder of the directorate's influence. In 1991 some *Land* representatives, seeking a better method of preparing themselves for the Thursday sessions, tried to persuade the directorate members to transmit a copy of their prepared remarks to them the previous day by fax machine. The campaign was unsuccessful. But it was an example of defiance towards the Frankfurt directorate which would have been barely conceivable in the 1960s or 1970s.

v. Persuading the president's men

In discussions on interest rate policy, the Bundesbank president and his deputy generally put to the council meeting a joint proposal for a particular course of action. Although Pöhl and Schlesinger occasionally disagreed at council meetings during the early 1980s, they normally avoided any serious dissonance. In 1987 came a notable exception. A seemingly inconsequential decision at the end of September that year to increase by 0.1 percentage points the Bundesbank's key money market interest rate for securities repurchase transactions from banks was taken at the behest of Schlesinger, against Pöhl's advice.[21] This came at a particularly delicate time, just before a meeting of the world's top finance ministers and central bank governors in Washington. When the news became public, it sparked anger at the US Treasury, which blamed the Bundesbank for impeding efforts to spur the German economy towards faster growth. During the course of October, James Baker, the US treasury secretary, complained fiercely after the Bundesbank raised the repurchase rate further later in the month. Somewhat ludicrously, Baker blamed Schlesinger and a hard money 'clique'[22]

* See chapter 7.

at the Bundesbank for triggering the notorious October 1987 stock market collapse.

Pöhl and Schlesinger occasionally disagreed on personnel matters, too. When in 1990 a replacement on the directorate needed to be found for Claus Köhler, the long-standing member responsible for banking and credit, Pöhl at first favoured the nomination of Ernst-Moritz Lipp, the young chief economist at the Dresdner Bank, as part of a bid to rejuvenate the Bundesbank's top floor. Schlesinger demurred, pointing out that Lipp would have difficulty asserting himself within the bank. Pöhl saw Schlesinger's point of view, and assented to Schlesinger's choice of Issing, who could rely on his orthodox monetary credentials from Würzburg university to make his authority felt.

From 1989 onwards, the consensus around the council table became much more fragile; the mood became still more fraught during the 1990 disagreements over German monetary union.* On two occasions, the president and vice-president were outvoted over interest rates. On 20 April 1989, the council reached fundamental agreement on the need to increase the discount and Lombard rates. For purely tactical reasons, Pöhl and Schlesinger wanted to postpone an increase to avoid discomfiting Theo Waigel, the new finance minister, nominated for office in a cabinet reshuffle a week earlier. A majority of other council members voted, however, to put into effect immediately a half point increase in the two rates, upsetting the attempt to smooth relations with the new minister.

This was a blow for Pöhl's authority, but hardly a major upheaval. The second episode was more spectacular. The decision to increase the discount and Lombard rates by a half point on 19 December 1991, a week after the EC summit in Maastricht, sent a shock wave around Europe. Pöhl's successor Schlesinger and his deputy, Tietmeyer, both argued at the council meeting that the increase in the Lombard rate should be limited to a quarter point to avoid upsetting Germany's EC partners. They were however over-ruled by a narrow 7 to 6 majority, with influential representatives such as Müller from Bavaria and Jochimsen from North Rhine-Westphalia joining forces to outvote the Bundesbank's top two executives.[23]

As the April 1989 and the December 1991 incidents illustrate, politics play an important part in determining the timing of interest

* See chapter 8.

rate changes.[24] A golden Bundesbank rule is to avoid increasing interest rates immediately before European summit meetings or important IMF gatherings. This type of politicking does not appeal to Helmut Hesse, the Lower Saxony central bank chief, who took up his post in December 1988. He says he found the general level of debate around the table 'disappointing' during his first year of council membership. As a result of his academic training and his membership of various Bonn government advisory bodies, Hesse had been expecting the council's deliberations to be a great deal more professorial. In fact, he says, 'A lot of decisions were not scientifically founded, but depended on politics. I learned in my second year that monetary policy is also high politics.'[25]

With a strong reputation for scholarly iconoclasm, Hesse is suspicious about the directorate's exposure to international pressures – and says its power needs to be held in check. 'If you are a member of the directorate, you are always in international conferences and working groups. Without knowing it, you lose contact with reality.' The *Land* central bank presidents, Hesse believes, form a vital counterweight precisely because they are not part of this political carousel. They have, he says, more opportunity to be objective:

> The monetary masters of the world meet regularly, they become personally close to one another. They call themselves not 'Mr President', but 'Karl Otto'. This is a good thing – but it is also a form of straitjacket which can be constrictive, because you have to take into account the personal interests of other people you meet. The Bundesbank president is certainly independent. But the *Landeszentralbank* president is a bit more independent – because he is totally unprejudiced.

Former chancellor Helmut Schmidt takes a diametrically opposite view of the power of the *Land* central bank chiefs. The experience of suffering the Bundesbank's high interest rates at the beginning of the 1980s – an important reason for the coalition bickering which forced him from office in 1982* – has left him embittered about the central bank's influence. Schmidt believes that *Land* representatives enjoy too great a policy hold. One of his favourite themes is that the *Land* central banks have been trying to block European monet-

* See chapter 7.

ary union because they would be emasculated by the establishment of a European central bank:

> Some people in the Bundesbank have arrogated for themselves the position enjoyed by the Constitutional Court in Karlsruhe. They have this ridiculous habit of taking votes, and not just following the lead of the president. The federalisation of the Bundesbank mechanism was an understandable policy in the 1950s when the Bundesbank was created, to counter the fear of too much centralisation. But it should be revised now.[26]

Leonhard Gleske, on the other hand, the former directorate member in charge of international monetary affairs, argues that the federal Bundesbank structure is necessary to counter undue concentration of power. A member of the central bank council for twenty-five years, Gleske says that federalism and independence are inextricably mixed:

> You need people in the council who reflect different developments in different parts of Germany. They come from different backgrounds, and are chosen by different procedures, corresponding to different political currents. Such a council makes it possible for a central bank to be independent. Otherwise, I would have my doubts about giving such a body so much independence.[27]

vi. 'He was incapable of diplomacy'

Faced with the task of steering the council in the direction he favours, a successful Bundesbank president needs to have an aptitude for psychology as well as finance. In order to win over the council, Karl Klasen, the president between 1970 and 1977, a man of commanding presence and disdain for detail, preferred a few cutting words. 'He had a tactic which he learned from Hermann Josef Abs,' recalls Karl Thomas of the Hesse central bank. 'He could make people who spoke too pompously look silly. There is nothing worse than to have a serious speech met by laughter.' Pöhl chose elegance, humour and sarcasm to make his point; Schlesinger prefers the driving force of complex macroeconomic exposés.

Otmar Emminger, the president between 1977 and 1979, was unique in choosing the method of the schoolmaster.

During the council sessions, Emminger developed an awe-inspiring capacity for long-windedness. 'I would ask a two-minute question, and he would give a fifteen-minute answer, just to show that he knew better,' says Johann Baptist Schöllhorn, the former state secretary at the economics ministry under Karl Schiller, who was president of the Schleswig-Holstein central bank between 1973 and 1989.[28] 'For all his personal charm and intellectual talent, he couldn't bear to be put in the shade by anyone else,' says Horst Bockelmann, a former head of the Bundesbank's monetary sub-department, who is now economic adviser at the Bank for International Settlements. 'He was incapable of diplomacy. He always wanted to be right.'[29]

Emminger was a supreme technician, with an able brain. His workaholic attention to detail extended to drawing some of the Bundesbank's monetary graphs himself. For many years, he recorded the proceedings of council sessions in his own shorthand. During Emminger's seven years as vice-president under Klasen, a period which included the stormy transition to floating exchange rates, the Bundesbank's 'foreign minister' saw his self-confidence growing with each international monetary meeting. For all his ego-centricity, Emminger had a down-to-earth touch, and used to take pride in carrying his own bag of documents to crisis gatherings. This was something neither the haughty Klasen nor the image-conscious Pöhl would ever do.

When he took over the Bundesbank reins at the beginning of 1980, Pöhl had spent two and a half years as Emminger's deputy watching in horror as the elderly president had antagonised the other council members. Pöhl vowed to do better. With his own brand of expertise and wit, he succeeded in turning the council gatherings into occasions which were, on the whole, agreeable as well as effective. But for all his veneer of bravura and bonhomie, Pöhl never found the council's atmosphere particularly sociable.

Compared with the sense of hierarchy and formality of the Bundesbank, Pöhl much preferred the easier, first-name-terms style of his monthly meetings (in English) with fellow central bank governors at the Bank for International Settlements in Basle. Never able to shake off completely his lowly origins, in a curious way Pöhl felt slightly elevated by the company of patricians. Old Etonian landowner Robin Leigh-Pemberton, or Jacques de Larosière of the Banque de France – who entertains guests for angling weekends in his wife's castle in Picardy – were a cut above the grey functionaries he would meet in the Bundesbank corridors.

Pöhl kept his distance from most of the other council members less because he was disdainful of their intellectual abilities than because of the relative colourlessness of their characters. As for the permanent staff at the Bundesbank's Frankfurt headquarters, Pöhl was torn between amusement and frustration at their stiffness. Pöhl was a member of the Bundesbank's directorate for fourteen years. Even after this long period, Pöhl still addressed all the other directorate members in the formal *Sie* form. Pöhl called four other members of the council *Du* – Nemitz, Nölling, Jochimsen (all three, like Pöhl, members of the Social Democratic Party), and the jocular one-armed Müller from Munich (who coaxed the reluctant president into a mutual *Du* relationship during a bout of social beer-drinking one evening in Bonn).[30]

Pöhl normally felt it beneath his dignity to turn up at the informal gatherings of *Land* central bank chiefs who convened for eve-of-meeting get-togethers in the Bundesbank guest-house. These Wednesday evening sessions were a regular fixture during the 1970s, organised by men like Hans Hermsdorf of the Hamburg central bank and Fritz Duppré from Rhineland-Palatinate, but during the 1980s far fewer *Land* central bank chiefs turned up at the gatherings. During his years as vice-president, Schlesinger sometimes put in an appearance. This was not so much out of a desire for conviviality; Schlesinger is on *Du* terms with no one on the council.[31] Rather, Schlesinger wanted discreetly to gauge opinion among the *Landeszentralbank* heads to prepare for a decision on interest rates the next day.

vii. Layers of responsibility

Notwithstanding the ritualism on the thirteenth floor, visitors to the Bundesbank generally witness a refreshing absence of stuffiness. The lifts and corridors are full of short-skirted secretaries and shirt-sleeved messengers ferrying cups of coffee and document files, or exchanging the standard midday greeting – *Mahlzeit* – on the way to lunch. The Bundesbank has its own ground-floor self-service staff canteen, full to bursting at midday; this is also the venue for weekly meetings of the Bundesbank's skat and chess clubs. In a smaller room next door, the Bundesbank boasts its own cafeteria, serving coffee and cakes. During the summer, chairs and tables are laid out on the lawn outside, creating an almost holiday camp atmosphere. The canteen serves a nutritious selection of midday meals, including, for some unfathomable reason, the occasional exotic rice dish from Indonesia. Bundesbank employees are not encouraged to over-indulge at lunchtimes. A large sign over the counter advertises the world-famous alcohol-free beer from the Upper Harz spa town of Clausthal-Zellerfeld near the old East–West German border.[32]

The Bundesbank sports club is an important focus of collegiate spirit. With around 3000 members – bank employees and their families, and pensioners – the club runs twenty-nine different activities ranging from angling, skat, model railways and photography to football, karate and shooting. The fee is well within the reach of Bundesbankers' pockets: DM3 per month. Several of the Bundesbank's more senior officials are regular skittlers. Few higher-ranking functionaries do anything energetic – although Dieter Hiss, the president of the Berlin central bank, occasionally uses the swimming pool, and Gerd Häusler, the young head of the credit department, is a basketball enthusiast. For its more literary employees, the Bundesbank runs a drama group attached to the sports club. It puts on well-attended performances of plays ranging from J. B. Priestley to Jean-Paul Sartre – as well as the occasional comedy.

Sporting engagements form a little-known part of international central banking cooperation. The Bundesbank takes part in regular sports events against the main European central banks.[33] The Bundesbank may win international anti-inflation honours, but its footballers have struggled to find their touch. Five Bundesbank v. Bank of England matches during the 1980s ended with three wins for the British and only one for the Bundesbank, with one game drawn. The Germans' worst performance came with a 7–1 drubbing from Threadneedle Street in 1984. The sports club with its distinctive red and white pennant was formed as recently as in 1968, but the sporting tradition was already firmly established at the Reichsbank. Jürgen Matthiessen, who has chaired the club since 1981, points out that international contests bring home a sense of the bank's 'broken history'.[34] Unlike most of its partners – the Bank of England and the Banque de France boast particularly sumptuous sports facilities – the Bundesbank does not have its own sports grounds. Instead, the Bundesbank has to hire municipal football pitches or local tennis courts.

For all the sense of informality in the corridors or on the sports grounds, a sense of hierarchy runs through every Bundesbanker's bloodstream. The bank's decision-making structure is highly compartmentalised, with communications organised vertically, up and down departments, rather than horizontally. Relations between different parts of the bank are the preserve of directorate members and heads of departments, referred to throughout the bank by a coded system of Roman or Arabic numerals and initials. Every person throughout the Bundesbank is known by a series of these symbols – the shorter the reference, the higher the rank in the pecking order.[35] In a system which originated in the Reichsbank, and was kept unchanged after the war, the president is referred to in internal bank documents simply as +, the vice-president as 0.[36]

If the directorate members are the Bundesbank's helmsmen, the engineers in the stoking room are found immediately below, on the eleventh floor. The lower ranking in the pecking order is indicated in a none too subtle way: the carpet colour turns from immaculate off-white to sickly yellow-green. The main task of the economics and statistics department on the eleventh floor is monetary analysis.[37] Information is disseminated through the Bundesbank's authoritative monthly[38] and annual reports, as well as through a proliferation of speeches and newspaper articles by directorate members. The bank prints 52,000 copies of its monthly report,[39] with special translated versions published in English, French and Spanish.[40]

The man who fostered the tradition of the monthly report was Eduard Wolf, the central bank's senior economist during the first two post-war decades[41] – a man whose impatient perfectionism could drive female staffers to tears.[42] Since the Wolf era, the department's size and output has increased dramatically. With so much of their work channelled towards the monthly report, Bundesbank economists rarely, if ever, publish original material under their own name. Outside economists, used to a more free-wheeling atmosphere in private research institutes or banks, find the Bundesbank's working style oppressive. Criticism is also sometimes voiced of the reports' relatively limited coverage, as well as of their laboured and unadventurous language. The monthly report rarely ventures into fields like international banking, securities markets innovation, banking supervision or payments systems – themes outside the Bundesbank's chief areas of preoccupation. Most readers however probably find reassuring the innate conservatism of the Bundesbank's regular publications.

When Wolf died of a heart attack in 1964, Helmut Schlesinger, then aged thirty-nine, took over as head of the economics and statistics department,[43] with the task of maintaining the Bundesbank's reputation and quality in the macroeconomics field.[44] Schlesinger's route up through the department has given him experience unmatched by anyone else in the bank; but it has been a rather narrow career path. Even during his years as the Bundesbank's vice-president, Schlesinger was able to sit down at almost any desk in the economics section and carry out each staff member's job. In earlier years, Schlesinger was notorious for patrolling the eleventh floor at 5.30 p.m. and asking why staffers were not at their desks. In the aftermath of Wolf's death, however, Schlesinger was seriously worried about his capability for the job. Looking back, more than a quarter of a century afterwards, he says, 'I found that very difficult. I thought I could not write as well as Wolf. I had to fight my way through'[45] – an unusual admission of anxiety from a man not normally known for self-doubt.

viii. Dealing in D-Marks

The hub of the Bundesbank's monetary trading with the outside world is its foreign exchange and treasury centre, located on the seventh floor. Because of a plethora of heat-radiating video-screens, this and the twelfth-storey directorate floor are the Bundesbank's sole office areas to enjoy air conditioning. The south-facing side of the seventh-floor office, looking towards the Frankfurt city centre, is taken up by the department investing and managing the Bundesbank's foreign exchange reserves. Less than 1 per cent of this sum is held in currencies other than the dollar; nearly all of the total comprises an amount of roughly $50 billion, held above all in US government Treasury bonds and Treasury notes of up to ten years' maturity.[46] Up until the mid-1980s, the New York Federal Reserve managed this huge portfolio on behalf of the Germans, but the Bundesbank has since taken a far more active stance in managing its own reserves. Daily turnover by the treasury dealing room fluctuates between $500 million and $1 billion.[47]

The Bundesbank's reserves include a large volume of European Currency Units, part of arrangements for partial pooling of reserves set up under the European Monetary System, but these are no more than book-keeping entries. In contrast to the Bank of England, the Banque de France or the Bank of Italy, the Bundesbank holds no 'private sector' ECUs (as opposed to the 'public sector' ones formed under the EMS arrangements); it has resolutely refused to go down the path of the multi-currency reserve system. The Bundesbank's distaste for the ECU is not simply a reflection of conservatism. It also illustrates a lack of enthusiasm for one of the central components of French plans for European Monetary Union.*

On the north side of the seventh-floor area, the Bundesbank's half-dozen foreign exchange dealers sit around an octagonal trading desk with a dollar note hanging symbolically on a thread in the middle. Along with a battery of screens, the room displays clocks telling the time in Tokyo, Singapore, Frankfurt, London and New York. The dealers' job is to maintain a watchful eye over the currency markets. If exchange rates become far out of line with those deemed appropriate, the Bundesbank can summon the might of its intervention capabilities to restore order.

The man in charge of intervention strategy is Franz Scholl, the head of the Bundesbank's foreign department, who joined the Bank deutscher Länder in 1952. He can lay claim to being a pioneer of the international central bankers' circuit. A burly man of rustic good humour, he was sent as a trainee to the International Monetary Fund immediately after West Germany joined the Washington-based institution in 1952. Unlike some senior currency officials at the Bank of England, Scholl does not have a miniature currency dealing screen at home; he generally dislikes being disturbed after hours. But colleagues at the Bank of Japan have his home telephone number, just in case he needs to be awoken at 4 a.m. to cope with a yen crisis.

When EMS currencies are trading quietly, or if the dollar is in a narrow range against the D-Mark, sterling or the yen, the Bundesbank dealing room can be a picture of tranquillity, with only one or two traders at their desks. There are however always routine

* See chapter 9.

deals. The foreign exchange department executes a variety of commercial operations for the German government. These range from handling regular dollar transactions for American troops stationed in Germany to paying out *Wiedergutmachung* pensions for Jewish victims of Nazi oppression living abroad.

When the currency markets start to fluctuate excessively, central banks need to act in concert if they wish to take action to stabilise rates. Since the largest single component of world foreign exchange transactions reflects sales and purchases of dollars against D-Marks, the Bundesbank generally takes the lead in European central bank intervention. The size of the Bundesbank's reserves, combined with its reputation for choosing the right psychological moment to intervene, often means that the mere entry of the bank into the market will calm the D-Mark/dollar rate. Scholl terms intervention strategy 'more art than economics'. He says, 'The important thing is that we must not be predictable. Concerted action works only if it is not a copy of others we have done in the past.'[48]

The Bundesbank reckons that, to be effective, it must spend at least $300 million in a day's transactions. The Bundesbank dislikes intervening to brake a well-developed 'fundamental' trend on the exchange markets; but it has a knack of getting its timing right. The Bundesbank normally trades with commercial banks in deals of $5 million a time, but can act for smaller amounts when dealing through money brokers. These latter deals have more effect, as the brokers through their communications networks signal instantly that the Bundesbank is flexing its muscles.

There is a paramount need for up-to-date reports on currency developments abroad and consultations with partner central banks. The Bundesbank switches in to telephone conferences with the foreign exchange rooms of the other European Community central banks four times a day – at 9.30 a.m., 11.30 a.m., 2.00 p.m. and 4.00 p.m. The New York Federal Reserve Bank is on the line at 1.00 p.m. to check on the morning's developments in Europe, and then takes part in the normal afternoon discussions.

Coordinated intervention, sometimes by as many as fourteen or fifteen central banks (including non-EC members like the Scandinavian countries, as well as Austria and Switzerland), is usually prepared several days in advance, with military precision. During the most active bout of intervention in recent years – on 7 January

1987, when the French franc suffered dramatic strains against the
D-Mark in the EMS – the Bundesbank and partner central banks
sold DM5 billion in one day. But such frantic activity is exceptional.
Even during periods of foreign exchange market turbulence – after
unexpected election results, or following the stock exchange crash
in October 1987 – the Bundesbank is normally more busy talking
to other central banks than intervening directly on the markets.

If the dollar is under pressure, European central banks invariably
press for participation by the Federal Reserve to convince the
markets that the authorities mean business. The Bundesbank however seldom knows until the last moment whether the Fed will be
taking part. The Bundesbank can act autonomously, since it owns
Germany's foreign exchange reserves. The New York Fed simply
manages the US reserves on behalf of the Treasury – and must
seek Washington's approval for its exchange market forays. Scholl
points to the New York Fed's lack of clout. He once told a colleague
at the Bank of England that the way the Fed functioned in the
currency markets reminded him of his cat. 'You never hear it. You
never know when it's operating. And you never know if it's caught
anything.'

ix. Burning money

Germans are peculiarly attached to wads of banknotes. Use of
cheques and automatic payments systems is generally less developed
than in other countries. The volume of notes and coins in circulation in Germany makes up 6.5 per cent of gross national product,
one and a half times as much as in the US and France, and twice
the proportion in Britain and Canada.[49] Perhaps because of the
history of currency debauchery, the Germans prefer their money
to be in good condition: more often than in other countries, the
public rejects tattered or dirty banknotes. The Bundesbank thus
faces a particular need to ensure that only top-quality notes remain
in circulation. It has developed considerable expertise not only in
producing banknotes – but also in destroying them in the cheapest,
safest and most environmentally sound way.

In 1990, the Bundesbank spent DM190 million printing money
– using 5000 tonnes of paper in the process.[50] In 1991 the costs
rose to an exceptional DM331 million. German banknotes have no
Queen's head on them; but the latest designs embody the next best
thing. The favourite personality depicted on the new notes is Clara

Schumann, the nineteenth-century pianist and wife of composer Robert Schumann. Her coolly elegant features adorn not only the DM100 notes but also compact discs of her music distributed as occasional promotional gifts by the Bundesbank's press department. When new notes are brought into circulation, a publicity drive is necessary – especially in view of the D-Mark's international importance. The Bundesbank sends out routine communiqués to foreign consulates in Frankfurt detailing the new issues, but still receives reports of hotels and banks in foreign countries refusing to accept unfamiliar designs.

At the other end of the life cycle of a banknote, the Bundesbank has traditionally destroyed old notes through burning them at the rate of two to three tonnes a day at a special incinerator in its Frankfurt headquarters. The Bundesbank normally destroys more than 500 million notes a year – worth between DM25 and DM30 billion. At 1100 degrees C, the process produces no smoke. But the Bundesbank for some years has been perturbed about the cost and laboriousness of the process. Additionally, in ecology-conscious Germany, eyebrows have been raised about the carbon dioxide escaping into the atmosphere. The Bundesbank has come up with an answer – an automatic high-speed shredding machine, costing about DM500,000, being rapidly installed in Bundesbank branches around the country, obviating the need for old notes to be brought to the central Frankfurt collection point.[51] The shredded notes are used as industrial filling material and for insulation; the Bundesbank has yet to find any more adventurous ways of turning old D-Marks to good use.

x. Over-rated and under-paid?

Pay is something of a problem for the Bundesbank. It is one area where its famed autonomy does not apply: the salaries of its 18,000-plus staff are laid down according to standard earnings scales worked out nationally between public sector unions and the government.[52] In recent years, booming earnings in the private financial sector forced the Bundesbank to make the occasional foray into the political ring to press for higher rewards to match higher salaries elsewhere. It makes such pleas at its peril: by appearing to depart from its usual anti-inflation rhetoric, the Bundesbank exposes itself to charges of double standards. Pointing out that his own

DM600,000-plus annual salary was only half what he could have received in a private bank, Pöhl liked to declare that Bundesbankers were 'over-rated and under-paid'. The Bundesbank's most senior staff – above all, the council members – are, in fact, generously treated and cannot complain. But for those lower down the pay scale, the Bundesbank's pay protestations have started to look increasingly justified.

Salaries of Bundesbank council members are laid down by individual contracts signed with the council. Their pay, however, is subject to approval by the government. During the 1950s, this was a matter of considerable irritation to Wilhelm Vocke, who did his best to thwart Bonn's control over Bank deutscher Länder salaries.[53] Another post-war central bank chief who believed that Bundesbank salaries should be higher was Karl Klasen. When Karl Schiller, the economics minister, approached him at the end of the 1960s and asked him to take over from Karl Blessing as Bundesbank president, Klasen was earning about DM500,000 a year as a board member of the Deutsche Bank.[54] Pointing out that he would be accepting a big drop in income, Klasen asked Schiller to boost the Bundesbank salary to roughly half what he was earning from private banking.[55]

During his spell as Bundesbank president, Klasen kept up his home in Hamburg. During his sojourns in Frankfurt, he spurned the attractions of the Bundesbank guest-house and occupied a suite (at his own expense) in the luxurious Schloss Hotel in Kronberg in the Taunus hills. Such was his taste for convenience that the Bundesbank requested permission to acquire a private aeroplane to fly Klasen to council meetings from his Hamburg home. The government turned the idea down after Schiller protested that purchasing an aircraft would have reduced the yearly profits the Bundesbank distributed to the finance ministry.[56]

As a young Social Democrat banker after the war, Klasen served as president of the Hamburg central bank between 1948 and 1952, giving him a seat on the Bank deutscher Länder council. Even in the early post-war years, pay comparability with the private sector was an important factor. Klasen and his central banking colleagues were anxious to underscore their right to small salary privileges similar to those in vogue in the private banking industry. In July 1948, shortly after the currency reform introduced on 20 June, Klasen pushed through a decision under which council members routinely received interest on their salary accounts.[57]

Money is a matter for discreet back-biting between Bonn and Frankfurt. Bundesbank council members earn roughly double the salary of top state secretaries in Bonn – who often have to work twice as hard.[58] Even though the central bank habitually criticises pay increases in the public sector, the basic element of a council member's total annual earnings of around DM370,000 is directly indexed to the annual wage settlement attained by German public employees.[59] In contrast to its normal transparency, the Bundesbank draws a veil of official discretion over the salaries of its council members – a sign that it is aware of the possibility of being accused of hypocrisy.

There is less largesse lower down the Bundesbank hierarchy. Standard Bundesbank salaries are often lower than those available in the private banking sector, and the gap has widened in recent years. This has led to problems in attracting and holding on to employees in sectors like dealing and information technology. A member of the Bundesbank's foreign exchange dealing team, for instance, can easily double his salary by joining a commercial bank. Computer specialists in 1992 earned two or three times as much outside the bank. A lower- to middle-ranking Bundesbank civil servant with seven or eight years' service in, say, the credit department, earned in 1992 around DM60,000 a year (£22,000), including allowances. In a post of similar seniority at a private Frankfurt bank, he would have received DM20,000 to DM30,000 a year more.

Working as a civil servant at one of the world's most celebrated central banks does, of course, offer distinct advantages: job security, freedom from normal social security insurance contributions, and help with housing loans.[60] None the less, Pöhl went to the lengths of writing a letter to Chancellor Kohl in April 1989[61] warning of 'difficult bottlenecks' in the personnel area. 'The maintenance of [our] customary standards of performance can no longer necessarily be guaranteed,' Pöhl claimed. Thomas Buch, the Bundesbank's personnel chief, admits that the quality of the intake into the Bundesbank's training college at Hachenburg in the Rhineland has suffered as a result of the relatively poor earnings prospects compared with outside banks.[62]

Another demotivating factor affecting higher-level Bundesbank officials is the lack of prospect of advancement to a directorate job. In the Bank deutscher Länder during the early years of the

Bundesbank, it was fairly common for the brightest and most dilig-
ent staffers to work their way right up to the top. During the 1970s
and 1980s, however, this path frequently became blocked, with the
government increasingly preferring to appoint outsiders on to the
council. One man who left the bank because of this obstacle was
Horst Bockelmann, the former Bundesbank monetary expert, now
at the Bank for International Settlements. Bockelmann points out
that compared with other international central banks, the Bundesbank has an unusually large number of 'outsiders' on its directorate.
'This can have a negative effect on the climate. There can be long-
term difficulty in attracting the right people if they know that their
career is likely to end as department chief.'[63] The promotion to the
directorate in May 1992 of two Bundesbank functionaries, Wendelin Hartmann and Helmut Schieber, was a direct attempt –
initiated by Schlesinger, the Bundesbank's classic insider – to
reverse the previous trend by rewarding home-grown Bundesbank
talent.

Underlining the relative modesty of Bundesbank salaries, a
higher-level official (*Bundesbankrat*) with ten years' service, perhaps
halfway up the hierarchy in the monetary department or working
as the head of a small branch office, earned about DM98,000
(£34,000) in 1992. This includes allowances and the traditional
end-year 'thirteenth month' bonus almost equivalent to one month's
pay. The chief of a larger branch office, representing the Bundesbank in a medium-sized town, or the head of a smaller sub-department in the Frankfurt headquarters (*Bundesbankdirektor*) earned
around DM120,000 (£41,000). The head of a main department
(*Hauptabteilungsleiter*) earned roughly DM210,000 (£72,000). A
young *Bundesbankinspektor* will earn around DM3100 a month
including allowances (DM40,000 a year, or £15,000, when the
bonus is added). A single twenty-six-year-old recruit starting off a
three-year period of preparatory service to qualify as a *Bundesbankinspektor* earns a far-from-princely DM1900 a month, including
allowances – making total annual earnings (with bonus) of less than
DM25,000 (£9000).

The Bundesbankers would like more pay – but are unsure how
to put their arguments to a public which expects them to plead for
austerity above all else. The central bank likes to hand down lofty
rebukes to the protagonists in the pecuniary squabbling outside its
portals. But the Bundesbank is an institution straddling the worlds

of public good and private greed; it has to adapt to the mores of both. The Bundesbank's men will preach the message of sound money with still greater certainty if they are satisfied that they are getting the right rate for the job.

4

Partner in Catastrophe

The future lives of our people, to the greatest possible extent, must be freed from the enormous burdens of the war. The instigators of this war have brought upon themselves the lead weight of billions of Marks; they will drag it through the decades to come, not we.
  Karl Helfferich, secretary of state at the Treasury, 1915[1]

It is not possible to run a central bank without being in harmony with the political principles of the government.
  Hjalmar Schacht, Reichsbank president, 1933[2]

National Socialist economic and financial policy, like National Socialist policy for freedom and equality, has taken upon itself the law of action. We will allow no one in future to strike this from our hand.
  Karl Blessing, senior Reichsbank official, 1935[3]

The Reichsbank was created in 1875 on the crest of a cascade of gold, amassed through reparations extracted from the coffers of the Paris government after the 1870–71 Franco-Prussian war. By the eve of the First World War, the German central bank had become a central pillar of the international monetary system based on the gold standard.[4] But as conflict erupted across Europe, Germany veered away from monetary rectitude by breaking the Mark's link with gold. Once again, as in 1870–71, the Reich hoped to finance the war with revenues from the vanquished. This was one of the most colossal gambles in history; and its failure had colossal repercussions. The heavy burden of reparations imposed on Germany in 1919 in the Versailles peace treaty – immediately denounced by the Reichsbank as 'unfulfillable'[5] – sowed the seeds of the inflation of the early 1920s, and of renewed catastrophe in 1939 as the world once again went to war.

In this doom-laden saga, the Reichsbank was normally a willing partner – though frequently passive, and all too often inept – in the economic policies pursued by successive inter-war governments. As an organisation close to the heart of German power, which for one and a half decades between 1922 and 1937 even enjoyed nominal independence from the German government, the Reichsbank occupied a clear position of influence within the administrative machine. This influence fluctuated and then subsided during the Third Reich. The Reichsbank covered its retreat from power in cravenness rather than glory.

The bank's ability to weather the traumas was weakened by its fundamental faults. It was self-satisfied, unaccountable, overstretched, and under-endowed with men of judgment. The Reichsbank's profoundly undemocratic nature made it, in a sense, a perfect tool in Hitler's hands. It shared with the Führer[6] the precept that monetary stability had to be dispensed from above, rather than created by the people themselves. When the Reichsbank briefly, and with less than whole-hearted conviction, rebelled against Hitler's monetary policies in January 1939, it was already much too late.

i. At the hub of the Reich

The establishment of the Reichsbank under the Banking Act of March 1875 was a seminal date in German and European history. It formed an essential link in the chain of events that was to transform Germany in the final quarter of the nineteenth century into the continent's industrial power-house – the position, after many vicissitudes and much strife, it holds still today.[7]

The Reichsbank emerged from a sea of fragmentation. In the first half of the nineteenth century, Germany was a slumbering patchwork of pre-industrial states, each protective of its boundaries and jealous of its sovereignty. For a unified currency, there was neither the will nor the wherewithal.[8] In contrast to the unified monetary conditions in England and France, there were seven different basic coinage systems across the German Confederation. The statutes of the Prussian-led *Zollverein*, the customs union put into effect in 1834, called for standardisation of German coinage. But rivalries between the main monetary systems – the thaler standard in northern states, including Prussia, and the gulden standard in the south (including Austria, which was not a member of the *Zollverein*) – delayed the breakthrough until after 1871.[9] In the year of the forging of the Reich after the defeat of France, the currency system was as heavily splintered as ever[10] – a significant brake on trade and commerce. Formation of a unified currency was a priority;[11] and the M4.5 billion French war reparations levy, promptly converted into gold bullion on the London market,[12] gave the Reich the means to carry out this aim. The arrival in Berlin of large stocks of bullion allowed the Germans to back the Mark with gold rather than silver, the currency standard in Germany and most of Europe hitherto.[13]

The state bank set up to oversee the new gold-backed currency was a reorganised Bank of Prussia, established in 1846 as the successor of a note-issuing institution founded by Frederick the Great.[14] The Reichsbank's functions were 'to regulate the circulation of money within the jurisdiction of the Empire, to facilitate settlements and to utilise available capital'.[15] Although owned by private shareholders, and enjoying a certain degree of administrative independence, the Reichsbank's place in the state hierarchy was firmly defined. According to the Banking Act, it was 'under the supervision and direction of the Reich'. The chancellor was the chairman of the federal council of curators (*Kuratorium*), the supreme body supervising the bank's functions. The day-to-day management of the bank was in the hands of the president and the other (normally eight) members of the directorate, who were appointed for life by the Emperor and enjoined 'to follow at all times the rulings and directions of the chancellor'.[16] The influence of the Reichsbank's private shareholders was limited. They were represented by a fifteen-member central committee (*Zentralausschuss*), made up largely of industrialists and bankers, who met once a month in an advisory function; they did, however, have the power to veto undue central bank financing of the state's cash needs.

By the time of the Reichsbank's foundation, the growing demands of the fledgling industrial sector had led to a great increase in the number of notes in circulation.[17] In 1871, thirty-three separate note-issuing banks were functioning across the Reich. Under the 1875 Act, the Reichsbank was given a central note-issuing role, but not a monopoly.[18] But by 1904, only four other banks of note issue were left – in the larger non-Prussian states of Saxony, Bavaria, Baden and Württemberg. Another curiosity of the 1875 Act was that banknotes were not made legal currency, reflecting the cautious view of the legislators that a large proportion of gold coins in circulation was the best way to guarantee a stable currency. This statutory discrimination against banknotes was lifted only with a change in the Bank Act in 1909.[19]

In spite of the Reich chancellor's theoretically unlimited power over the Reichsbank, there were only a few cases of direct government interference.[20] The automatic regulation of the gold standard proved to be the most important constraint on the Reichsbank's behaviour. Invariably, rises in the discount rate were linked to the need to attract funds from abroad to increase the gold reserves above the legally required minimum, rather than as part of policy action to dampen credit growth. However, as Germany grew restless with its place in the hierarchy of international power, politics started to intrude into monetary policy. After the Agadir crisis erupted in 1911 (prompted by Germany's expansionist ambitions in North Africa), the Reichsbank directorate became increasingly preoccupied by contingency planning for war. Consequently, it took action to build up the bank's gold stocks. The Reichsbank's gold reserves had fluctuated in the range of M500 million to M700 million in the two decades between 1890 and 1910. They roughly doubled to M1.1 billion in 1913 as the bank converted a large proportion of its foreign securities into bullion.[21] The operation closely resembled the action taken by the Reichsbank to protect its reserves on the eve of the Second World War.*

The Reichsbank knew that the gold stocks were insufficient to cover the large increase in demand for cash likely to be created by the outbreak of hostilities. It therefore made preparations for legislative changes to suspend gold convertibility and increase the printing of paper money. This change in the law, eventually enacted in August 1914,[22] was prepared in 1911, when the Reichsbank declared disingenuously that abandonment of the formal link to gold laid down in the 1875 Act would have 'no factual importance'.[23]

The 1914 legislative change opened up for the first time the possibility for the state to borrow unlimited sums from the Reichsbank. This created an inflation machine which was switched on fully only after the 1918 defeat. The August 1914 legislation set up 'special loan offices' as supplementary branches of the Reichsbank. Their aim was 'above all to support the operation of trade and commerce'[24] through loans (against goods or securities as collateral)

*See chapter 5.

paid out through issues of a new form of paper money, *Darlehnskas-senscheine* (loan office notes). The law maintained the formal rule that one third of notes in circulation should be backed by gold. But the constraint was side-stepped by the ruling that the Reichsbank's own holdings of the new loan office notes would count as part of the gold reserves. Gold was put aside as a regulator of the currency: one form of paper money was turned into backing for another.[25]

ii. Misplaced trust

Germany girded itself for a war which would be – like the conflict of 1870–71 – blessed, short, victorious and indemnified by the enemy. It turned out to be none of these. A key member of the German financial oligarchy whose calculations went drastically awry was Karl Helfferich, state secretary in the Treasury between February 1915 and May 1916. The man controlling the Reich's fiscal policies was an arch exponent of financial wishful thinking. Helfferich, like all bad finance ministers, believed he was spending money in a good cause. The problem of raising the necessary revenues would solve itself: provided the war went according to plan.

Helfferich was a conservative journalist and academic economist, who joined the board of the Deutsche Bank in 1908. He also helped look after Deutsche Bank's interests on the central committee of the Reichsbank. Speaking to the Reichstag in March 1915, Helfferich declared that Germany and its principal ally, Austria-Hungary, were determined to fight the war without tax increases. Pouring scorn on England's attempts to raise revenues through extra taxes, Helfferich pointed proudly to the buoyancy of Reich war bonds compared with British issues. Helfferich relied on the earning power of the German army:

> The present war is being fought not just for the present, but above all for our future. We are sticking to the hope of being able to present our opponents at the conclusion of peace with the bill for the war forced upon us.[26]

Helfferich maintained his confidence when he next spoke before the Reichstag in August 1915. He repeated the pledge not to raise taxes, even though the conflict was costing a staggering M2 billion a month – one third more than the total costs of the 1870–71 war.

'Concerning the raising of resources ... we should take the path of bond issues ... As long as there is no pressing necessity, we do not want to raise taxes and thus increase the considerable burdens which our people have to bear during this war.'[27]

There have been few examples of trust so sorely misplaced. Helfferich's reliance on war financing through long-term bond issues did not end the need for large short-term loans raised from the Reichsbank and private banks.[28] As the conflict lengthened, inflation accelerated in line with the heavily increased volume of cash in circulation.[29] Consumer prices roughly trebled between 1914 and 1918.[30]

As late as August 1918, on the eve of the sudden weakening of Germany's armies in the west, it was still possible for the German people to believe in the success of the Reich's military and financial strategies. That month, Russia agreed to transfer to Germany punitive amounts of gold and goods as part of the Carthaginian peace settlement imposed on the Bolsheviks at Brest-Litovsk in March. The accord came shortly before the Allies paved the way for German defeat by pressing home their September counter-offensive. The booty from the Tsar boosted the Reichsbank's gold reserves to a record M2.5 billion on 7 November. The bullion entered the vaults just two days before the Kaiser abdicated – plunging the country into transition and tumult.

As Germany drifted towards anarchy, political power threatened to pass to the communists. At the end of 1918, a council of revolutionary sailors besieged the chancellery and, for a time, held the government captive. Amid increasing worries about the breakdown of food supplies as well as of civil order, the government drastically increased its short-term borrowing to defray the costs of the demobilisation and the disruption in its wake. By the end of 1918 the Reichsbank's reserves were top heavy with Treasury bills – M27 billion, thirteen times as much as four years earlier.[31] The Reichsbank was certainly aware that excess monetary growth would lead to ruinous inflation. But, assailed by conflicting priorities, it simply watched helplessly as the tide rose all around.

Firm monetary action would have caused pain. It would, though, have been preferable to the agony of the currency depreciation which followed.[32] The crucial factor behind the coming monetary breakdown was the question of reparations. Uncertainty and dismay about the total indemnities set by the war victors sapped the will of the Reichsbank to resist the government's demands for ever more short-term finance.[33] When the terms of the Versailles treaty were published in early May 1919, most Germans were aghast at the vindictiveness of the Allied powers. Chancellor Philip Scheidemann accused the victor powers of trying to make the Germans 'slaves and helots'.[34] In fact, reparations accounted for only a small fraction of state expenditure in the early 1920s. Yet the political and psychological effect of the payments proved a burden from which the republic never recovered.

Confidential Reichsbank letters to the government from 1919 onwards illustrate how the central bank warned about sharply deteriorating monetary trends, but then became resigned to the inevitable. There are intriguing similarities with the admonitory statements made in private by the East German central bank, the Staatsbank, in the 1970s and 1980s: warnings which, again, did nothing to prevent the eventual collapse.* The Reichsbank sent routine letters to the Reich chancellor to accompany publication of the Reichsbank's annual report each spring. The objective was to inform the government of developments which were too sensitive to be dealt with in the published report. In the first few post-war years, two sets of messages – one reassuring, the other doom-laden – were transmitted in parallel. The 1918 annual report, published in March 1919, before the Versailles terms became known, broadcast in relatively confident tones that the demand for cash 'was able to be satisfied in full and without difficulty by the Reichsbank until well into the second half of 1918'.[35] The accompanying unpublished letter, however, pointed out ominously that gold covered only 6 per cent of total cash in circulation (including the *Darlehnskassenscheine*) by the end of 1918, against 40 per cent at the beginning of the war. It spoke of a 'breakdown in German monetary conditions'.[36]

As the government stepped up its short-term borrowing, two further letters in July 1919 – a month after the signing of the Versailles treaty – pointed out that continued Reichsbank credit was creating 'the most serious dangers'.[37] The central bank delivered a melodramatically worded ultimatum:

There is an ever more pressing need to make immediate and considerable cuts in expenditure and to raise new revenue . . .

*See chapter 8.

If this is not accomplished, and the floating debt rises further, the day will not be far removed when we will have to suspend the unrestrained discounting of Treasury bills, in order to stop the Reichsbank and the entire German economy from being destroyed.[38]

Nine months later, the Reichsbank's mood changed again – from defiance to resignation. The Reichsbank's confidential letter to the government at the time of publication of the next annual report – in April 1920 – simply recorded the 'disadvantageous consequences' of a 50 per cent increase in cash in circulation throughout 1919.[39] The bank's threat the previous summer to cut off the flow of funds to the government was all too quickly forgotten.

iii. The crumbling of the mark

In 1920 cash in circulation rose by a further 60 per cent.[40] The Reichsbank recorded that the volume of short-term debt – which had risen more in 1920 than during the whole of the war – was 'a dangerous threat for the Reichsbank'.[41] The war victors meanwhile set a reparations total of 132 billion gold Marks stretching for decades ahead, to be paid, in dollars, through a series of punitive bond issues. In 1921, the Berlin government made the first payment by selling newly printed Marks for the US currency on the foreign exchanges. This transaction contributed to a sharp decline in the Mark's value on the currency markets: the beginnings of a downward spiral. At home, strikes and social unrest worsened. Some companies – such as the Hugo Stinnes conglomerate – profited by grotesquely inflating away their debt payments. But the overall result of the economic chaos, exacerbated by the forced transfer of Upper Silesia to Poland, was a self-fuelling decline in industrial confidence.

In 1921, as cash in circulation again rose by 50 per cent,[42] the vicious circle became still more virulent. The Reichsbank admitted that continuation of massive short-term loans to the government was 'unavoidable'.[43] Rudolf Havenstein, the hapless Reichsbank president, conceded that the threat in July 1919 to cease financing the government's needs had been a bluff.[44] Reparations now became, in the Reichsbank's view, the chief cause of monetary disorder. The central bank emphasised that, as long as the payments to the victors continued at the punishing level demanded, it would continue to take into its reserves all the Treasury bills the government wished to issue.[45]

An important landmark in the Reichsbank's history came in May 1922 with the passing of a law – at the behest of allied creditor nations – making the central bank autonomous from government.[46] The Reich chancellor ceased to be the head of the Reichsbank, and the directorate – although still under government 'supervision' – was theoretically free to make policies on its own.[47] Although Havenstein wrote that the Reichsbank's new statutory position would 'strengthen its authority in its own country', he added revealingly: 'For limiting inflation, today's autonomy of the Reichsbank is but a very small expedient.'[48]

Havenstein's words proved ominous. The granting of the Reichsbank's independence had no effect on controlling inflation, which ran at 1300 per cent in 1922. The Reichsbank continued to discount Treasury bills at an exponential rate.[49] This was the counterpart to floods of paper money being printed round-the-clock. The *coup de grâce* came in January 1923 when the Ruhr was occupied by the French and Belgian armies after Germany had fallen behind on reparation transfers. The Reich government promptly declared its backing for a campaign of peaceful resistance against the foreign troops. The ensuing economic dislocation opened up still more yawning gaps in the state's finances – filled by uninterrupted issues of Treasury bills to the Reichsbank. The central bank put the blame squarely on the reparations policies of the Allied governments. Casting aside any pretence at traditional central bankers' moderation, in May 1923 the Reichsbank assailed the Allies for plotting 'the wholesale destruction of our Fatherland'.[50] In an accompanying letter to the government, the central bank complained that 'the ever quickening collapse of the Reich finances and of the currency' was 'necessarily [the result of] the intolerable burden of the Versailles Diktat'.[51]

A few months later, the Reichsbank's despair deepened further. The Mark's decline against the dollar continued relentlessly as a wave of strikes spread across the country between June and August 1923. 'Enormous demand' for banknotes was certain to cause 'a considerable new inflation far exceeding that seen hitherto', the Reichsbank stated in August 1923.[52] The printing presses were turning out M60 trillion a day in new banknotes; the daily production of money would increase still further once the new M100 million notes were brought into circulation. The Reichsbank declared that it would continue discounting the government's new Treasury bill issues totalling up to M1000 trillion; this was simply a question of 'fulfilling state needs'. The Reichsbank continued to press for budgetary discipline, but it knew that – as long as reparations continued – its pleading was likely to fall upon deaf ears. Like a sanctimonious old lady distraught by innuendoes about her virtue, the Reichsbank recorded its concern about a possible deterioration of its image:

> We foresee attempts in public opinion to make the Reichsbank responsible for the enormous new burdens of increasing inflation and acute payments difficulties. We expect that the Reich government will take care to inform the people and reject these recriminations as unjustified.

Catharsis came in the final quarter of 1923. Currency in circulation, a mere M120 billion in 1921, reached the level of the most surreal of nightmares: M2,500,000 trillion in October 1923, M400,000,000 trillion in November, M497,000,000 trillion in December. Consumer prices measured by the official index rose nearly 2 billion-fold during 1923. At the height of the inflation, a young man named Adolf Hitler was arrested in Bavaria, two days after he attempted to lead his stormtroopers on a march on Berlin on 9 November 1923. The countdown to calamity was under way.

Since the Mark was becoming unusable, economic experts were vying with each other to produce ideas for monetary reform. For several years, economists and professors had been discussing a return to stability through linking the Mark to a 'real' yardstick of unimpeachable value. Attention turned to the idea of issuing bonds repayable in gold and dollars as a means of stabilising government revenues.[53] Private sector companies had already made a start by launching bonds and investment certificates secured against coal, potassium or electricity, as well as agricultural commodities such as rye.[54]

Of the reform alternatives put forward in summer and autumn 1923, the government of Gustav Stresemann turned down a commodity-based scheme for a currency geared to the market price of rye. It favoured the Rentenmark plan, based on a mortgage on all the property in the country. Under these proposals, bearing a name put forward by Hans Luther, the new and tough-minded finance minister, notes would be issued under the aegis of a new institution, the Rentenbank, against the collateral of industrial and agricultural land. Of far greater importance than the technical aspects, the public was persuaded to place their trust in the new currency. The day after the issue of the first Rentenmark notes on 15 November 1923, the Reichsbank stopped discounting Treasury bills. It put out an injunction declaring that massive volumes of 'emergency money' (*Notgeld*) – improvised paper money issued by municipalities and companies – would henceforth no longer be accepted as legal payment. The Reichsbank's holdings of Treasury bills, which reached a high point of M190,000,000 trillion in mid-November, were reduced to zero by the end of the year.[55] Stresemann's minority government was close to falling; but he had put in train the measures necessary for currency stabilisation. The way was open for the introduction of the Reichsmark.

The conversion rate of the new currency was set at one-trillionth of a Mark. This was based on the foreign exchange rate of M4.2 trillion per US dollar at which the currency was stabilised on 23 November – the day when Stresemann's government finally stood down. Public belief in the authorities' resolve to defend the new currency was fostered by Luther's energetic budget cuts. This led to a speedy return to stable money, but without two of the conditions long deemed to be vital prerequisites: a permanent solution to the reparation problem, and a return to the gold standard.[56] On the political front, there was little reason for optimism. The stabilisation of the Mark incurred costs whose full impact was to be felt only later – in Germany, and around the world.

iv. Ambition and ambivalence

The 1923 currency crisis propelled to the monetary helm a man who, at the age of forty-six, had not yet ventured into public life. Once, however, he took over as Reichsbank chief, Hjalmar Horace Greeley Schacht[57] was never in any doubt that both he and his country would profit from the experience. Bumptiously intelligent and imposingly self-confident, Schacht arrayed the job during two periods in office (1923 to 1930 and 1933 to 1939) in a unique garb of ambition and ambivalence. The cherub-faced theorist in the high-wing collars brought a touch of devilry into a central banking profession which previously had been the preserve of the staidest of bureaucrats.

As 'Hitler's magician',[58] who made possible the Führer's 1930s economic miracle, Schacht was to earn wider notoriety than any other financier in history. To Montagu Norman, the governor of the Bank of England, who had a soft spot for Schacht and was the godfather of his grandchild,[59] the Reichsbank president was 'the sane man among a party of dangerous totalitarianists'.[60] Wilhelm Vocke regarded him as 'a great man' prone to 'great errors'.[61] Hitler believed Schacht was the banker who could outsmart the rest of the world – including the Jews:

> Before each meeting of the International Bank at Basle, half the world was anxious to know whether Schacht would attend or not and it was only after receipt of the assurance that he would be there that the Jew bankers of the entire world packed their bags and prepared to attend. I must say that the tricks Schacht succeeded in playing on them prove that even in the field of sharp finance a really intelligent Aryan is more than a match for his Jewish counterparts.[62]

Schacht started his career as an academic trade expert who occasionally dabbled in journalism.[63] In 1903 he joined the Dresdner Bank as head of its economic statistics department, and later became an assistant director. He served during the First World War in the office of the German currency commissioner in occupied Belgium, and afterwards moved to the smaller National Bank, where he took on the post of chief executive. In 1922 the bank merged with the Darmstädter Bank to become the Darmstädter und National Bank (Danat), one of the Big Four in German banking. On 12 November 1923 Schacht was appointed by the Stresemann government in the new post of currency commissioner. His job was to supervise the Reichsbank's over-burdened and ailing Havenstein.[64] For several months, the government had been trying to dislodge Havenstein, but the sixty-six-year-old – who had been appointed for life – refused to depart. On 19 November Havenstein wrote a defiant letter expressing his 'painful regret' at not being able to accede to the government's request for his resignation.[65]

The next day, Havenstein resolved the matter by conveniently dying of a heart attack.

Schacht was a staunch advocate of a return to the gold standard. But in the fateful month of November 1923, he was a key figure in putting into effect the alternative Rentenmark proposal supported by Karl Helfferich. A man who still enjoyed the best possible reputation in conservative circles in spite of his war-time miscalculations, Helfferich had become Schacht's arch-rival for the vacancy as Reichsbank chief.[66]

In the month after Havenstein's death, squabbling over the rival plans to stabilise the Mark overshadowed deliberations on choosing his successor. Although the Reichsbank had attained independence the previous year, the government retained great influence over nominating its president.[67] The Reichsbank directorate favoured Helfferich for the post and unanimously rejected Schacht's candidature. In an extraordinary letter to the Reich chancellery on 17 December 1923 the Reichsbank directorate claimed that Schacht did not meet the test of possessing 'a past absolutely free of blemishes'. The men of the Reichsbank stated: 'Dr Helfferich is the only personality known to us who possesses the full qualifications as Reichsbank president.'[68] Schacht was labelled as 'in no way suited for the post of Reichsbank president' since he lacked the 'creative energy necessary to re-establish our currency'. The directorate repeated a virulent anti-Schacht allegation arising from his work in the First World War, complaining that Schacht had committed irregularities by favouring the Dresdner Bank in transactions connected with the Belgian currency commission.[69]

This assault on Schacht's competence cut little ice with the government. At the beginning of the 1920s, Schacht had not yet embarked on his move to the far right of the political spectrum. He was valued as a conservative of strong Republican credentials, enjoying good contacts with bankers in foreign countries. The cabinet under Stresemann's successor as chancellor, Wilhelm Marx of the Centre party, came to the conclusion that the bourgeois Schacht was better suited to deal with the economic crisis than Helfferich, linked to the ultra right through his membership of the Nationalist Party.[70] Schacht was formally appointed as Havenstein's successor on 22 December.[71] He was immediately anxious to establish his international connections. Schacht insisted on making a visit to the

Bank of England before taking up his post at the beginning of the New Year.[72]

At his first meeting with the directorate in January 1924, Schacht acknowledged the reasons for the Reichsbank's disapprobation, referring to the Belgian currency episode as a case where 'I stole silver spoons'.[73] But Schacht voiced his hope for cooperation – optimism which proved justified. Wilhelm Vocke, a member of the directorate which had unanimously voted against Schacht, later recorded how he and his colleagues changed their mind on Schacht's character: 'We recognised that he was the unsurpassed master in his and our business,' he told the Nuremberg tribunal in 1946.[74]

Schacht's 1920s stewardship of the Reichsbank brought relief from post-war pain and perturbation – but the respite was short-lived. The stability of the newly introduced Reichsmark, successful efforts to cut budgetary expenditure and an understanding with foreign creditors at the Dawes Conference led to a period of rapid economic growth. The clouds of gloom over Germany momentarily parted. Schacht, at the helm of a bank which seemed miraculously to have recovered some of its pre-war status and authority, was pleased to take full credit for the rescue. He later recalled receiving a gushingly grateful letter from a railway conductor describing how his family had been able to lay out presents under the Christmas tree for the first time in years.[75]

Establishment in March 1924 of Schacht's brainchild, the Gold Discount Bank, a central banking institution with the right to issue notes in sterling, helped mobilise foreign credits to overcome Germany's capital shortage. The new Banking Law of 30 August 1924 confirmed and extended the Reichsbank's independence from government[76] – but greatly increased the influence over the central bank of Germany's foreign creditors. In an attempt to ensure that Germany would indeed live up to its reparations obligations, foreign representatives were given seats on the bank's new governing council (*Generalrat*). This body was the successor to the *Kuratorium*, which had the power to elect the Reichsbank president and the other members of the directorate.[77] The law also formalised the new gold-exchange standard, under which the Reichsbank was obliged to cover 40 per cent of its notes in gold and foreign exchange.[78] Economic recovery came in spite of heavy reparations payments of more than RM2 billion a year. But the relative economic tranquillity unleashed by the Dawes plan proved a false dawn. Germany was borrowing from US banks to meet its reparations payments. The country was slowly rebuilding capital destroyed by inflation; but burgeoning foreign debt was storing up problems for the future.

Having set up the Gold Discount Bank to garner funds from abroad, Schacht was the first to recognise the drawbacks of the process. He had long opposed fiscal laxity, pointing to the government's inability to raise taxes during the world war as one of the main reasons for the 1923 inflation.[79] In a series of speeches in the second half of the 1920s, Schacht emerged as a fierce advocate of central bank independence, and a propagator of the *Stabilitätspolitik* which was to become the hallmark of the Bundesbank. He declared that Germany was spending income from abroad not on productive investments, but on 'luxuries' – public projects such as stadia, swimming pools and theatres, mostly built, Schacht complained, by spendthrift, Socialist-run municipalities.[80] He insisted that the only way to financial salvation was through balanced budgets.

At the beginning of 1929, the Reichsbank summed up the problem in the starkest terms:

Once again, reparations during the past year were paid not from economic surpluses, but from borrowed money. There are grounds for ever more serious anxiety about how long this process of indebtedness can continue.[81]

In February 1929, a final international effort was launched to solve the reparations imbroglio. The Reich government led by the new Social Democrat chancellor Hermann Müller nominated Schacht and the steel industrialist Albert Vögler as Germany's expert representatives on a reparations committee headed by Owen Young, a US businessman. Although he had been given the right to negotiate independently of government instructions, Schacht considerably overestimated his freedom of manoeuvre. He gambled monumentally – and lost. He proposed reducing Germany's annual reparation payments to RM1.6 billion – on condition that the Allies agreed to return both its colonies and the Polish Corridor ceded as part of the Versailles settlement. His demands were rejected. Beset by a foreign exchange crisis and under pressure from Stresemann, the foreign minister, Schacht was forced to back down ignominiously.

At the end of a tortuous series of negotiations, Schacht in June 1929 reluctantly signed the Young reparations plan. Though reducing the reparations total, the agreement maintained Germany's obligations to its former enemies for a further half a century. The plan was designed to find a permanent means of reconciling Germany's interests with those of its creditors. At Schacht's initiative, the Bank for International Settlements, an institution owned by international central banks based in Basle, was created to coordinate the Young payments planned to stretch out up to 1987–88.[82] Within a few years, the reparations plan was torn up; and with it was buried the fragile spirit of international economic cooperation.

Schacht found himself facing the dilemma of both defending the Young plan and denouncing it. His position became increasingly untenable after the New York stock market crash in October 1929, which sparked off the fear of financial unrest around the world. Although he was not yet ready to go into full opposition to the Weimar republic, Schacht had been moving steadily to the right.[83] Perhaps sensing the fatal threat to democracy which lay ahead, Schacht brought his disagreement with the government to a theatrical climax. He announced his resignation from the Reichsbank on 7 March 1930, on the grounds that the Young plan gave foreign creditors an excessive hold over the German economy.[84]

The manner of Schacht's exit in 1930 could hardly have been in greater contrast to his brusquely received arrival just over six years earlier. Friedrich Dreyse, who had taken over as Reichsbank vice-president in 1926, told a reception to mark Schacht's departure that, 'No other event since the world war has so moved the hearts of the Reichsbank functionaries.' Schacht's name had become, Dreyse added, 'a firm guarantee for the security of the German currency'.[85] Schacht, too, sensed the drama of the occasion. Delivering his farewell speech to the Reichsbank, Schacht praised the 'collegiate' spirit of the directorate before going on to criticise the government for abandoning the 'moral basis' for future handling of reparations.[86] His parting words were:

> I do not leave with any feelings of pessimism. The German people, so much in ferment at the moment, are far too full of life that they should not once again find a way out of this confusion. I hope, gentlemen, that we shall meet again on that

road, and shall call to one another: 'Lo – A friend and comrade
in the fight!'

v. 'The national windstorm will not die down'

Schacht's Reichsbank colleagues lived for three years under the
command of the arch-conservative Hans Luther. Together with
Chancellor Heinrich Brüning, the new Reichsbank president put
into effect the toughest of deflationary policies to try to withstand
financial collapse in Germany's ever more stretched economy. After
the central bank's tight money policy ended up exacerbating the
effects of the depression, in 1933 the men of the Reichsbank indeed
met their former master again, just as Schacht had predicted in
1930. The road, though, led not to salvation but to disaster.

Schacht's personal history, perhaps unfairly, will forever be
associated with the story of National Socialism. Although he was
never a member of the Nazi party,[87] and leading figures in the
movement frequently treated him with the utmost suspicion,[88]
Schacht's ideology in the early 1930s drew gradually closer to that
of the Nazis. Schacht's true attitude towards the party is inevitably
obscured by the tissue of obfuscation, half-truths and lies surrounding his pronouncements on the subject. One of the most
accomplished of Schacht's talents was his skill in dissimulation;
nowhere was this craft exercised with greater adroitness than on
the treacherous sands of the Third Reich.

The antipathy Schacht attracted from leading Nazis like Heinrich
Himmler, Hitler's SS Reichsführer,[89] later spilled over into downright hostility which eventually cost him his freedom and almost his
life. However, during the first half of the 1930s, Schacht undoubtedly ranked as one of Hitler's most vocal and influential supporters
within the German economic establishment. After the end of the
war, Schacht was one of many who chose to distort the truth,
claiming: 'I stood in opposition to Hitler from the first day.'[90]

During his three years out of office between 1930 and 1933,
Schacht refused to remain on the sidelines. On the day of the
general election in September 1930 which gave the National Socialists the second largest tally of votes in the Reichstag, Schacht left
Germany for a nationwide tour of the US, during which he gave
forty speeches.[91] After arriving by boat in New York, Schacht told

American inquirers that the size of NSDAP support was a vote against the Treaty of Versailles.[92] The trip appeared to coincide with a marked pro-Nazi swing in Schacht's political beliefs.[93] Schacht met Hermann Göring, Hitler's future Reich marshal, for the first time in December 1930. Göring introduced him to Hitler the following month. At the same time, Schacht's opposition to reparations became ever more intense.[94] In 1931, using one of the laborious metaphors of which he was inordinately fond, he said the Allies' attempts to 'extort' payments from Germany were 'as senseless as trying to harvest bananas at the North Pole'.[95]

The collapse in May 1931 of the largest Austrian bank, the Kreditanstalt, prompted the step Schacht had long feared: widespread withdrawal of foreign loans to Germany by bankers, who, after the years of boom, suddenly became worried about risk. Germany won respite on the reparations front when a moratorium on war debts was suggested by US President Herbert Hoover in June 1931. But the danger to Germany's financial standing seems to have heightened Schacht's sense of nationalism. In October 1931 standing on the same platform in the obscure hillside town of Harzburg as Hitler and Alfred Hugenberg, chairman of the National People's Party, Schacht declared his hope that 'the national windstorm blowing through Germany will not die down until the road to self-determination and economic success is once again made free.'[96]

In August 1932, Schacht wrote ingratiatingly to Hitler: 'You can rely on me as your dependable helper.'[97] After the Reichstag elections of 6 November 1932 – which resulted in the NSDAP's first big setback on the road to power – Schacht signed a letter to President Hindenburg along with a number of influential industrialists recommending that Hitler form the next government.[98] Later that month, Schacht informed Hitler that he had 'no doubt' that the Nazi leader would become chancellor.[99] The prediction was fulfilled when Hitler secured the presidential consent to become chancellor of a coalition government on 30 January 1933.[100]

Given the degree of Schacht's support for Hitler, it was no surprise that – after a fund-raising campaign to gather RM3 million for the NSDAP and its allies[101] – Schacht on 17 March 1933 dislodged the luckless Luther and was back again at the helm of the Reichsbank. Just as in 1923, Schacht appeared the right man for the job. He combined loyalty to the government of the day with an international reputation for financial orthodoxy which seemed to place him above the mire of politics. Even if Hitler had not had a ready-made candidate, he would certainly have asked Luther to step down. At their first meeting after Hitler's election as chancellor, the incumbent Reichsbank chief immediately provoked the Führer's irritation by offering him no more than RM100 million to spend on extra armaments programmes. Hitler delivered a semi-comic description of how, brusquely side-stepping the Reichsbank's nominal independence, he persuaded Luther to leave.

> Luther again gave me the figure of RM100 million. Further comment was superfluous, so I simply asked the Reich president to remove the man from office. This, however, was not possible without further ado, as the Reichsbank was still an international organisation. I was then compelled to try to reach an amicable settlement . . . and then I offered him the post of Ambassador to Washington, if he would voluntarily resign his present position. This he declared himself ready to accept, provided I would add an allowance of RM50,000 a year to his pension. I can see him still, his eyes modestly downcast, assuring me that it was pure patriotism which caused him to fall in with my suggestions![102]

In contrast to the largesse granted to Luther, Schacht took an annual pay cut of 60 per cent – more than RM80,000 – compared with his predecessor's salary.[103] The sacrifice was designed to emphasise the Nazis' early desire for austerity.

For a while, Hitler and Schacht formed one of history's most incongruous political tandems.[104] These two most disparate men were, at first, linked by a fateful bond of mutual admiration. From 1936 onwards, however, disillusionment set in, and Schacht fought an increasingly desperate battle to maintain his influence. He saw his authority within the government progressively weaken as economic power was transferred to Hermann Göring. He grew increasingly worried about the effects of the harassment of the Jews (as well as of other economically influential groups such as Freemasons) on Germany's economic performance and on its financial standing abroad. Most of all, he became convinced that, unless checked, Hitler's economic policies would lead to a repeat of the 1923 trauma of inflation and ruin. Yet Schacht retained up to 1939 a naive belief that he could wield sufficient clout to persuade the Führer to switch course. Schacht's eventual failure was one of judgment. Long after he had ceased to trust Hitler, the Reichsbank president maintained a colossally misplaced faith in his own ability to manipulate events. Had Schacht been pushed by his later-expressed doubts about the Nazis to resign from the Reichsbank in 1937, the course of history might have been different. Schacht was not, however, the only contemporary player – both in Germany and abroad – who failed to estimate the momentum pushing Hitler towards the brink.

vi. 'This government will avoid monetary experiments'

In the early years of the Third Reich, Schacht's public support for Hitler knew no bounds. On 18 March 1933, a day after he returned to the Reichsbank post,[105] and five days before the Reichstag passed the Enabling Act giving Hitler absolute power, Schacht made a radio broadcast to the German people. He identified himself categorically with the goals of the new regime. 'Monetary policy and the banking and credit sector cannot be thought of as having a separate existence, run according to some mathematical formula. Rather, they are interwoven to the closest possible extent with the national economic interest and that of the entire German people.'[106] Like many central bankers in more modern times, Schacht emphasised the message that, whatever happened, the currency would remain stable. 'Future monetary policy will adhere with unchanging steadfastness to the task of maintaining the value of the Mark.' On 23 March 1933, the day when Germany voted itself into dictatorship, the Führer, too, did his best to calm the nerves of Germany's economic conservatives. In his opening speech before the Reichstag, ringed by black-shirted SS guards, Hitler declared: 'This government will avoid monetary experiments.'[107]

In the national plebiscite of 12 November 1933, Schacht campaigned for a nationwide 'Yes' for Hitler 'to show the whole world that our whole people adheres to the Führer to the last man'.[108] On the day of the death of President Hindenburg in August 1934, Schacht ascended further in the hierarchy when he joined Hitler's government as economics minister, maintaining his job as Reichsbank president.[109] Schacht energetically supported Hitler's elevation to the new head of state, combining the offices of chancellor and president. 'All power must be transferred to Adolf Hitler,' he proclaimed in a radio speech drawn up by the Reichsbank's economics and statistics department.[110] Schacht gushingly praised the 'natural and consistent insight of Adolf Hitler into economic processes and necessities . . . Precisely in the simplicity and clarity of his economic thought processes lies the great secret of the Führer's economic policy success.'[111] The Reichsbank president's statement contrasted strangely with his oft-repeated post-war assertion that Hitler 'understood nothing about economics'.[112] It also made nonsense of Schacht's 1948 claim that he joined Hitler's government 'as a conscious opponent'.[113]

Schacht was well aware that his reputation as a government internationalist earned him the misgivings of Nazi die-hards. He launched a typically tortuous initiative to bolster his domestic credentials in a speech at the Leipzig Fair in 1935, in which he pointedly warned foreign governments against believing that he was opposed to National Socialist theories:

> I can assure you that everything that I say and do has the absolute approval of the Führer, and that I would not do and say anything, which did not have his approval. The guardian of economic reason is not I, but the Führer. The strength of the National Socialist regime stems from the will of the people unified by and channelled through the Führer.[114]

In June 1935, Schacht reinforced the message by organising a public vow of loyalty to the Führer at an extraordinary Reichsbank ceremony. The occasion was the unveiling of a bust of Hitler in the entrance foyer of the Reichsbank building. Schacht's *laudatio* was characteristically elaborate; his affinity to the language of totalitarianism was absolute:

> Whoever has experienced the Führer in his work, delivering one of his great speeches, or taking part in difficult negotiations, will recognise the Hitler whose likeness has been captured here, and who has been propelled into the midst of the Reichsbank's daily work-flow. Just as the essence of real art is that it leaves no passer-by unmoved, and gives continuous benefit to those who approach it with an open mind, so should this work impart its spirit to all those who pass, because it

encapsulates something of the life-awakening spirit of Adolf Hitler.[115]

In a letter to Hitler the previous month, Schacht outlined the two essential objectives of his Reichsbank presidency. Rearmament was 'the task to which all else must be subordinated', but at the same time, everything had to be done to prevent inflation – 'a snake which bites its own tail'.[116] In a boast which he knew would carry particular appeal for the Führer, Schacht revealed that foreigners' frozen Reichsmark accounts were being secretly channelled into the arms industry: 'Our armaments,' he gloated, 'are being financed partly with the deposits of our political opponents.'

Schacht's greatest contribution to the arms build-up came through the invention of the so-called 'Mefo bills'. These financing instruments transformed short-term liquid funds into long-term capital for the defence sector. As a machine for monetary creation, the device was as unconventional as it was shameless.[117] A total of RM12 billion of these bills of exchange were issued by big industrial corporations through their Mefo financing subsidiary. The bills were discounted by the Reichsbank and used to pay debts to contractors and manufacturers.

Whatever the zeal he displayed for building up the weapons industry, Schacht's interest in armaments was, however, primarily political and financial. There is no evidence that he was ever actively engaged in preparations to wage war. Practicality always had the edge: 'What is the use of thousands of aeroplanes if we only have enough fuel for fourteen days?' he asked Hess in 1934.[118] In a confidential speech at the Reich war ministry at the end of that year, Schacht said, 'The irrefutable task of coming years is to shore up the Wehrmacht financially and economically in such a way as to avoid a future war ... If, God forbid, fate imposes upon us a new war, we will be able to fight it with prospect of success only if our economy and our finances are well-ordered and healthy.'[119]

As the 1930s wore on, Schacht's pleading for financial rectitude became increasingly insistent. As the political divide between the Reichsbank chief and the regime widened, his power, almost inevitably, began to wane. In one of his most celebrated speeches, at Königsberg in August 1935, he declared that 'the material implementation of the tasks we have set ourselves causes me great headaches.'[120] In a confidential memorandum finalised shortly afterwards, Schacht complained about Germany's 'dependence' and 'vulnerable position' vis-à-vis the world outside.[121]

In April 1936 – after Schacht repeatedly complained that currency shortages were hampering fulfilment of the government's rearmament objectives[122] – Göring took over responsibility for foreign exchange transactions. In October 1936 the Four Year Plan was introduced – with Göring given the dominant voice. Schacht suggested a 'pause' in armaments production in a letter to Göring in April 1937.[123] In summer 1937, within earshot of witnesses at Hitler's Berchtesgaden residence, he engaged in a heated argument with the Führer over rearmament policy.[124] In November 1937, Hitler finally agreed to Schacht's repeated request to be relieved of his economics minister's post; he was replaced by Walther Funk, the propaganda ministry state secretary who had become one of Hitler's closest economic advisers.* The Führer however expressed fulsome thanks for Schacht's 'excellent performance', and maintained him as personal adviser and minister without portfolio. Hitler expressed confidence that Schacht would remain Reichsbank president 'for many years'.[125]

vii. A role in repression

The Reichsbank was only rarely an initiator of Nazi policies. In two controversial fields of pre-war policies – the repression of the Jews, and the annexation of Austria – the Reichsbank was at first unenthusiastic in its support for government actions. It regarded persecution of the Jews with initial distaste, and believed that the currency *Anschluss* with Austria took place at the wrong exchange rate. None the less, once the government's mind was made up, the Reichsbank carried out with faithful precision its role as executor of the state's demands.

The bank's reasoning on the Jewish question was pragmatic: official anti-semitism would spark off widespread emigration, and this would greatly damage Germany's stock of productive capital and its financial position abroad. As anti-Jewish discrimination increased during the 1930s, the Reichsbank emphasised its view that such action was economically counter-productive.[126] A Reichsbank memorandum in 1935 recorded that Jewish emigrants since

*See chapter 5.

1933 had already transferred RM125 million out of the country; the total sum which could potentially flow abroad, Schacht estimated, amounted to well over RM1 billion.[127]

Schacht used his Königsberg speech in August 1935 not only to declare that Jewish 'influence' had disappeared 'for all time' but also to criticise arbitrary attacks on Jewish business life.[128] Warning of the difficulties of preventing Jews from exporting banknotes and securities, a sharply worded internal Reichsbank document in autumn 1935 concluded that the government's toughening of anti-Jewish measures 'will cause a new wave of Jewish emigration and thereby a considerable deterioration of our foreign currency position'.[129]

The Reichsbank directorate wrote to the Reich interior minister in November 1935 to express disquiet over the falling value of the Reichsmark on the Amsterdam foreign exchange market. It ascribed this to selling of Reichsmark notes smuggled out by Jewish emigrants. Uncertainty about the details of the government's not-yet-finalised anti-Jewish legislation was also depressing bond issues, the letter said. Above all, capital flight amounted to a drain on foreign exchange resources at a time when 'every piece of foreign currency is required for imports of food and raw materials for work creation and rearmament'.[130] In a similar vein, Schacht warned in December 1935 that 'the economic and legal treatment of the Jews' amounted to 'impairment of our armaments tasks'.[131]

In 1936, the Reichsbank warned that the Nazi party's desire to 'drive Jews out of economic life' would cause 'unfavourable effects on employment and on the financial position of the Reich'.[132] The bank put forward a straightforward solution: measures to take over Jewish companies. Aryanisation would prevent such companies from going out of business altogether, but lack of 'well-capitalised Aryan purchasers' was a hindrance, it said. The Reichsbank drew up a list in May 1937 showing that 345 of 915 registered private banks were 'non-Aryan', making a share of 38 per cent; measured by the size of balance sheets, the non-Aryan percentage was even higher, at 57 per cent.[133] A year later, a 'highly confidential' list, showing that only 178 Jewish banks were still active, carefully recorded how far Aryanisation had proceeded.[134]

After the orchestrated attacks against the Jews on *Reichskristallnacht*, 9 November 1938, in which more than 250 synagogues were set on fire, nearly a hundred Jews died, and 26,000 were sent to concentration camps, Schacht voiced his disquiet in public. He did so, however, in a manner indicating that he hardly expected his voice to carry any weight. He told a Christmas gathering of Reichsbank employees that the events of *Reichskristallnacht* – triggered by the murder of a German diplomat in Paris, Ernst vom Rath, by a young Polish Jew – were a 'cultural disgrace' which should make 'every decent German red with shame'. Turning to the Reichsbank messengers, he glowered: 'I only hope that none of you office boys were there, since there would be no place for such persons at the Reichsbank.'[135]

For all Schacht's carefully controlled outrage, the Reichsbank was extensively involved in the government's efforts to inflict sanctions on the Jews as a form of racial reparation for vom Rath's killing. Three days after *Reichskristallnacht*, the government levied a collective fine of RM1 billion on the nation's Jewry, amounting to 20 per cent of individual Jews' wealth, to be paid in four instalments. The Reichsbank was concerned that the Jewish community might raise cash for the levy by selling large amounts of securities, which would then depress bond prices. At a meeting chaired by Göring on 12 November 1938, Karl Blessing, by then a member of the Reichsbank directorate, declared that 'the Jews could sell Reich bonds in their hundreds of thousands in the next few days', thus hindering placement of further issues.[136] To counter the risk, the government imposed a ceiling on Jewish securities transactions. The new regulations were implemented through Reichsbank notices sent out during the next few months, establishing a monthly RM1000 limit for Jewish securities disposals.

As with the government's policy towards the Jews, the Reichsbank's attitude towards the *Anschluss* was never one of wholehearted approval. However, the Reichsbank played an important behind-the-scenes role in preparing the monetary technicalities for Hitler's move on Austria in March 1938. Schacht was a general supporter of linking Austria to the Reich, but he affirmed at Nuremberg that he knew nothing about Hitler's plans until one day before the Wehrmacht marched in on 12 March 1938.[137] The truth is more complex. Germany had been proposing a currency union since 1936 as a means of ending the inconvenience of a mounting bilateral trade deficit. The Austrian National Bank strongly opposed the idea, above all on the grounds that the schilling would be weakened by attachment to the 'soft' Reichsmark.[138] At the begin-

ning of 1938, German desire to bring Austria fully under its economic control was increased by reports that large amounts of Jewish
capital were escaping abroad from Vienna. At a top-level meeting
on 23 February, the Reichsbank emphasised that economic and
monetary union would have to go hand in hand. In an argument
very similar to that used by the Bundesbank in 1990 concerning
German monetary union,* the Reichsbank declared that disparities
in the two countries' economic structures made a simple currency
merger 'not possible'.[139] With political pressures building up for a
complete *Anschluss*, the Reichsbank was told to intensify its preparations. A seventeen-page memorandum drawn up by the economics and statistics department on 26 February 1938 came to a
blunt conclusion:

> From the German point of view, it would without doubt be
> most suitable to extend the Reichsmark to Austria (full disap-
> pearance of the Austrian currency), with the National Bank
> being simultaneously taken over by the Reichsbank.[140]

Technical discussions on the by exchange rate for the *Anschluss*
took place on 1 March.[141] A Reichsbank document at the beginning
of March declared that monetary union 'would represent from a
practical point of view the decisive contribution to a complete
integration of Austria into greater Germany'.[142] Friedrich Wilhelm,
a long-serving Reichsbank official and later member of the Nazi
party,[143] who was the bank's currency specialist, was commissioned
by Schacht to fly to Vienna on 12 March to manage foreign
exchange matters there.[144] Wilhelm joined the Reichsbank directorate after the January 1939 dismissals, weathered the war and its
aftermath, and continued his central banking career in West Germany after 1948.† On 14 March 1938, he organised the last annual
meeting of the Austrian National Bank. Wilhelm ensured that the
gathering broke up after fifteen minutes, by removing unnecessary
items from the agenda and winning Berlin's approval to continue
dividend payments to shareholders.[145]

Settling the Reichsmark/schilling conversion rate was more prob-
lematic. The Reichsbank's recommendation of a 2 for 1 exchange

---

*See chapter 8.
†See chapter 7.

between the schilling and the Reichsmark was overturned by Hitler, who insisted on a 1.5 to 1 relationship[146] – amounting to a revaluation of the schilling of around 35 per cent. In another remarkable parallel with German monetary union in 1990, the higher exchange rate was intended to make the *Anschluss* more palatable by giving a purchasing power bonus to the people whose currency was being suppressed.[147] In May, the schilling was fully replaced by the Reichsmark. The Austrian National Bank was put into liquidation, and its offices were transformed into branches of the Reichsbank.[148] Austrian newspapers taken into the Nazi propaganda network had already proclaimed in March 1938 that the Austrian National Bank would close its doors for ever.[149]

viii. Reaching the limits

The annexation of Austria clearly overstretched Germany's resources. Schacht's economic speeches became progressively more cautious; his demands that the Reich government take the path of austerity grew more insistent. Schacht was however anxious to protect himself from the political backlash he knew would result from his requests for economic rigour. As a result, the Reichsbank president wove into his words of financial orthodoxy extravagant praise for Hitler. In one of the most striking examples of his backing for Hitlerian economics, Schacht gave an unqualified welcome to the change in the Banking Law in February 1937. This ended the Reichsbank's legal independence from the German government, severed the foreign ties agreed during the fruitless years of reparations negotiations, and brought the bank formally under Hitler's control.[150] The presence of foreign creditor representatives on the bank's general council had been ended in 1930, and the general council itself had been abolished in 1933. But the Reichsbank had still been required up to 1937 to seek foreign central bank approval for important changes in its policies, for instance, for changing regulations on the note issue. Schacht declared that the new law of February 1937 'removed the last traces of Versailles' by restoring 'German monetary sovereignty'.[151] Denouncing the previous separation of the central bank from the government as a 'constitutional anomaly', Schacht proclaimed that placing the Reichsbank under Hitler's direct jurisdiction was 'the best possible guarantee for maintaining monetary stability'.[152]

As a sign, perhaps, of Schacht's increasingly desperate search for political legitimacy, his eulogies of Hitler increased throughout 1938. After the war, Schacht's supporters claimed that, by this time, the Reichsbank president had become the Führer's 'bitter enemy'.[153] Schacht's public pronouncements during that year were calculated, however, to snuff out any spirit of resistance. Schacht later claimed that he had been merely trying to 'divert the suspicion of the Gestapo'.[154] Schacht's post-war protestations, like most of his statements, contained a grain of truth, but a much stronger element of self-delusion. Speaking to the employees of the Austrian National Bank shortly after the *Anschluss*, Schacht declared in March 1938: 'Not one of us can find his future unless he holds true to Adolf Hitler with all his heart.'[155] In a toughly worded memorandum to staff in April 1938, Schacht proclaimed: 'I expect and trust that all members of the Reichsbank will bear in mind always that they are National Socialists, not only in their actions but also in their words. Those who infringe against the rule can reckon with the strictest disciplinary measures.'[156] In the same month, he went on the offensive against fear-mongers: 'Rumours over the safety of the currency have no part in the German economic community . . . Forward and up with our Führer Adolf Hitler!'[157]

In a typically double-edged address to the Deutsche Akademie in November 1938, Schacht declared that, since Germany had regained full employment in the spring, further extension of Reichsbank credit to the state would be 'not only senseless but also damaging'.[158] Schacht claimed that, during the past six months, the Reichsbank had forced the government to finance its spending needs only from tax revenues and long-term bonds: recourse to central banking credit had ceased. But he added that Germany's economic recovery had all been the Führer's work: 'There has been no German financial miracle; rather, there has been the miracle of the re-awakening of German national consciousness and German discipline, and for this miracle we must thank our Führer Adolf Hitler.'

The contradiction between the Reichsbank president's acclamatory public rhetoric and his private forebodings became steadily greater. In the summer of 1938, Schacht told his hostess at a private dinner: 'We have fallen into the hands of criminals!'[159] A confidential Reichsbank minute in October 1938, used as a draft for the celebrated memorandum delivered the following January, indicates how matters were coming to a head. Pointing to imbalances in the economy caused by the proliferation of arms financing, the document stated: 'In spite of all the efforts we have made, full stability of the German currency no longer exists. Rather, a certain, barely recognisable, inflation of the Reichsmark has now appeared. Since the Reichsbank believes it has fully discharged its duty and its expertise in the interest of protecting the currency, the Reichsbank should have no fear of admitting this publicly.'[160]

Full public admission of the risks was however clearly out of the question.[161] The climax came when, at the end of 1938, the government was confronted with the need to repay RM3 billion of Mefo bills in the first quarter of 1939. The finance ministry's reserves were exhausted, and the Reichsbank refused to make the cash available for the redemption.[162] Hitler told Schacht at Berchtesgaden at the beginning of January 1939 that he was intent on using the printing presses to bridge the financing gap. This appears to have provided the impetus for the directorate to put the finishing touches to their long-prepared anti-inflation memorandum finalised on 7 January 1939. The message was dire.[163] Reichsbank gold and foreign exchange reserves were 'no longer available'; the trade deficit was 'rising sharply'; price and wage controls were no longer working effectively; the volume of notes in circulation had been accelerating worryingly fast,[164] and state finances were 'close to collapse'. In a vain attempt to mollify the Führer by emphasising the soundness of his economic views, the Reichsbank directorate emphasised that Hitler himself had always 'rejected inflation as stupid and senseless'. The central bank appealed to Hitler to switch course by clamping down on spending, toughening wage and price controls and restoring the authority of the Reich finance ministry and the Reichsbank over all spending and borrowing decisions.

To give it maximum weight, the Reichsbank message was, unusually, signed by all eight of the directorate. Apart from Schacht, the other signatories were the vice-president Friedrich Dreyse (who was anyway due to retire), Karl Blessing, Carl Ehrhardt, Ernst Hülse, Max Kretzschmann, Emil Puhl and Wilhelm Vocke. Puhl, Kretzschmann and Blessing were members of the Nazi party: they must have signed with mixed feelings. Hitler angrily rejected the Reichsbank's recommendations as 'mutiny'.[165] Within the next few weeks, six of the eight received their dismissal notices. Schacht, Dreyse and Hülse were removed on 20 January: Walther Funk took over as president, while Rudolf Brinkmann, another high-flyer from the economics ministry, was appointed vice-president; both retained their ministry posts. The dismissal of Vocke, Ehrhardt and Blessing was announced at the beginning of February. They were replaced by Friedrich Wilhelm, Kurt Lange and Walther Bayrhoffer: all men whom the Führer could trust.

Vocke and Blessing remained to the last minute loyal executors of the state's wishes. One of the last acts by Vocke and Blessing was to sign a routine Reichsbank notice affirming the monthly RM1000 limit on Jewish sales of securities.[166] The six who left the bank were treated in a gentlemanly manner; they received full pay or pensions. Additionally, Hitler sent Schacht a fulsome letter thanking him for his work on rearmament[167] – much to the former Reichsbank president's irritation seven years later when he went on trial for war crimes at Nuremberg.

For the second time in less than a decade, Schacht bade the Reichsbank farewell with a valedictory letter to the staff. There was not even the most flimsy of code-words to signal misgivings to the outside world. For this reason, the letter – although existing in the Bundesbank's archives – is not mentioned in any of Schacht's numerous accounts of the Hitler era:

When I started my second period of office [in 1933], the legacy of the past crisis had to be liquidated. At the same time the Reichsbank took up the great tasks set for it by the National Socialist state of financing job creation and rearmament, and went to the limit of its powers to achieve the success of these national goals. When the Führer conferred upon me, too, the leadership of the Reich economics ministry, the Reichsbank's support allowed me to bear and overcome this double burden. In the last few years the annexation of Austria and the Sudetenland demonstrated the success of the armaments policy, to which the Reichsbank has contributed its share. Territorial enlargement created new and important challenges for the Reichsbank, and the old tasks have not become smaller . . . I take leave of you with the request that, loyal to good Reichsbank tradition, you will continue to dedicate yourselves to your work with full strength, upright consciences and joyful devotion, in the proud knowledge that the Reichsbank, wherever it is brought into action, will always be at the front line: for the nation and for the Führer.

Heil Hitler!

Hjalmar Schacht[168]

During the next six years of hubris and acrimony, the Reichsbank indeed stood at the front line – before it disappeared over the brink with the rest of the shabby paraphernalia of totalitarianism. Schacht's parting words were tinged with the sheen of sunset. They formed an apt send-off for the Reichsbank's journey into the darkness of war and, when the dawn eventually came, oblivion.

The March of the Reichsmark

We embody the iron commitment not to defraud the German people through inflation.
  Rudolf Brinkmann, Reichsbank vice-president, in a letter to Heinrich Himmler, 1939[1]

It appears certain that a new European currency bloc under German leadership is now becoming established.
  Otto Pfleiderer, economist at Reichs-Kredit-Gesellschaft, 1940[2]

We heard already during the time of the Nazis that monetary stability was based on the work of the nation. But this was only a half truth, and therefore a lie.
  Ludwig Erhard, West German economics minister, 1948[3]

The Reichsbank went to war in September 1939 with sound money emblazoned on its banner. It subsided in 1945 under the ruin of the Third Reich's matchless contradictions. The rubble left after its demise provided the first foundation stones for the later construction of the Bundesbank.

The Reichsbank relentlessly reassured the German public that the war would not damage the Reichsmark. But the central bank, with an ambivalence typical of so many episodes in German monetary history, frequently had a different message, in private, for the government: that monetary instability would impede accomplishment of Germany's economic and foreign policies. Some Reichsbank officials certainly had their doubts about the morality or desirability of Germany's aims; others were fully wedded to these objectives. Their qualms, in so far as they could be expressed at all in a totalitarian state, invariably focused on the means employed by Hitler, not his goals.

After the end of hostilities, many Reichsbankers tried, understandably enough, to put the best possible interpretation on their actions under the Third Reich. They affirmed that Hitler's tyranny had stopped them from speaking out against him; but they declared that they had none the less carried out some form of resistance. As ever, Hjalmar Schacht's misrepresentation of the past was unrivalled in its extravagance. On the one hand, Schacht claimed that if he had carried out more active resistance to Hitler – for instance by cutting off war funding – he would have ended up 'mute in a grave'.[4] On the other hand, Schacht also made the ludicrous boast that the Reichsbank was the sole arm of German government which carried out 'open resistance'.[5]

Although threats of hardship and death certainly existed, there is no evidence that any senior Reichsbank official suffered real disadvantage as a result of speaking out.[6] Wilhelm Vocke, who departed in 1939, claimed that the bank was 'raped and misused by Hitler'.[7] That was a considerable over-simplification. A system held together by dictatorship and cruelty allows institutions and the men who run them almost limitless room to claim afterwards that they were not responsible for their deeds. It does not, however, give them clear consciences.

i. 'A very weak human being'

Walther Funk took over from Hjalmar Schacht as Reichsbank president in January 1939, and remained at the central bank's helm during the Second World War. He was a man of unappealing versatility. Technocrat, thinker, propagandist and drunkard, he brought a unique amalgamation of sophistry, populism and crudity to the top job in German central banking. Born into a literature-loving farming family in East Prussia – the philosopher Immanuel Kant had once browsed in the bookshop later owned by his uncle – Funk excelled in his boyhood as a piano prodigy.[8] His career was to bring him a profusion of high as well as low notes. After his conviction as a war criminal at Nuremberg, it ended in Spandau prison, on the most self-pitying of adagios.

During the 1920s he became editor-in-chief of the *Berliner Börsenzeitung*, a well-regarded economics daily which showed implacable hostility to the Weimar political system. He joined the Nazi party in 1931, and soon became personal economic adviser to Hitler. The post included the responsibility of raising funds from the world of business and finance.[9] In 1933 Funk took over as the Hitler government's press chief, and then was promoted to state secretary in Joseph Goebbels' propaganda ministry. Before being made head of the Reichsbank, Funk had already replaced Schacht as economics minister in 1937.[10] In contrast to his predecessor, Funk always told Hitler exactly what he wanted to hear. Like Rudolf Hess, Funk was a believer in astrology. There were traces of mysticism in his economic forecasting. Perhaps it was Funk's undoubted visionary quality that most appealed to the Führer. 'Today I laid my financial ideas before the minister of economics,' declared Hitler in October 1941. 'He's enthusiastic. He foresees that in ten years Germany will have freed itself from the burdens of the war without letting our purchasing power at home be shaken.'[11]

Even the acolytes called to testify on Funk's behalf during his war crimes trial at Nuremberg found it difficult to identify the positive side of his character. Funk wept frequently in his cell, 'overwhelmed by maudlin self-pity', according to the Nuremberg psychiatrist.[12] 'A greasy, shifty-eyed paunchy little man whose face always reminded this writer of a frog,' was the description of the American journalist William L. Shirer.[13] 'A very weak human being,' says Hermann Josef Abs,[14] the honorary chairman of the Deutsche Bank. In his capacity as board member of the Deutsche Bank during the war, with a seat on the Reichsbank advisory board, Abs knew Funk well – and echoed some of the Reichsbank president's basic economic thoughts during his own war-time declarations.[15]

A warped pioneer of European unity, Funk enthusiastically backed Hitler's plans for a new international 'order'.[16] Funk professed the traditional central banker's belief in international cooperation, and was a strong admirer of the Bank for International Settlements (BIS) in Basle. Funk believed that, once victory was secured, the BIS would provide a forum 'where the threads of new economic cooperation can be knotted together'.[17] On Funk's first visit to the 'central bankers' bank' in March 1939, he enthusiastically suggested that the bank should study using the Reichsbank's *Arbeitswährung* ('work currency') concept in international financial relations.[18] This laid down – as Hitler once put it – that, 'What backs a currency is economic production: not a bank, or a strongroom full of gold.'[19] In postulating that a currency's strength should stem not from gold, but from the output of the economy behind it, Hitler was unwittingly laying down one of the basic edicts of modern monetarism.

At the March 1939 central bankers' gathering in Basle, Funk

told Montagu Norman of the Bank of England that 'meetings of this kind, whatever the differences between those taking part, could only be helpful, provided that both parties stated their views frankly, realistically and, where necessary, brutally.'[20] The Bank of England's representative in Berlin, had, in fact, already bluntly set out his views in a confidential dispatch the previous year. The UK official, Charles Gunston, was an admirer of Hitler; he had even spent his 1934 summer holiday at a German labour camp.[21] However, Gunston – who was later to play an important role in setting up the Bank deutscher Länder* – was no fan of the new Reichsbank president: 'Funk, so his critics say, is lazy, fuddled by drink, and evades responsibility either by not knowing what is going on or (where he must) by getting Göring [his superior, with overall responsibility for the Four Year Plan and the economy] to take decisions for him.'[22]

Schacht, too, was well aware of Funk's personality defects. Schacht told his Allied interrogators in 1945:

> Funk is certainly stupid and has no knowledge of finance. He understands other things ... On the whole, Funk was a harmless little man. He came from a humble family and worked his way up to be commercial editor of the *Berliner Börsenzeitung* ... He was removed from the *Börsenzeitung* on account of his homosexual tendencies, and in the party he became a member of the large group of men of his ilk.[23]

Funk's reputation for mendacity[24] and unorthodox sexual adventure[25] was rivalled only by his penchant for drunken bawdiness. Friedrich-Wilhelm von Schelling, a Reichsbank official and NSDAP member,[26] who subsequently helped build up the Bank deutscher Länder and later became president of the Hamburg *Landeszentralbank*, recalls Funk throwing a glass of cherry brandy over him at a war-time reception in Berlin's Hotel Kaiserhof. Schelling suspected this was a failed attempt to opportune him. He was given a cognac by Funk's adjutant to make up for the spill.[27]

Funk showed an alarming mixture of assurance and self-deceit. In August 1939, just over a week before the invasion of Poland,

*See chapter 6.

the Reichsbank president reported to Hitler that the central bank was well prepared:

> I can most obediently inform you that, as a result of the measures taken in the last few months, I have succeeded in making the German Reichsbank internally so strong and externally so impregnable that even the most severe reverberations on the international money and capital markets will have absolutely no effect on us. In the meantime I have converted all identifiable foreign assets of the Reichsbank and the whole of German industry into gold.[28]

After the opening of the second front against the Soviet Union, Funk proclaimed in spring 1942: 'War in the East serves the new construction of Europe – victory in the East will bring this to fruition!'[29] The shadows and illusions of Funk's nether-world grew longer and deeper as the war progressed. Defeat for Germany, he claimed in 1944, would bring to the whole of Europe 'the destiny of slavery'.[30]

As the Reichsbank suffered the full force of the nightly hail of Allied bombing, Funk showed his mastery of surreal rhetoric. He told the bank's annual shareholders' meeting in February 1944: 'The bombs of the air pirates have torn deep wounds here, but they cannot break the Berliners' will to live; their power of resistance and their love of work.'[31]

Right up to the end, Funk kept up his defiant message: that the Reichsbank was helping to build a new Europe. In November 1944, five months after the Allied armies swarmed ashore on the Normandy beaches, the portly swastika-emblazoned figure assembled the staff of the Reichsbank in the Berlin state opera house for one last desperate attempt to revive morale. 'Germany is fighting not just for the freedom and the life of its people, but for Europe and the survival of western culture ... We will win because we must and can win, and because we have the historic duty to bring victory!'[32]

The main torrent of Funk's spleen was reserved for US Treasury Secretary Morgenthau and his short-lived plan to reduce Germany to a 'pastoral' economy.[33] The Reichsbank chief's words rang round the opera house, chilling in their venom – and in their twisted sense of prophecy:

We know that our enemies do not want simply to defeat us; they want to destroy completely the substance and force of our people. Driven by Old Testament hatred, our enemies plan that the German people should be cast back to the idyllic state of sheep- and goatherds. But how should European industry exist without German coal, without German iron and German potash, without the high-performance produce of the German chemical and electrical industries? Germany delivers 40 to 50 million tonnes of coal a year to Europe. England cannot replace this coal, for even today she does not produce enough for her own needs. Between 60 and 70 per cent of Germany's foreign trade is with Europe, which makes up more than half of world trade, and after England, Germany's trade in Europe was always decisive for world trade. The fanatics of hate have not thought of that!

Indeed, they had not. The Americans soon perceived that the Morgenthau plan was counter-productive; it was never put into effect.[34] Funk's own power of resistance was however shattered in 1945 when the state's gold stocks he had striven so hard to maintain – augmented by Nazi plunder from occupied territories – fell into the hands of the Allies in Thuringia.[35] Goebbels accused Funk of 'criminal dereliction of duty' for not showing greater vigilance.[36]

For three years after the end of the war, vast quantities of Reichsmark notes in circulation bore Funk's signature, until they were withdrawn with the introduction of the D-Mark in 1948. By the time the currency reform was carried out, the Reichsbank chief was serving a life sentence in Spandau. Suffering from cancer of the gall bladder, Funk was released from the crumbling Berlin fortress in 1957, on compassionate grounds, a decade after the Nuremberg tribunal.

Wilhelm Vocke, ensconced as president of the directorate of the Bank deutscher Länder, knew the value of Reichsbank solidarity; he himself had drawn his full Reichsbank salary during the war after quitting in 1939. In 1957, he displayed sympathy for an ex-Reichsbanker in need. The central bank had already been paying Funk's wife Luise a maintenance grant of DM600 a month. With Walther (or 'Dr Funk' as he was pompously and erroneously called in Bank deutscher Länder documents in the 1950s) out of jail, the bank decided to increase the Funks' monthly allowance to

DM1000. The Bank deutscher Länder also paid Funk's medical bills – starting off with a lump sum of DM3000.[37] The central bank's magnanimous treatment of this most unappetising of Nazis was carried out with the utmost discretion. West Germany had started a new life, and men like Funk belonged to a past which suddenly seemed to have happened a long time ago.

ii. A bank with National Socialist character

In January 1939, along with the nomination of Funk as president and Brinkmann as vice-president, Hitler signed on to the statute books a new Reichsbank Law significantly extending the legal measures of February 1937. The Reichsbank – now preceded by the official appellation 'Deutsche' – was brought fully under the Führer's control. Details of the law were kept secret until the summer. But, as preliminary indications were published in the Nazi press, there could be little doubt in the public mind that the overall shake-up was part of contingency planning for war. One leading economic journal commented that the 'reunification of the Reichs-bank and the Reich economics ministry' served the interest of 'discipline and uniformity of economic leadership' in order to meet 'the great military and economic challenge of the Four Year Plan'.[38] Hitler told the Reichstag at the end of January that the changes were part of moves to infuse all Germany's national institutions with 'National Socialist character'.[39] In the same speech, he made an ominous threat against European Jews:

> If international Jewish finance, within and outside Europe, should succeed in plunging the world once again into war, then this will result not in world Bolshevisation and victory for Jewry, but in the destruction of the Jewish race in Europe!

The new law on the Reichsbank was published in June, revealing that the bank was 'unconditionally subordinated to the sovereignty of the state'.[40] The official Reichsbank reaction was one of unalloyed enthusiasm: the move could only make the Reichsmark stronger. Karl Frede, an official in the bank's economics department, wrote, 'The date of 15 June 1939, when the Führer put into effect the Law on the Deutsche Reichsbank and accomplished the full integration of the Reichsbank into the organism of the Third Reich, is a memorable day in the history of the central bank of the German people.'[41] Frede joined the Nazi party in 1940.[42] After the war, he became a senior regional official of the Bank deutscher Länder and Bundesbank – and quickly adjusted to the new ways of independence.[43]

Towards the end of 1939 – after the outbreak of hostilities – Frede's thoughts were echoed by Eugen Einsiedel, the bank's chief economist. He declared – just as Schacht had done when the previous law was passed in 1937 – that the new Banking Law would help maintain monetary stability. Einsiedel neatly turned on its head the argument that independence was the key to financial soundness: in fact, he declared, precisely the opposite was true. Since 'highest decision-making power' in the bank would henceforth be subordinated to the Führer, stability of the currency would be assured, Einsiedel proclaimed. He added: 'The destiny of our currency ultimately depends on the same factor on which hangs the well-being of our nation [*Volk*] and the well-being of each one of us, namely, on the victorious outcome of the war. And of this outcome, we are all certain.'[44]

The new legislation emphasised how the Reichsbank was rapidly becoming a mere appendage of the Nazi state. Later, in 1942, the Reichsbank was to be awarded the title of a National Socialist 'model'.[45] The personnel changes served the same purpose. Whereas, at the end of 1938, only three out of the then nine-man Reichsbank directorate had been NSDAP members, a year later all seven men on the remodelled board carried the party card.[46]

The new leadership made clear its objective was to stabilise the currency – not to debauch it. A key figure was Rudolf Brinkmann, the new vice-president, a member of the SS and a leading functionary from the economics ministry, who had been one of Schacht's early protégés.[47] In one of his first statements after his appointment, Brinkmann affirmed in February 1939 the highest commitment to currency stability. 'Only fifteen years ago, the German people suffered the effects of inflation on their own lives . . . For an economy to grow and deliver the highest performance, a stable currency is absolutely necessary.'[48] A memorandum from the Reichsbank's statistics department emphasised that the Nazi leadership's more rational attitude to 'the overall question of financing' formed a vital difference between Germany's economic policies in the two wars.[49]

In an unusually frank speech in Cologne in early 1939 – details of which leaked out to the foreign press – Brinkmann bitterly complained about Germany's growing budget and trade deficits, as well as increasing inflationary pressures.[50] Some of Brinkmann's policy statements may have appeared sound; but it soon became apparent that his appointment as the Reichsbank's second-in-command was highly irresponsible. Brinkmann's devotion to the National Socialist cause went beyond the merely fanatical. He was growing increasingly mentally unhinged.

In his painful eagerness to please, Funk liked to amuse the Führer by describing Brinkmann's eccentricities. In one notorious episode, Brinkmann distributed newly printed banknotes – all bearing Funk's signature – from his briefcase on the main thoroughfare of Unter den Linden in the centre of Berlin. With an ear for the pun (*Funk* means 'spark' in German), Brinkmann would ask bewildered passers-by, 'Who wants some of the new Funks?'[51]

Directorate colleagues started to complain about Brinkmann's bad language. His many other idiosyncrasies also attracted attention: Brinkmann had his office repainted bright red, kept a loaded revolver on his desk, and entertained Reichsbank cleaning ladies to impromptu violin concerts.[52] A heated meeting involving Reichsbank officials and his arch-protector, Göring, took place to discuss the unseemliness. Despite this, more bad behaviour by Brinkmann ensued at a party to celebrate the Führer's birthday on 20 April 1939. The Reichsbank vice-president took refuge from Berlin in a guest-house in Lower Saxony. From there, he was physically removed by police and medical orderlies and taken to a mental hospital in Bonn. In early May, Brinkmann bitterly complained after Himmler stripped him of the right to wear his SS uniform or carry the ceremonial dagger. In a letter of chilling sympathy which signalled the end of Brinkmann's part in the German war effort, the SS Reichsführer replied, 'I am sure you will survive the period of your illness so long as you have the will to become healthy.'[53]

The Brinkmann affair, though exceptional in its surreality, was in line with the dream-like atmosphere which pervaded the wartime Reichsbank. The monetary misgivings which led to the January 1939 memorandum never completely disappeared.[54] But as the Wehrmacht's initial success in Poland was followed in 1940 by sweeping victories in the west, the Reichsbank's mood became little short of euphoric.

'Our economic rearmament has not lagged behind our military

rearmament,' declared in 1940 Friedrich Oechsner, an official in the economics and statistics department and long-time Nazi party member, who was destined for a top Bundesbank post in southern Germany after the war.[55] Rudolf Windlinger, another member of the economics and statistics department, who after 1948 took up a senior position with the Bank deutscher Länder,[56] wrote in November 1940:

> One of the many false impressions with which the western powers entered the war in September 1939 was that of Germany's unavoidable economic and financial collapse. In the meantime this hope, like so many nurtured by the enemy, has been wrecked. The German economic system – and above all the system of German war financing – has entered into operation without any problems at all, and has brilliantly surmounted its baptism of fire.[57]

The economic hierarchy continually restated its belief that German dominance was leading inexorably to a new European economic order. Emil Puhl, a Nazi party member[58] who became the bank's managing vice-president in 1940, declared, 'In the re-ordering of the European economy, the Axis powers will be the leaders.'[59] Culminating a long Reichsbank career which started with a lowly clerk's post in 1913 and brought him to the directorate in 1934,[60] Puhl served alongside Kurt Lange, the other vice-president.[61] Lange, a long-time Nazi and crude propagandist moved from the Reich economics ministry, was put in charge of personnel matters and safeguarding National Socialist principles at the bank. Since Funk rarely entered the Reichsbank building, Puhl was in charge of day-to-day banking operations throughout most of the war. He was the key go-between in an arrangement with Himmler and the SS under which jewellery, watches, spectacle frames, dental gold and other gold items taken from Jewish concentration camp victims were deposited in the vaults of the Reichsbank from August 1942 onwards.[62] In 1949, Puhl was jailed by the Americans for his complicity in this arrangement.[63] After his release from the fortress of Landsberg, Puhl resumed his career, taking up a senior job with the Dresdner Bank in Hamburg.[64]

Otto Pfleiderer, an economist at the government-owned Reichs-Kredit-Gesellschaft, held similar views to Puhl. Later he became a long-serving president of the *Landeszentralbank* Baden-Württem-berg and, for twenty-four years, an influential member of the Bun-desbank council.* Later, Pfleiderer won acclaim for his financial acumen; in the early years of the war, however, he showed a distinct absence of foresight. Pfleiderer wrote in October 1940 that Berlin would be Europe's 'liquidity centre', the natural home for European countries' reserve currencies, while Germany would also be the 'natural provider of capital for the great investments needed to develop Europe after the end of the war'.[65]

The same prognosis was spelled out by Pfleiderer's boss, the head of the Reichs-Kredit-Gesellschaft economics department, Bernhard Benning. He spent five post-war years in Soviet captivity, including a long spell at the Buchenwald concentration camp near Weimar in East Germany. In 1950 he was freed, crossed to the west, and gained a job on the directorate of the Bank deutscher Länder. He remained in this position when the Bundesbank was set up, and stayed on until his retirement in 1972. 'There is no argument about the position of the Reichsmark as Europe's leading currency,' he wrote in 1943. 'Berlin will take over a similar position – albeit significantly stronger – to that occupied formerly by London within the sterling area.'[66]

To ensure economic dominance, the men of the Reichsbank knew that morale must be sustained. In 1941, Alphons Diehl, a leading member of the economics and statistics department – who took up a senior regional Bundesbank position after the war[67] – issued a vibrant rallying call to employees to mark the eighth anni-versary of Hitler's accession to power. The language bore little resemblance to the studied moderation of central bankers' tra-ditional utterances: 'After a victory march without parallel, the bearers of German arms are ready to do final battle against our ultimate enemy... When the weapons are stilled and a greater Germany is secure for the rest of time, none of us should be allowed to say to himself that, at this decisive time, he ever failed.'[68]

iii. The plan for European Economic Union

In summer 1940, as the Wehrmacht rampaged across Europe, the success of the Blitzkrieg convinced the Reichsbank – like many

*See chapter 6

others – that the fighting would soon be over. The central bank and the Reich economics ministry actively laid plans for post-war monetary union across a large part of Europe, with the Reichsmark the dominant currency.

In June 1940, the Reichsbank's economics and statistics department prepared a detailed analysis for Funk and the rest of the directorate looking ahead to 'problems for external monetary policy after the end of the war'.[69] The document concluded that the Reichsmark would be the 'leading currency in a German economic area'[70] and one of the world's two 'standard currencies' (along with the US dollar). Germany would demand war damages from the vanquished in the form of raw materials, gold and reductions in the Reich's foreign debt. The Reichsmark's link with gold would remain, though 'in sharply relaxed' form. Additionally 'within the German currency bloc', fixed exchange rates would be introduced 'to ease the way later to a currency and customs union'. The memory of Germany's harsh treatment after the First World War had left its mark: but in their plans for future reparations, the Reichsbank's experts were surprisingly magnanimous:

> Even though we do not wish to repeat the mistakes of Versailles by making the attempt, for decades on end, to suppress economically a defeated opponent, a significant one-off sum of war damages is none the less appropriate.

The Reichsbank estimated that reparations payments of RM16 to RM17 billion – to be borne jointly by both Britain and France – would be 'tolerable'.[71] After the war, German officials denied any knowledge of these reparations plans. During his pre-Nuremberg interrogation, Funk dismissed the existence of such proposals as 'unthinkable'.[72]

In fact, by July 1940, the Reich economics ministry had already drawn up detailed plans for a 'Bank for European Settlements', also to be called the Europabank ('Bank of Europe'), as the pivot of the planned post-war monetary system. The bank, to be based in Vienna, would be owned by individual governments and central banks, which would pay in share capital in proportion to their existing pre-war financial obligations.[73] All payments between member countries would be made through the Europabank, which would also have the ability to grant Reichsmark credits to members to back export activity. The bank would have the power to levy minimum reserves from central banks 'to control expansion of credit of member states'.

Countries eligible for participation in the proposed 'Central European Economic Union' included the Netherlands, Denmark, Slovakia, Romania, Bulgaria and Hungary. The Reich economics ministry suggested that Belgium, Norway and Sweden would also be associated. Special 'arrangements' would have to be made in a future peace treaty with Britain and France 'in order to secure the economic recovery of Central Europe'.

Although the Reichsmark would clearly stand at the centre of Europe's financial arrangements, the government was well aware of the political disadvantages of proceeding to a single European currency. The Reich economics ministry believed that a single currency would be 'the most simple [method] to carry through from an administrative point of view'. In an intriguing foretaste of the Bundesbank's views half a century later on European monetary union the economics ministry added: 'For political reasons it could be undesirable to damage the self-esteem of member states by eliminating their currencies.' Initial plans were thus based on individual countries maintaining their own currencies, but agreeing to permanently fixed exchange rates against the Reichsmark.

Schacht was gone. But the old Schachtian delusions continued, in new form. One reason for the Reichsbank's early 1940s confidence was its belief that it had invented an unbeatable method of war financing. By systematically tapping the banking sector's short-term liquid funds – through the system of so-called *geräuschlose Finanzierung* (noiseless financing) – the Reich authorities avoided the stream of state bond issues favoured by the US and Britain. The inflationary spuriousness of the German financing method was fully admitted after 1945. Bernhard Benning however wrote in 1943 that the system combined low cost and 'technical simplicity'; it was a system, he wrote, which was only possible in a 'total war economy', with a 'continually perfected apparatus of price and wage controls'.[74]

The system of *geräuschlose Finanzierung* led to a steadily growing build-up of short-term government debt to the commercial banks. In a repetition of developments towards the end of the First World War, most of the debt was accumulated after 1943 in the form of Treasury bills lodged directly with the Reichsbank. As the money supply soared towards the end of the war, the Reichsmark was reduced to near worthlessness. Ironically, however, because the Third Reich managed to avoid large volumes of public bond issues, subsequent German governments were left with a beneficial legacy. The wiping out of asset values in the 1948 currency reform affected above all savings deposits rather than public bond issues. Since the state's own name as a borrower did not unduly suffer, the German government's reputation was not spoilt as a reliable debt issuer. By avoiding the need to rebuild an image as a borrower, successive post-war governments have reaped a curious benefit from Nazi Germany's economic practices.

The Reichsbank's optimism about war funding was juxtaposed with new pride in Germany's international financial stature. The Reichsbank hammered out the incessant Leitmotif that, through conquest and occupation, Germany was bringing monetary order to the rest of Europe. In his first speech to the Reichsbank's central committee, shortly after the German army marched into Prague, Funk declared: 'An intolerable hotbed of disturbance and danger in central Europe has been eliminated, and a new order has been established.'[75] At the Reichsmark's finest hour, the men of the Reichsbank believed that order had moved in to stay.

iv. Persistent pursuit of orthodoxy

Emil Puhl, the Reichsbank's joint vice-president from 1940 onwards, applied himself with trenchancy and persistence to the goal of extending Germany's financial influence throughout the continent. A man of exemplary ambivalence, Puhl had signed Schacht's anti-inflation memorandum of January 1939 – without suffering the least setback in his career. After the war, Puhl claimed that it had been 'ever more recognisable' that Hitler's policies would lead to inflation.[76] All along, Puhl had a foot in both camps; early on in the war, he was a discreet participant in obscure financial negotiations with the central banks of the Allied powers at the Bank for International Settlements in Basle.[77]

In Puhl's public statements in the early 1940s, there was no ambiguity or doubt. In words of unconstrained clarity, Puhl stated that, with the Reichsmark run by the Nazis, European monetary affairs were in the best possible hands. Puhl used a propaganda radio address in May 1940 to mock the Cassandras abroad who had warned that the Nazi leadership would plunge Germany into inflation.[78] This simply showed how little foreigners understood German monetary policy, he said. Describing the June 1939 Banking Law subjugating the Reichsbank to Hitler as 'the most modern central banking law in the world', Puhl emphasised the Nazis' attachment to total financial orthodoxy. 'In no land more than National Socialist Germany does honest effort, in whatever way it is applied, receive greater protection and higher respect. It is self-evident that the National Socialist leadership unconditionally rejects all monetary experiments, as these could endanger the savings of millions of hard-working German people.'

Puhl maintained that German economic domination would benefit the entire continent. In 1941, he spelled out how the *Reichskreditkassen*, the local money-issuing offices set up in the occupied territories as the elongated arm of the Reichsbank, 'had to replace the entire money and credit apparatus in Poland, where the monetary sector was totally destroyed'.[79] The Reichsbank carried out similar operations in Denmark, Norway and the Netherlands. 'In Belgium and the occupied parts of France, we faced much harder tasks, because the central banks here were only gradually ready to work with us.' Nearly everywhere around occupied Europe, the Reichsbank introduced Hitler's 'work currency' (*Arbeitswährung*) concept to replace the 'gold currencies';[80] the gold, meanwhile, usually ended up in Berlin. As the war reached its turning point with Hitler's move in June 1941 to turn his armies towards the might of the Soviet Union, Puhl explained how the Reichsbank's generosity towards countries crushed by German arms was simply a question of duty:

> The monetary aid which the Reichsbank has extended to Serbia has already been made available to all occupied areas. Recognising that orderly monetary conditions form the fundamental basis for economic recovery, Germany has lent its support to all these countries in a manner going well beyond the international practice of former times. In spite of differences in the details, everywhere we have applied the same thoroughness, speed and expertise in rebuilding the currencies which were destroyed before the war. We have proved that we recognise and fulfil the economic obligations which come from European supremacy.[81]

After the Wehrmacht moved eastwards, Puhl reported in December 1942 that the Reichsbank's work 'in the service of the European economic community' had been extended to the Soviet Union and Bulgaria.[82] The Reichsbank was 'stepping into the future', he declared in 1943, 'with the confidence that the Reichsmark will always match up to the greatness and dignity of the National Socialist German Reich.'[83]

One man who played an intriguing role in spreading German values eastwards was Fritz Paersch, a dedicated and long-serving Reichsbank official who in September 1939 became a board member of the *Reichskreditkassen* organisation. In 1940 Paersch was chosen to head the new German-sponsored central bank running the occupied Polish territories. He remained in this post in Cracow until the end of the war, and was plainly proud of his work. Paersch organised the disappearance (at a punitive rate of exchange) of the old zloty notes; the old Bank Polski, the Polish central bank, as he put it in 1941, had become 'unoperational'.[84] Since then, Paersch wrote, the new zloty had been established as an *Arbeitswährung* based on 'economic performance'. It had won the confidence of the people 'in a surprisingly short time'.

Though not a Nazi member, Paersch was held in the highest regard both by the Reichsbank directorate and by Hans Frank, the sadistic Nazi governor of Poland,[85] later executed after being found guilty of war crimes charges at Nuremberg. Since his loyal service to the Nazi state had been embarrassingly well documented, Paersch met considerable difficulties after the war in winning de-nazification clearance from the Allied authorities, and was turned down for a job as the Bank deutscher Länder's directorate member for banking and credit. It was however impossible to keep a good Reichsbank man down.* Paersch was given a lower-profile post as vice-president of the Hesse *Landeszentralbank*, where he remained between 1949 and 1957. Long after normal retirement, at the age of nearly seventy, Paersch continued to find employment in Frankfurt. He was brought in as an official liquidator of the tortuous affairs of the Reichsbank, which was still in the midst of legal winding-up throes two decades after the end of the war.[86] The Reichsbank continued to look after its own, long after it had ceased formally to exist.

*See chapter 6.

v. 'German order is being destroyed'

The private voice of the Reichsbank was a good deal less confident than the one heard publicly. As early as January 1942, immediately after the Japanese attack on Pearl Harbor brought the US into the war, an internal Reichsbank memorandum voiced the fear that the rapid rise of money in circulation made inflation inevitable:

> Our currency is endangered on two fronts: on the monetary side, from the permanent increase in purchasing power, on the goods side, from the continued fall in consumer goods production. If present developments continue, the time cannot be too far off when the dams of price and goods controls – the only factors protecting the currency from decline – will collapse under the pressure.[87]

The document emphasised that inflation would not simply cause 'bitterness' among the population, but would also 'seriously reduce the will to resist at home and on the front'.

In a description which could also have applied to the position in East Germany forty-five years later, the document continued: 'The permanently increasing surveillance and control of every individual is a source of general discord. In spite of nominal price stability, the value of money is falling considerably, as, for a large part of people's money, there are no goods to buy.'[88]

As late as 1943, the Reichsbank maintained a desperate optimism that Germany would be spared defeat and inflation. Both consequences however started to look increasingly probable as the US entered the conflict and German armies were repulsed in the east. In October 1943, Rudolf Windlinger from the bank's economics department was still trying vainly to foster optimism. He used exactly the same words as in his essay of November 1940 to point out the enemy's error in predicting Germany's 'economic and financial collapse'.[89]

In June 1943, the Nazi vice-president Kurt Lange crudely extolled the state's 'elastic' financing methods before an audience in Budapest, and – echoing Hitler – declared: 'In an authoritarian state, there can be no inflation.'[90]

At a meeting of the fifty-nine-strong Reichsbank advisory board in June 1943 – both Hermann Josef Abs and Karl Blessing were present – Walther Funk presented a sobering balance of the effect of Allied bombing on consumer goods production.[91] At a later advisory board meeting, in February 1944, Funk maintained his forecast of victory and said this would require Germany to switch industry away from armaments and into rebuilding.[92] The Reichsbank asserted in its 1943 annual report that monetary problems were still being 'mastered'.[93] But the figures told a story reminiscent of a saga the Reichsbank had sworn would not be repeated: the inflation which followed the ending of the First World War. As the Reich finance ministry pumped out ever-rising quantities of Treasury bills, Reichsbank notes in circulation – RM12 billion at the end of 1939 – tripled to RM34 billion by December 1943. The figure reached RM50 billion by the end of 1944 and exceeded RM70 billion by the time of the capitulation in May 1945.

'The rise in Reich indebtedness,' lied Lange in a radio broadcast in October 1944, 'is in no way disturbing.'[94] The massive quantities of debauched money flowing through the torn country were in fact already preparing the way for the next currency reform – and the 1948 birth of the D-Mark. As the Germans lurched towards total defeat after a total war which had cost 55 million lives, Funk complained to his Reichsbank employees in the Berlin opera house: 'German order is being brutally destroyed.'[95]

vi. The magician's fate

Hjalmar Schacht, 'Hitler's magician', saw out the war in distinctly unmagical circumstances. After his dismissal from the Reichsbank, Schacht became associated with the opposition movement, and was implicated in the 20 July 1944 plot to assassinate Hitler.[96] The Führer ordered Schacht's imprisonment on 23 July, declaring that the Reichsbank president should have been shot before the start of the war on account of his attempts to hamper rearmament.[97] Schacht was shunted between a number of Nazi prisons and concentration camps: Ravensbrück and Potsdam, Berlin and Flossenbürg. He was brought to Dachau in April 1945, before being liberated by the Americans in South Tirol at the end of April. He was then promptly re-imprisoned. In 1946, no one was more surprised than Schacht to find himself in the dock at the Nuremberg tribunal accused of war crimes. He told the court that he had never been a 'convinced supporter' of Hitler,[98] and had even wanted to kill the Führer himself.[99] Symptomatic of Schacht's quicksilver ability to steer several different courses at once, one of his most celebrated 1930s pronouncements – at Königsberg in 1935, when he spoke out both for and against the Jews – was used in Nuremberg by two sets of counsel: for the prosecution, and for the defence.[100]

One of Schacht's crucial contentions was that his frequent flattering remarks about Hitler were necessary to maintain the confidence of the Nazis by 'disguising' his true feelings.[101] After putting up a self-assured defence, brilliantly assembled by his counsel Rudolf Dix, Schacht was acquitted on all charges. One remarkable fact which escaped notice at Nuremberg emphasised both Schacht's anxieties about his own future during the Third Reich and his extreme capacity for duplicity. At the end of the 1930s, he actively tried to defect from Nazi Germany with the help of the US embassy.[102] Schacht ignored the episode in post-war books or public statements – perhaps because it would have undermined his contention that he was acting all along in the best patriotic interests of Germany. He did however reveal that he had asked Hitler for approval to travel to the US at the beginning of 1940 to conduct peace talks with President Roosevelt.[103] The idea was turned down by Joachim von Ribbentrop, the foreign minister.

As Germany started to rebuild, Schacht was once again a free man. The former Reichsbank chief refashioned his life with aplomb, becoming a small-scale private banker and perpetual publicity-hungry thorn in the side of the Bundesbank and successive Bonn governments.[104] Schacht's 1945 forecast assuring an Allied interrogator that he would not write his memoirs[105] was premature. He achieved fresh renown with a series of books on the Hitler years, his 'resistance' becoming slightly stronger with every new account.[106] He died in 1970 at the age of ninety-three. With the quixotism of old age, Schacht insisted right up to the end that, by agreeing to the 'abandonment of the Reichsbank', West Germany had given up the old Reich. This had helped cause the 'lasting separation' of the two parts of the divided nation.[107]

Although the full story of the Reichsbank's war-time tribulations was never told, the lessons – moral and monetary – of the Reichsbank's ruin served an important purpose. The bank's demise represented a powerful reminder of the need for utmost rectitude in the monetary affairs of the now truncated nation. The message sunk home. As the Germans learned it by heart, they reaped the rewards of a rejection of profligacy. No one could have predicted that, within a short span of years, a new and more permanent order would rise from the smoking ashes of the Reichsmark.

6

Continuity and Change

> I hope it will prove possible to put our currency on to an
> orderly footing.
> *Ludwig Erhard, Bavarian economics minister in US occupied
> zone, 1945*[1]

> The suggestion that 'the best German' put his name to the
> new currency is excellent, and we shall of course attempt
> to follow it . . . Persons too predominantly associated with
> the Nazi past are also prominently identified with the fact
> that the Reichsmark has been discredited.
> *Jack Bennett, financial adviser to Gen. Lucius Clay, US
> military governor, 1948*[2]

> The central bank is forced, depending on circumstances,
> to take unpopular measures. It must be better for the
> government, from a political point of view, that these
> measures do not have to depend on the outcome of
> parliamentary debates.
> *Wilhelm Vocke, president of directorate of Bank deutscher
> Länder, 1950*[3]

For ordinary Germans who survived the ending of the war, the
first few years of peace brought pause, but little relief. For the
dispossessed inhabitants of demolished towns and cities, the pound-
ing of the bombs was replaced by the threat of slow starvation. In
an early post-war call for the British government to send more
grain, Britain's Field Marshal Lord Montgomery – not a man
suspected of softness towards the Germans – pointed out that the
average rations given to Germans in the British zone were the same
as those latterly granted to inmates of the Belsen concentration
camp.[4]

The Morgenthau proposals to reduce Germany to an agricultural
economy had long been abandoned as official policy. Yet an unin-
itiated visitor to ruined Germany might have thought that the plan
was being put into effect after all. During the savage winter of

1946–47, industrial production fell to a level last seen in the nineteenth century.[5] The proud men of the Reichsbank now had humility thrust upon them. Rudolf Eicke, an economist who had been one of the pillars of the old Berlin bureaucracy, was given a job at the Hamburg office of the Reichsbank. Since the bank's headquarters in the Soviet zone in Berlin had been closed by the Russians, the so-called *Reichsbankleitstelle* in the northern city on the Elbe served as the rump of the old central banking structure, and a home for those Reichsbankers who had escaped from the East. It was also the effective central bank of the British occupation zone in northern Germany. Eicke was not in a cheerful mood. 'Through the great distress in which we are, life in Germany is burdened by an ever increasing despair and lethargy,' Eicke wrote in haltingly bureaucratic English at Christmas 1946 to a sympathetic official at the Bank of England.[6]

Amid the devastation and decay, the birth of the Bank deutscher Länder on 1 March 1948 marked a small step towards the resumption of normal life. German monetary history could restart: the country had a new central bank. The organisation which served as the forerunner of the Bundesbank was established initially in the US and British zones, and extended promptly to the French area of occupation. It was the first post-war German institution, and its limitation to the western zones marked a precursor of the political division which was formalised in 1949 with the establishment of separate East and West German states. A further forty-one years were to elapse before the West German central bank system was transferred to the region under Soviet control in the East.

i. A hybrid takes shape

The bank created at the behest of the western victors was a hybrid. It was constructed on the shallowest of foundations, enlarged by diverse means, and designed to serve a panoply of contradictory objectives. The officials chosen to take the helm of the Bank deutscher Länder showed masterful ability in carving out a new role. In 1957, when the Bundesbank was established to take over the bank's functions, the D-Mark was still not freely convertible into foreign currency, and West Germany remained a junior partner in international monetary affairs. But the country's economic and political recovery was in full swing, and the new central bank had won a reputation for determination and independent-mindedness. With surprising speed, an edifice embodying characteristics of the American and British central banking systems, as well as many traits of the old Reichsbank, established itself as a brand new German institution.

The Bank deutscher Länder's headquarters were in the book-crammed offices of the old Reichsbank branch in Frankfurt off the Taunusanlage thoroughfare in the west of the bomb-devastated city. It was without foreign exchange reserves, without sovereignty and without esteem, bolstered only by hope, and the desire of strong-willed men to fill the vacuum left by the demise of the old order. The Bank deutscher Länder grew in stature and purpose partly by design, partly by accident. Its early development was driven as much by the clash of personalities as by the unfolding of high-flown principles. Its struggle to secure a role in the new German state was accompanied by elements of drama, tragedy and farce, as well as by a grim resolve not to repeat past mistakes.

Established more than a year before the birth of the Federal Republic in May 1949, the Bank deutscher Länder could only be a strongly federal institution. If it was made independent from government, that was partly because, at the time of its establishment, there *was* no central government.[7] The bank was owned jointly by western Germany's regional central banks (*Landeszentralbanken*), analogous in some ways to the components of the Federal Reserve in the US.[8] The *Landeszentralbanken* themselves were created shortly after the war in the Allied zones as part of the victors' desire to break up the centrally controlled apparatus of German power.

The Bank deutscher Länder was conceived above all as a coordinating agency for monetary decision-making. Its functions were defined as follows:

> To promote in the common interest the best use of the financial resources of the area served by the member *Land* central banks, to strengthen the currency and the monetary and credit systems, and to coordinate the activities of the *Land* central banks.[9]

The decision to establish the bank ended more than two years of acrimonious argument between the US and British governments on the make-up of the new German central banking system. Although the US won the day, features of banking centralisation favoured by the British gradually came into favour. More important still, the bank's foundation supplied the essential precondition for an event which was to take on almost mystic significance: the June 1948 replacement of the Reichsmark by the D-Mark.

The American goal of decentralisation did not mean that the new bank would have no power. The US intended the Bank deutscher Länder to have greater influence over the banking system than that exerted by the largely passive Reichsbank. The bank was buttressed by new instruments of monetary control, above all, the capacity to levy minimum reserves on banks' deposits. These levies gave the Bank deutscher Länder greater control over interest rates than the Reichsbank had enjoyed. If the bank tightened minimum reserve ratios, it would automatically reduce the supply of credit in the economy; by lowering the ratios, the central bank could increase the flow of funds.[10] To guard against any resumption of inflationary lending to the state, the bank's ability to provide bridging finance to the economic administration of the western zones was subjected to strict limits.[11] To keep the bank at arm's length from the commercial banking world, it had no supervisory role over the banks. Unlike the Reichsbank, the Bank deutscher Länder was barred from lending money to private customers.[12]

Article 3 of the Law on the Bank deutscher Länder specifically stated that the new institution 'shall not be subject to the instructions of any political body or public non-judicial agency'.[13] Yet it was clear that the Allies would not countenance full independence. At least until occupation came to an end, the bank was placed under the tutelage of an Allied supervisory body, the Allied Bank Commission.[14] The new institution was theoretically able to give instructions to the central bank, but its practical influence over German monetary policy turned out to be extremely limited.[15]

Although the Bank deutscher Länder, as an institution, could lay claim to being new, the men behind it clearly were not. As in other areas of West German life, the Allies' denazification procedures did not extend very far beyond ensuring that leading Nazis were barred from attaining the first batch of senior posts. The western powers quickly realised they needed a stable West Germany as a bulwark against Soviet expansion. West Germany required experienced functionaries to run its central bank, just as the foreign ministry had to employ well-established diplomats for its embassies, and the judiciary called on seasoned judges for its benches. Many of the new German central bankers – particularly those in the *Landeszentralbanken* – came from the Reichsbank. If they had not actively supported Nazism, they had certainly acquiesced in it.

For many officials who joined the Bank deutscher Länder, a new commitment to monetary rectitude was perhaps a painless form of personal atonement for past sins and omissions. Many had been guilty, in varying degrees, of opportunism, short-sightedness, naïveté or cowardice. As for their basic economic creed, it needed simply to be adjusted, rather than to undergo wholesale change. German society still strove for sound money – just as it had done under Hitler. This time, however, the circumstances were more propitious.

Germany's dramatic monetary history had the effect of enhancing rather than weakening the status of West Germany's first generation of central bankers. In 1957, when the Bundesbank Law came into effect, German parliamentarians formally transferred sovereignty over the D-Mark to an organisation outside their jurisdiction. Past experience had eroded the politicians' confidence in their ability to master inflation. The new central bankers grew quickly accustomed to their independence. Very soon, they guarded it as a basic right; they sensed that no government in Germany was ever likely to be sufficiently strong – or foolhardy – to remove it from them.

ii. A tussle between Allies

Everything about the Bank deutscher Länder was a compromise – even the name. In their eagerness to avoid centralisation, the Americans at first suggested 'Länder-Union Bank'. This was then shortened simply to 'Union Bank'. German experts involved in the negotiations turned this down and favoured 'Deutsche Zentralbank'. To satisfy all sides, 'Bank der deutschen Länder' was put forward. The name – 'Bank of the German States' – gave the impression however that all the German *Länder* would participate, not just those in the western zones. So at the last moment the word 'der' was dropped from the appellation and the bank was baptised, with becoming vagueness, 'Bank of German States'.[16]

The bank's policy-making council was made up of the heads of the eleven *Land* central banks existing in western Germany in

1948.[17] They were appointed by *Länder* governments. Another two members formed a dual leadership: the president of the council and the president of the directorate, the bank's management board which handled day-to-day operations. The council itself voted the appointment of both presidents, as well as the other members of the directorate, subject to the approval of the Allied representatives grouped in the Allied Bank Commission. Directorate members attended meetings of the council, but had no vote. This changed with the enactment of the Bundesbank Law in 1957, when directorate members were given equal voting power with those on the council.

The Bank deutscher Länder acted as a form of financial clearing house for the *Land* central banks, and thus for the banking system as a whole. It was, for instance, the central collection point for the minimum reserves levied by the *Land* central banks. Unlike the Reichsbank, the Bank deutscher Länder possessed a monopoly on banknote issuance. After the foundation of the Federal Republic, it handled the state's foreign financial transactions. The bank also supervised all the country's payments with the rest of the world under an administered system which ended only when the D-Mark was made freely convertible in 1958. Under the European Payments Union, set up in 1950 to settle trade among European countries on a clearing basis, automatic credit was extended to countries running balance of payments deficits – a mechanism which proved to be of great value to the fledgling Federal Republic.

The Allied aim was to make a clean break with the past, as the US and British military governments made clear:

> Unlike the old Reichsbank, the bank of the German *Länder* will not compete directly with the other banks for private funds, and will not be subject to domination by the state. On the other hand, it will have even greater influence over general monetary conditions, by virtue of its power to influence reserve ratios. It is felt it will therefore be possible to avoid many of the undesirable monetary and credit policies followed by the German central banks in the past.[18]

Reaching unanimity between the two war-time Allies required much effort. Since the ending of the war, plans to rebuild the German monetary system had provided fertile ground for quarrelling. Britain believed that the old centralised Reichsbank, stripped of the most obvious Nazis, could be used as the basis of the new central bank in the western zones. Responsible for the struggling coal and steel industry in their northern zone of occupation, the British were deeply concerned that wholesale banking upheaval would worsen the problems of the German economy. Influenced by the friendship between Montagu Norman and Hjalmar Schacht, Bank of England officials had established good connections with their opposite numbers at the Reichsbank during the 1930s. British officials in charge of post-war financial policies generally believed that German financiers and industrialists involved in the war effort had behaved little differently from their counterparts in the US or the UK.

The Americans were more rigorous – and less forgiving. If the war-weary British took the line of least resistance, many US officials were determined to maintain the ideology of defeating Nazism. America's motive was to exert retributive justice; and this would be best done, according to the US argument, by demolishing the old structures behind the German war economy – including the last vestiges of the Reichsbank.[19]

Joseph Dodge, previously president of the Detroit Bank and Trust Company, was brought to Germany in 1945 as the head of the Finance Division of the US Office of Military Government (Omgus).[20] The American goal, he proclaimed, was 'to ensure that the German financial hierarchy will never play any part in disturbing the peace of the world'.[21] Dodge in 1946 described US proposals for the new central bank in terms of a string of negatives:

It should be emphasised that the suggested bank is not a government-owned institution; it is not an individually owned institution; it is not a central financial department, although it can act in some respects as a substitute for one; and it is not, as is customary, an institution created at the national level and spreading downward, but one created from the bottom upward, with its roots in the banks of the *Länder*, but which can serve Germany as a whole.[22]

Britain underlined its opposition to the US-inspired decentralisation measures by deciding immediately after the war to maintain the old northern Reichsbank operation in the form of the Hamburg

Reichsbankleitstelle.[23] This office took over control of the central bank's north-western branches, which had been cut off from any central direction after the closure of the Berlin headquarters. As president and vice-president respectively of the Hamburg office, the British chose two former Reichsbank directorate members who had departed after the January 1939 memorandum – Ernst Hülse and Wilhelm Vocke.[24] Both Hülse and Vocke were well-known to the British through the Bank for International Settlements, where Hülse had served as assistant general manager between 1930 and 1935.[25]

In early 1947 Britain stepped up its campaign against the American decentralisation proposals, arguing that the three-power Potsdam agreement of August 1945 had agreed the need for 'central financial control' of Germany.[26] The Bank of England's Charles Gunston, on good terms with former Reichsbank officials who solidly opposed the break-up of the old central bank,[27] called Dodge's proposals 'lunatic'.[28] In an unusually heavy-handed memorandum, the British authorities warned that the American plan could prepare the way for a return to totalitarianism. 'If an over-decentralised system is introduced which leads to financial catastrophe such as that which occurred in Germany in 1926–32, an opportunity would have been provided for a centralising and militarising party to gain popularity, and perhaps power, as in 1933.'[29]

General Lucius Clay, the US military governor, although a strong supporter of decentralisation, was more conciliatory towards Britain than his financial adviser, Jack Bennett.[30] In autumn 1947, recognising the need to stabilise the western part of Germany as a bulwark against Soviet expansion, Washington indicated readiness to compromise. Clay's view was that 'A *Länder* Union Bank, in which the capital is held by the several *Land* banks who select the board of directors, does not constitute in itself a strong centralisation which would be apt to become dangerous in the future ... With much of the evil of the Reichsbank system ended, I would be prepared to accept this arrangment as a compromise measure with the British.'[31]

In the struggle to withstand a decentralised banking system, the British authorities realised all along that they had little alternative but to 'bow before the dollar pressure'.[32] But, in return for giving up the idea of re-establishing a Reichsbank-type system, the UK extracted important concessions from the US.[33] The two sides agreed to create a bizonal budget, relieving the strain of expensive subsidies for coal and steel in the British zone. The US and Britain also reached accord on setting up a bizonal Reconstruction Loan Corporation – the Kreditanstalt für Wiederaufbau – to finance industrial recovery in areas like the British-run Ruhr.[34]

Cameron Cobbold, the deputy governor of the Bank of England, declared that the structure agreed for the Bank deutscher Länder was an improvement on US proposals. But Cobbold claimed that the 'lack of centralised Treasury or central bank control in the zone' was still an element of weakness.[35] Once the Germans took over the full running of the Bank deutscher Länder, the ex-Reichs-bankers were destined to make this point with ever greater persistence.

iii. 'The Yanks nearly passed out'

The meeting on 2 April 1948 of the policy-making council of the Bank deutscher Länder was a landmark. The bank was already more than a month old. No one, however, was running it. The council's task was to elect two presidents – of the council, and of the directorate; the second president would function as the deputy of the first. Nearly two tortuous months were to pass before the matter was settled. The meeting provided the scene for the first battle of wits between the bank and its nominal overseers on the Allied Bank Commission – and produced the first post-war stirrings of central banking independence.

By voting for Otto Schniewind, a pre-war member of the Reichs-bank directorate,[36] and Hermann Josef Abs, the most prominent war-time board member of the Deutsche Bank,[37] the council issued an unmistakable signal of defiance. Both men were opposed by the US occupying authorities. As the result of American objections, the election of these two well-established and politically ambivalent financiers never took effect. None the less, by resisting the wishes of the occupying powers, the council served up a message often to be repeated in coming decades: the bank was determined to run affairs as it, and no one else, thought best.

Both Schniewind and Abs presided over ample reserves of three vital qualities necessary to build a banking career during the Third Reich: quick brains, technocratic ability, and political agility. They had profited from good connections with top figures in the Nazi regime; later, they had both become associated with Hitler's opponents. Following the July 1944 plot against the Führer, Schniewind was interned by the Nazis after the Gestapo realised that his name appeared on a putative post-Hitler cabinet list drawn up by the conspirators.[38] Abs, destined to become the most powerful commercial banker in post-1945 Germany, never pretended to have participated in resistance to the Hitler regime. Abs was a banker, not a hero. One of his favourite sayings was 'A man who has not been imprisoned or hanged or shot by the Nazis cannot claim to have opposed Hitler.' In 1948, he was well on the way to making himself as helpful to the British in the northern zone as he had been to the economic rulers of the Third Reich.[39]

On 2 April, the man presiding temporarily over the council's landmark deliberations was Otto Veit, the president of the Hesse central bank. He was a former economic journalist: scholarly, opinionated and vain. Veit's relations with the Nazis had not been helped by the fact that his mother was both English and 'non-Aryan'. None the less, he had been talented enough to have held down a job at an Aryanised banking firm during the war.[40] After gathering written proposals from the assembled council members, Veit warned his colleagues that the Allies had already made their feelings plain about a number of potential nominees. A total of thirty names had been put forward for the central bank's three top jobs: president of the council, and president and vice-president of the directorate.[41] The Bank Commission had already classified several names on the list as 'non-acceptable', Veit revealed – including, as a result of US objections, both Abs and Schniewind.[42] The US misgivings were not surprising. In a recently completed Omgus investigation into the Deutsche Bank's war-time activities, Abs' name figured prominently as an architect of the bank's predatory incursions across occupied Europe.[43]

Although fully aware of the Allied objections, the central bankers decided to ignore them. For the job of president of the council, they elected Schniewind by 8 votes to 3; for the post of his deputy, the president of the directorate, Abs was selected by a margin of 7 to 4. British and American officials from the Finance Division of the bizonal government sat in on the council's gathering. One Bank of England man there recorded the Americans' shock that the council should ignore their recommendations: 'When Abs' name was announced, the Yanks at the meeting nearly passed out.'[44]

Schniewind and Abs were also surprised. Alerted to the news, the two bankers told the council of their 'reservations' about accepting the posts – 'above all because we must be doubtful whether we can count on the approval of the occupying powers.'[45] Both men realised they were not liked by the Americans; and neither wanted to be rejected outright. What followed next was a face-saving exercise of Byzantine complexity. As a condition for taking on the top jobs, they set down a requirement which they knew would be virtually impossible to fulfil: a change in the Bank deutscher Länder law to increase the influence of the president and his deputy compared with that of the *Land* representatives. Insisting that the proposal was 'essential' for maintaining anti-inflation policies, Schniewind and Abs called for the right to veto proposals over the granting of central bank credits to government authorities.[46] For the two bankers, the proposals provided a convincing and cunning means of cutting short their candidature for jobs which the Americans were anyway not disposed to give them.[47]

At the next meeting, on 14 April, American hostility to Schniewind and Abs came fully into the open when US representatives deposited with the council dossiers on the two men's war activities. Neither had been a member of the Nazi party, and they had both been exonerated in post-war denazification procedures.[48] But, in the documents handed to the council, Schniewind was alleged to have lied about his membership of the Reich civil servants association, and to have profited from the Aryanisation of Telefonbau und Normalzeit, a formerly Jewish-owned telephone company of which he eventually became management board chairman.[49] The material on Abs was weightier: a nine-page memorandum detailing the banker's role as 'one of the foremost German bankers during the Third Reich' who had helped carry through Aryanisation measures and 'proved very valuable to the Party and to the Government by using his bank to assist the government in doing business in the occupied countries'.[50] To make their antipathy to Abs still clearer, the Americans ostentatiously placed on one of the meeting room chairs the five-volume Omgus report on Deutsche Bank's war-time operations.[51]

The next gathering of the council was on 21 April. The council members formally asked the Allied Bank Commission to change the Bank deutscher Länder Law to meet Schniewind's and Abs' demands; as had seemed likely all along, the Commission rejected

1. Rudolf Havenstein, Reichsbank president 1908–23.
Died of a heart attack after the Great Inflation.

2. (*left*) Hjalmar Schacht, Reichsbank president 1923–30 and 1933–39.
'Hitler's magician' believed he could control the Führer,
but he was outmanoeuvred. Schacht finished the war in a concentration
camp.

3. (*right*) Hans Luther, Reichsbank president 1930–33. Put into effect
disastrous deflationary policies. Dislodged as soon as Hitler took power.

4. An early Bank deutscher Länder meeting
under Karl Bernard (*centre*) and (*to his left*) Wilhelm Vocke in 1948.

5. (*left*) Walther Funk, dissolute Nazi. Reichsbank president 1939–45.
Given life sentence at Nuremberg. Received monthly allowance from the
Bank deutscher Länder after his release from Spandau in 1957.

6. (*right*) Wilhelm Vocke: an unshakable belief in his own infallibility.
Member of the Reichsbank directorate 1919–39. President of the
directorate of the Bank deutscher Länder 1948–57.

7. The 19th-century Reichsbank building on the Jägerstrasse. Badly damaged by war bombing. 'The bombs of the air pirates have torn deep wounds here, but they cannot break the Berliners' will to live.'

8. The Reichsbank extension in Berlin. Marble-cladded and studded with sculpture, under the Third Reich it was 'the most modern bank building in the world'. Now back in use as the Bundesbank's HQ for east Germany.

9. Karl Blessing, ambitious
and ambivalent technocrat,
Bundesbank president
1958–69. War-time career
at the heart of the Nazi
economic establishment.

10. Karl Klasen, autocratic
Hamburg Social Democrat,
Bundesbank president
1970–77. A man of
commanding presence. 'He
could make people who
spoke too pompously look
silly.'

11. The old Reichsbank building in Frankfurt: home of the Bank deutscher Länder (1948–57) and the Bundesbank before it moved to its new quarters in 1972.

12. The Bundesbank building on the north-west outskirts of Frankfurt: erected on a green swathe of land wrested away in the late 1960s from local allotment gardeners.

13. Chancellor Helmut Schmidt visits the Bundesbank's 13th floor in November 1978 to harangue the council on the European Monetary System. Flanked by Hans Matthöfer, finance minister (*left*) and Otmar Emminger, Bundesbank president 1977–79.

14. Karl Otto Pöhl, Bundesbank president 1980–91. Seldom at a loss for a well-honed phrase – but stumbled over German unity.

15. Dispute at the Bundesbank over German unity in May 1990. Pöhl at council meeting with Theo Waigel, finance minister (*left*) and Schlesinger.

16. The Bundesbank council meets for the first time under Schlesinger in August 1991 – and decides to increase the discount rate by 1 percentage point to counter inflation.

17. Pöhl welcomes Margaret Thatcher, the British prime minister, to the Bundesbank in February 1989. 'Let me tell you something about Karl Otto. At some time or another, you will find, he has said everything.'

18. (*left*) Helmut Schlesinger, who took over unexpectedly from Pöhl as Bundesbank president in 1991. Orthodox and wooden, but more patient than Pöhl; the Boy Scout of German central banking.

19. (*right*) Hans Tietmeyer. Became Bundesbank vice-president in 1991. Combines missionary enthusiasm with the charm of a blunderbuss.

the idea.[52] Two fruitless council meetings later, on 5 May, both men withdrew from the race.[53] Among those to declare his disappointment was Konrad Adenauer, still more than a year away from becoming West Germany's first chancellor.[54]

Later during the meeting on 5 May, the Bank deutscher Länder council tried again to elect a dual leadership. It chose as council president Karl Bernard, a former Reich economics ministry official who had helped put into place Brüning's emergency legislation in 1931. Bernard, who had fallen foul of the Nazis on account of his Jewish wife, had spent the war as a director of a Frankfurt mortgage bank.[55] For the second job, that of president of the directorate, the council opted for Wilhelm Vocke, the former Reichsbanker, fresh from his experience of helping the British at the *Reichsbankleitstelle* in Hamburg. Bernard accepted the post as president of the council, but – contacted by telephone midway through the meeting – Vocke turned the job offer down.[56]

The council persisted. It promptly elected as president of the directorate another ex-Reichsbanker – Bodo von Wedel, former head of the central bank's foreign exchange department. Von Wedel had a reputation as an opponent of the Nazis.[57] During the latter part of the war, he had been custodian of the property of British and US banks in Germany – a job which assured him close contacts with the Anglo-American financial community. However, the central bankers' wishes were again thwarted. Still convalescing from illness, von Wedel had been living in the Swiss mountains for nearly four years, and had no wish to return to Germany. In a melodramatic letter to Veit, the former Reichsbank man introduced a culinary note of peevish incongruity into the haggling over the job: 'I am a strict vegetarian and total abstainer. Apart from that, I also refuse certain other food and almost all luxury food. On the other hand I require fresh fruit and vegetables, cereals and vegetable shortenings. I request the respective Allied authorities to guarantee supplies of such food.'[58]

After von Wedel's rejection, the council turned once more to Vocke, who on 19 May changed his mind and signalled his willingness, after all, to accept the post of president of the directorate.[59] He was elected by 8 votes to 3. With a lawyer's natural caution, Vocke sent a telegram to Bernard pointing out that he would accept the job only if the occupation authorities approved him. They did.[60] Vocke travelled to Frankfurt in time for the next council meeting on 1 June 1948, and stayed until the end of 1957. The sixty-two-year-old ex-Reichsbanker, backed by a bevy of former comrades-in-arms, ensured during the next nine and a half years that some of the old Reichsbank traditions were kept alive. A quarter of a century later, he recalled with pleasure how he and his colleagues had succeeded in thwarting the Americans' decentralisation plans for the new central bank. Setting up a centralised central banking system for West Germany was, Vocke wrote, exactly what the Americans did not want. 'It remains a mystery,' he added smugly, 'how we accomplished it after all.'[61]

iv. A certain flexibility

The presidents of the eleven regional central banks who sat on the first council of the Bank deutscher Länder council were a heterogeneous collection of functionaries, bankers and economists. Several were drawn from the so-called 'conclave' of German experts brought in to advise the Americans and British in the two months before the June 1948 currency reform. The group, which met in a well-guarded barracks at Rothwesten near Kassel, put forward valuable technical suggestions for reducing the huge overhang of Reichsmarks left after the collapse of the Third Reich.[62]

The 'conclave' had no influence on the decision of the date for the currency switch, which was announced on Friday 18 June, to come into effect on the following Monday, and the Bank deutscher Länder was not directly involved in the process. On Sunday 20 June the first stage of the currency conversion was put into place, when an initial sum of DM40 per head was paid out to the West German population.[63] Although current payments like wages and pensions were maintained at one new D-Mark for each old Reichsmark, assets were written down drastically. When savings deposits were converted the following October, individuals received an entitlement of just DM6.50 for every RM100 of savings.[64]

Ludwig Erhard, holding the position of economics director in the US-British bizone, issued a radio appeal for confidence: 'When I try to strengthen our people's trust in our new currency, I am appealing not to some vague, shadowy belief in miracles, but to the commonsense and insight of all of you.'[65] The birth of the D-Mark provided the incentive for the appearance of hoarded goods, brought out into the shops by the realisation that money of real value was now available to pay for them. However, the conversion also caused great hardship among savers – particularly older people who could not believe that their deposits had all but disappeared. Many families ended up with virtually nothing in the bank. 'Only heartless people could fail to be moved by the sorrow, bitterness, the sadness and the tears,' wrote an official from the Wetzlar savings bank in October 1948, describing distressing scenes at the bank's counters. 'An eighty-three-year-old widow sold her property in 1920 and deposited the savings with us,' wrote the Rheinprovinz savings bank. 'She lost three quarters in the first inflation [1923]. RM15,000 was left in the bank, which before the currency reform would have lasted a long time. Now she has only DM1000, and has to rely on charity.'[66]

Tales like this illustrated the challenges facing the council of the Bank deutscher Länder. Flexibility, as well as steadfastness, proved of great virtue. The council members shared two obvious characteristics: they were survivors; and they had made themselves amenable to the Allied occupation powers. At the outset, only two members of the Zentralbankrat – Ernst Hülse, a stiff technocrat in charge of the *Landeszentralbank* of North Rhine-Westphalia in the British zone, and Karl Mürdel from the Württemberg-Hohenzollern central bank in the French zone – came from the Reichsbank.[67] The British government had shown their regard for Hülse by making him head of the Hamburg *Reichsbankleitstelle*, and had favoured him as president of the central bank council. Precisely because he was firmly bound to the old Reichsbank ways, the US authorities, however, showed Hülse great hostility and flatly rejected making him the head of the new central bank.[68] Bennett, the US military government's financial adviser,[69] declared that a decision to make 'this former right-hand man of Schacht' head of the Bank deutscher Länder council would be 'catastrophic'.[70]

Allied policy in 1948 was geared to keeping ex-Nazis out of public life. The only ex-Nazi among the eleven presidents of the *Landeszentralbanken* in 1948 was Mürdel[71] – showing a surprising lack of stringency among the political masters in the French zone. As Allied influence waned, and former Nazi functionaries stepped up efforts to reclaim their jobs, the proportion of former Nazi party members on the council started to increase dramatically. In 1958, the first full year of operation of the Bundesbank, when the council was expanded to include the directorate members as well as the *Land* central bank presidents, its nineteen members included five former National Socialists.[72] By 1968, there were eight former Nazi card-holders on the twenty-strong council.[73] When the names of the other leading officials of the *Landeszentralbanken* are taken into account, the trend is even more marked.[74] In 1958, of the Bundesbank's total leading executives (members of the council, together with other board members of the *Land* central banks), thirteen out of thirty-four (38 per cent) were former Nazi members. By 1968, the figure had grown to eighteen out of thirty-four (53 per cent).[75]

In 1948, the members of the Bank deutscher Länder council came from a wide mix of backgrounds. One of the more distin-guished members was Wilhelm Boden, a former Centre Party member and Prussian state functionary, who was expelled from office when the Nazis took over in 1933.[76] During a short period in 1946–47 he had been the first prime minister of the newly-formed state of Rhineland-Palatinate. Another man with a favourable political past was Karl Klasen from Hamburg: a Social Democrat who finished the war in US imprisonment after starting a career with the Deutsche Bank in the 1930s. Max Sentz, rep-resenting Lower Saxony, was another banker. Between 1936 and 1946 he had been managing director of the Deutsche Girozentrale, the central organisation of the German savings bank movement. In what he affirmed later had been a purely representative capacity, Sentz sat on the Reichsbank's advisory council during the war.[77] Two other bankers in the council's ranks were Hermann Tepe, representing Bremen,[78] and Otto Burckhardt, the president of the Schleswig-Holstein central bank, a well-established financier, who in 1938 had helped to 'Aryanise' the Essen-based Jewish private bank Simon Hirschland. The bank was subsequently rebaptised Burckhardt und Cie.[79]

A man who quickly established himself as a vocal member of the council was Otto Pfleiderer, the dome-headed economist who was the president of the *Land* central bank in Württemberg-Baden.[80] With a solid academic background at four German universities behind him, as well as a long spell at the Reichs-Kredit-Gesell-schaft, Pfleiderer was singled out by the Americans shortly after the war as a potential high-flyer. Before 1945, Pfleiderer had been a persuasive advocate of economic nationalism and Reichsmark hegemony in Europe,* greatly underestimating the financial burdens Germany was shouldering as a result of the war effort.[81] In 1945 he was appointed to a senior post in the Württemberg-Baden finance ministry,[82] and in 1948 he became one of the experts in the 'conclave' advising the Americans on the currency reform.[83] Pfleiderer had now become an arch-critic of the Reichsbank. Pfleiderer exerted an important influence by helping to appoint a group of non-Reichsbank economists from Berlin on to the early Bank deutscher Länder directorate: men like Erich Zachau, Bernhard Benning (Pfleiderer's superior at the Reichs-Kredit-Gesellschaft), Eduard Wolf and, later, Otmar Emminger.[84]

Another Bank deutscher Länder council member with a chequered history was the former Reichsbank directorate member Hülse, whose relationship with the Nazis had been more than usually complicated. Before his dismissal from the Reichsbank in 1939, Hülse – in public at least – had given the Nazi economic leadership the benefit of the doubt.[85] Hülse, in fact, had little choice but to make congratulatory public pronouncements: he had been an object of suspicion because of his part-Jewish wife, and attracted direct criticism during the mid-1930s from the radical Nazi publication *Der Stürmer*.[86] During his three and a half years on the central bank directorate from 1935 onwards, Hülse did his best to restrict use of central bank credit to finance the arms build-up.[87] Hülse stated after the war that he had been the only member of the Reichsbank directorate not regularly invited during the 1930s to 'representative functions of the Party and of the Reich government'.[88] His obvious misgivings about the regime made all the more ironic his signing of Reichsbank notices asking banks to limit loans to Jewish companies[89] or requiring punctual attendance at Nazi party ceremonies.[90]

If Hülse cut a traditional central banking figure, Veit, the council's temporary chairman in 1948, was distinctly less orthodox. For all his renown as a monetary theoretician, Veit was primarily a historian and philosopher. His horizons stretched far beyond exchange rates and price indices; he liked to wander through the intricate byways of metaphysics and ethics. Veit was fascinated by a quality often found in central bankers: ambivalence. He rejected the comfortable notion that the world could be governed by rules.

*See chapter 5.

In an address in 1948 to admiring friends celebrating both his fiftieth birthday and his recent accession to a professorship, Veit spelled out his agnostic – almost anarchic – view of the world. 'The only law of history worthy of scientific analysis is that there is no law.' This was particularly marked, he said, in the development of the human spirit:

> Here we see crass contradictions, yes, ambivalent tendencies, which can exist side by side in an era, in a nation, in an individual person. The roots of the Second World War, which stretch back to the time of the Enlightenment, or further still, cannot be analysed unless one recognises such areas of contradiction and ambivalence. One example from the period we have just been through would be the coexistence of the most extreme elements of good and evil in the attitude of most Germans towards tyranny and its superficial success. Where can one glimpse here any sign of a law, or some kind of historical 'order'?[91]

Veit's analysis of ambivalence could have been applied to his own views on Hitlerian economics. Like many economists in Germany and abroad, Veit during the 1930s took a firm line favouring state intervention. The conditions in Germany, he suggested in a book published in 1937, were better than elsewhere:

> The [National Socialist] system, whose strength at the beginning was doubted by many, was put into effect with astonishing consistency and unexpected success. An important condition was the firm footing of the National Socialist state. In democratically run countries, it is hardly possible that such a system of directed intervention would work.[92]

The world needed, Veit wrote in 1938, 'a systematic support of investment, along the lines put into effect in Germany with widely admired success'.[93] Two months after the outbreak of war, he stated: 'Germany and perhaps the other participants in the war are in the process of proving that investment projects which are either profitable or promoted by the state are in all cases feasible. The question of financing is always secondary.'[94] In fact, as the Reichsmark's fate showed, the question of financing turned out to be anything but secondary. By 1961, Veit – like everyone else – was a good deal wiser:

> It is hardly necessary to point out to German readers examples of how the long-term consequences of monetary policies can be underestimated ... In the Second World War, it was thought that war financing could be carried out 'invisibly' or 'noiselessly', and thus without consequences. This was simply relying on technical methods – systematic tricks.[95]

v. The return of the old guard

Once Vocke started to build up the Bank deutscher Länder directorate, it became clear that – whether the Allies liked it or not – many former Reichsbank staff would be returning to take up senior positions. Four of the first six officials to join the directorate (including Vocke) came from previous careers at the old central bank.[96] Up until 1969, the year of Blessing's departure, there were never less than four ex-Reichsbank men on the eight- or nine-man directorate.

Not all of these officials were archetypal representatives of the old system. Vice-president of the directorate under Vocke's stewardship was Wilhelm Könneker, an ex-Reichsbank official who had become highly disillusioned with the old central bank, and who had shown genuine resistance to the Nazis. As director of the branch of the Reichsbank in Limburg, an antique town with a famous hill-top castle between Frankfurt and Cologne, Könneker ran into difficulties with local Nazis over his refusal to join the party. He disobeyed an injunction in 1938 to cease credits to a Jewish horse-dealer[97] who eventually went out of business. After 1945, Könneker's independence of mind impressed the Americans, and they made him trustee for the now defunct Reichsbank in the US zone. The Bank deutscher Länder council elected him to the vice-presidency in June 1948.

Another early directorate member was Erich Zachau, a banker and auditor who, like Bernard and Hülse, had faced opprobrium during the Nazi period because he was married to a Jewess. In August 1948 he took up responsibility on the directorate for administration and organisation.[98] Zachau was in charge of an extensive construction programme of apartments for employees of the central

bank, with the result that the Bundesbank at the beginning of the
1960s owned a stock of 1200 homes rented out to staff. One of
Zachau's colleagues, Hans Treue, had followed a more traditional
career path. He had been in charge of the Reichsbank's foreign
exchange dealing department before leaving to join the Dresdner
Bank at the beginning of the war – when he also joined the Nazi
party.[99] A man of his experience was in July 1948 the obvious choice
to become the Bank deutscher Länder directorate member in
charge of its international section.

The directorate job in charge of banking and credit was taken
over in March 1950 – after five years of internment by the Russians
– by Bernhard Benning, previously head of the economics department at the Reichs-Kredit-Gesellschaft.*[100] Benning, arch-propa-
gator of the war-time dictum of 'noiseless financing' of German
deficits, defended the new economic theses with the same thoroughness with which he had once supported the old ones.

If Benning represented one small strand of continuity between
the old and the new systems, a much more important link was
provided by Friedrich Wilhelm, a gruff, self-possessed monetary
technician who had been a member of the Reichsbank directorate
between January 1939 and capitulation in May 1945. Reverting to
his baptismal name of Karl Friedrich Wilhelm, he took up his old
job after the war, becoming the Bank deutscher Länder's directorate member responsible for foreign currency affairs in November
1948. He remained in this post until his retirement five years
later.[101] Although the Allies at first objected to his re-employment,
Wilhelm proved as useful, in his technocratic way, to the purveyors
of democracy as he had been to the forces of totalitarianism. Here
was a man who saw the world in terms of balance sheets rather
than ideology. 'I never concerned myself with politics,' he said after
the war.[102]

Wilhelm joined the Reichsbank in 1914 and headed the bank's
exchange department during the 1930s. After proving his worth
during the *Anschluss* with Austria in March 1938,† he was brought
into the Reichsbank directorate after the January 1939 memorandum affair.[103] Immediately following the directorate reshuffle,
Wilhelm was the only member of the new directorate not to own a

*See chapter 5.
†See chapter 5.

Nazi membership card; he conformed, however, to requirements by joining the party at the end of 1939.[104] Wilhelm maintained sanctimoniously after the war that his decision to join the Nazis had reflected his dedication to the Reichsbank. He wanted at all costs to remain at the bank, he said, 'to ensure that the Reichsbank, which represented my life's work, was not deprived of my indispensable technical abilities'.[105]

Wilhelm remained doggedly true to Reichsbank principles. He resisted, for instance, a Nazi proposal for the central bank to print large stocks of forged rouble banknotes with which to flood the Soviet Union after the invasion in June 1941. So that no blame could be attached to the central bank, Wilhelm recommended to the Nazi leadership that 'a special organisation should be set up' for this job.[106]

At the end of the war, Wilhelm was arrested in Berlin by the Red Army. He was released in December 1945, in poor health, after suffering the deprivations of seven different internment camps. Informed that Vocke at the Bank deutscher Länder wanted Wilhelm to take up his old duties again, the military government in western Germany at first rejected the idea.[107] The bank however stuck to its desire to employ the old Reichsbanker – and persistence paid off. In November 1948, five months before his denazification procedures had been concluded,[108] the council voted Wilhelm on to the directorate. Ignoring the lack of formal approval from the Allied Bank Commission, Wilhelm started work at the beginning of 1949. Only in May 1949 did the Commission issue a letter confirming Wilhelm's appointment. It was one more sign of how the Allied watchdogs were fast losing their teeth.[109]

vi. 'Not the slightest guilt falls upon the Bank . . .'

In June 1948 the Bank deutscher Länder council seemed to have found the ideal incumbent for the post of the directorate's chief economist: a bright forty-one-year-old economist, Victor Wrede, chosen by unanimous vote. A respected former member of the Institut für Konjunkturforschung, the Berlin economic research institute, Wrede arrived at the Bank deutscher Länder fresh from taking part in the currency reform conclave advising the Allies.[110] Wrede seemed to have every chance of a model career. In fact, his spell at the Bank deutscher Länder was short and doom-laden.

After less than eighteen months at the bank, Wrede was forced to step down following the discovery that he had contracted heavy debts. He and his wife then committed suicide at Christmas 1950 in their luxury home at Bad Homburg on the outskirts of Frankfurt. The affair was immediately enveloped in a cloak of secrecy. The full circumstances lay buried in official files for more than forty years.

'Not the slightest guilt falls upon the Bank deutscher Länder for this affair,' wrote Bernard, the council president, in one of a series of confidential letters to leading politicians. 'It is a case which could have arisen in any administration or in any company.'[111] This was true only up to a point. Wrede was a leading member of an institution which relied for its public credibility on maintaining exemplary standards of rectitude. In matters of money, those in positions of responsibility at the Bank deutscher Länder had to be beyond reproach – particularly as the bank at the end of 1950 was pushing through a controversial high interest rate policy, at a time of high unemployment (11 per cent of the labour force), to combat the inflationary upsurge generated by the Korean war.*

Had details of Wrede's grotesque financial laxity leaked out, the revelations would have rocked confidence in the Bank deutscher Länder at a delicate time in German economic history. The central bank had good reason for remaining silent.

Wrede never appeared likely to cause trouble. He had left school with the highest of grades. He had not been a member of any political party, and left the Protestant Church in 1940 – he said later – because he was displeased with its lack of resistance to the Nazis.[112] He spent the war quietly at his Berlin economic research institute, responsible for regular economic publications as well as for classified reports for the military authorities. His post-war denazification formalities were cleared without problems, and Wrede was quickly given approval by the Allied Bank Commission to start his new job in Frankfurt.[113] Tension however arose in the economics department between Wrede and his deputy Eduard Wolf, a hard-driving man who was three years older – and disliked being upstaged by a man he plainly considered inferior.[114]

Upset by the bickering, Wrede started to look around for another job from mid-1949 onwards. But before that, emboldened by the

*See chapter 7.

enhanced social status stemming from his new position, Wrede and his wife Eva had embarked on a course central bankers are supposed to disdain: borrowing extremely large amounts of money. Alarm bells flashed within the Bank deutscher Länder in November 1950. An official examination of the accounts of a Hamburg bank, the Handels- und Verkehrsbank, which had run into financial difficulties, showed that Wrede and his wife owed the bank DM102,000 – more than three times his annual salary of DM30,000. The Bank deutscher Länder council was told on 13 December that Wrede had amassed total debts of DM225,000 from various sources since the June 1948 currency reform. The debts were covered by no more than DM120,000 worth of assets, including the luxuriously appointed and newly built family home in Bad Homburg.[115]

The council took a stern view of Wrede's extravagance. It told him that, unless he agreed within six days to resign voluntarily, he would be sacked. The council did however state its readiness to 'consider' granting Wrede a loan (in addition to an already granted housing credit of DM9900) to help him restructure the debts. There was an important condition: that a formal assessment of Wrede's assets and liabilities should show no significant change from the bank's provisional analysis. The council also held out the promise of making Wrede a DM5000 grant to tide him over immediate payments difficulties.

The next day, Wrede duly wrote his resignation letter to Bernard. But the bail-out never took place. On 18 and 19 December, when Bank deutscher Länder officials visited the Wredes in Bad Homburg, they discovered disquieting details. The loans raised by the couple had been used to finance a supremely extravagant life-style. They had bought antique furniture and an expensive wardrobe for Eva, and embarked on lavish foreign travel. Later, after the deaths, there were rumours that Eva had been a frequent visitor to the Bad Homburg casino. The overall net debt to be cleared up was higher than the council had first thought – around DM125,000. A final disturbing point was to prove decisive. Asked about the extraordinary, largely unsecured credit from the Handels- und Verkehrsbank, Wrede admitted that at the end of 1948 he had helped the bank improve its credit rating by signing a declaration testifying to the bank's good standing.[116]

Informed of these findings, the Bank deutscher Länder council, meeting in emergency session on 20 December, took a markedly tougher line than a week earlier, turning down any question of bailing out the hapless economist. On 21 December Bernard sent Wrede á letter of exceptional severity: 'The central bank has come to the conclusion that, under the circumstances, the granting of bank funds – in other words, of public money – to pay for a foolish and unrestrained pursuit of the pleasures of life could never be justified vis-à-vis the political authorities. In comparison to this, the central bank considers it a lesser evil to have to suffer the news of the financial collapse of one of the members of its directorate.'[117]

Bernard rounded off the letter on a note of paternalism:

> Believe me, I write this with a heavy heart! Especially for me, the only leading member of staff in the Taununsanlage to have always supported you, this state of affairs . . . means a great human disappointment. None the less, I give you my sincere wishes that you will succeed in recovering from this collapse. Do not lose courage! . . .

This was however just what Wrede did. On receiving Bernard's message, the luckless directorate member scribbled on the back that the letter amounted to 'a death sentence on an exceptionally dedicated and loyal employee'. On 25 or 26 December, he and his wife killed themselves by poisoning. Bernard discovered that Wrede had despatched a number of suicide notes, putting the blame for the affair squarely on the Bank deutscher Länder. Bernard wrote a confidential letter to Chancellor Adenauer to counter the dead man's claims, maintaining that Wrede had been suffering from a 'delusion'.[118]

Shortly after the suicide, Wolf secured the job he had so plainly desired. He was appointed Wrede's successor, with effect from 1 January 1951, and held the post with distinction for the next thirteen years. Wrede became nothing but a dim and unhappy memory, fading fast.

vii. The battle for independence

Created under the conditions of the occupation regime, the Bank deutscher Länder was a long way from being master of the currency. A decision in April 1948 establishing a fixed exchange rate of RM3.33 to the dollar – compared with the notional war-time rate of RM2.50 – was announced by the Allied bizonal authorities without any consultation with the Bank deutscher Länder.[119] In September 1949, when the D-Mark was devalued in the wake of the British government's decision to devalue the pound by 30 per cent, the occupation authorities went through the formalities of consulting the Bank deutscher Länder. But the new D-Mark rate was none the less chosen by the Allies, not the Germans.[120] The three victor powers set a devaluation of 20 per cent to DM4.20 to the dollar. This overruled a vote by the Bonn cabinet for a higher devaluation of 25 per cent. The Allied decision however embodied a symbolic advantage: it returned the German currency rate to the old pre-1933 dollar/Reichsmark parity.[121]

Despite its lack of influence over external currency matters, the bank progressively won clout in domestic monetary affairs. By the end of 1949, the Allied Bank Commission's ability to influence the bank's interest rate decisions virtually came to an end.[122] As early as June 1948, the bank rejected an Allied wish to maintain the discount rate at 8 per cent; the rate was set at 5 per cent[123] before being reduced in two stages to 4 per cent by summer 1949. With evident meekness, the Allied Bank Commission wrote to Bernard in August 1948: 'It is not our intention to interfere in your deliberations.'[124] In November 1948, the Allies attempted to re-assert some authority over the Bank deutscher Länder. The Commission sent a letter to the bank complaining about an article in its first monthly report calling attention to the high level of occupation costs (paid for by the Germans). Vocke icily refrained from even sending a reply.[125]

As the Bank deutscher Länder grew less dependent on the Allies, it gradually carved out for itself the chance to break free of government influence. Vocke's stubborn propagation of central banking independence earned him Adenauer's suspicion – and, later, the chancellor's downright opposition. Article 88 of West Germany's 1949 constitution made clear that the Bank deutscher Länder had only provisional status; it had eventually to be replaced by a fully fledged federal bank: the future Bundesbank. The task of working out the new bank's statutes considerably strained relations between Bonn and Frankfurt.

Two separate pieces of legal renewal were necessary. The 1951 ending of the first phase of occupation required redrafting of the law on the Bank deutscher Länder. This would have to be harmonised with the preparatory work on the Bundesbank Law. In both cases, Vocke was determined to stop the government from taking over the legal control hitherto vested in the Allies. He wanted the *Länder* to retain their stakes in the new Bundesbank, and also favoured maintaining the council's power to elect its own president and the president of the directorate.

Vocke wrote to Adenauer in 1949 that making the state the shareholder of the new Bundesbank would break with the tradition of the Reichsbank – and would unsettle the financial community at home and abroad. Vocke's arguments were couched in his customary high-handed tone:

> Confidence in the D-Mark, which has been established to a relatively high degree at home and abroad, is still of very recent date . . . Therefore ideas currently being discussed, that the government should set up a new 'Bundesbank' instead of the Bank deutscher Länder, or that the capital of a 'Bundesbank' should be fully owned by the federal government (which was never the case for the Reich and the Reichsbank) should be dismissed as totally unworldly and unpractical. Our task is to defend and secure with all means the trust which the D-Mark and the Bank deutscher Länder have been able to achieve. Although we must naturally provide room for discussion of wishes and possibilities of various kinds, we must refrain absolutely from disturbing the foundations of the Bank and the currency.[126]

Recognising that the Allied Bank Commission had little power left, Vocke cynically attempted to persuade Adenauer to maintain notional dependence on the Allies for as long as possible.[127] In 1950, Vocke vigorously fought government proposals to make the central bank dependent on a 'Bundestag committee for monetary and economic policy questions'.[128] As late as March 1951, Fritz Schäffer, the finance minister, proposed replacing the Allied Bank Commission by the government as the body exercising jurisdiction over the Bank deutscher Länder. Vocke's arguments however won the day. When the legislation on the Bank deutscher Länder was revised in 1951 to phase out the role of the Allied Bank Commission, the central bank's independence from the German government remained intact.[129]

A further six years of political and legal argument elapsed before the long-discussed law on the new central bank was promulgated in July 1957, and the Bank deutscher Länder was turned into the Bundesbank. Ludwig Erhard, the economics minister, gave Vocke crucial support in his efforts to persuade Adenauer and Schäffer of the merits of an independent central bank.[130] As late as September 1956, the chancellor stirred alarm in Frankfurt by suggesting that the Bundesbank should be set up in Cologne to place it closer to Bonn. In the end, the Bundesbank stayed in Frankfurt, at arm's length from the government. Although the Bundesbank Law strengthened the government's hand by giving it the right to choose the central bank's directorate, the bank's fundamental independence was solemnly inscribed in law. After Adenauer, no other German chancellor ever again seriously contemplated taking it away.

A Question of Interest

A central bank which is so much dominated by its own government as to have no independence or initiation, and even no right of protest, is not in a fair position and therefore cannot play its part either within its own country, or, still more, alongside other central banks.
  Montagu Norman, governor of the Bank of England, to Rudolf Havenstein, president of the Reichsbank, 1921[1]

You see, we live in the realm of politics. We do not have it as easy as you.
  Franz Etzel, finance minister, speaking to Bundesbank council, 1961[2]

It was always a cheap policy to make the Bundesbank a scapegoat for the errors and failings of others.
  Karl Otto Pöhl, Bundesbank president, 1981[3]

Since the birth of the Federal Republic in 1949, the country's goals and decisions have been framed within an institutionalised system of political and economic consensus where the organised sections of society – the political parties, the leaders of big business, the employers' organisations and the trade unions – all find their place. The most important conflicts seldom flare in the open; the altercations which matter most are confined to the banking parlours, the negotiating tables and the smoke-filled rooms of parliamentary caucuses.

Within this complex network for managing the nation, the Bundesbank occupies a pivotal position. Its statutory right to set interest rates gives it a firm hold over a vital area of policy-making – and classic potential to generate strife. The lesson of forty years of post-war history is that tangling with the Bundesbank is dangerous for the government's health. Yet the men running the central bank know instinctively that they will do their job better if they are not identified too frequently and too publicly as a challenge to the elected political leadership. Both sides share a common interest in playing down the Bundesbank's potency. The central bank wants to avoid creating an exaggerated impression of dominance, while the politicians have no wish to expose their vulnerability. The arrangement is a delicate one; yet both sides have the advantage of knowing where they stand.

i. 'The central bank can topple the government . . .'

Fritz Schäffer, West Germany's first finance minister, was acutely aware of the uncomfortable implications of the central bank's sway over monetary policy. Schäffer spelled out his misgivings in a series of exchanges with Wilhelm Vocke at the Bank deutscher Lander during the long 1950s tussle over the Bundesbank Law. Commenting on the finance ministry's initial proposals (later abandoned) to bring the central bank under government control, Vocke complained to Schäffer in 1950: 'The main theme running through your newly drawn-up regulations is a certain mistrust towards the central bank. As you say yourself, your primary concern is that "the central bank can topple the government".'[4]

The next decades proved Schäffer's prediction right. The political history of the Federal Republic has been one of exemplary stability. Yet, where governments have fallen and coalitions switched colours, the central bank has arguably had greater influence than the electorate in bringing about the changes.

Karl Otto Pöhl, in a moment of candour, once admitted that the Bundesbank was 'a form of a state within the state – an economic policy counterweight to the government'.[5] From his own experience, both in analysing the Bundesbank as a journalist in the 1960s and then, later, as a practitioner of monetary policies, Pöhl was well aware that the unelected functionaries of the central bank formed an inner policy-making élite. Both Pöhl and his successor, Helmut Schlesinger, have normally been highly cautious in defining and delineating the central bank's sphere of competence. '*Die Bundesbank ist keine Nebenregierung*' ('The Bundesbank is not a shadow government') was one of Pöhl's favourite expressions;[6] 'We are not a government,' declared Schlesinger in early 1992.[7] Precisely because their statements were not completely credible, this was one particular message of reassurance which both men had continually to repeat.

Although a central player within the consensus system, the Bundesbank also occupies the role of referee. If it feels inflationary pressures are getting out of hand, the central bank reserves the right to confront the politicians, industrialists and trade unionists who exert the main influence on corporate Germany. The threat to squeeze the economy by tightening monetary policy is maintained discreetly, just beneath the threshold of political debate. The central bank's finger is never very far away from the monetary equivalent of the nuclear button.

The Bundesbank's job is to enforce self-discipline. All sides realise that the less often the central bank has to resort to the weapon of higher interest rates, the greater the effectiveness of its anti-inflation deterrence will be. If the politicians none the less understand very well the nature of the Bundesbank's message, it is because they have precise, and normally painful, memories of the weapon being used. On a dozen occasions during the life of the Federal Republic, the Bundesbank and the Bonn government have been in serious disagreement over policy on interest rates or on the exchange rate of the D-Mark. Over interest rates, the Bundesbank has nearly always got the better of the squabble. On the question of currency adjustments – where, in formal terms, the final decisions on revaluation rest with the government – the Bundesbank has also, more often than not, finished on the winning side.

Three chancellors – Ludwig Erhard in 1966, Kurt Georg Kiesinger in 1969 and Helmut Schmidt in 1982 – owe their downfall directly or indirectly to the actions of the Bundesbank. All three leaders were ousted not by defeat in general elections, but as a consequence of shifts in coalitions, sparked off by controversies over monetary policy. The Bundesbank's high interest rates played a role, too – though only a secondary one – in the resignation of Chancellor Willy Brandt in 1974. Although the political background differed widely each time, there were significant similarities in the economic circumstances surrounding the departures of Erhard, Brandt and Schmidt. All three were dislodged shortly after peaks in the Bundesbank's interest rates, when an earlier period of credit easing had been followed by drastic monetary tightening. Kiesinger's downfall came at a different point in the economic cycle, coinciding not with a period of high interest rates but with unrest over the second post-war revaluation of the D-Mark. The Bundesbank was loosening credit but was at the same time attempting to force the chancellor to abandon his opposition to an upward movement in the D-Mark's exchange rate against the dollar.

Compared with this long list of political casualties, Germany's post-war central bankers – profiting from their long periods of appointment and their statutory protection from being sacked – have enjoyed highly durable periods of tenure. Pöhl's decision to quit in 1991, well before the expiry of his second term, represented a unique case of early departure. The only president apart from Pöhl who (briefly) considered resigning over a policy issue was Blessing, during the imbroglio over the first revaluation of the D-Mark in 1961.

This story of regular conflict between the Bundesbank and government provides an object lesson for countries such as Britain which have tied themselves to a Bundesbank-style monetary policy. The German central bank's independence from government interference has not – contrary to some illusions abroad – opened up an economic 'virtuous circle': that happy state of affairs where a low rate of price rises somehow painlessly and automatically produces sustained, non-inflationary economic growth. To maintain the country on a low inflation path, the presence of the Bundesbank's hand on the tiller has been an important influence, but it is not enough; from time to time, confrontation with the government has been necessary. This has normally involved a price in terms of lost economic output as the Bundesbank steps on the monetary brakes. The price in Germany of bringing down inflation to a 'core' level of 2 or 3 per cent may have been less than for other, more inflation-prone countries; but it has had to be paid, all the same.

The Bundesbank's institutional authority transcends personal relationships. Two past episodes of clashes between the central bank and the government are particularly revealing. During the final unhappy phases of the Erhard and Schmidt administrations in the mid-1960s and early 1980s protégés of the two chancellors – Blessing and Pöhl respectively – were in each case at the helm of the central bank. Both times, they presided over decisions to increase interest rates which contributed towards unseating their former mentors. Germany is one of the few countries where central bank presidents know that tough and unpopular measures can win them a place in the history books. The loyalty which Bundesbank presidents may occasionally feel towards the chancellor in Bonn is subordinate to greater allegiances. The reputation of the Bundesbank, and the cause of sound money, at all times take precedence.

ii. Discord and harmony

The relationship between a central bank president in Frankfurt and the Bonn chancellor is normally one of extreme delicacy. Bound by the common desire to maintain confidence in the conduct of state affairs, the two are condemned to harmonious co-existence. In the interest of decorum, public manifestations of irritation or animosity are normally avoided. Beneath the surface, there can be bitterness; Kohl's outburst of indignation against Pöhl in March 1991 – after the central banker criticised the terms for German monetary union* – was however highly unusual in that it brought differences directly into the public eye.

There have, in fact, been relatively frequent clashes of personality. Angered by the rigidity and stubbornness of the president of the Bank deutscher Länder, Konrad Adenauer in private called Wilhelm Vocke 'an over-cooled ice-box'.[8] For Hans Matthöfer, finance minister for four crucial years under Helmut Schmidt, Otmar Emminger was 'a terrible know-all' – although the finance minister voiced clear respect for Emminger's grasp of financial affairs.[9] Schmidt himself became increasingly embittered with the Bundesbank's leadership. In his latter years, he dismissed Pöhl, once his right hand man at the finance ministry, as a mere 'technician' – one of the most scathing words in the ex-chancellor's political vocabulary.[10] Schmidt tended to get on better with Emminger – who showed him great respect – than with Pöhl's long-time deputy during the 1980s, Helmut Schlesinger. Schmidt terms the latter 'a German nationalist', above all on account of his well-publicised opposition to European monetary union.[11]

Pöhl's relations with Christian Democrat Ministers after 1982 were, on the whole, less complicated than those with the Social Democrats who were in office at the start of his period in office. The relationship with Kohl however cooled sharply towards the end of Pöhl's tenure. With Schmidt and Matthöfer, Pöhl was used to having long (and sometimes controversial) discussions on technical matters, above all on the establishment of the European Monet-

* See chapter 8.

ary System. By contrast, during the central bank president's nearly nine years of co-existence with the Christian Democrats, Pöhl could not recall one satisfactory conversation on economic affairs with chancellor Kohl.[12]

Theoretically, ministers and top Bonn officials have the right to take their grievances directly to the central bank. Visitors from Bonn often take part in the Bundesbank's council meetings. They can voice their opinion, but they have no vote. Central bankers from Frankfurt – normally the president or the vice-president – participate from time to time in Bonn cabinet meetings. Partly because of Helmut Kohl's much lower interest in economic affairs compared with that of Helmut Schmidt, but also reflecting the lack of monetary policy controversy in the first five years of Kohl's rule, overall personal contacts between Frankfurt and Bonn subsided during the 1980s. Karl Klasen, the Bundesbank president during the 1970s – and a close personal friend of Schmidt – took part in on average seven or eight Bonn cabinet meetings a year.[13] In the late 1980s, Pöhl participated in no more than one or two such sessions per year. During the imbroglio over German monetary union, Pöhl's views were conspicuously ignored.*

Another indication of close contacts between Bonn and Frankfurt in the 1970s was that Pöhl, in his capacity as state secretary in the finance ministry, took part in twenty-one Bundesbank council meetings between 1973 and 1976. Tietmeyer, while serving in the same job in the 1980s, participated in only eleven council meetings between 1983 and 1989 – half Pöhl's attendance figure in double the length of time. There was another, more prosaic, reason for the closeness of ties between the Bundesbank and the finance ministry in the late 1970s. Matthöfer, the finance minister, whose electoral constituency was in Frankfurt, lived in Kronberg on the outskirts of the city and often arranged informal weekend discussions – sometimes over dinner – with senior Bundesbank officials. During the time of the Kohl government, this form of routine socialising with the Bundesbank came to a halt.

The Bundesbank Law gives the government the means to hold up Bundesbank decisions by two weeks in cases of fundamental disagreement. (Under the legislation establishing the Bank deutscher Länder, the government had the right to delay decisions for

* See chapter 8.

one week.) It is a mark of both sides' desire to avoid spectacular confrontation that this veto power has never been used. In practice, when the government disagrees with the Bundesbank, it normally tries to argue its case with the central bank in private, and to minimise the public import of the episode.

In 1958, the Bundesbank correctly foresaw that both sides would normally have no interest in playing out their conflicts in public:

> These regulations [determining relations between the Bundes-bank and the government] may turn out to be uncomfortable in individual cases. But generally it must be assumed that the government and the Bundesbank will act in accord with one another and that unavoidable differences of opinion will be settled ... so that real cases of conflict which could lead to a postponement of important Bundesbank measures will be rare.[14]

The government came close to deploying its veto in February 1961 when the central bank wanted to ease minimum reserve require-ments as a way of forestalling a D-Mark revaluation. On other occasions, when the government has learned of an impending Bundesbank interest rate rise, it has sometimes informally prevailed on the central bank council to postpone the measure by two weeks.[15] The best-publicised episode of near-deployment of the Bonn veto was at the beginning of January 1979. This opened a three-year battle of attrition between the Bundesbank and Bonn which even-tually led to the fall in October 1982 of Chancellor Helmut Schmidt's coalition.

Manfred Lahnstein, who had taken over from Pöhl in 1977 as state secretary in the finance ministry, travelled to Frankfurt for the council's fortnightly meeting on 18 January 1979. Lahnstein, a brisk blond-haired technocrat with a penchant for playing jazz, briefly became finance minister in 1982 in the months before the fall of the Schmidt government.[16] At the beginning of 1979, the Bundesbank, under the direction of Emminger, was concerned about over-heating in the economy. On 18 January it took the relatively modest step of increasing the Lombard rate from 3.5 per cent to 4 per cent.[17] Lahnstein spoke out against the measures during the council meeting – and, unusually, spelled out the government's objections at a press conference immediately afterwards.

More than a decade later, Lahnstein admitted that he realised all along that making a public stand against the Bundesbank was a losing battle. In the eyes of public opinion, and especially in the view of the columnists of influential conservative newspapers such as the *Frankfurter Allgemeine Zeitung* or *Die Welt*, such action stigmatised the government as being on the wrong side of the struggle for sound money:

> We regarded the credit tightening as exaggerated – for reasons of growth, but also in view of external imbalances. The European Monetary System was just starting, which added to the sensitivity. Differences of opinion between the central bank council and the government are no more unusual than differences within the council itself. The difference was that I announced my dissent openly, at a press conference afterwards. It was not a dramatic point. I knew how difficult it was – because of the support it receives from the conservative press – to operate against the Bundesbank. Emminger won, and he could be happy. I lost, but it didn't spoil my even temper or my relationship with the Bundesbank.[18]

Looking back at the episode, a long-standing member of the Bundesbank directorate, Claus Köhler, said that, had Lahnstein announced a formal veto, this would simply have resulted in needless polarisation. 'Lahnstein didn't want to inflame the disagreement. He saw that a majority was for the concept [of raising interest rates]. A veto would have led only to a delay, and wouldn't have changed anything in the end.'[19]

The Lahnstein fracas proved good news for Emminger. Lahnstein's tabling of formal disagreement gave the central bank president a public relations coup by heightening his image of independence. 'I was pleased that, for once, such a conflict with the government emerged into the open, and did not take place, as is normally the case, out of the public eye,' Emminger wrote.[20] He gleefully pointed out that dissent from Bonn did not stop the Bundesbank from continuing its policy of monetary tightening during 1979. As inflationary pressures grew, the central bank raised its discount and Lombard rates by a full percentage point in May 1979. Emminger claimed that Schmidt told him later that year that he regretted Lahnstein's January show of resistance: 'Impressed by the strength of the economic upswing, he [Schmidt] told me that he now saw that the Bundesbank's restrictive policies were justified.'

When Schmidt's chancellorship ended in October 1982, it marked the climax of several years of misfortune within the coalition formed by the Social Democrats and Free Democrats. A widening budget deficit stemmed from the consequences of an over-hastily conceived reflation package in 1978, while the sharp rise in 1979 in the international oil price led to a marked weakening in the economy. Both these factors depressed the D-Mark and produced an unusual three years of current account deficit between 1979 and 1981.

The Bundesbank had eased monetary policy – with hindsight, by too much – during the D-Mark's sharp appreciation against the dollar in 1977–78. In both years, it allowed its monetary target to be overshot. It applied the monetary brakes from 1979 onwards, bringing the discount rate up gradually to a post-war record of 7.5 per cent in May 1980. Then, in February 1981, the Bundesbank intensified the anti-inflation drive by suspending its normal Lombard rate for emergency lending to commercial banks, and imposing a punitive 'special' Lombard rate, initially at 12 per cent. Money market interest rates soared to 30 per cent. The ensuing 1981–82 recession left unemployment near 2 million – double its level two years earlier[21] – and sharply reduced the aura of omnipotence which had earlier been Schmidt's chief hallmark.

After months of behind-the-scenes tussling, the Free Democrats decided to abandon the coalition, and again forged an alliance – as they had done during the 1950s and 1960s – with the Christian Democrats. In the climactic Bundestag debate on 1 October 1982 which sealed the fate of his government and brought Chancellor Kohl to power, Schmidt launched an unusual public broadside at the Bundesbank. He warned that the central bank would have to 'contribute decisively to a fall in interest rates' in order to stimulate investment. 'I am warning about the consequences of deflation!' he declared.[22] The episode underlined how, at crucial moments, the Bundesbank does indeed act as a political arbiter. The greater the indecisiveness in Bonn, the more likely it is that the Bundesbank will enter the arena.

iii. Setting a standard

The Bundesbank's monetary policy independence during the 1970s and 1980s was built on foundations laid down during the earliest years of the Bank deutscher Länder. An important milestone came in October 1950, when the Bank deutscher Länder, under the leadership of Vocke, was just two and a half years old. The bank deemed necessary a sharp increase in the discount rate to choke off inflationary pressures stoked by the outbreak of the Korean war and by a programme of import liberalisation put into effect by Erhard, the economics minister. A string of monthly trade deficits had nearly exhausted the Federal Republic's credit lines within the newly constituted European Payments Union, the financing mechanism set up to finance European trade. With the country's slender currency reserves dwindling fast, Vocke wrote to Adenauer in early October that the central bank had entered 'dangerous and stormy waters . . . Everything depends on the central bank being able to master the situation, confound the dangers, strengthen its authority and thus secure confidence in the currency.'[23]

The West German economy was growing fast in response to the stimulus of the 1948 currency reform. But unemployment was still rising as the result of a dramatic influx of refugees from Germany's former eastern provinces and from East Germany. Adenauer's chief concern was to avoid a further rise in the unemployment total – which during 1950 averaged 1.9 million or 11 per cent of the workforce. In view of the mounting trade deficits, Adenauer knew that Vocke favoured credit tightening. The chancellor did his best to pre-empt it, but his rearguard action failed dismally. A meeting of the Bank deutscher Länder council was convened on 26 October 1950 in the chancellor's office in Bonn, lodged at the time in the König museum near the Rhine, normally full of stuffed animals.[24] Adenauer voiced strong objections to higher interest rates: the Bank deutscher Länder's plans would prove counter-productive by triggering further demands for wage increases. They would cause 'general political turbulence', he protested.[25] The chancellor's arguments were backed by Schäffer, the finance minister, but were opposed by Erhard, the economics minister, who said higher interest rates represented the only way to reduce the trade deficit. Adenauer's intervention failed to change the minds of the council. After the chancellor left the meeting, the council voted 8 to 5 to raise the discount rate, and with a narrower margin of 7 to 6 decided to increase it from 4 to 6 per cent.

When, nearly a quarter of a century later, Vocke described the 1950 meeting, he painted it in the most dramatic of colours:

> The struggle lasted many hours. There was much resistance to my proposal on the central bank council. Additionally, I failed to receive support from finance minister Schäffer. Finally Adenauer left the battlefield. Bernard, the chairman of the central bank council, came over to my side, and there was a majority for an increase in the discount rate from 4 to 6 per cent. The danger was averted . . . The stability of the currency was rescued.[26]

The bank's tight money policy was maintained for a further nineteen months, up to the early summer of 1952. It produced a sizeable improvement in the balance of payments. The trade deficit fell sharply in 1951, and the following year West Germany registered the first in what turned out to be a lengthening series of growing surpluses. Unemployment, on the other hand, failed to show anything more than a gentle decline in the next two years – and remained above 1 million until 1956.[27]

Vocke kept up the anti-inflation pressure – and maintained a string of alarmist letters to Adenauer. In February 1951, describing a further import-induced build-up in West Germany's foreign debt, Vocke warned the chancellor of the danger that the country would have to leave the European Payments Union – which would mean 'the death sentence for the idea of Europe . . . and also for the German economy'.[28] Extending the bank's policy suggestions into areas which in later decades would have been regarded as outside its sphere of jurisdiction, Vocke proposed wage incentives to increase coal output, higher tariffs to dampen the flood of imports, and further credit restrictions to hold down demand. 'Should we not use unorthodox methods, if we want – at the last hour – to try to stay alive?' Vocke concluded melodramatically.

In 1954 Vocke sent another high-handed letter to Bonn complaining that Adenauer had given too favourable an impression of Germany's improving foreign exchange position. The chancellor had boasted in a speech in Hamburg that cash in circulation would soon be 100 per cent covered by gold or dollars; Vocke pointed out icily that the percentage was in fact only 47 per cent. 'I believe that we should judge our international monetary situation with caution, especially as our position is more fragile than that of many other countries.'[29]

In April 1956, Vocke went on the offensive again, drawing up a five-point anti-inflation plan to compensate for 'serious errors' threatening the stability of the D-Mark. He lectured Adenauer on the need for moderation in defence spending, drastic cuts in general public expenditure, as well as in public building and other investment, and reductions in depreciation allowances. Of course, Vocke added with customary acerbity, the bank would also need to continue its restrictive interest rate policy.[30]

Next month, the bank underlined its concern by raising the discount rate 1 point to 5.5 per cent – the second increase within two months. The measure had won the prior approval of both Erhard and Schäffer.[31] Adenauer, however, was of a different opinion. Influenced by the complaints of industrialists that the tightening would severely weaken the upturn, Adenauer expressed his irritation in blunt fashion, speaking of 'a severe setback for the German economy' in a speech to the Federation of German Industry in Cologne. 'The guillotine is hitting the small fry,' he protested, adding, 'I have not yet been persuaded that such a step was necessary.'[32]

In 1957, when the Bank deutscher Länder was transformed into the Bundesbank, the jobs of president of the directorate and president of the council – held up to then by Vocke and Bernard respectively – were merged. The hope of the seventy-one-year-old Vocke that he would be asked to stay on after the end of the year as Bundesbank chief was in vain. Adenauer and Vocke had fallen out, and Vocke's term of office – which had already lasted nine and a half years – was not renewed. Vocke complained afterwards that he learned from the newspapers that Adenauer and Erhard had approached Blessing – then at Unilever – to take over the top job in German central banking. Blessing wrote a commiseratory note to Vocke in July 1957: 'What has happened in the last few days is anything but pleasant . . . Bonn's behaviour towards me can also hardly be said to have employed a great deal of tact. I did not seek the candidature, and would be happy if the chalice were to pass me by.'[33]

Of all Vocke's irritating characteristics, it was his carping which seems to have most vexed Adenauer.[34] In his memoirs, Vocke suggested that one important reason why his mandate was not renewed was his implacable opposition to a revaluation of the D-Mark.[35] The revaluation issue was not, in fact, the main consideration convincing Adenauer of the need for a change at the top: Adenauer was no supporter of a revaluation, and Blessing was, to begin with, just as much opposed to the move as Vocke had been. Vocke's experience showed that a central bank president who loses the means to communicate with Bonn also loses his hold on policy. Of this underlying fact of Bundesbank life, the discord between Pöhl and Kohl thirty-five years later provided another graphic illustration.

iv. Discovery of a dilemma

In the 1950s, the West German economy drew its energy and dynamism from the population's resolve to rebuild the shattered country. But the upturn was also fuelled by an extraordinary boom in foreign demand. Annual exports rose ninefold between 1949 and 1957, from DM4 billion to DM36 billion, and the balance of payments registered large trade surpluses[36] at a time when Britain and France were battling with recurrent deficits. In view of the competitiveness of German goods on world markets, the D-Mark started to look under-valued; as sporadic revaluation speculation surfaced on the currency markets, both the central bank and the Bonn government were forced to issue regular denials of rumours that the D-Mark would be up-valued.

Vocke and most of his colleagues on the directorate were infused by the 'stable money' ideals of the Reichsbank; to them, any idea of a parity change was anathema. '[The currency] is stable, it will be kept stable, and it will certainly not be revalued!' proclaimed Vocke in August 1956.[37] When Blessing took over in January 1958, he too was vehemently opposed to revaluing the D-Mark. The question of the external value of the currency was in fact an area where the central bank was due to receive a strong rebuff to its image and authority. The revaluation which eventually took place in March 1961 was decided by the Bonn government, against the wishes of the Bundesbank. Unlike in 1955, when Erhard supported the Bank deutscher Länder in its interest rate battle with Adenauer, in 1961 the rotund economics minister opposed the will of the central bank. Faced with disruptive inflows of foreign exchange caused by revaluation speculation, Erhard became convinced that allowing the D-Mark to rise would moderate the risk of 'imported inflation' from the rest of the world. Erhard's policy was at first opposed by Adenauer, but in the end the economics minister's views prevailed.

The 1961 episode brought a sizeable dent in the Bundesbank's credibility: on this occasion at least, it was out-trumped by the Bonn government – after several years of argument. Vocke, backed by the majority of the directorate and *Land* central bank chiefs, had always believed that any change in the exchange rate would lower public confidence in the currency. Otmar Emminger, who since 1953 had been the Bank deutscher Länder's directorate member in charge of international monetary affairs, took a diametrically opposite view – but, for several years, it remained a minority opinion. Emminger believed that an under-valued exchange rate would be a source of inflation. Together with another directorate colleague, Heinrich Irmler, he was the first German official to identify the dilemma between internal and external monetary stability, which was to become a central preoccupation for the Bundesbank during the next four decades.[38] In an inflationary world Emminger pointed out, maintenance of external currency stability could endanger the goal of stabilising internal prices. The more the central bank attempted to ward off revaluation pressure by lowering interest rates, the greater was the danger of an upward spiral in wages and prices.

Emminger warned in several public speeches of the threat of 'imported inflation'. In a confidential internal memorandum to Vocke at the end of 1956, he emphasised that the old taboo on revaluation had to be broken: 'In the interest of internal monetary stability, it is unavoidable that we will eventually have to consider a revaluation of the D-Mark.'[39] Emminger favoured a revaluation of 6 per cent by widening the D-Mark's fluctuation bands against the dollar within the Bretton Woods system.[40] Vocke at first refused to allow the directorate even to discuss the matter; when it eventually met to consider Emminger's suggestion, the idea was brusquely turned down.[41] Erhard, who had been considering the advantages of a revaluation for imposing extra discipline on the price front, attempted in vain to change Vocke's mind; after a long discussion in May 1957 at Vocke's home in Frankfurt, the central bank president sent the economics minister a nine-point letter explaining, 'Why I am still a clear opponent of a revaluation of the D-Mark', attacking the proposal as 'an experiment with a highly uncertain outcome'.[42] Vocke proclaimed a short while afterwards: 'There are two things which we want to avoid: revaluation and the inflation of other countries.'[43] In fact, as Emminger was trying ceaselessly to point out, resistance to revaluation was increasing rather than hindering the risk of price rises.

With upward pressure on the D-Mark momentarily abating after a sizeable devaluation of the French franc in August 1957, foreign exchange market speculation died down. An autumn increase in the UK bank rate was coordinated with a cut in the Bundesbank's discount rate to lower selling pressure on sterling. Early in 1958, in one of his first statements as Bundesbank chief, Blessing declared that revaluation would be a 'mistake'. 'The present parity will not be changed. That is it!'[44]

The Bundesbank's dilemma over the exchange rate sharpened towards the end of the 1950s as the trade surplus soared during a domestic economic boom. In a letter to Erhard in August 1959, Blessing strongly criticised public sector construction programmes as contributing to an excessive boom, warning that, unless the government took action to slow down building orders, price and wage rises would prompt the central bank to 'deploy the weapon of [tighter] credit'.[45] The Bundesbank carried out the threat, raising its discount rate in three stages to 5 per cent by summer 1960. Emminger lobbied for a 7.7 per cent revaluation against the dollar in an internal paper in January 1960, in which he pointed out that raising the value of the currency would have a 'salutary impact' in reducing economic over-heating.[46] A majority of the Bundesbank council continued, however, to rule out the idea. In October 1960, shortly before a meeting with Adenauer in which top ministers and the Bundesbank chief unanimously rejected revaluation, Blessing went so far as to declare to the directorate that he would resign if a revaluation took place – a statement which he was later to regret.[47]

In an effort to dampen international demand for the D-Mark, the Bundesbank took the controversial step of reversing its monetary tightening, in order to reduce the interest rate return for foreign depositors. In November 1960 the central bank cut the discount rate from 5 per cent to 4 per cent. This was followed by a further reduction to 3.5 per cent in January 1961, when it also announced a cut in banks' minimum reserve ratios. Although the new finance minister Etzel had now joined Erhard in favouring revaluation, Adenauer, backed by a group of influential advisers including Abs of the Deutsche Bank and Fritz Berg, the president of the Federation of German Industry, was still refusing to adjust the currency on the grounds that it would weaken exporters' competitiveness.[48]

Events in Washington increased the pressures on Bonn. A firm refusal by President Kennedy to devalue the dollar heightened the foreign exchange markets' belief that Germany would have to act unilaterally to raise the value of the D-Mark. As it became clear that foreign inflows of 'hot money' were posing an acute threat to the Bundesbank's statutory duty to prevent inflation, Erhard finally gained the upper hand. The climax came at the end of February 1961. Faced with a fresh speculative barrage from abroad, the Bundesbank indicated to the government that it was preparing to reduce minimum reserves still further. Erhard and Etzel warned Blessing that they opposed a further easing of credit since it would be inflationary: one of the extremely rare occasions when a Bundesbank move to ease monetary policy has met with the disfavour of the government.[49] Unless Adenauer could be persuaded to revalue, Etzel proposed the drastic step of foreign exchange controls to block inflows into Germany. Blessing admitted that the Bundesbank had gradually lost control of the situation[50] and seriously considered the idea of quitting.[51] At a meeting in Bonn with Erhard, Etzel and Blessing on 27 February, Adenauer – influenced by Robert Pferdemenges, his Cologne banker friend and adviser – changed his mind over the revaluation issue with surprising speed. The chancellor gave his blessing to a revaluation of 5 per cent,[52] and the decision was ratified at the cabinet meeting on 3 March. Blessing had no choice but to agree.

On the afternoon of 3 March, Erhard travelled to the Bundesbank to secure the council's formal approval for the move. Significantly, the bank was not asked for its opinion on the size of the rate change.[53] 'We have come to the conclusion that there are really only two alternatives,' Erhard told the Bundesbank men. 'Either we let things slide still further and allow an inflationary process to attain more momentum, or we draw the conclusion that we must revalue.'[54] The council accepted what was being spelled out as a virtual *fait accompli*, and voted 16 to 3 in favour. Erhard justified the decision on the need to keep faith with German savers who had amassed DM125 billion in deposits since the currency reform, and who needed reassurance that their savings – unlike in 1923 and 1948 – would be protected: 'We keep telling the German people . . . that we will do everything in our power to protect the stability of our currency. That means that we have to take energetic measures when needed.'

For the central bank, acceptance of revaluation broke the traditional commitment to stable exchange rates.[55] Blessing admitted:

> For a long time the Bundesbank resisted an adjustment of the currency. For a central bank, the exchange rate parity is sacrosanct, something which can only be changed when all other methods have proved unsuccessful.[56]

Erhard could hardly conceal his delight. In one of the sweeping pronouncements for which he became famous, the economics minister declared, 'The overwhelming majority of the German people welcome this decision of the government and owe gratitude for its courage.'[57]

German consumers in fact benefited from the import-cheapening effect of the revaluation, while exporters, as expected, suffered disadvantages.[58] West Germany appeared well on the way towards curbing its massive foreign surpluses, and thus brought a measure of stability to the Bretton Woods system. The revaluation indeed brought several years of hard-won tranquillity on the external economic front; but it marked only a period of calm before the ultimate monetary storm.

v. Consequences of a conversion

For Blessing, the loss of public credibility caused by his conversion to revaluation was a chastening experience; but this was only one of a number of U-turns carried out during a long career. This supreme practitioner of the skills of German corporate in-fighting, the man who had survived Schacht, Funk, Hitler and two years of post-war imprisonment by the Americans, was tough and flexible enough to recover his poise. Compared with the austere Vocke, Blessing brought a distinct change of style; Vocke's Prussian high-handedness was replaced by southern German charm. The charm, however, had its limits. The revaluation episode stiffened Blessing's conviction that the best way to deal with the government was through a policy of uncompromising monetary rigour. The Bundesbank's attachment to 'stability policies' had to be established beyond doubt. The consequences proved uncomfortable for the two chancellors who succeeded Adenauer, Ludwig Erhard and Kurt Georg Kiesinger.

Already in the earliest post-war years, Blessing had given plenty of evidence of his resilience and his aptitude for pulling strings at the highest level. The former board member of Kontinentale Öl had renewed his business career with conspicuous success, and had soon recovered his place at the heart of the German economic establishment. In July 1948 Blessing rejoined the board of the German subsidiary of Unilever which he had left in 1941; he became chairman in 1952.

During his post-war years as a private businessman, Blessing enjoyed the confidence of Adenauer and the comradeship of Erhard, with whom he had periodically conversed in Berlin during the war. He showed no inhibitions about bringing his influence to bear with his former Reichsbank colleagues at the Bank deutscher Länder. In 1949, in a memorandum to the central bank council warning that 'our situation is extraordinarily fragile', Blessing mounted a well-argued plea for tax cuts and for the creation of new forms of money market paper to channel surplus short-term funds into private investment.[59] In 1950, Blessing told Vocke that a rumoured move by the Bank deutscher Länder to make internal company bills of exchange no longer eligible for discounting would drive up margarine prices causing 'unpleasant discussions, particularly with trade union representatives and with parliament'.[60]

Another reminder of Blessing's prime role in corporate Germany came in 1955, more than two years before he took over the top job at the Bundesbank. He was a central figure in a series of complicated exchanges with Erhard over price cuts in the margarine industry and the government's planned cartel legislation. Together with its associated companies, Unilever controlled 75 per cent of West German margarine sales. Thus it had a clear interest in the anti-trust rules being drawn up at top level at Erhard's economics ministry. Erhard hinted to the margarine industry that he would countenance a degree of price fixing in this sector, provided that the margarine industry was ready to lower overall prices.[61] The Unilever companies were only too happy to meet the minister's requirements. In September 1955, Unilever agreed to follow the economics ministry's recommendation to reduce prices for a variety of margarine brands;[62] in return, the economics ministry agreed to moderate the proposed cartel legislation. Blessing was well aware of the *quid pro quo*. At the end of September 1955, Blessing sent a message to Roland Risse, Erhard's key official at the economics ministry, expressing the hope that 'our sacrifice will not be in vain'.[63]

In power struggles during the Third Reich, Blessing had shown his ability to win the confidence of competing factions. At the end of the 1950s, the man who was now at the helm of the Bundesbank again played the role of a political mediator. The occasion was an incident in 1959, during one of the frequent squabbles between Adenauer and Erhard over the latter's campaign to secure the chancellorship. Adenauer, who all along regarded his economics minister as unfit for the highest government office, enlisted Blessing's help in a vain effort to persuade Erhard to give up his designs on the chancellorship.[64]

When Erhard eventually took over from Adenauer in 1963, his previous smooth relations with Blessing gave him every hope of good cooperation with the Bundesbank. In fact, three years later, the 'father of the economic miracle' was dispatched unceremoniously from the chancellorship – and Blessing bore an important part of the responsibility. For the first few years after the 1961 revaluation, the German monetary scene was calm. In 1962 the country's balance of payments on current account registered a small deficit for the first time since 1950. There followed two years of minor surpluses. The discount rate remained at the low post-revaluation level of 3 per cent for four years between 1961 and the beginning of 1965, when the Bundesbank declared, somewhat prematurely, that the threat from 'imported inflation' no longer existed.[65] However, with the reemergence of a sizeable current account deficit for 1965 of DM5 billion, the Bundesbank moved again to tighten money. In tones very similar to those used by Pöhl in 1990 to berate the Kohl government's failure to cut budget spending, Blessing delivered a stern warning against 'euphoria' generated by the years of economic boom. 'We have reached a point where there must be a turn-round. If we do not moderate our behaviour, events will force us to recognise realities.'[66] Inflation topped the 4 per cent mark; the Bundesbank became particularly concerned about the inflationary impact of extra social spending decided by the Erhard government in preparation for the general elections of 1965.

Blessing admonished the government in severe terms, spelling out the consequences of failure to attack the budget deficit: 'The less it is supported by fiscal policy, the tougher monetary policy has to be ... Prices cannot continuously rise without producing dangerous economic, social and even political consequences.'[67] The Bundesbank made good its threat, by forcing up the discount rate in three separate steps to 5 per cent by summer 1966. This helped precipitate West Germany's first post-war recession. With unemployment rising fast (tripling from an average of only 166,000 in 1966 to 459,000 in 1967), Erhard cut a beleaguered figure. He was forced to bow out of office at the end of October 1966 after a coalition dispute over balancing the budget. Next month the Christian Democrats agreed to form a Grand Coalition with the Social Democrats under Kurt Georg Kiesinger, a former Christian Democrat deputy who had retired to Baden-Württemberg after Adenauer refused to make him foreign minister. There was little doubt in Blessing's mind that the Bundesbank's action had sizeably contributed to Erhard's ousting. In an interview shortly before his death in 1971, Blessing admitted that in 1966 he had used 'brute force to put things in order'.[68]

In his first parliamentary statement as chancellor, in December 1966, Kiesinger called on the Bundesbank to ease credit. However, by then, the central bank was well used to resisting government pressure. The Bundesbank cut interest rates only gradually. This brought fresh complaints from Karl Schiller, the former Hamburg senator who had become economics minister in the Grand Coalition, who criticised the Bundesbank for responding far too cautiously to the economic slowdown.[69]

As a result of the diverse consequences of the upswing which started after 1966–67, the next conflict soon followed. The Bundesbank encouraged the recovery by reducing its discount rate from 5 per cent to 3 per cent in the first half of 1967; but the previous slackening of economic activity produced a dramatic improvement in the balance of payments, which quickly moved into a large surplus on current account.[70] This attracted massive flows of speculative funds from abroad into the D-Mark – further disrupting the sorely pressed international exchange rate system.

Sterling was devalued in November 1967, while the French franc came under heavy selling pressure after the riots in Paris in May 1968. The Bundesbank had learned its lesson from its embarrassing defeat in 1961. This time it came out strongly in favour of a D-Mark revaluation, recommending this course to the economics ministry in September 1968 as a means of dampening inflationary pressures. Schiller, however, assumed the role of defender of the exchange rate that Blessing himself had played until February 1961. In spite of Schiller's inner doubts about whether the D-Mark parity was tenable, he declared in a speech in September 1968 that revaluation would be 'an absurdity'.[71] Kiesinger declared that, as long as he remained chancellor, the D-Mark would not be revalued.[72]

As the currency turmoil continued, a surreal and unproductive monetary conference convened in Bonn on 20 November 1968.[73] Protestors picketed the conference building at the Bonn ministry of economics bearing placards proclaiming 'Save our Mark!'[74] Before the gathering began, the German government rejected the D-Mark revaluation which had been worked out (together with a franc devaluation) in technical discussions between the Bundesbank and Banque de France,[75] and imposed instead a special tax increase on exports and tax reductions on imports. In the midst of the monetary conference, the Bundesbank's council sent a telex to Bonn – subsequently leaked to the press – calling for an upward shift in the D-Mark's value. Afterwards, amid further huge flows of currency into Germany, Schiller underwent his own conversion to the cause of changing the D-Mark parity, and in March 1969 adopted the Bundesbank's recommendation for a revaluation. The move which the whole world was awaiting was however delayed by a further six months, above all because of the stubbornness of Kiesinger and his advisers.

As in 1961, export-dependent West German industry fought against revaluation, claiming that it would damage foreign sales and hurt economic growth. Again, as had been the case with Adenauer in 1961, Kiesinger was influenced by the advice of Abs and the now retired Vocke, who came out publicly against revaluation. The question split the cabinet, with the Social Democrats for and the Christian Democrats against a revaluation; the matter was settled only after the September 1969 elections, following a campaign in which the revaluation question played an important role. Although the conservatives gained 46 per cent of the vote, this was not enough to prevent Kiesinger's fall from power. The Social Democrats and

Free Democrats decided to form a coalition. After a turbulent month in which the D-Mark was allowed to float freely against the dollar, the new government on 24 October agreed to revalue the D-Mark by 9.3 per cent. The long tussle over the currency had contributed to the Christian Democrats' downfall; Kiesinger admitted afterwards that the question of revaluation had been 'our biggest political mistake'.[76]

Emminger, the Bundesbank's chief proponent of revaluation, was a close personal friend of Kiesinger. Had the Christian Democrat chancellor remained in power, Emminger would have succeeded Blessing as Bundesbank president when the latter bowed out at the end of 1969 at the age of sixty-nine.[77] In view of the change of government, Karl Klasen, the autocratic Social Democrat from the Deutsche Bank, took over as the new central bank chief, with Emminger taking the job of vice-president. Together, they soon plunged into a fresh currency crisis.

vi. The end of Bretton Woods

Klasen had already declared himself sceptical about the advantages of revaluation in curbing price rises.[78] The initial events after the 1969 parity change seemed to vindicate this argument. Just as German inflation initially rose after the 1961 revaluation, price rises accelerated after October 1969.[79] Emminger claimed – with some justification – that this was due to the long delay in 1968–69 in deciding the move; none the less, the rise in inflation damaged the claims of the revaluationists. At the same time, it became clear that the revaluation had patently failed to bring the international currency markets to order. The German current account surplus, which in 1968 soared to DM13 billion, fell fourfold in the first few years of the 1970s. But as a result of a 1970 switch by the Federal Reserve towards an easy money policy, massive volumes of interest-sensitive capital flowed across the Atlantic towards the Federal Republic.[80] Attempting to stem the attractiveness of the D-Mark for international investors, the Bundesbank cut the discount rate from a high point of 7.5 per cent in summer 1970 to 5 per cent in spring 1971.

As the inflows reached a high point in May 1971, Schiller – who had become joint economics and finance minister in the new coalition government – attended a Bundesbank council meeting to urge a switch to floating exchange rates. A majority led by Klasen opposed the idea, pleading instead for capital controls to deter inflows. The Bundesbank's solution was in the end turned down by the government, which won international agreement temporarily to free the Bundesbank from the obligation of intervening on the currency market, allowing the D-Mark to float freely with other European currencies against the dollar. This interim solution lasted until December, when the D-Mark was revalued against the dollar by 13.6 per cent as part of an agreement in Washington realigning world currency rates.[81]

During the Washington talks, Schiller insisted to Klasen and Emminger that the Bundesbank should further ease interest rates to compensate for the dampening impact on the economy of the D-Mark revaluation. As a result, the Bundesbank cut the discount rate in two stages to 3 per cent by December 1971.[82] The Washington outcome brought an uneasy truce between Schiller and Klasen. With sterling under extreme pressure, in June 1972, Britain decided to leave the European 'snake' exchange rate mechanism, which had been established in April that year as a means of limiting European currency fluctuations.* Floating the pound unleashed a fresh wave of speculative demand for the D-Mark. As a result, supported by the rest of the Bundesbank directorate, Klasen proposed at a cabinet meeting in Bonn on 28 June a system of capital controls subjecting foreigners' purchases of German securities to prior authorisation. At the same time, the Bardepot exchange control scheme was made still more restrictive. Schiller bitterly opposed capital controls as running counter to the principles of market economics.[83] His alternative – to seek collective floating of European currencies against the dollar – was unanimously rejected in a cabinet vote.[84]

Angered by the cabinet rebuff, the economics 'super-minister' tendered his resignation a few days later – and was surprised when Chancellor Brandt immediately accepted it. The exchange controls dispute was not the prime reason for Schiller's resignation; his argumentativeness and *hauteur* in cabinet meetings, as well as his attempt to swing the spending axe to carry out large cuts in the 1973 budget, had already made him unpopular, and Brandt was patently relieved to find an opportunity to adjust his governmental line-up.[85] Schiller's successor was Helmut Schmidt. The new fin-

* See chapter 9

ance minister had been one of the main proponents of capital controls to dampen revaluation pressure. Later, though, in 1973, he bowed to the inevitable and prompted the move to floating exchange rates.

The episode was an extraordinary example of how the Bundesbank's views could prevail over those of one of the country's most popular ministers. Klasen and Schiller had been close friends; but, once the cabinet lined up fully on the Bundesbank's side, Schiller had little choice but to leave. The affair had an ironic postscript. In March 1973, a further currency storm caused the ultimate collapse of the Bretton Woods system.[86] After being forced to buy up a record $2.7 billion to defend the dollar on 1 March, the Bundesbank suspended its intervention operations. The central bank also prevailed upon the government to call an emergency meeting of European finance ministers, which decided that European currencies should float freely against the dollar. After two and a half weeks of crisis closure of the international foreign exchanges, Schiller's proposals for a system of floating European exchange rates against the dollar were approved – nearly a year after he had fruitlessly proposed the idea.

Looking back at the turbulence of the 1970s, Schiller declared in 1991:

> During 1971–73 the Bundesbank was completely on the wrong track. It was obsessed with the idea of fixed exchange rates – even if it meant calling in the Bundesgrenzschutz (federal border police) ... People there like [Johannes] Tüngeler [the directorate member responsible for international monetary affairs] had experienced the time of capital controls with the Reichsbank. They were no great advocates of market economics.[87]

Somewhat forgetting his own defence of fixed exchange rates in autumn 1968, Schiller claims that the real reason for Klasen's implacable 1972 defence of fixed exchange rates lay in the monetary conservatism inherited from his long career with Germany's biggest bank. 'Klasen had the *Weltanschauung* of the Deutsche Bank ... It was the mentality of Hermann Josef Abs.' Schiller admits that, already before the dispute with Klasen in 1972, his 'temperamental contributions' to cabinet meetings had irritated the harmony-loving

Brandt. Schiller conceded that general opposition to his budgetary proposals was a strong factor behind his departure.[88]

The ending of fixed exchange rates – like the aftermath of the 1969 revaluation – left a legacy of inflation.[89] Recognising that its previous obligation to defend fixed dollar/D-Mark parities had acted as an impediment to controlling inflation, the Bundesbank used its new-found freedom to step hard on the monetary brakes. The priority was now the goal of reducing the annual rate of price rises, in 1973–74 running at roughly 7 per cent.

Most industrialised countries in 1974 registered double digit inflation, but the Bundesbank took on the role of the world's anti-inflation ice-breaker. The central bank succeeded in reducing inflation – but at the cost of a domestic recession. It sharply increased interest rates, raising its discount rate to 7 per cent in June 1973 and suspending its normal Lombard rate for routine lending on the money market – a measure which drove up day-to-day money market rates to 38 per cent in July 1973. At the same time, the government introduced an austerity programme of spending cuts and tax increases. The credit-tightening campaign was prolonged as a result of the quadrupling of oil prices in autumn 1973 sparked by the Yom Kippur war, which not only increased recessionary trends in the world economy, but also sparked off a round of 15 per cent wage demands for West German public sector workers. Chancellor Brandt's administration had emerged strengthened from the 1972 elections. But with high interest rates and a decline in exports contributing to a fall in industrial output, by the end of 1973 economic difficulties were starting to weigh down the government. When a political scandal broke over the discovery in April 1974 of an East German master-spy in the Bonn chancellery, a simmering power struggle in the Social Democratic Party came rapidly to the surface. A casualty of party intrigue, his own weariness with power, economic uncertainties and the Bundesbank's high interest rates, Brandt resigned to make way for Schmidt.

Looking back at the years of breakdown of the post-war monetary system, Schmidt said in 1977: 'The freeing of exchange rates added to uncertainty and therefore contributed to the world recession in 1975. But, in view of inflationary financing in so many countries, it was unavoidable.'[90] Schmidt praised the Bundesbank's decision taken on 1 March 1973 to abandon intervention to support the dollar. 'In the aftermath [the Bundesbank] was able to deploy its range of monetary instruments with real success in stabilising the D-Mark.' In distinct contrast to his frequent unflattering comments on the central bank in later years, he added this tribute: 'From the government's point of view, cooperation with the Bundesbank worked so well not despite the autonomy of the Bundesbank, but because of it.'

vii. Searching for a system

Some supporters of floating exchange rates believed that the ending of the Bretton Woods system would free the Bundesbank of all external constraints, and allow it to concentrate purely on the task of reducing domestic inflation. This view was soon exposed as an illusion. Given the openness of the West German economy – exports made up around 20 per cent of gross national product in the 1960s, rising to more than one third by the end of the 1980s – Germany had no choice but to take account of external economic circumstances in drawing up its monetary policies, whether it was in a fixed-rate system or not.

Additionally, the Bundesbank and the government recognised the necessity of finding new yardsticks for steering and controlling monetary performance. One result soon followed with the end-1974 introduction of annual money supply targets. These were designed partly as a technical exercise to guide the Bundesbank in its lending to the banking system, and partly to establish a public framework for influencing expectations in wage bargaining. The Bundesbank's mixed record since then in adhering to the targets* has not, in general, undermined its credibility, but has allowed it to maintain its freedom of manoeuvre. The Bundesbank has normally convinced the financial markets that occasional failure to meet the targets has not substantially increased inflationary risks.[91] Belying his image as an unbending technocrat, Helmut Schlesinger spelled out as long ago as in 1985 that the Bundesbank takes a flexible approach over the targets: 'Pragmatic monetarism as accepted in the Federal Republic must not be confused with rigid adherence to scholarly doctrine.'[92]

Another prime result of a search for a Bretton Woods substitute

*See chapter 1.

came in the external currency field. Reflecting both the increasing share of German trade within the European Community, and the political need to forge closer monetary cooperation with Germany's trading partners, Chancellor Schmidt and President Valéry Giscard d'Estaing supplied the initiative for establishing the European Monetary System, which took effect in 1979. This extended and formalised the European 'snake' scheme which had started life in April 1972; Schmidt saw it as one route for organising an eventual return to fixed exchange rates. The Bundesbank, jealous of any encroachment, was at first wary of the Franco-German initiative. The central bank's view however became more favourable during the 1980s as it became clear that the EMS brought advantages as well as pitfalls.*

Schmidt himself visited the Bundesbank in November 1978 to persuade the central bank council of the merits of the EMS plan.[93] This provided the occasion for the most passionate and politicised speech ever made on the Bundesbank's thirteenth floor.[94] Schmidt delivered a lengthy harangue on the need for Germany to take an active role in bringing about European monetary integration. When making statements on economics, the chancellor took notorious delight in encompassing a wide sweep of history.[95] During his visit to the Bundesbank, Schmidt performed true to form. His remarks extended well beyond the theme of exchange rate stability. He started off by dwelling on the legacy of Auschwitz, and then dealt with Germany's future as a national state, the need to maintain the country's firm western links, and the threat of Euro-communism.[96] 'He gave a real Schmidt speech,' said Hans Hermsdorf, the former head of the Hamburg central bank, and a close colleague of the former chancellor.[97]

Schmidt's address carried a sting. If the Bundesbank were to put forward strong opposition to signing the agreement setting up the EMS, Schmidt hinted that he might ask parliament to reduce the Bundesbank's independence through a change in the Bundesbank Law.[98] Speaking in 1991, the former chancellor summed up the episode as follows: 'I made them see that they should not overstretch their independence.'[99]

Schmidt's threat was not really serious. It is extremely doubtful whether he really favoured such an initiative; moreover, the chancellor realised that far-reaching changes to the Bundesbank Law would

*See chapter 9.

be highly difficult to push through parliament. Schmidt probably failed to influence any Bundesbank council member to change his mind on the EMS issue.[100] None the less, the visit left the Bundesbank with the lasting impression that, if ever the EMS were to grow towards a system of irrevocably fixed European exchange rates, the central bank would come under fierce pressure to back Bonn's political line. The 1978 confrontation with Schmidt provided the Bundesbank with a foretaste of coming strife. The greatest strains did not arise for another decade, with the emergence of the twin challenges of German unification and European monetary union.

The Challenge of Unity

In spite of general yearning for reunification in today's torn Germany, many of our people – including the refugees – are worried that the merger, together with the efforts accompanying it, would bring an intolerable reduction in living standards.
 Ludwig Erhard, West German economics minister, 1953[1]

May the day come when a central bank in a reunited Fatherland will be able to serve the whole German people!
 Karl Blessing, Bundesbank president, 1967[2]

From 1 July 1990 there are 16 million more reasons for the Bundesbank to care about stability.
Karl Otto Pöhl, Bundesbank president, in publicity leaflets distributed in East Germany, 1990[3]

German monetary union on 1 July 1990 was not the only example of economic annexation in German history. Yet it took place under by far the most favourable auspices. Less than eight months after the breaching of the Berlin Wall, the D-Mark crossed the forty-year-old dividing line between capitalism and communism; and the divide itself passed into history. The D-Mark was the herald of liberal democracy, foreshadowing profit and (for some, at least) prosperity. West Germany discovered its most successful export product – its own currency. It moved eastwards as the first step in the acquisition of a country which was falling to pieces. Once the East Berlin government gave up its financial sovereignty with the extinguishing of the East Mark, the dissolution of the East German state three months later on Unification Day, 3 October 1990, was almost a foregone conclusion. Germany's peaceful *Anschluss* was complete. Although the takeover was acclaimed by governments throughout the world, there were fears abroad, as had been the case in 1938, that Germany might, once again, be growing disruptively large. Most foreign observers, however, did not realise that the greatest threat to the rest of Europe would come not from the success of German reunification – but from its failure.

After four decades of drabness, inefficiency and brutality, the East German population opened their arms to the arrival of the D-Mark. Even the army contributed to putting into place the new monetary order. As part of preparations for the replacement of the East Mark, the Bundesbank transported across the Elbe DM27.5 billion worth of D-Marks at the end of June 1990. A total of 460 tonnes of notes and 600 tonnes of coins were carried in a fleet of lorries. Unknown to the public, the East German National People's Army (NVA) gave the Bundesbank crucial help by making barracks available for temporary storage of the huge cash hoard.[4] The institution which had been at the heart of the East German state contributed to its demise. The currency change-over was indeed enacted with military precision. The events which followed, however, ran a great deal less smoothly.

i. An enterprise of epic proportions

Monetary union between the two parts of Germany was an enterprise of epic proportions. It brought unique opportunities and unique risks. Chancellor Helmut Kohl comprehensively abandoned the dictum of 'no experiments' which had guided West German economic policy for four decades. The financial terms for the East–West German merger were as audacious as in a highly leveraged stock market takeover. It was always clear that dismantling East Germany's Byzantine communist system and repairing its manifold faults, failings, inanities and crimes could not be an easy task. Some of the problems which ensued were inevitable; others were compounded by policy errors in Bonn.

The mistakes reflected lack of preparation as much as lack of competence. Kohl never possessed anything like a blueprint to take over East Germany. After the November 1989 fall of the Berlin Wall, Bonn was beset by worries that the Soviet Union might intervene to curb the growing disruption in the East. Kohl's government had to act first and think afterwards. It showed an impressive capacity to improvise. But it did not always make the correct decisions.

Kohl was undoubtedly right when, early in 1990, he instinctively decided to press for rapid monetary union between East and West

Germany. This choice went against the advice of the Bundesbank. Ludwig Erhard as long ago as 1953 had however recognised that the first step towards reunification would have to come through a transfer eastwards of the West German currency.[5] Delay would simply have postponed the economic difficulties – and would have led to still greater complications in negotiating the withdrawal of the Soviet army from a country which represented Moscow's main prize of the Second World War.

Kohl and his ministers however greatly underestimated the crippling effect on the East German economy of the introduction of the D-Mark. Moribund East German industrial enterprises were not only exposed for the first time to the full brunt of western competition. They were also weighed down by an effective revaluation of the East Mark by 300 to 400 per cent as part of the terms of the 1 July conversion.[6] As a result, East German factories were sucked into a vortex of destruction. The Bonn government hoped that new industries would rise from the old. It forgot, or pushed into the background, that this would only happen over a ten-year period, and that much hardship would have to be endured before the recovery came. Horst Bockelmann, the former Bundesbank official who is now monetary adviser to the Bank for International Settlements, commented in 1991: 'It was not a surprise that the East German economy should collapse. If you wanted to ruin an economy, that was the way to do it.'[7]

After unification, East Germany became the European Community's largest and most problem-ridden depressed region. Output per head in 1991 was only about 30 per cent of the West German level.[8] Infrastructure was crumbling, the factories outdated, the environment polluted and the people psychologically scarred. The cost of trying to put all this right was part of the burden of German history. Before the events of November 1989, most Germans had regarded the legacy of problems in East Germany as a matter beyond their immediate concern. Yet, after political union on 3 October 1990, the responsibility for repairing the damage wrought first by the Third Reich, and then by Stalinism, had to be borne by the whole of Germany.

If Kohl had possessed the skills to convince his compatriots that unification posed an unprecedented challenge, demanding unprecedented efforts, he would have greatly increased the chances of success. Instead, Kohl propagated to the electorate two comforting and fundamentally contradictory messages. The chancellor told Germans in the east that they could relatively quickly attain western living standards. Germans in the west were assured that the whole operation would not cost too much. Each proposition, taken on its own, was extremely doubtful. The likelihood that they would come true simultaneously was vanishingly small.

The chancellor's central premise was that the takeover of the failed communist state would virtually finance itself during the first half of the 1990s. Theo Waigel, Kohl's finance minister, an amiable and deeply conservative Swabian, built his fiscal policies on highly over-optimistic predictions of future tax receipts. Unity, so the two men and their advisers declared, would generate self-perpetuating economic growth. This would automatically bolster tax revenues sufficiently to allow Bonn to channel extra public subsidies and investment grants to the east without the need for any special tax-raising measures to increase budgetary resources. 'As a result of a brilliant economic outlook up to 1993, we will have extra tax revenues of DM115 billion,' proclaimed Waigel in June 1990. 'I believe it is right to forgo tax increases.'[9] 'No one will have to give up anything for German unity,' trumpeted Kohl at the same time. Although the circumstances were undoubtedly much more positive, the refusal to consider higher taxes in 1990 was a miscalculation reminiscent of Karl Helfferich's refusal in 1915 to increase taxes to finance the First World War.*

The politicians' tendency to indulge in wishful thinking was considerably heightened by almost continuous election campaigning during 1990. East Germany held its first ever democratic elections on 18 March. Although the East German Social Democrats (SPD) held a sizeable lead in the opinion polls during most of the campaign, the election produced a clear majority for Chancellor Kohl's Christian Democrats – a vote unambiguously in favour of speedy unity with the west. Two months after Unification Day, the whole of Germany went to the polls on 2 December: an election which, again, ended in triumph for the Christian Democrats. In the frenetic months leading up to the first democratic vote for a united German parliament since 1932, Kohl and Waigel repeated their pledges not to increase taxes. Pressed by the Social Democrats to admit that his estimates for the cost of unification were over-optimistic, Kohl

* See chapter 4.

stuck stubbornly to his ground. When Oskar Lafontaine, the SPD candidate for the chancellorship, forecast in July 1990 that unification would cost the public exchequer DM100 billion a year, he was ridiculed.[10] In fact, Lafontaine's figure turned out to be an under-estimate.

Kohl's optimism about the costs of unity was challenged not only by the Social Democrats, but also by President Richard von Weizsäcker, who became increasingly frustrated by what he regarded as the chancellor's refusal to face facts. At the Unification Day ceremony on 3 October at the Berlin Philharmonic concert hall, von Weizsäcker issued a discreet plea for tax increases: a remark which brought a visible wince to the face of the chancellor sitting in the audience. Von Weizsäcker summed up his point in two pithy sentences:

> There is no way of avoiding the conclusion: in order to be united, we will have to learn to share. German unity cannot be financed simply through high-yielding bonds.[11]

With the 2 December elections won, as reality dawned of the size of the budgetary needs in the east, the Kohl government quickly decided a massive one-year tax raising package to garner funds for unification.[12] Kohl was guilty not so much of electoral duplicity, but rather of lack of understanding of the scale of the transition confronting his country. Kohl did not consciously lie to the voters. His sin was perhaps more damning: he believed his own forecasts.

Unification gave the western part of Germany a powerful economic impetus. The West German economy registered a sizeable spurt between 1989 and 1991. Companies in the west seized on their chances of expanding eastwards, in a boom fuelled by the sharp expansion of demand caused by large public sector deficits. Higher economic growth in 1989–91 benefited the whole of Europe, boosting demand for industrial products from Germany's neighbours. It was, however, a different story east of the Elbe.

In eastern Germany, the economic downturn exceeded all expectations. Kohl and Waigel had hoped that the introduction of the D-Mark on 1 July 1990 would spur the same sort of economic revival in the east as that seen after the currency reform in the western sectors of occupied Germany in 1948. In fact, East German industry simply collapsed. In western Germany in 1948, industrial output rose 50 per cent in the first six months after the currency reform.[13] Although unemployment remained high until the early 1950s,[14] producers and consumers reacted favourably both to the new currency and to the liberalisation measures brought in by Ludwig Erhard. The contrast between events in 1948–49 and 1990–91 could hardly have been more marked: industrial production in eastern Germany in the twelve months after the introduction of the D-Mark fell by 50 per cent. The depth of the slump was caused above all by the over-generous terms of the 1 July monetary conversion, together with large wage rises granted to East German workers in the months afterwards. A collapse in exports to the Soviet republics and other parts of the former communist trading bloc contributed to the severity of the downturn. Long-pent-up East German consumer demand was satisfied as western products poured into the new part of the Federal Republic. Outmoded, overmanned and inefficient East German factories were powerless to compete – resulting in a steady tide of plant closures and a steep rise in unemployment.

Unschooled in economic thought, Kohl failed to see that the 1948 and 1991 episodes were not comparable. Three years after the end of the Second World War, much of German industry had been devastated, but twelve years of National Socialist rule had left less deep psychological marks on the population than forty years of Stalinism. With the rest of Europe weakened by the aftermath of war, and the D-Mark still protected by foreign exchange controls, the exposure to outside competition in 1948 was nothing like as drastic as that experienced in eastern Germany in 1990. In an obscure treatise published nearly twenty-five years earlier, Helmut Schmidt, Kohl's predecessor, had forecast that opening up East Germany to unrestricted access for western goods would cause the country's economic collapse.[15] Had Schmidt been chancellor, he would have been far more aware of the dire economic consequences of the sudden entry of the D-Mark. This would have made him much more cautious in taking advantage of the opportunity for German unity which arose in 1990. It remains an intriguing hypothesis that, as a result, the chance might have been missed altogether.

The slump in the east had a direct impact on the government's finances in the west. Public sector transfers from west to east Germany proved far larger than expected. In 1991 and 1992, 16 million East Germans required annual net public sector subsidies from the west of around DM150 billion a year to cover social security programmes, support investment, tackle environmental pollution and build new infrastructure. The figure – roughly three times finance minister Waigel's estimate in summer 1990[16] – made up 5 per cent of Germany's overall gross national product. East Germany in 1991 accounted for only 6.8 per cent of total economic output in united Germany – but absorbed 13 per cent of overall German economic resources.[17] Funding from west to east of at least DM100 billion a year will probably be necessary until the end of the 1990s.[18]

For an economy of Germany's size and resilience, transfers on this scale are manageable; they imply however a massive shift in resources. The 1991 tax increases came too late to avoid a drastic increase in Bonn government borrowing. Since the willingness of the West German electorate to accept further tax increases is limited, the cost of bailing out the eastern part of Germany makes large and persistent German budget deficits virtually inevitable during the 1990s. Total German public sector debt is forecast to rise from DM1.2 trillion at the end of 1991 to DM2 trillion at end-1995 and DM2.5 trillion by the year 2000.[19] The sharp deterioration in Germany's internal finances is mirrored by a worsening in its traditionally extremely healthy external payments position. Triggered by above-average expansion of the domestic economy, and a slackening of foreign demand for German exports, the German current account balance of payments swung from a surplus of DM77 billion in 1990 to a deficit of DM34 billion in 1991.

This fundamental swing in the underlying state of Germany's finances, together with growing inflationary pressures, left the Bundesbank with little alternative but to tighten credit significantly in 1991–92. As a result, economic growth slowed not only in Germany but also in other European countries which make up Germany's prime export markets. This, in turn, dented the prospects for rapid recovery east of the Elbe, and increased the financial costs of keeping the East German economy afloat.

Failure to put the economic management of German unification on to a sound footing has several long-term consequences:

• Reflecting the sharp build-up of German public sector debt, both taxes and interest rates in Germany will be higher in the early

1990s than would otherwise have been the case. This may place an important dampener on Germany's future economic dynamism.

• Resentment has increased in wealthier German regions about sharing out the financial burdens of unity. This could eventually lead some richer states to try to opt out of the system for distributing financial resources among the German *Länder* – a step which would fundamentally undermine the German system of federal government.

• Because of the international role of the D-Mark, Bonn's mishandling of the financing of unity is producing political and economic pain not just in Germany, but across the whole of Europe. This constitutes a considerable impediment to the plan for European monetary union.*

ii. A meek counterweight to authority

There was one particularly ironic reason for general surprise in West Germany about the economic disintegration in the east. Before 1989–90, the Federal Republic generally believed East Berlin's propaganda claiming East Germany was the world's ninth or tenth most important advanced economy. An industrial machine of this prowess – so many West as well as East German experts believed – could not simply crumble within a few months. Erich Honecker, East Germany's long-time communist leader, boasted right up to the end: 'The masses have proved they can determine their fate without capitalists.'[20] Oskar Lafontaine showed his credulity by declaring in summer 1990, 'Up until the fall of the Wall, East Germany was a leading industrial country.'[21] As Kohl himself put it in March 1990, 'For a long period, East Germany appeared as a monolith. But it was a house of cards, and it simply fell down.'[22]

Ever since the East German state was formed in 1949, subterfuge and lies about its economic performance were routine. In 1953, an article in the East Berlin party newspaper *Neues Deutschland* claimed that the Bank deutscher Länder had drawn up a confidential memorandum concluding that East Germans enjoyed lower prices and higher salaries than in the west.[23] Wilhelm Vocke, president of the directorate of the Bank deutscher Länder, sent an angry letter to

* See chapter 9.

Chancellor Adenauer declaring that the article was 'invented from start to finish'.[24]

In later decades, East Germany kept up the disinformation campaign: it was an edifice built on spurious statistics. Amid this web of distortion, the Staatsbank, the East German central bank, played an intriguingly double-sided role. Its function, like that of all central banks, was to maintain a public façade of confidence in the currency. But it also delivered to the government an annual report on the economy, never published, whose very existence was known only to insiders.[25] The bank used this document to warn regularly about economic failings which could never be referred to in public. In its role as a meek counterweight to the central authority of the East Berlin regime, the Staatsbank resembled the Reichsbank in its indecisiveness and its ultimate failure. None the less, the Staatsbank – like the Reichsbank – can claim some credence for having pointed to economic weakness in the system, long before these defects brought the downfall of the state.

In its annual report for 1965, for instance, the Staatsbank stated that imbalances between supply and demand in East Germany had caused the development of a potentially inflationary 'monetary overhang' – meaning that too much money was chasing too few goods. As a result, the Staatsbank earned powerful criticism from the SED that it was using 'bourgeois' economic terminology. In 1966, the Staatsbank drew attention to shortfalls in capital investment, productivity and the trade surplus.[26a] 'In important areas, the planned economic targets have not been fully reached,' the bank said.

In 1975, the Staatsbank again focused on the need for higher productivity and also on the growing cost of social housing programmes.[27] It warned that borrowing from foreign capital markets to finance investment 'cannot be continued in coming years'.[28] Foreign indebtedness had reached a level 'which can no longer be enlarged', the Staatsbank declared. The only way to reduce the debt, the Staatsbank concluded wearily, was to register a series of trade surpluses in the forthcoming five-year planning period.

The Staatsbank's most outspoken warning came early in 1989, in a report on 'the stability of the currency of the German Democratic Republic'.[29] It pointed out that money supply since 1975 had risen by 165 per cent, while national income had increased by only 77 per cent – widening the potentially inflationary demand gap. Belying the official government boasts of stable prices, the Staatsbank recorded lugubriously that inflation in industry, construction and agriculture had totalled an overall 56.9 per cent since 1975. Foreign debt had continued to grow, and the free market exchange rate of the East Mark against the D-Mark was less than half the 1976 level, the bank pointed out.[30]

The man formally responsible for central banking affairs under the regime of Erich Honecker was Horst Kaminsky. The crinkle-haired functionary had worked his way up to the Staatsbank presidency after starting out as a humble book-keeper in a state-owned *Kombinat*. For years, Kaminsky held court in the Staatsbank's once ornate nineteenth-century building on the corner of Charlottenstrasse, priding himself on his place in the cheerless hierarchy of East German life. He stayed on for a few months after the elections in March 1990, then was asked to take early retirement at the age of sixty-three. He received a pension of only DM1400 per month – one-fortieth of the salary of the president of the Bundesbank. After unification, Kaminsky was one of the many to feel the effects of the new lack of job security. He remarked glumly in May 1991: 'In the former German Democratic Republic, nobody had to worry about his job.'[31] Kaminsky claimed, however, that the bank had been worried for several years about negative economic trends. 'From the middle of the 1980s we could recognise the problem caused by our lack of production efficiency, which opened up a growing gap compared with consumption . . . I had the feeling that reform was necessary to correct policies in certain areas.'

Bruno Meier, a Staatsbank official who served as a deputy president under Kaminsky, admitted – more than six months after unification – that the East German central bank had long realised that its days were numbered. During the 1980s, the Staatsbank had come to the basic conclusion, Meier said, that, 'The socialist system would not survive in competition with the west.'[32] None the less, even after the breaching of the Wall, the Staatsbank was confident that it would still enjoy some form of diminished role as the two German states worked out improved economic cooperation.[33] As Meier put it, 'We expected three or four years to elapse' before monetary union between the two parts of Germany. Meier expressed the Staatsbank's envy towards the Bundesbank – a central bank in charge of a real currency, not an artificial one. 'We respected the Bundesbank for making the D-Mark one of the most stable currencies in the world,' Meier said. He particularly admired the Bundesbank's ability to speak out independently. 'The Bundesbank president is allowed to irritate the chancellor. If Kaminsky had said something critical, he would have been immediately sacked and persecuted as a western agent.'

No one foresaw the speed with which the East Mark was abolished, and the Staatsbank was simply made redundant. The miscalculation was made not simply by officials at the East Berlin central bank; it was shared, too, by the top echelons of the Bundesbank in Frankfurt.

iii. 'The idea of monetary union is unrealistic'

Unlike some of his compatriots, Karl Otto Pöhl had never shown false sentimentality towards East Germany. He once told a TV interviewer that the characteristics which most impressed him about the east were 'the poverty, the backwardness, the bad air'.[34] He was one of many West Germans who would have been happy to see East and West Germany continue to co-exist, as separate, democratic states.[35] Pöhl's reaction to the fall of the Berlin Wall was essentially pragmatic, like that of many of his colleagues on the Bundesbank council. Although he knew that German reunification was now on the international agenda, Pöhl wanted to avoid any hasty monetary steps which would endanger his main objective: upholding the stability of the D-Mark. As calls for a merger of the D-Mark and East Mark multiplied at the beginning of 1990, Pöhl and his colleagues maintained a public tone of polite but firm scepticism.

The Bundesbank based its misgivings about monetary union, and particularly its opposition to a 1 for 1 conversion rate, on sound economic logic. At the beginning of 1990, the rate used for exchanging East Marks against D-Marks in commercial transactions was 4.5 to 1. On the free exchange market (illegal according to the East German authorities), the rate was 7 to 1. Monetary union on a 1 for 1 basis would involve a substantial revaluation of the East Mark which would cripple East German industry, by sharply increasing East German companies' costs, making their output uncompetitive.

In the twelfth-floor offices of the Bundesbank, there were voices speaking out in favour of monetary union. Claus Köhler, the directorate member responsible for monetary affairs, a bow-tied figure radiating almost permanent bonhomie, was more enthusiastic about reunification than the rest of the Bundesbank council. One of the rare Keynesians on the central bank board, Köhler, born in Berlin, was always thought slightly suspect by Schlesinger, the archetypal monetarist. The two indulged in frequent altercations around the council table, but they also shared a sense of comradeship; nearly every day, they buried their differences over lunch together in the directorate's dining rooms. On 22 November 1989, at the first meeting of the council after the fall of the Berlin Wall, Köhler put forward a thirteen-page plan for 'step by step' replacement of the East Mark by the D-Mark.[36] The idea was briefly discussed; and Pöhl and Schlesinger made clear their doubts about the plan's practicality.

Events, however, dictated that the momentum behind monetary union soon became uncontrollable. In the months after November 1989, the East German regime lifted the most draconian controls along the guarded East–West German border. East Germans were even permitted access to special D-Mark allowances to give them the wherewithal to travel to the west. At the beginning of 1990, an average of 2000 dissatisfied East Germans were leaving their country every day to settle in the Federal Republic.[37] Many East Germans doubted whether the ramshackle and repressive system under which they had lived for forty years was capable of orderly change. The migration wave was a striking sign of the magnetic pull of West Germany's prosperous democracy. Yet there was no rejoicing in Bonn. Worried that the inflows were putting strains on western social security, housing and jobs, the West German government was trying hard to keep the disruptive emigration within bounds.

The East Germans were no longer fleeing to freedom. That was, after all, now being introduced in the east. The migrants wanted to avoid the turmoil which they sensed was on its way in East Germany – and they wanted direct access to the West German currency. Their refrain was growing more insistent: 'If the D-Mark does not come to us, we will go to the D-Mark.' Later, the plea hardened in favour of a 1 to 1 exchange rate: '1 for 1, or else we will never be one.'

Willy Brandt, the former Social Democrat chancellor, had emerged as the patriarch of German unity. At large rallies in East Germany before the elections on 18 March, Brandt urged Bonn to introduce economic and monetary union as a way of persuading more East Germans to stay. The Bundesbank was unmoved. Pöhl believed that the East German government would not accept the shift in monetary sovereignty to Frankfurt which would result from monetary union between the two states. In an interview at the end of January 1990, Pöhl dismissed the suggestion as 'fantastic'.[38] Equally unbendingly, Schlesinger declared at the end of January: 'The idea of monetary union at the moment is very unrealistic.'[39]

In view of the mounting pressures on the East German state, at around the end of January 1990 Kaminsky of the Staatsbank telephoned Pöhl to suggest a top-level parley between the two central banks.[40] Without great enthusiasm, Pöhl agreed to travel to East Berlin, accompanied by Schlesinger, for talks with the Staatsbank. Kaminsky and Pöhl were old hands at hatching discreet financial deals. Their first encounter had been in the early 1970s, when each held the rank of state secretary in Bonn and East Berlin. Then, they had worked on the small print of abstruse East–West German financial claims, unravelling conundrums over child support payments, property transactions and bequests bogged down in the East–West quagmire. Pöhl's contempt for his communist opposite number was mixed with rueful admiration for Kaminsky's negotiating skills. Pöhl once admitted that the East Berliner had emerged from their 1970s dealings with by far the better of the bargain.

During the 1980s, the German banking duo had sometimes exchanged subdued small talk at annual meetings of the Bank for International Settlements in Basle. Communist and capitalist central bankers from around the world habitually mingled at the summer beanfeasts to study balance sheets and drink cocktails under Swiss sun umbrellas. The two men had even started a half-hearted practice of making annual visits to each other's central banks. Up to now, these occasions had been largely ceremonial. In February 1990, as the bankrupt East German state slid further into terminal decline, there was – for the first time – something serious on the two presidents' agenda.

Pöhl and Kaminsky made a singularly ill-matched pair as they strode before the media in East Berlin on Tuesday 6 February 1990. The two central bankers had just emerged from talks held in a chintzy first-floor Staatsbank meeting room festooned with red curtains and an assortment of communist glass light fittings. The

TV cameramen instinctively homed in on the debonair Pöhl, radiating sleek self-confidence in his well-cut suit. The communist functionary at his side was all too clearly the underdog. As the two men appeared before the reporters on the steps of the Staatsbank, a crackle of expectancy filled East Berlin's sulphur-polluted air.

During their meeting in the first-floor Staatsbank office, Pöhl and Kaminsky discussed the need for East German reforms. They agreed to examine steps towards monetary union. First, though, the East Mark would have to be turned into a convertible currency. In view of the disparities between the two states' economies, both men agreed that the goal was a long way off. Speaking to the waiting reporters outside the Staatsbank on the prospect of monetary union, Pöhl said both he and Kaminsky believed it was 'premature' even to consider 'such a far-reaching step'. Pöhl was unaware that Chancellor Kohl, the same morning in Bonn, was holding a crisis meeting on monetary union with senior coalition politicians – and that he was about to announce a decision to press for the extension of the D-Mark to the east.

Before returning to the Kempinski hotel near the West Berlin Ku'damm, Pöhl held talks with Christa Luft, the East German economics minister. He also saw Ibrahim Böhme, the head of the East German Social Democratic Party, which was widely – but wrongly – predicted to emerge as the strongest party from the 18 March elections. Schlesinger held a separate meeting with Lothar de Maizière, the East German Christian Democrat leader destined to become prime minister. Schlesinger spelled out strong opposition to the idea that East German wages and savings could possibly be converted into D-Marks on a 1 for 1 basis.[41]

East Berlin was not Pöhl's favourite city, but he reflected that the trip had gone well. His composure was shattered by a telephone call to the Kempinski late in the day from a harassed Rudolf Seiters, Kohl's chancellery minister in Bonn. Seiters apologetically informed Pöhl that the chancellor had gone before the TV cameras in the afternoon to spell out an offer of 'immediate' monetary union with East Germany. Theo Waigel, the finance minister, later put forward an unconvincing reason for the chancellery's failure to inform the Bundesbank president immediately. Bonn had been unable to contact Pöhl, Waigel said, because of the poor state of the East Berlin telephone lines.

Pöhl had good reason for feeling slighted. Kohl had had every opportunity to warn him; but the chancellor chose not to. Pöhl was particularly vexed at having been made to look foolish before the media representatives outside the Staatsbank. The previous morning – Monday 5 February – Kohl had telephoned Pöhl at his twelfth-floor office in the Bundesbank. They discussed East Germany for thirty minutes – an unusually long conversation between the two men. Kohl was clearly probing Pöhl's attitude on monetary union – but dropped no hint that he was planning an immediate decision.

Before flying to Berlin, Pöhl – accompanied by Schlesinger – travelled to Bonn on Monday afternoon for two hours of talks with Waigel in his cramped Rhineside finance ministry offices. Pöhl had never completely forgiven Waigel – the chairman of the Bavarian Christian Social conservative party in Kohl's coalition – for having opposed his nomination to the Bundesbank job both in 1979, when his appointment was decided, and in 1987, when it was renewed. Pöhl however generally enjoyed Waigel's sense of humour. On Monday afternoon, the finance minister was in wise-cracking mood, commenting jocularly about the war of nerves now under way with East Berlin. Yet Waigel, like Kohl, gave no indication of an immediate move towards German monetary union.

Pöhl later described the lack of consultation with Bonn as 'unusual and irritating' – deliberate understatement.[42] In reality, his indignation went a great deal deeper. Once he heard the news from Seiters on Tuesday evening, Pöhl briefly considered resigning. He quickly rejected the idea, however, concluding that it would be wrong to over-react to a 'protocol' matter at a time of historic significance for Germany. Later, Pöhl reflected, 'I didn't want to play the insulted prima donna.'[43] Instead, he headed for Berlin airport – to catch an aeroplane for Bonn, where Kohl had requested his attendance at a hastily arranged cabinet meeting on German monetary union called for the morning of Wednesday 7 February. There was one added inconvenience: Pöhl had failed to pack a clean shirt for an extra night away from home.

iv. The chancellor changes his mind

Some officials sympathetic to Kohl and Waigel subsequently suggested that the two politicians had strongly indicated their leanings towards speedy monetary union on Monday 5 February, but that

Pöhl had simply ignored these hints. This version does not fit the facts. On 5 February, Kohl assembled his experts on East Germany for a meeting in the chancellery. They decided that a gradual move to monetary union based on achieving step-by-step economic convergence was still the most practicable approach.[44] Up to late Monday, Kohl was still balking at the costs and complications of rapidly introducing the D-Mark into the east.[45] That evening, however, Kohl held a crucial meeting in East Berlin with East German Christian Democratic leaders – including Lothar de Maizière.[46] They warned him that despair in the east about future prospects made immediate entry of the D-Mark the only way to guard against further damaging migration to the west.[47] This convinced Kohl that a rapid move to take over East Germany on Bonn's terms would probably be less onerous than waiting for the communist state to disintegrate.[48]

Horst Teltschik, the chancellor's foreign affairs adviser, and a key figure in behind-the-scenes unity discussions, confirmed sixteen months later that the breakthrough came only on Tuesday 6 February. 'On Monday, neither Kohl nor Waigel knew anything [about a plan for monetary union].'[49] At 10 o'clock on 6 February, at a meeting in the chancellery with Seiters and Teltschik, Kohl took the historic decision to propose 'immediate' talks on extending the D-Mark east of the Elbe.[50] This would have been the time to have tried to inform Pöhl in East Berlin; but the thought simply slipped the chancellor's mind.

Kohl later declared that West Germany was bringing to the negotiating table 'our strongest economic asset – the D-Mark'.[51] The D-Mark became the instrument of reunification; but it was also a potential casualty if, along the path of rapprochement, something was to go wrong. Risky though the plan was, it also embodied considerable political advantages. Kohl reasoned that, in the East German election campaign, announcement of a plan for bringing in the D-Mark would give a considerable boost to the Christian Democrats' fortunes and take the wind out of the sails of the Social Democrats. The prediction proved devastatingly correct. By paving the way for the expiry of the East Mark, Kohl's decision sounded the death knell for the SPD's hopes of holding political power in the former communist state.

The main impetus for the decision, however, as Kohl admitted later, was fear of migration: 'I don't have any alternative. If we don't carry out economic and monetary union, then we face the risk that in the summer we will have 500,000 people coming here from the GDR.'[52] The chancellor tried to put the most positive gloss on the decision by forecasting that it would spark a revival in the *Länder* of eastern Germany comparable with that produced by Erhard's measures in 1948. Kohl rejected the cautious 'book-keeping' approach of the Social Democrats as being contrary to Erhard's vision. 'If Erhard had thought like that, then today we would still be buying shoes with rationing coupons.'

Kohl's colourful forecast of the effects of the entry of capitalism to East Germany was based on his views about human nature, rather than on his knowledge of economics:

> I wouldn't know the Germans if there was not to be straight away an enormous car boom. The Germans have a tendency towards eating, drinking, cars and travel as the priorities. The car is the status symbol. And when the East Germans have a lot of cars, then, of course, they will need repairing. Then there will be an incredible push in construction. They [the East German communists] have done nothing to repair old buildings, and the new ones are terrible. In East Germany you have the highest proportion of working women – 90 per cent. So you have two incomes. And what does the wife say: 'At last I want a decent bathroom' – just like in the magazines. And this will give a unique chance for the plumbers and handymen.[53]

Later in 1990, Kohl declared: 'I have no doubt that we will see a broad wave of investment . . . In a few years, in three or four years, we will see a flourishing landscape in Thuringia, in Saxony-Anhalt, in Saxony, in Mecklenburg, in western Pomerania, in Brandenburg . . . If Ludwig Erhard had acted in the way that many are advising me to behave, then what was possible after the currency reform would never have happened.'[54]

Kohl encouraged the belief that East Germany would be able to catch up with the west within a few years; but the prediction was hopelessly flawed.[55] The chancellor's predictions were in fact far more rosy than those put forward by his own advisers. Several leading Bonn officials were predicting 'chaos' east of the Elbe. Horst Teltschik did not hide his belief that 2 million people might lose their jobs in the former communist state. Günther Krause, the East Berlin state secretary who headed the East Berlin delegation during negotiations on monetary union, predicted that only one third of East German companies would be capable of surviving the advent of the D-Mark without help.

Kohl admitted in 1991 that he had under-estimated the scale of problems in the east. Top-level Bonn officials were particularly rueful about the misjudgment over taxation. Teltschik conceded that the failure to increase taxes earlier had been 'a spectacular wrong decision'.[56] According to Volker Rühe, general secretary of the Christian Democratic Union,* this was 'a big mistake'.[57] Otto Schlecht, the veteran state secretary in the economics ministry, admitted:

> We deceived ourselves about the size and depth of the restructuring crisis. We gave prominence to the positive elements [about East German economic prospects] and forced the negative ones into the background. This was because we wanted people to take heart – and because there was an election campaign.[58]

The chancellor, however, stuck to his basic belief in the correctness of his overall policy. His faith was mixed with a defiant desire to see the Bundesbank's caution proved wrong. 'If I had followed the recommendations of the Bundesbank,' he declared in 1991, 'we would not have introduced the D-Mark on 1 July.'[59]

v. The conversion takes shape

Three days after Kohl's announcement of the monetary union plan in February 1990, Pöhl made his forebodings plain when – in a highly unusual move – he called a press conference in Bonn on 9 February. Sporting his favourite red tie, Pöhl said the Bundesbank would support government policies, as it was bound to do according to its statutes. Monetary union was, after all, a political decision – for the government to take, not the central bank. But he recited a long list of financial and legal obstacles to the idea of introducing the D-Mark east of the Elbe.[60]

The Bundesbank president warned that German monetary union

---

* Rühe was appointed defence minister in April 1992.

had to be seen as part of an overall move to reunification. Bringing in the D-Mark would require 'enormous transfer payments' to the east if it were to go through without 'social upheaval'. Pöhl pointed out that the monetary union plan would require 'a radical change of East Germany's economic structure ... This cannot happen overnight.' If wages paid in East Marks by the East German state enterprises were suddenly converted into D-Marks, 'most would go bankrupt', he forecast – an accurate prediction of what actually happened. He expressed diplomatically worded unease at Kohl's change of mind, describing the chancellor's proposals as 'cryptic'. Asked about the general surprise caused by Kohl's decision, Pöhl replied: 'I always advise the government to consult the Bundesbank first.' Pöhl dropped a clear hint that tax increases might be necessary to help defray the costs of unity. He said it was 'shabby' for politicians to talk of the vision of reunification for thirty years and then, when the chance came, not to want to pay for it.

The press conference marked the onset of a summer of discontent between Bonn and the Bundesbank. During his first eight-year term at the helm of the central bank, Pöhl's relations with the Kohl government had been much more harmonious than with Schmidt's Social Democrats. Pöhl established a good *modus vivendi* with Kohl's first finance minister Gerhard Stoltenberg, who held the job between 1982 and 1989 – a man whom Pöhl regarded as decent, reliable and humourless. Sluggish economic growth in the mid-1980s allowed the Bundesbank to follow a relatively easy interest rate policy but also to achieve year-by-year progress in bringing down inflation; it was also a period of quiet within the European Monetary System. In 1986–87, as the expiry of Pöhl's first eight-year term of office drew closer, he toyed with the idea of quitting and turning to a more highly paid job in private banking. But when it became clear that Kohl was backing him for a second presidential term, Pöhl resolved to stay on. Ever conscious of his image, Pöhl saw the reappointment of a Social Democrat Bundesbank president by a Christian Democrat chancellor as an inestimable tribute to his qualities. It was too good an opportunity to turn down.

Relations with Bonn, which had already started to worsen during the aftermath of the 1987 stock exchange crash,* became more

* See chapter 2.

delicate still at the beginning of 1990 when Hans Tietmeyer joined the Bundesbank directorate. A fervent Christian Democrat, Tietmeyer enjoyed the confidence of Chancellor Kohl. Pöhl regarded the acerbic and insistent former state secretary in the finance ministry as a highly competent monetary expert and negotiator; but Pöhl also saw in Tietmeyer a rival for his job. Tietmeyer joined the Bundesbank to take over the responsibilities of Leonhard Gleske – who had retired in September 1989 – for international monetary affairs. But it soon became clear that the new man in Frankfurt would be playing a central role in the process of German unification. At Pöhl's suggestion, Tietmeyer was seconded to Bonn from the beginning of April 1990 onwards, serving as the special adviser to Chancellor Kohl on monetary union with East Germany. He headed the West German delegation in the monetary talks with the new East Berlin government of Lothar de Maizière which took office after the 18 March elections. Tietmeyer's dual role gave the Bundesbank a clear hand in the negotiations on the terms of the D-Mark's move eastwards. The new directorate member's enhanced position however became a source of additional tension within the Bundesbank council. Tietmeyer was suspected by some members of the council of accumulating far too much power.

As preparatory talks on monetary union got under way in February–March 1990, the Bonn government asked the Bundesbank for its recommendation on the vital question of the D-Mark/East Mark conversion rate. The dilemma was acute. Too low a level for the East Mark against the D-Mark would sharply cut East German incomes, and encourage more migration to the west. Too high a rate would, on the other hand, spark greater unemployment – and this would also spur desperate East Germans to seek the prosperity of the Federal Republic.

At the end of March, the Bundesbank suggested that East Mark assets and payments should be converted into D-Marks on the basis of 2 to 1. This itself was a compromise between the Bundesbank's desire to see a still lower rate established for the East Mark, and the fear that such a rate would encourage great social problems. The central bank was, however, overruled by Bonn – not least because of protests from easterners complaining that anything less than 1 to 1 would unfairly reduce their savings, and would leave them with wages of only about one quarter of western levels. Agreement on a more generous conversion rate, based on 1 to 1 for smaller savings deposits, was announced on 23 April. The overall exchange rate for all financial assets was 1.8 to 1, reflecting different treatment of larger savings accounts. The conversion of East Mark savings into D-Marks led to a once-and-for-all increase of about 15 per cent in overall German money supply.[61] This was more than double the increase which would have been warranted by the relative size of the East German economy – one factor behind the acceleration in German money supply growth which increasingly worried the Bundesbank in 1991–92.

De Maizière admitted afterwards that the conversion of East German savings accounts ('backed by nothing') into solid D-Mark balances amounted to a 'gift'.[62] However, even after agreement on the conversion rate, there were still voices in eastern Germany complaining that Bonn's parsimony was somehow turning the former communist state into 'a low wage country'.[63] Tietmeyer took a critical view of the outcome, commenting in 1991 that the Bundesbank's 2 to 1 proposal 'would have been more favourable both for the competitiveness of East German industry and for the necessity of maintaining wage differentials [between the two parts of Germany]. Unfortunately, it was not possible to put the proposal into effect.' The result, he added grimly, was much lower East German competitiveness after monetary union – and higher unemployment.[64]

The complex monetary union treaty was negotiated in just over three months: a formidable undertaking. On 18 May 1990, when the treaty was formally signed in Bonn, sanguineness was in the air. The ceremony took place in a tapestry-strewn chamber of the Palais Schaumburg, Konrad Adenauer's former chancellery headquarters. The event was held in Bonn rather than Berlin for a highly characteristic reason: afterwards, Kohl had to attend a birthday celebration nearby for an old acquaintance. In a short speech, the chancellor declared that the D-Mark gave East Germany not just the chance but also the 'guarantee' of soon becoming a 'flourishing landscape'.

Amid all the well-publicised wrangling over the conversion rate, discreet technical preparations for the currency change-over had already been proceeding for several weeks. On 2 April, four Bundesbank officials and three functionaries from the Staatsbank met in a state-run East German hotel near the site of the Buchenwald concentration camp outside Weimar to work out the basic details.[65] Bundesbank officials toured East Germany examining Staatsbank buildings – many of them formerly owned by the Reichsbank – to find appropriate sites for the central bank's planned network of new branches. There were several unseemly tussles with the Deutsche Bank and Dresdner Bank, which were also hunting for new premises.[66] The Bundesbank invested a total of DM60 million in the new network of fifteen provincial offices in eastern Germany. Half of the funds went on improving security. Bundesbank officials were astonished to find that the strongrooms in many Staatsbank offices were fitted with locks and doors dating from the period of the Reichsbank. The Bundesbank's historical archives section prevailed upon colleagues working in the east to bring back some exhibits for the Bundesbank's museum.

The Bundesbank launched its own eastern modernisation drive by bringing in up-to-date computers for the new East German network. Requiring sophisticated frequency regulating apparatus to improve supplies of electricity to the new offices, the Bundesbank fell foul of western technology transfer rules. It had to apply for a special dispensation from controls operated by the shadowy CoCom watchdog body. Telephone lines were a particular problem. But once the Bundesbank gained entry to the old Berlin Reichsbank extension building on the Werdersche Wiese, officials realised they could make use of high-performance secret police lines to connect up provincial branch offices.

vi. Strains in the council

For all the technical challenges, the installation of computers and telephone lines in eastern Germany proceeded with only minor hitches. Within a few months, the Bundesbank succeeded in establishing a working central banking network on virgin eastern territory, staffed by 250 officials from the Federal Republic and 900 local employees – a remarkable feat of energy and organisation. However, the task of coordinating policies between Bonn and Frankfurt proved far more of a headache. Already vexed by the snub over the conversion rate, Bundesbank officials in mid-May 1990 were given a fresh reason for irritation. The finance ministry faced unexpectedly large demands for transfers of public funds to eastern Germany. In agreement with the *Land* governments, the ministry reacted by deciding to set up a new financing vehicle –

the German Unity Fund – to shift borrowing for East Germany outside normal budget procedures.

The plan was of critical significance for the Bundesbank. Extra government borrowing carries the risk of increasing inflation; the central bank would normally be consulted on such an initiative as a matter of course. This time, however, top officials of the Bundesbank – with the exception of Tietmeyer – were not informed. Horst Köhler, Tietmeyer's successor as state secretary at the finance ministry, telephoned Schlesinger on the morning of 15 May 1990 to inform the Bundesbank about the Unity Fund innovation. By then – much to the Bundesbank's annoyance – the first reports of the launch of the fund were already in the press.

Pöhl was well aware that tension was rising. He remained silent, for fear of exacerbating the government's difficulties. Others on the Bundesbank council were less restrained. Wilhelm Nölling, the quick-tempered president of the Hamburg *Landeszentralbank*, gave a newspaper interview on 23 May in which he sharply criticised Bonn's repeated failure to consult the Bundesbank. 'The government has to stop acting as if the autonomy of the Bundesbank has been put aside for the process of reunification.' Pointing out the danger that this could dampen confidence in the D-Mark, he added that disregard for the central bank's views 'could start to damage the Bundesbank's reputation'.[67] Helmut Hesse, the Lower Saxony central bank president, gave a similar warning in a lecture in Kiel, in which he complained that the Bundesbank was being stripped of its 'leadership role' in monetary policy. He emphasised the inflationary dangers of the over-generous conversion rate. The consequence, he said, would be 'higher real interest rates'.[68]

These two uncompromising statements were made for different reasons. Nölling's was a calculated effort to express the Social Democrats' lack of sympathy for Chancellor Kohl's go-it-alone approach to German unity. Hesse's lecture was an academic contribution to the debate rather than a bid to make a political point. Whatever their motives, the publicity given to the two men's declarations caused Pöhl acute discomfort. The Bundesbank president felt squeezed from both sides – from the government, for his lack of enthusiasm over monetary union, and from within the council, for not having protested loudly enough when, during the last few months, the Bundesbank had been side-stepped or ignored.

Pöhl took the unusual step of calling the Bundesbank council to order. On 23 May – the day the Nölling interview appeared – Pöhl sent a letter to all council members asking them to tone down their public comments. On 30 May, he used a speech in Frankfurt to criticise rumours of 'confrontation' between Bonn and Frankfurt. The next day, 31 May, the Bundesbank council convened for its regular fortnightly gathering. To try to counter the growing public impression of discord between Bonn and Frankfurt, both Theo Waigel and Horst Köhler participated as guests around the Bundesbank's thirteenth-floor table. The TV cameras were allowed in, as usual, at the beginning of the session to record the show of solidarity. But the meeting which ensued afterwards – as always, closed to the media – proved unusually tempestuous. In his opening remarks, Pöhl came straight to the point, regretting that the 'wrong image' of the Bundesbank had lately been projected in public.[69] This was due to 'the statements of individual council members', he said. From now on, Pöhl warned his colleagues around the Bundesbank's top table, such behaviour had to stop.

From the normally tactful Pöhl, this was exceptionally strong language. The two members at whom the admonition was aimed – Nölling and Hesse – reacted in different ways. Nölling angrily complained at being reprimanded, and defended his right to make public criticisms of monetary policy. The less rumbustious Hesse took the criticism in silence. His stoicism was however misleading; he was seething with anger. 'No professor likes to be told off by someone he regards as a student,' a Bundesbank council member commented subsequently. The session ended with the council agreeing a face-saving statement pointing out that the Bundesbank had indeed been involved 'from the start' in negotiations with East Germany on monetary union.

Nearly a year afterwards, Hesse commented on the passions unleashed around the council table on 31 May. He and Nölling had been made 'scapegoats' for mistakes over unification, he declared. 'I was badly affected [by Pöhl's reprimand]. It wasn't a very human thing to do . . . This didn't do the reputation of our president any good, and it had a negative effect on the whole of the central bank.'[70]

Although the effects were not immediately apparent, the emotional May meeting damaged the council's *esprit de corps*. Pöhl's relaxed style of management seemed no longer to be working. In September 1990, when the council met for its annual 'external' session, this time in Bremen, the strains again rose dramatically to the surface. For years, Pöhl had been seeking a way of streamlining the council's cumbersome decision-making structure. Reunification seemed to provide an ideal opportunity. Ever since the Bank deutscher Länder's creation in 1948, each *Land* had sent one representative to the council. Pöhl regarded the system as increasingly unwieldy. Incorporation into united Germany of a further five *Länder* from East Germany would, if applied to the Bundesbank, lead to an administrative log-jam. If the system was continued, there would be no less than sixteen *Land* central bank presidents on the council – a development which would mean that the number of directorate members would have to be increased too. A 25- or 26-strong council would be unmanageable, Pöhl reasoned. Radical restructuring steps were needed.

In Bremen, Pöhl consequently suggested a cut in the number of *Land* representatives on the Bundesbank's top policy-making body, from eleven in West Germany to eight in united Germany. The plan was logical enough: one new East German representative would be taken on to the panel, and through regrouping of the West German *Land* central banks, the number of West German representatives would be cut to seven. Pöhl's ability to detect trouble seemed, however, once again to have been dulled. His suggestion immediately attracted the wrath of a group of seven *Land* central bank presidents, who accused the Bundesbank chief of trying to strengthen the directorate's influence over the *Länder*. For Bundesbank insiders with long memories, the proposals had striking similarities to those put forward in an ill-fated report in January 1970, recommending that the posts of *Land* central bank presidents should be abolished.[71] The 1970 report, never made public, proposed that the *Land* central banks be run by Bundesbank civil servants – in the same way that the provincial offices of the Reichsbank had been. The plan would have led to a marked centralisation of the Bundesbank's operations. It was never put into effect. After having attracted the combined opposition of the *Land* presidents and the directorate, the document was consigned to the archive files.

Faced with opposition from heavyweights on the council such as Reimut Jochimsen from North Rhine-Westphalia and Lothar Müller, the Bavarian central bank chief, Pöhl tried to enlist Kohl's support for the streamlining plan. But a letter from Pöhl to Kohl on 18 January 1991 went unanswered for many months. Jochimsen angered both Pöhl and Schlesinger by sending a rival letter to the chancellor on 21 January. This set out a proposal backed by the seven dissident *Land* central banks, urging that each German *Land* should continue to be represented on the central bank council by a regional central bank president. The Byzantine wrangling over the restructuring plan added to the complications bequeathed by Pöhl to his successor. A compromise government plan for nine regional central banks ran into heavy *Land* opposition at the end of 1991, but the plan was eventually due to go into effect at the end of 1992.

vii. Disaster in Brussels

In the catalogue of misunderstandings between Bonn and Frankfurt over German monetary union, the stormy events of 19 March 1991 occupy a special place. Pöhl was in Brussels, making an appearance before the economic committee of the European Parliament to talk about European monetary union. During off-the-cuff comments (in English, where he is always less circumspect than in German), Pöhl incautiously declared that East Germany had been ill-prepared for monetary union, and that the aftermath had been a 'disaster'.[72] The remarks were designed to back up Pöhl's views about moves towards a single European currency. Pöhl believed that, if the European Community proceeded too rapidly towards full monetary union, those countries which were not ready to take on the burdens of a hard currency would inevitably suffer from a widespread loss of competitiveness and closure of factories – just as East Germany had done. Transmitted to the international money markets by news agency reporters in the committee room, the comments however caused a sensation. The spotlight of the world's foreign exchanges immediately focused on discord between Bonn and Frankfurt – and the D-Mark fell several pfennigs against the dollar.

It had hardly been Pöhl's aim to weaken international confidence in the management of the German economy. But this was the result. Kohl, ever on the lookout for conspiracies, believed that Pöhl was deliberately trying to undermine him. Once the Brussels committee session was over, Pöhl – dismayed by the reaction on the foreign exchanges – took the highly unusual step of telephoning Dieter Vogel, the senior Bonn government spokesman and a former journalist colleague in Bonn. Pöhl explained how the remark had been unpremeditated, and that he had no intention of stirring up a public row. Kohl however was in no mood to accept any olive branches.[73] The chancellor believed that Pöhl had stepped beyond the bounds of mere independence; he was becoming downright troublesome.

Before an audience of bankers and industrialists meeting to discuss the progress of German unity at the chancellery the next day, Kohl subjected Pöhl to an unusual public reprimand. Pöhl sent Kohl a semi-contrite letter saying he 'regretted' the commotion, giving an unusually full explanation of what he had actually said in Brussels:

> The theme of my nearly two hours of discussion with deputies from the European Parliament was European, not German monetary union. In order to illustrate the problems which can arise in a monetary union between two strongly divergent economic areas, I put forward German monetary union as an extreme and drastic example. I expressedly said that I never disagreed with the political necessity for this, and that I did not criticise the government's decision. The result, none the less, was a 'disaster' . . .
>
> Under current conditions, by far the majority of enterprises in East Germany are not competitive – with all the consequences we now know, which were certainly foreseeable, although perhaps unavoidable. That is a 'disaster'. If I had foreseen the effect this would have, perhaps, I would have used another description.
>
> As you know, Chancellor, the Bundesbank and I personally have done everything in our power to make German monetary union possible – and thus to pave the way for German unity. We will carry on like this in future, and I ask you not to ascribe the affair in Brussels more importance than it really merits.[74]

The letter failed to heal the rift. At the end of March, Pöhl travelled to St Moritz with his family for an Easter skiing holiday. He spent much time dwelling on the affair, and reflected that his position was becoming dangerously exposed. The Brussels episode had been a relatively minor mishap, triggered by his own lack of prudence, as well as by his genuine misgivings over the way the D-Mark had been extended into eastern Germany. Kohl's irascible reaction had come as a shock. Pöhl concluded that if ever in the future he was to make a really serious policy error, he could expect no backing from the government. The Bundesbank president had ascended the monetary heights; but now, like Icarus, he was flying too close to the sun.

viii. A mind made up

Ever since the day of surprises in Berlin on 6 February 1990, Pöhl had been inching towards a decision to leave the Bundesbank. His mind was made up by a tragedy on 1 April 1991. After a glorious day of Alpine skiing during his Easter break, Pöhl was stunned to learn of the murder of his friend Detlev Rohwedder, a former Social Democrat state secretary at the economics ministry, gunned down by terrorists at his home in Düsseldorf. The two had been close colleagues during the Schmidt government years. Rohwedder had switched to a career in industry. During a successful decade, he had presided over the Ruhr steel group Hoesch. In 1990, at the request of the Kohl administration, Rohwedder was catapulted into one of the most important and thankless jobs in reunited Germany: that of chief executive of the Treuhand state holding company, the owner of the former East German state's sprawling collection of industrial and property assets. As the man charged with either privatising or closing down numerous enterprises from the bankrupt East German era, Rohwedder had already attracted a good deal of political flak; but he had been intelligent, talented and principled enough to take it in his stride.

The killing – by the Red Army Faction (RAF), the urban guerrilla grouping which had murdered several top members of the German establishment during the previous fifteen years – was a cold-blooded and senseless act of terrorism. Pöhl's wife Ulrike had been on particularly close terms with Rohwedder's elegant spouse Hergard. Pöhl knew that he, too, was one of the élite group of German policy-makers on the RAF 'hit list'. For some time, Pöhl had been growing restive with the tight security precautions with which he and his family had to live. Rohwedder's murder brought home to the Bundesbank president not just the intensity of the threat but also the futility of a top-flight career which might be snuffed out by an RAF bullet. Pöhl was worried above all about the strains on his family. Unsettled by the constant attention of bodyguards, Pöhl's young son had started to ask his father whether he would be the next victim.

Pöhl waited a month to tell his colleagues at the Bundesbank, and the politicians in Bonn, that he was quitting. The first to be let into the secret was his deputy Helmut Schlesinger, informed on Monday 6 May. Despite their differences in temperament and personality, Schlesinger was by far Pöhl's closest confidant at the Bundesbank. The older man was surprised by the news; with only slightly more than a year to go before his own planned retirement at the age of sixty-eight, Schlesinger had given up any hope of scaling the last Bundesbank summit. The next day, 7 May, Pöhl travelled to Bonn to inform Theo Waigel and President Richard von Weizsäcker;[75] Kohl was absent from Bonn that Tuesday afternoon, on his way to a meeting with political leaders in Bavaria, and so heard the news later from his finance minister. On 8 May, at their regular Wednesday meeting, Pöhl told the rest of the Bundesbank directorate.

If the chancellor and the Bundesbank president had enjoyed a better relationship, they would have found time to discuss the matter on 7 May. They did not in fact meet for another week. By then, Kohl had already made up his mind that Schlesinger would receive the job. The chancellor decided that the switch might even be beneficial, and was determined to make the best of it. Remarking that Pöhl was envious of the seven-figure salaries earned by the commercial bankers whose skyscrapers he could see from his Bundesbank office, a jovial Kohl declared later that Pöhl was simply leaving to earn more money.[76]

Although the news was not yet official, it was Germany's worst-kept secret. Considerable media speculation about the switch at the top of the Bundesbank coincided with a birthday party in Bonn. On the evening of 15 May, a few hours after meeting Kohl, Pöhl attended a festive dinner to celebrate the eightieth birthday of Karl Schiller, the former Social Democrat economics minister, who had been responsible at the beginning of the 1970s for plucking Pöhl out of journalism and into government service. On the menu was an excessive selection of indigestible speeches. Impatiently slumped into his chair, the Bundesbank president allowed his sardonic wit full flower as he listened to the dapper Jürgen Möllemann, the bombastic economics minister, launch into a self-laudatory address on the virtues of the government's *Aufschwung-Ost* ('Upswing East') programme to pour money into East Germany. In a wry aside, Pöhl remarked that the financing burdens placed on western Germany might well trigger a simultaneous *Neidergang-West* ('Downfall of the West').

Pöhl left the dinner early to prepare his resignation statement. Back in the Bundesbank's Frankfurt headquarters at 9.30 the following morning, Pöhl ran into Wilhelm Nölling, the Hamburg central bank president, on the way to the council meeting on the thirteenth floor. The two men had been friends within the SPD for years. They had fallen out badly over Nölling's notorious May 1990 newspaper interview over German monetary union. Although they had lately patched up their disagreement, relations remained tense. Travelling in the lift up to the council gathering, Pöhl told the astonished Nölling that he had considered resigning over the issue a year earlier.

As the meeting got under way, Pöhl outlined the mixture of reasons for his departure. He had already carried out the job longer than almost anyone in the Bundesbank's history. The burdens of office were growing heavier. He outlined the differences with the government over German unity. He mentioned the strain of the security precautions. In his capacity as the longest-serving president of the *Land* central banks, Kurt Nemitz, the Bremen *Landeszentralbank* chief, made an emotion-charged speech asking Pöhl to rethink his decision. During the last fortnight of soul-searching, Pöhl had been privately disappointed that neither Kohl nor Waigel had done anything to try to dissuade him from leaving.[77] Now, as Nemitz put forward the plea, Pöhl was grateful that it had been made, but adamant in rebutting it – as everyone around the table knew he would. Shortly afterwards, he strode before the cameras in the Bundesbank guest-house to announce his resignation. The Bundesbank president became one more victim of unity.

ix. The aftermath of unity

The consequences of German unity were paradoxical in the extreme. The D-Mark's transition across the Elbe represented both blessing and bane. Günter Mittag, who under Erich Honecker had occupied the post of economic supremo in the East German Politbüro, had been one of the most feared men in East Germany until the fall of the Wall. For years Mittag had been at the helm of East Germany's ruinous policy of concentrating economic resources on giant state-owned *Kombinate*. The tsar of the conglomerates had been a firm upholder of East German sovereignty; a masterful propagator of boasts about East Germany's industrial prowess; a much-vaunted negotiator in wheeling-and-dealing with the west. Any East German courageous or foolish enough to talk of the possibility of reunification in Mittag's presence would have been arrested and confined at the pleasure of the secret police. After unification, Mittag underwent a metamorphosis; his dictatorship was nothing but tinpot. He declared in 1991 that, without unity, 'East Germany would have faced an economic catastrophe with unforeseeable social consequences.' Claiming that he had made an attempt in 1989 to persuade Honecker to change economic course, Mittag proclaimed that he had been aware before the Wall fell that 'East Germany, on its own, was not capable of surviving for long.'[78]

Unity also changed Helmut Kohl. His belief in the inevitability and justice of German unification had never flagged throughout his political career; and he seized the opportujity when it came with courage and decisiveness. Yet, installed at the pinnacle of German politics, enshrined in the history books as 'the chancellor of German Unity', Kohl failed to master the economic consequences of unification. In a moment of candour, he once admitted, in 1988, that he would probably never live to see the two parts of the nation brought together again. Like so many, he was unprepared. For Kohl, success and failure came at the same time.

The Germans who lived east of the Elbe were certainly taken aback by the scale of the transition wrought by the arrival of the D-Mark and the entry of market economics. Before the fall of the Wall, the East German workforce totalled almost 10 million; by 1992, the total had shrunk to 6 million, of whom 1.4 million were unemployed, and 1 million were on short-time or in work creation schemes. Massive western transfers and support measures failed to spark the self-fuelling recovery expected by the politicians in Bonn. With gross domestic product increasing in western Germany by 3 per cent in 1991, and slumping 30 per cent in the east, the whole of Germany registered zero economic growth that year. In 1992, although recovery finally got under way in the east, growth in the west fell sharply. Germany was revealed as an economic giant – with giant problems. However, the French finance ministry, watching these developments from the Seine, was aware that the difficulties would probably turn out to be only temporary. In a confidential memorandum at the end of 1990 on the result of German unification, it forecast that the Germans would soon win back their strength:

> The first paradox of unification is that it will result in the first instance in a weakening of the German economy ... Once these problems are surmounted, at the end of the century Germany will be – even more than today – the dominant economic power in Europe.[79]

Fears of German dominance added impetus to French efforts to secure a commitment from Chancellor Kohl for European monetary union. By forging a single European currency, other countries would gain entry into the Bundesbank's monetary domain, and the Germans would serve notice that, in spite of unity, they were still 'good Europeans' after all. Kohl agreed at the Maastricht summit in December 1991 to a firm timetable for European monetary union – a step which would spell the demise of the D-Mark. The chancellor adhered firmly to his favourite adage that 'German unity and European unity are two sides of the same coin'. He did not foresee that the two sides of the coin could both become tarnished at once.

9

The Quest for Europe's Money

In a unified monetary area, monetary policy and other central
banking matters can be executed only from a central point.
  Hjalmar Schacht, Reichsbank president, 1938[1]

I would like to put the question of how the intended 'internal
market relationships' across the Common Market can be
realised if, within the individual regions of this large internal
market, currencies keep fluctuating? . . . Our next goal
must be to make the European Economic Community an
island of monetary stability. That would also brake
inflationary tendencies in the other industrialised countries.
  Otmar Emminger, Bundesbank directorate member, 1965[2]

No one is ready to give up the stable Deutsche Mark for an
unstable currency. That is absolutely self-evident.
  Helmut Kohl, German chancellor, 1991[3]

The elusive dream of European economic and monetary union
(Emu) is almost as old as the European Community itself. The aim
of irrevocably fixing exchange rates between European currencies,
accompanied by continent-wide harmonisation of economic policies, has always been much more than a mere financial stratagem.
The idea springs from a multitude of motives: to improve economic
cohesion, to heal post-war political wounds, to shield Europe from
currency turbulence abroad, to promote a wider sense of European
identity and, in latter years, to increase industrial competitiveness
compared with the US and Japan. Behind the various European
Community exchange rate stabilisation schemes which have
unfolded during the last thirty years has stood another common
theme. European monetary integration has been conceived as a
powerful political tool to help maintain post-war Germany firmly
and securely in the western community of nations. There is a neat
and successful symmetry in place here. By providing the D-Mark

as the currency anchor across the whole of Europe, Germany itself has been anchored to the west.

The vision of Emu was first promulgated by the EC Commission in 1962, four years after the Treaty of Rome came into force setting up the six-member Community. Following the success of the European Payments Union, the early post-war clearing mechanism for financing European trade, monetary union among European states seemed a natural addition to the institutional arrangements of the Bretton Woods exchange rate system. It was the logical way forward for a continent desirous of assembling a new order based on multilateral economic cooperation. The turmoil caused by the growing US balance of payments deficit during the 1960s however weakened and then destroyed Bretton Woods, pushing monetary union well down the list of European priorities. As the world switched over to floating exchange rates in the early 1970s, the goal slid beneath the breaking waves of monetary unrest, and was lost from view. Yet it was never completely forgotten.

At the end of the 1980s, with the EC's original membership of six doubled to twelve, the Emu objective was reinstated as part of efforts to strengthen the Community's '1992 programme' to build a genuine common market across Europe. The creative forces of free movement of goods, people and capital, so the proponents of the scheme declared, could never be completely unleashed as long as eleven different national currencies* were circulating. For the Community to reach its full potential, national currencies had to be replaced by a single European money. Hans-Dietrich Genscher, the West German foreign minister, gave the idea considerable political impetus in a discussion paper launched in February 1987. The effect of the 'single market' in intensifying the search for European integration was amplified by the dramatic events in the east between 1989 and 1991. The collapse of communism, the unification of Germany and the break-up of the Soviet Union provided further catalysts for change. As a result of all this, since 1990, the quest for European monetary union has been conducted in tandem with a bid to realise something much less clearly defined: European political union.

Since Germany is Europe's pivotal power, Europe will move towards such a union only at a pace to which the Germans agree.

---

* Monetary union already exists between Belgium and Luxembourg.

Germany has the capability to accelerate the process, or to slow it down; to bring it to fruition, or, if the Germans so desire, to stop it ever happening.

If a single European currency were adopted by all EC countries, the D-Mark would disappear, along with the British pound, the French franc, the Italian lira and all other national currencies. The Community's planned supranational central bank would become Europe's pivotal monetary institution – the role at present played by the Bundesbank.

Through membership of the European Monetary System, Germany's EC partners have already effectively transferred to Frankfurt decision-making over monetary affairs. In European monetary union, rather than losing independence, these countries would regain power by helping to influence the operations of the EC central bank. The principal net loser, though, by a wide margin, would be Germany itself.[4] At a time of serious strains in the newly reforged nation, the German electorate is being asked to accept the dethronement of the currency which has become Germany's national symbol, and the emasculation of the institution which controls it. Precisely at such a time of upheaval, the Germans regard the prospect with extreme reluctance.

German monetary union and European monetary union are different in essential respects. Yet, as part of a political process unfolding across the continent, they are inextricably intertwined. Monetary union in Germany was an experiment on the scale of a nation. The aim of establishing a single currency across the whole of Europe is much more ambitious – and fraught with still greater risks. Under German monetary union, the Bundesbank extended its sovereignty eastwards; under European monetary union, it would give it up. At the time of German monetary union, the Bonn government clung to the belief that it would somehow enhance prospects for European monetary union. The Bundesbank's view was that the former was likely to impede the latter. The Bundesbank has turned out to be right. German monetary union helped spawn the fresh attempt at European monetary union; but Germany's post-unity difficulties pose an increasing threat to the chances of its realisation.

i. At the crossroads of Europe

At the European Community's summit meeting in December 1991, one all-encompassing issue dominated the agenda. The Community was called upon to amend the Treaty of Rome to establish political and monetary union among the states of western Europe. The gathering was held in a supremely appropriate setting. As a location for contorted international diplomacy, Maastricht, an elegant city on the Maas (Meuse) river at the southern tip of the Netherlands, offers unrivalled geographical advantages. Maastricht is the capital of the Dutch province of Limburg, a sliver of land only six miles wide at its narrowest point. Comfortably sandwiched between its neighbours Belgium and Germany, the city sits at the crossroads of the continent.

Limburg's long list of rulers registers the peaks and troughs of Europe's oscillating balance of power. A former Roman province, Limburg blossomed 1200 years ago as part of the Frankish empire under the reign of Charlemagne. During the seventeenth, eighteenth and nineteenth centuries, France and Spain, Austria and Prussia, the Netherlands and Belgium played out their power struggles here. Between 1848 and German unification under Bismarck in 1871, Dutch Limburg was a member of the German Confederation, before afterwards becoming part of the Netherlands.[5]

The remains of Maastricht's fortified walls still stand. But today the city's garrisons have been replaced by chic fashion boutiques, and restaurants draw multilingual tourists from the prosperous reaches of Europe. On the second weekend of December, Maastricht was the meeting place not of armies but of politicians, brought together in a circular conference room, listening through headphones to the tones of interpreters. The summit venue was Province House: a brick building looking like a lavish municipal library set on an island in the Maas, usually home to the Limburg provincial government. As the heads of government of the European community's twelve member states arrived at the military section of Maastricht airport, the city was decked out with Christmas decorations and the flags of many nations.[6]

The event represented the culmination of months of work. It brought to a close the Netherlands government's controversy-ridden six months' presidency of the EC Council. Only a year earlier, two inter-governmental conferences on political and monetary union had started in Brussels, under an initiative launched by Chancellor Kohl and French president François Mitterand. Now, the twelve summiteers had their eyes fixed on the highest of objectives. The centrepiece of their deliberations was a radical project to establish by the end of the century a single European currency run by a European central bank: innovations which would mark the renewal of Europe.

Draft texts on a political and monetary union treaty had been exhaustively debated by myriads of ministers and officials in pre-summit sessions. They were attempting to build on the lessons of the past. Europe had taken its first steps towards a similar objective at the end of the 1960s. In 1970, the then six EC governments formally adopted a portentous monetary plan laid down under a committee led by Pierre Werner, the Luxembourg prime minister.[7] The aim had been to accomplish step-by-step harmonisation of economic policies, and to complete the process with monetary union in 1980. The plan was killed off by the exchange rate instability 1971–73. The idea was formally abandoned at a meeting of heads of government in Paris in December 1974.

The damage wrought to the world monetary system by the gyrations of the dollar ruined the aspirations contained in the Werner Report. It did however furnish western Europe with a considerable incentive to seek greater monetary independence from the US. The European Community started the exchange rate 'snake' in 1972 to dampen fluctuations among European currencies.[8] The 'snake' lived through much turbulence and frequent realignments. After Britain's short-lived membership in 1972, France departed from the system in 1974, re-joined the next year, and then left again after another bout of unrest hit the French franc in 1976. But, after another round of dollar instability towards the end of the 1970s, Europe responded to the trans-Atlantic challenge by upgrading the 'snake' and developing the European Monetary System as a more institutionalised zone of foreign exchange stability. The architects of the scheme were West German chancellor Helmut Schmidt and French president Valéry Giscard d'Estaing.[9] All nine EC members except Britain became members of the exchange rate mechanism of the EMS when the scheme started operations in March 1979.

The EMS was part of what Schmidt liked to call, in later years, his 'grand strategy for integrating Europe'.[10] In 1987, Schmidt revealed that a vital, though unspoken, reason behind the creation of the EMS was his wish to provide an additional 'anchor' for West Germany's ties to western Europe. Since the time of Konrad Adenauer, the desire to bind the country into an irreversible commitment towards the west has been one of the more permanent features of post-war European foreign policy. The aim was however seldom explicitly spelled out. Precisely because the strength of that commitment has sometimes been doubted, it is never publicly called into question.

The EMS at first attracted intense suspicion from the Bundesbank. The central bank feared being drawn into massive automatic intervention commitments to shore up weak currencies. As under the Bretton Woods arrangements, the Bundesbank believed that the EMS would be yet another inflationary attempt at sustaining an over-rigid exchange rate regime. But during the 1980s, the EMS became a permanent and highly successful feature of the international monetary scene. The system proved its worth by helping the stabilisation of the D-Mark during 1980–81 when the German currency was unusually weak. Additionally, as other countries became far more wedded to rigorous German-style economic policies, inflation rates started to converge, and exchange rate realignments – before the EMS upheavals of September 1992 – became far less frequent.[11]

The EMS helped produce more stable conditions for European business. Two aspects of the system did not, however, live up to expectations; and, in both of these, the Bundesbank played an important role. Schmidt and Giscard originally planned that the EMS should be built around the European Currency Unit (ECU), the Community's composite accounting unit which was foreseen as eventually growing into a fully fledged currency. When EC heads of government formally decided to set up the EMS in December 1978, the ECU was proclaimed as the 'central point' of the new system.[12] Here, the architects of the EMS miscalculated. The pivot of the EMS became not the ECU, but the D-Mark.[13] Karl Otto Pöhl, who in his capacity as Bundesbank vice-president had played an important role in setting up the EMS in 1978–79, showed considerable satisfaction when he looked back in 1991 at the Bundesbank's accomplishment: 'The Bundesbank turned the original concept [for the EMS] on its head by making the strongest currency the yardstick for the system.'[14]

The goal of setting up a European Monetary Fund (EMF) also failed to be realised. This institution was foreseen as a European-style International Monetary Fund. It would pool part of member countries' foreign exchange reserves, subsume other Community institutions such as the European Investment Bank and provide loans to states in balance of payments difficulties. Particularly wary of losing control over Germany's monetary reserves, the Bundesbank all along opposed establishing the EMF.[15] The plan for the new institution – originally designed to be put into effect as early as 1981 – was quietly dropped.[16]

Simply by surviving for much longer than its initial critics had predicted, the EMS started to look like an embryo which could grow into monetary union. In the mid-1980s, the concept of a single European currency was given fresh impetus by Jacques Delors, the former French finance minister who became president of the EC Commission in 1985.[17] His roots firmly planted in the catholic Socialist trade union movement, Delors won renown in 1983 for introducing unpopular austerity policies in Paris to steer the new French Socialist government out of its early economic difficulties. After three devaluations of the French franc in the Socialists' first two years in office, France switched to accepting fully the disciplines of EMS membership. Ending President Mitterrand's early flirtation with reflationary policies, and switching towards German-style anti-inflation rectitude, represented a milestone not just for France, but for the whole Community. The Paris government realised that France would achieve Germany's full respect only if it succeeded in eradicating the inflation mentality which had pervaded French economic life since before the Second World War.

Afterwards, ensconced at the EC commission, Delors was determined that France's monetary virtue should be extended to other countries; and that virtue should be properly rewarded. Delors believed that monetary cooperation represented the key to wider political integration. Over the longer term, Delors reasoned, it was unacceptable that other EC members should live under a system in which one country – Germany – effectively set monetary policy for the rest of the continent. Concrete action towards monetary union, Delors believed, would not only improve the functioning of the Community's post-1993 'single market'. It would also mark a giant political step forward. Additionally, by taking away the dominance of the D-Mark, it would represent a more equitable method of distributing economic power.

As part of Delors' overall strategy, the goal of monetary union was enshrined in the Single European Act which came into effect in 1987.[18] Preparations for monetary union started in earnest with the setting up in 1988 of a study group to examine the matter, chaired by Delors and composed mainly of EC central bank governors. The Delors report, published in 1989, proposed a three-stage process for moving to monetary union, on the firm condition that countries would first have to show a sizeable degree of economic convergence.[19]

The Emu project gained considerable momentum during the hectic count-down to German unity in 1990. Following a dictum laid down by Adenauer, Chancellor Kohl insisted that German unity must be part of a wider union of Europe. The precept was both morally appealing and politically shrewd. Many of Germany's European neighbours, above all France, were uneasy about the renaissance of a reunited nation of 80 million people. As the merger between the two unequal Germanies got under way, Bonn urgently needed to reassure the rest of the continent that it would remain a reliable and cooperative partner. Holding out the promise of a single currency was the best way of convincing Germany's partners of its goodwill.

The Bundesbank gave the project its general backing; since the policy had been given the imprimatur of the Bonn government and its most important European partners, the central bank could hardly do otherwise. Its misgivings, however, were plain to see; if Emu ever became a reality, the Bundesbank would be the principal loser. Karl Otto Pöhl succinctly summed up the position in June 1989, shortly after the Delors committee report was unveiled. As the dominant European central bank within the European Monetary System, he remarked: 'We can live very well with the status quo.'[20] More than two years before anxieties over the future of the D-Mark started to make headlines in Germany, Pöhl correctly predicted that the proposed relinquishment of the currency would spark a storm of complaint:

> If the idea spread and the German population understood what it [European Monetary Union] is about – namely, that it centres on their money, and that decisions on it would be

taken not by the Bundesbank, but by a new institution – then I would imagine that considerable resistance might arise.

When German unification led to signs of accelerated moves towards European Monetary Union, Helmut Schlesinger, Pöhl's then deputy, voiced public scepticism about the feasibility of carrying out both undertakings at once.[21] The Bundesbank realised more quickly than the politicians in Bonn that the plan for European monetary union was above all a means of undermining German power. Accurately summing up the political power-play with the Paris government Pöhl complained consistently that France was trying to 'get a grip on the D-Mark'. As Wilhelm Nölling, president of the *Landeszentralbank* in Hamburg, put it in early 1991: 'We should be under no illusions – the present controversy over the new European monetary order is about power, influence and the pursuit of national interests.'[22]

Hans Tietmeyer, newly nominated as the Bundesbank's vice-president, voiced the Bundesbank's misgivings with exceptional bluntness in a statement in 1991 which markedly toughened the Bundesbank's pre-Maastricht position:

> German unity should not slow down the European unity process. But neither should it speed up the tempo of European monetary integration. It is problematic that attempts are being made to put political pressure on Germany . . . United Germany has much to lose in the forthcoming reordering of European currencies, namely one of the most successful and best monetary constitutions in the world.[23]

Tietmeyer's remarks broke the long-standing taboo against German politicians and officials speaking about European integration in anything except the most positive terms. As the one member of the Bundesbank's senior hierarchy who had earned Chancellor Kohl's unqualified confidence, Tietmeyer knew that his words would make an impact. They represented a harbinger of the virulent debate which lay ahead. As the heads of government settled down for their deliberations in Maastricht, a basic question hung over the conference table. Did the Germans really want to give up the D-Mark?

ii. A lopsided agreement

The decisive meeting at Maastricht took place before the summit had even started. Normally, at such gatherings, François Mitterrand was the last participant to arrive. This time, he turned up early. It was a clear indication of a pre-emptive strike. On the evening of Sunday 8 December, the French president met veteran Italian prime minister Giulio Andreotti, the only summit participant who had been present at the setting up of the European Monetary System thirteen years earlier. Both nearing the end of long and tortuous political careers, the two leaders, master-practitioners at the art of finessing their opponents, were well known for the subtlety of their manoeuvrings. The plan they conceived over dinner at Mitterrand's out-of-town hotel did full justice to their reputations. The deal they had hatched would, they believed, make European monetary union inevitable by the end of the century. And there was nothing the Germans could do about it.

During months of pre-summit meetings, European finance ministers had agreed that Emu would be based on strict anti-inflation criteria. Monetary orthodoxy would be given priority over other macroeconomic targets like lowering unemployment. There was also accord that the proposed European central bank should be independent from governments and geared wholeheartedly to achieving price stability – ingredients which were vital for winning German support. A prime stumbling block had however been the refusal of the Bonn government and the Bundesbank to accept a firm timetable for moving to Emu. This was construed in Paris and Rome, as well as in other capitals, as implying that Germany's political commitment to the scheme was less than rock solid.

To repair this fundamental flaw, Mitterrand and Andreotti chose an ingenious formula. They proposed making monetary union obligatory in 1999 for all EC countries which had fulfilled a set of rigorous economic targets. Budget deficits had to be limited to 3 per cent of a country's gross domestic product, while the overall stock of public sector debt had to be brought down to 60 per cent of gdp.*[24] In their inflation and interest rate performances, only countries which had achieved levels close to those of the most stable members of the Community would be allowed to participate in monetary union.[25] If a majority of EC member countries had

* See appendix.

attained these criteria by 1997, union could start by that date; otherwise, it could go ahead in 1999, even with a minority of states.

By associating a firm starting date with tough criteria to ensure monetary and fiscal rectitude, the plan was designed to appeal to everyone. It satisfied countries like France and Italy, which wanted an unambiguous political signal in favour of Emu. It met the objections of members like Britain and Germany which were wary about proceeding too fast towards monetary union unless the economic conditions were right. Above all, it fulfilled a key requirement of the Bundesbank and the Bonn government, which had argued for months that not all EC member states could simultaneously accede to Emu. European monetary union had to be 'two speed'; otherwise, it would not happen at all. Low inflation countries could proceed along a 'fast track' and join as soon as monetary union was established. Higher inflation countries in southern Europe would have to wait. In the EMS, full membership had been restricted to those countries willing to stick to German-style *Stabilitätspolitik*, and it had worked well.[26] If Emu had any chance of functioning, it would have to follow the same principle of refusing membership to the laggards in the inflation stakes until their economic performances had improved.

The next day, 9 December, the Franco-Italian compromise was presented to the other EC leaders. As Dutch police floated past the Province House windows in patrol boats, guarding against the threat of terrorist attacks, the twelve leaders gave the monetary union plan their blessing. As a pivotal element, the heads of government decided to set up a new 'cohesion fund' to channel resources from higher income countries to the EC's four poorer members, Spain, Portugal, Ireland and Greece. The financing mechanism was part of efforts to promote structural changes in EC economies to help all members up to the challenges of a single currency. In view of the economic divergences between the north and south of Europe, Mediterranean states would be plainly unable to accept the disciplines of monetary union unless their economies were first brought more into line with those in the north. The plan for 'cohesion money' was destined to spur political opposition among the biggest contributors to the EC, above all Germany and Britain. If a single currency were to become reality everyone suspected that large sums of money would be required.

At a meeting with journalists late on Monday night at the Golden

Tulip hotel next to the conference centre, Kohl was enthusiastic about the breakthrough. He hailed the economic performance criteria as assuring that European monetary union would be established on the soundest possible basis.[27] He expressed jubilation that Germany's idea for setting up an independent central bank had been fully accepted. Prime minister John Major was still stoutly defending Britain's position of keeping its options open on whether or not to become part of Emu. But Kohl declared how much he had been impressed by Major's quiet, determined performance, which he colourfully contrasted with the 'hammer-swinging' style of Margaret Thatcher. Britain would join in 1997, at the first possible date for proceeding to a single currency, the chancellor proclaimed. With Europe firmly embarked on the road to unity, Kohl believed that not even the British would want to be left out.

Kohl's fervour about the monetary deal was not shared by more cautious members of the large German government delegation. They were worried about a growing drumbeat of opposition on the home front. For months, German newspapers had been ignoring the question of the possible replacement of the D-Mark by a European currency – even though the subject had been on the political agenda for more than two years. Belatedly, the German media had woken up to the story – and, for several days, had been sounding the alarm about the threat to monetary stability. German officials in Maastricht were concerned that a campaign against monetary union had been launched simultaneously by the *Bild-Zeitung*, Germany's most popular daily newspaper, and by *Der Spiegel*, the best-selling news magazine. The two publications normally operate at different ends of the political spectrum: the raucous tabloid *Bild* is unashamedly conservative, while *Der Spiegel* leans heavily to the left. Yet the editor of *Bild*, Hans Hermann Tiedje, and the publisher of *Der Spiegel*, Rudolf Augstein, were united in their criticism of Kohl's apparent readiness to give away the D-Mark. The front cover of *Der Spiegel* – on prominent display in the press room at Maastricht – read '*Angst um die D-Mark*' (Fear for the D-Mark).

One German official at Maastricht said that the chancellor had to take seriously the warnings in the newspapers. 'He knows the power of the *Bild-Zeitung*.' Another Kohl adviser declared that the outbreak of worried headlines made it imperative that Kohl secured agreement on bringing the European central bank to Frankfurt –

to assure the public that, even if a European currency were introduced, the Germans would still be in control. 'It's a time bomb which could explode under Kohl,' he commented.

The Maastricht agreement did, however, meet several long-standing, crucial German conditions. In the legal statutes for the EC central bank – the area where Bonn had anticipated most opposition from other countries – the EC had agreed that the new institution would be virtually a clone of the Bundesbank. In recognition of Germany's success in achieving price stability, the central bank would be deliberately set up as an imitation of the Bundesbank. Six directorate members (including the president and vice-president) would be joined on the governing council by the presidents of the central banks of participating EC member states. The central bank would be owned by national central banks – just as the Bank deutscher Länder had been in the hands of the *Länder* central banks. Independence of the members of the governing council and the directorate would be statutorily guaranteed. Those EC countries (the majority) whose central banks were not independent of governments would have to change their own central banking laws in line with this stipulation.

In some ways, indeed, the proposed legislation for the European central bank contained tougher safeguards than those in the Bundesbank Law. The main aim of the EC central bank would be to maintain 'price stability'. This was an unambiguous statement of anti-inflation intent. It contrasted with the less clear cut phrase in the Bundesbank Law committing the German central bank to 'safeguarding the currency' – an expression capable of being interpreted as giving priority to exchange rate stability.* Furthermore, the EC central bank would have no power to bail out the government by granting credits to the public sector. The Bundesbank Law, on the other hand, allows the central bank to make loans to the public sector, subject to certain narrow limits. In the crucial field of exchange rate policy, the EC council of ministers would have the final decision. But in the case of the Bundesbank, the government, too, has the final say over exchange rate policy.

Despite satisfaction about these advances, officials in Kohl's entourage believed that opposition in Germany was likely to grow rather than diminish in coming months. Their doubts were increased by the chancellor's noticeable failure to secure agreement

* See chapter 6.

on one important condition at the Maastricht meeting. In public statements before the summit, Kohl had insisted he would not agree steps towards monetary union unless there was a matching accord on European political union. In fact, compared with the concrete terms of the treaty on monetary union, the Maastricht summit agreed only vague steps forward towards a genuine federal Europe. In fields like defence, social policy, immigration and powers for the European parliament – all areas where Germany had been insisting on progress – Maastricht saw only modest advances. As was pointed out to Kohl with increasing virulence in the months ahead, the Maastricht accord looked lopsided.

At his hotel press conference near midnight on 9 December, Kohl rejected with surprising vigour the idea that the planned new European currency should be called the Ecu (for European Currency Unit) as the French and Italians had suggested. There would be years to decide this, Kohl said. The first part of the text of the new treaty stated that the EC's single currency would be called 'the Ecu'. However, confirming Germany's reluctance to accept that the Maastricht accord would lead to automatic abandonment of the D-Mark, Kohl affirmed: 'You don't baptise a child before it is born.'[28]

Peter-Wilhelm Schlüter, a European monetary expert from the international section of the Bundesbank, attended the Maastricht summit as the central bank's official observer in the German delegation. Schlüter, one of the few Bundesbank officials to sport a beard, is a keen supporter of European monetary union. He raised his eyebrows on hearing Kohl's anti-Ecu remarks at the Golden Tulip. In addition to his European monetary duties, Schlüter is the head of the Bundesbank's arts and entertainment group, responsible for laying on theatre shows and brass band concerts in Frankfurt. Chancellor Kohl's midnight display of misgivings about the Ecu was a portent of ructions to come; it represented the first, somewhat surreal, act in a memorable and long-running piece of German political theatre.

iii. 'Such a lovely couple'

On 11 December, the day after the end of the Maastricht meeting, the *Bild-Zeitung* chose a melodramatic headline to sum up the outcome.[29] '*Das Ende der Mark*' (The End of the Mark), it proclaimed on the front page, next to a picture of a bashful-looking Kohl tenderly clutching a larger-than-life version of the prized coin. 'Helmut, you were such a lovely couple,' ran the caption. An editorial went on to the offensive: 'The days of the D-Mark are numbered . . . This is praised as progress in Bonn, but the population thinks otherwise . . . It is the fault of those who cannot explain how the Ecu will bring any advantages . . . The end of the D-Mark could be damned expensive.' The newspaper prominently reported the suggestion by Theo Waigel, the finance minister, that the new European currency should not be called the Ecu, but the 'Euro-Mark'. In *Der Spiegel* that week, Rudolf Augstein voiced the opinion that Germany's EC partners, jealous of the country's new-found power, had conspired to tie down the country 'like Gulliver'.[30]

Kohl's vulnerability to criticism was heightened by his abject failure to win approval from EC partners for full-scale political union. In a speech only ten days before the Maastricht conference, Kohl set down his conditions for the summit with great care.

> Political union and economic and monetary union are insepar-
> ably linked. The one is the unconditional complement of the
> other. We can and will not give up sovereignty over monetary
> policies if political union remains a 'castle in the air'.[31]

Set against these German expectations, 'castle in the air' was a good description of the relatively low-key commitment to political union which emerged from Maastricht.

Kohl's statements on the need for political as well as monetary union had been fully backed by the Bundesbank. In a declaration in September 1990, the Bundesbank pointed out: 'A monetary union is an irrevocably sworn cofraternity – "all for one and one for all" – which, if it is to prove durable, requires, judging from past experience, even closer links in the form of a comprehensive political union.'[32] The statement added that 'an early irrevocable fixing of exchange rates and the transfer of monetary policy powers to Community institutions would involve considerable risks to monetary stability.'

The Bundesbank statement was the work of Hans Tietmeyer, the directorate member for international monetary affairs. Underlining how his influence had spread at the Bundesbank since he joined at the beginning of 1990, Tietmeyer's draft, drawn up in the late summer of 1990, was approved practically without change by the other members of the Bundesbank council.[33]

Hard-nosed economic logic, not any sentimental attachment to the ideals of a federal Europe, dictated the Bundesbank's views on the importance of political union. It knew that welding together a fully fledged European monetary bloc was likely to be practicable only if there was a unified system for allocating fiscal resources. Monetary union, the Bundesbank believed, required common budgetary and tax policies, as well as complete solidarity among tax-payers in different regions of the currency area. These were conditions which the Bundesbank held to be virtually unattainable. Although a firm supporter of greater European monetary cooperation, Tietmeyer was highly sceptical about Emu's chances of success. His attitude had been moulded by his earlier experience at the Bonn economics ministry of helping prepare Germany's position on the 1970 Werner Report. Tietmeyer and Schlesinger were also following, with remarkable consistency, the line the Bundesbank had taken thirty years previously when Emu and a European central bank had first been mooted by the European Commission. In 1963, Karl Blessing, the first Bundesbank president, set down his objections with the same arguments used in 1992:

> The final goal of the Commission is a European monetary union ... As a European, I would be ready to approve of European monetary union and to accept a centrally directed federal central banking system; as a responsible central banking practitioner, and a realist, I cannot however avoid pointing out the difficulties which stand in the way. A common currency and a federal central banking system are only feasible if, apart from a common trade policy, there is also a common finance and budget policy, a common economic policy, a common social and wage policy – a common policy all round. In brief, this would only happen if there was a [European] federal state with a European parliament with legislative powers in respect of all member countries.[34]

After analysing the aftermath of German monetary union, the Bundesbank could draw on another cautionary experience to back up its Emu viewpoint. In a lecture in Rotterdam in November 1991, a month before the Maastricht talks, Schlesinger forcefully laid down the gospel.[35] History had shown, the Bundesbank president said, that monetary union needed an accompanying political commitment to iron out economic and fiscal discrepancies within the currency area.[36] Schlesinger's basic worry was the same as that articulated by Pöhl when he made his notorious 'disaster' remark about German monetary union in Brussels seven months previously.* The new Bundesbank president, however, put his concern a great deal more diplomatically:

> A monetary union will prove permanent only if there is a dominant political will to take social measures to deal with the serious economic effects . . . In the last resort, this calls for a political union too.

In their hypotheses on the result of too hasty a move towards Emu, Schlesinger, Tietmeyer and Pöhl were all making fundamentally the same point. They were worried about the economic effects on weaker countries – and also about the reverberations in Germany. Permanently fixing exchange rates between countries of different structure and performance would remove an essential element of flexibility in their economic relationships. Economic adjustments could no longer be made by exchange rate changes. So they would have to be carried out through alterations in costs and output, as the less well-off nations adapted suddenly to a hard currency.

The outcome had already been seen in East Germany. Similarly, binding sterling to the D-Mark in October 1990 subjected Britain to a milder form of the same unpleasant competitive stresses. On a Community-wide scale, this would confront the better-off nations with large demands for funds to compensate for problems in poorer EC countries. The volumes required to accompany Emu would add to the large payments being channelled to East Germany. The main country to be asked to foot the bill would be, as always, Germany. At a time of already great strain on German fiscal policy, this, according to the Bundesbank, would be simply unacceptable.

iv. 'Nothing will come of Emu'

Before Maastricht, the Bundesbank had had plenty of practice in

* See chapter 8.

marshalling its arguments over European monetary union. But the debate had always been theoretical. Men like Pöhl had seen the potential threat several years previously. But they failed to recognise the acuteness of the danger until it was virtually too late. Like the rest of Germany, the Bundesbank had been preoccupied for too many months by the drama of reunification. In its tussle with the government over the terms for German monetary union, the central bank had already seen how its monetary wishes could be overridden by the force of political expediency. None the less, the result of the Netherlands summit took it by surprise.

Confronted with the growing attention paid towards Emu from the late 1980s onwards, the Bundesbank had changed its tactics on several occasions. Originally, the bank believed that proposals for European monetary union were not practicable, and would collapse under the weight of their own contradictions. After the creation of the Delors committee in 1988, and the delivery of its report a year later, the Bundesbank realised that the plans had to be taken seriously. Realising that outright opposition to Emu would be sterile and counter-productive, the Bundesbank opted for a more subtle line of assault. If the bank could not bring down the Emu from outside, it had to try to disable the edifice from within.

As the Bundesbank's Otmar Issing put it:

> For a long period, we said nothing will come of Emu. We have the better monetary policies. Why should we take over a worse currency? Then we saw that if we remained on the sidelines, we would be confronted with difficulties. So we decided to advance to the head of the movement, with the aim of making the Bundesbank's position clear at a European level.[37]

The Bundesbank's chosen method was to give ostensible backing to the aim of European monetary union, but to seek to obstruct it by posing conditions which would simply not be acceptable to the other countries. It voiced constant concern about the dangers of tampering with the Bundesbank's autonomy. This was backed up by warnings that monetary union could only take place if there were guarantees that the new system would be at least as stable as the one based on the D-Mark. In June 1989, Pöhl spelled out that, if a European inter-governmental conference on monetary union was called too early, it would risk being badly prepared. This could split the Community and lead to failure of the Emu ideal – a prospect which the Bundesbank, in private, did not find repugnant.[38]

In his public statements, Chancellor Kohl always gave the Bundesbank's line full support. In January 1988 – when the Paris government under prime minister Jacques Chirac was pressing for an EC central bank to stop the EMS becoming unduly dominated by the D-Mark – Kohl issued a brusque public rebuttal of French ideas.[39] In March 1990, when momentum towards German unity was growing towards full speed, the chancellor was again adamant that European monetary union would only be feasible on Bundesbank-style conditions.[40] The well-honed phrases of German political rhetoric, however, generally serve to hide rather than expose differences; the true signs of discord are found between the lines.

Despite Kohl's welter of supportive statements, the Bundesbank had become increasingly fearful of a political deal over monetary union between the French and German governments. One signal of Kohl's susceptibility was the chancellor's statement in April 1990, in a joint declaration with President Mitterand, that economic and monetary union would 'become effective' on 1 January 1993.[41] The Franco-German pronouncement was worked out in secret between the federal chancellery and the Elysée palace without the knowledge of the Bundesbank. Although the declaration provided the political impetus behind the amendment to the Treaty of Rome which was eventually agreed at Maastricht, it gave an unrealistic impression of the speed at which Emu could become a reality. The significance of the statement was political. It improved Germany's credentials as a supporter of European union during a hectic phase of international diplomacy over German unification.

The Bundesbank was worried that, at a late-night EC summit bargaining session, the chancellor might forget altogether about the primacy of *Stabilitätspolitik*.[42] At Maastricht, the Bundesbank's fears were realised: but the outcome emerged in a way which it had not expected. At the Netherlands summit, Kohl's emotional need to show the other EC partners that the Germans were still 'good Europeans' was as strong as ever. Additionally, Bonn's own bargaining position had been weakened by the sharp deterioration in the public sector budget induced by German unification. The main reason for the unexpected Maastricht accord centred, however, not on Germany but on its partners. By accepting Germany's own maximalist conditions for the EC central bank, the Maastricht players laid back down on the table trump cards taken from Germany's own hand.

After his departure from the Bundesbank, Karl Otto Pöhl watched the summit from the political sidelines. He was surprised that the Community's heads of government accepted the Bundesbank-inspired regulations for the independence of the EC central bank. Pöhl and his colleagues had not anticipated that countries like France and Italy, long used to their central banks being dependent on the government, could agree to such a far-reaching innovation. The other EC members, however, were bidding for the highest of stakes. Up until the last moment, the Bundesbank did not realise that, to release themselves from the grip of the D-Mark, the French and Italians were ready to promise almost anything.

v. Fighting for the D-Mark

The Maastricht deal caught the Bundesbank off guard. Its initial riposte was confused, equivocal, and distinctly *sotto voce*. It was so muted, in fact, that several influential members of the Bundesbank council voiced private indignation that Helmut Schlesinger, celebrated for years for his stern monetary hawkishness, suddenly appeared to have gone soft.

A quirk of the calendar determined that, on the evening of 11 December, Schlesinger had a long-standing engagement to make a speech in Paris.[43] From a political and psychological angle, this was the least suitable place to unleash an attack on the summit outcome. Schlesinger stuck to a diplomatically formulated address in which he praised the Community's general successes in monetary integration and beating inflation. Schlesinger repeated the Bundesbank's well-known calls for existing Community central banks to be made independent before the final third stage of Emu. He pointed to the economic costs of a premature move to monetary union, and warned that the 'real work' still lay ahead.

Schlesinger admitted coyly that, in the Maastricht accord, 'There are some details which the Bundesbank would have wished otherwise.' But, anxious not to add to Kohl's post-Maastricht difficulties, Schlesinger refrained from commenting on the lack of advance towards political union. The Bundesbank president conspicuously failed to follow up his Rotterdam lecture given a month previously, in which he had stated that monetary union without political union would fail. Schlesinger wound up his address with benign sanguineness: 'There is really good reason to look with hope to the future of European monetary integration.' Several members of the Bundesbank council, when they met in Frankfurt a week later to ponder an increase in German interest rates, were worried that Schlesinger seemed to be losing his bite. His tame Paris showing appeared to indicate that the Bundesbank would accept Emu without a fight. The council decided to show the world that this was not the case.[44]

The first member of the Bundesbank council to express public opposition to the Maastricht accord was Reimut Jochimsen, the president of the North Rhine-Westphalia central bank, speaking in London on 17 December. Kohl's agreement on giving up the D-Mark without first achieving an accord on political union was 'courageous, but maybe suicidal', Jochimsen said.[45] 'Too rigid a timetable' had been agreed for the passage to Emu.

On 19 December, the council assembled in Frankfurt for its last meeting of 1991. The acceleration in Germany's own inflation rate, the worries over the budget deficit and Kohl's compliance in Maastricht all made it necessary to issue a strong interest rate signal. But, above all, the weakness of Schlesinger's reaction required firm steps to keep alive the Bundesbank's anti-inflation credibility. As Karl Thomas of the Hesse central bank put it, 'Especially now, we must show we are serious.' Lothar Müller, the baroque president of the Bavarian *Landeszentralbank* – who had argued unsuccessfully for an interest rate increase on 5 December, before Maastricht – led the call for a full-blooded response. This earned him a strong rebuke later from Theo Waigel, the finance minister and leader of the Bavarian Christian Social Union, who regarded Müller's role as distinctly unhelpful. The desire of Schlesinger and Tietmeyer for an increase of only a quarter point in the Lombard rate was over-ruled by a one-man majority.* This was a severe blow to Schlesinger's authority.

In the months afterwards, the Bundesbank stepped up its sniping against monetary union, accompanied by continued protests in the German press about the forthcoming demise of the D-Mark. The Bundesbank could not – and, indeed, did not want to – sabotage the Maastricht agreement directly. Since so many of the conditions

* See chapter 2.

agreed in December had been of its own making, a frontal onslaught would have looked distinctly churlish. The Bundesbank believed, however, that giving publicity to its residual misgivings was entirely legitimate. The central bank was well aware that public unease about the future of the D-Mark was likely to be exploited by Germany's Opposition parties – both the Social Democrats and the far right. Opposition to the Maastricht treaty would be uncomfortable for the government; but it would be even more unpleasant, the Bundesbank reasoned, if the D-Mark were swept away by an unstable currency system.

Associated with its forebodings about the future of Europe's money were the Bundesbank's separate fears about the D-Mark. The bank calculated that, unless it took a firm stand on Emu, the German currency was likely to weaken under the impact of a lowering of the Bundesbank's credibility. This would send out negative ripples across Europe. As Helmut Hesse of the Lower Saxony central bank put it: 'If Germany does not have price stability, the rest of Europe cannot be stable. A high inflation rate in Germany leads to higher inflation in the rest of Europe.'[46] Defending the D-Mark and attacking the terms of Emu thus coalesced into a single policy: what was good for Germany and the D-Mark would be good for Europe.

The Bundesbank published a statement at the beginning of February to emphasise its scepticism about some aspects of the Maastricht accord. This was the result of spirited debate among members of the council.[47] Again, the draft was written by Tietmeyer. It was highly sensitive work. When first intimations of the tenor of the document reached the press, Tietmeyer – who had not been responsible for the leak – telephoned the federal chancellery to apologise for the apparent indiscretion.[48] In highly cautious language, the statement acknowledged that the recommendations of the Bundesbank 'on all major technical issues and problems' had been taken into account in 'important clauses' of the Emu treaty.[49] The bank warned that the dates set for the entry into force of the third stage of Emu should not take priority over the goal of achieving convergence. And it pointed out that the Maastricht decisions 'do not yet reveal an agreement on the future structure of the envisaged political union'.

Far stronger were some of the individual statements of complaint by Bundesbank council members. Dieter Hiss, the president of the

Berlin *Landeszentralbank*, was a former adviser to Chancellor Helmut Schmidt. He traditionally ranked as one of the most moderate members of the council. Yet Hiss called the automatic mechanism for passing to the third stage of Emu in 1999 'exceptionally dubious'.[50] Since Germany's anti-inflation priority was a product of history, Hiss questioned whether it was capable of being transferred abroad. The key to German mentalities, as always, lay in the experience of hyper-inflation:

> Germany's great awareness of the need for stability is the result of a painful learning process, still present in people's minds, which wiped out savings twice within a period of less than thirty years. This form of behaviour based on experience cannot simply be passed on to others.

Karl Thomas from the Hesse central bank focused on the psychological impact of Maastricht on 'the man in the street'.[51] He pointed out: 'The Germans first have to accept that they will be giving up the D-Mark. Then they have to swallow the setting up of the "cohesion fund" into which the Germans will have to contribute to help the poorer European countries. And then they should also have to accept that Frankfurt is taken away from them as the site of the European central bank?'

Lothar Müller, the president of the Bavarian central bank, called for fresh negotiations to improve the Maastricht results on political union; a demand he knew to be impossible.[52] Müller's unlikely ally was Wilhelm Nölling, the Social Democrat *Land* central bank chief from Hamburg – a man who had already given ample proof of his independent-mindedness during the row over German monetary union in 1990.

As a member of the Social Democratic Party, Nölling – like Jochimsen – was able to launch a personal attack on Kohl's handling of the Maastricht deal.[53] 'It is now clear that the elimination of the D-Mark is now a serious possibility. Understandably, this has excited a good deal of attention, and many people are rubbing their eyes in disbelief... The advantages for Germany are difficult to recognise; it is also difficult to back up the justification that the new Ecu currency will be as stable as the D-Mark.'

Somewhat in desperation, the Bonn government ran a series of press advertisements pleading for public acceptance for the Maastricht deal. 'Stable currency, stable future' ran the slogan. 'In a united Europe, the common currency will remain as strong as the Mark.' Pointedly, the advertisements made no mention of the ECU.

The government's own premonitions over the unpopularity of Maastricht proved justified. Ultra right groups registered unexpectedly large scores in state elections in Baden-Württemberg and Schleswig-Holstein in April 1992.[54] The gains were caused above all by protest voting over the excessive number of immigrants streaming into Germany, as well as the general economic consequences of German unity. But a contributory factor was disquiet stirred up by the far right about the future of the German currency.[55] German officials sensed that the pro-European spirit of Maastricht was no longer supported by a majority of voters.[56]

In April 1992, one top Bonn official wryly described the scale of the problem:

> It used to be that the German government could automatically rely on the voters' backing for policies of European integration. That is no longer the case. After Maastricht, the politicians looked around behind us to see if the public were supporting them. Not only were the people not there; they were two kilometres down the road, and heading in the opposite direction.

vi. Residual conditions

The Bundesbank is famed for adhering to the highest of standards. Its objections to Emu are not only of predictably top quality, but are also continually updated. As soon as Germany's EC partners consent to a set of the Bundesbank's conditions, the bank is normally flexible enough to think of some more. After Maastricht, the following six points represented the Bundesbank's main grounds for continuing resistance:

● Stability. No other country, the Bundesbank sometimes likes to imply, can be as stability-minded as the Germans – because none has experienced the same history. Schlesinger stressed in January 1992: 'On paper, the preconditions for a stable European currency are given. They still have to prove effective in reality . . . There is a *Kultur* of stability in Germany; that is what we need in Europe as well.'[57]

• Central bank. Although the statutes agreed for the proposed EC central bank are based on an improved version of the Bundesbank Law, the Germans stress that there is no substitute for experience. According to Hans Tietmeyer, 'Whether and to what extent the future European central bank succeeds in winning its own stability-orientated profile will be of great importance. In contrast to German monetary union, the institution taking over responsibility will not be tried and tested.'[58]

• A wider Europe. The Bundesbank has always believed that widening the Community will probably have to take precedence over deepening. Sweden, Austria, Finland and Norway are likely to become EC members from the mid- to late-1990s.[59] Although the proponents of monetary union say this increases the need for reform of the present Community institutions, the Bundesbank take a radically different view. During the period of flux before the addition of new members, it believes the existing EMS should be extended and improved before any far-reaching changes are made on the way to monetary union. Wilhelm Nölling of the Hamburg central bank adds that, in view of the large-scale circulation of D-Marks in eastern European states, these countries are likely to become 'confused' if the D-Mark is taken away.[60]

• Convergence. Many studies suggest that there has been little improvement in economic convergence since 1987.[61] That which did take place occurred as the result of a deterioration of the German economy – hardly the most positive augury of success for Emu. Economic slowdown in Europe as a result of high German interest rates is automatically expanding budget deficits – making the Maastricht target still harder to meet.

• Conversion. Working out the interest rate conversion for replacing the vast stock – around DM1 trillion – of foreign holdings of D-Marks (both official and private investors) represents a legal and political quagmire. Very little thought has been given to this. According to Horst Bockelmann of the Bank for International Settlements: 'The losses (for either creditors or debtors) could in individual cases take on dimensions amounting to expropriation.'[62]

• Public debts. Under monetary union, interest rates would be aligned among member states. Unless all members of Emu brought down public sector deficits to near the lowest possible levels – and kept them there – borrowers from the more prudent countries would be disadvantaged. Profligate governments would be able to draw from the overall available pool of capital, raising the general level of interest rates, but escaping the specific sanction of weakness in their own individual capital markets. Governments which carry out this type of activity would be unfairly 'jumping on to the running boards' of more thrifty countries, according to Tietmeyer.[63]

vii. Fears and the future

Horst Köhler, state secretary at the Bonn finance ministry and the most trusted economic confidant of Kohl and Waigel, is a boyish figure of charm and confidence. He also brings to his job an almost Latin streak of over-optimism. One of his tasks in Bonn – where his predecessors in the job were Karl Otto Pöhl, Manfred Lahnstein and Hans Tietmeyer – is to tell the Germans that they should learn to love to abandon the D-Mark. In April 1992, Köhler voiced satisfaction that, through the plan for European monetary union, 'a good piece of German identity' was being exported to the rest of Europe.[64] 'We should not fear that the others are taking away the D-Mark and our stability.' In the next breath, Köhler however admitted that the fears were very real. He warned that the other EC states had to accept Frankfurt as the site for the central bank: in order to allay Germans' anxieties that a prize was, indeed, being stolen from them. 'We also need symbols. Frankfurt would perhaps calm our citizens down a little.'

As Köhler implies, Germany is encircled by competing fears. Foreigners are afraid that reunified Germany may become a different country. One of these is André Szasz, an executive director of the Nederlandsche Bank, the Dutch central bank, and one of the most experienced figures in European central banking. He believes that Germany is ripe for change – unless it is constrained by outside forces such as Emu:

> Left to itself, Germany, in the next two decades, will become a different nation. The western European country we are so familiar with will be replaced by a central European power, with interests of its own which may differ significantly from ours. The present generation of Germans in leading positions made their careers in the context of close west European cooperation. They were aware of its huge benefits to Germany and Europe. They are aware of the risk that this may change,

and they are therefore ready to ensure Germany's further integration into western Europe . . . Thus there is an incentive on both sides to establish economic and monetary union which was previously lacking.[65]

Wolfgang Schäuble, Kohl's closest adviser among top Bonn politicians, is the chancellor's most likely choice of successor – despite being bound to a wheelchair after an assassination attempt in October 1990. One of the most able and intelligent men in Bonn, Schäuble is worried that, without assistance from its friends and partners, Germany may become unpredictable. Schäuble, who led the West German team negotiating the unification treaty with the East Berlin government in 1990, is now parliamentary leader of the Christian Democrat and Christian Social Union grouping in the Bundestag. In April 1992, Schäuble admitted: 'I think our western friends should think very hard about how the Federal Republic, sitting in the middle of Europe, can be ever more firmly anchored in western Europe, and not tempted backwards and forwards between east and west.'[66]

In the equation of German emotions, the dominant fear is that of German might. Ex-Chancellor Helmut Schmidt recognises the worries – at home and abroad. A man who has campaigned for years for a single European currency, Schmidt says that the quest for Europe's money is a race against time. If Emu is not accomplished before 2000, Schmidt says, then it will not happen at all.[67] By the end of the 1990s, he predicts, one of two things will have happened. Either the D-Mark will have been replaced by the Ecu. Or else it will be the 'dominating, overwhelming currency because of the overwhelming formation of capital in a state of 80 million Germans.' By then, he says, Germany will have recovered from the turbulence of unification, and the country will be in 'a position of great leverage over the whole of Europe' – and neither the German government, nor the German financial community, will wish to give it up.

Schmidt's message was well understood by other members of the European Community. France and Italy were in the vanguard of efforts to maintain stable exchange rates within the EMS in 1990–91 as an important part of the overall policy of making Emu acceptable to the Germans. Beneath the surface, however, unprecedented strains had been building up. The EMS unrest in September 1992 brought to an end 5¾ years without a significant realignment; and it also destroyed the illusion that the EC could proceed uniformly towards Emu. Both Italy and Britain 'suspended' their membership of the exchange rate mechanism on 'Black Wednesday' – September 16 – while Spain devalued the peseta.[68] During these episodes, as well as during a subsequent – successful – effort by the Bundesbank and Banque de France to maintain the D-Mark/franc parity, the Bundesbank was forced into unparalleled foreign exchange intervention.[69] The monetary unrest effectively split the EMS into a 'core' of currencies closely linked to the D-Mark, and a 'floating' group of more peripheral, less stable, currencies – including sterling and the lira. On the monetary front, Europe was clearly now moving at two (or more) speeds.

Helmut Schlesinger received a large – and mainly unjustified – amount of blame from the British Government for having allegedly provoked the assault on sterling.[70] For the Bundesbank president, the September unrest came as no great surprise. The Bundesbank had long believed that both the lira and sterling were overvalued.[71] The Bundesbank's view was that the EMS devaluations simply compensated for higher inflation rates elsewhere in the EC.[72] Schlesinger's deputy, Tietmeyer, preparing to take over the Bundesbank reins in autumn 1993, was adamant that the upheavals could have been avoided. He blamed other EC states for not having realised the necessity for a realignment shortly after German reunification in 1990.[73] The autumn 1992 turbulence vindicated the Bundesbank's suspicions about the difficulties lying along the road to Emu. But the episode also had another, more insidious, effect. The D-Mark's sharp rise against other important EC currencies, by adding to the problems facing Germany's export industry, tipped the German economy into recession. Already overshadowed by the burdens of unification, Germany's political skies darkened further: a highly unpropitious climate for European integration. The EC knew all along that, to win German support for an abandonment of the D-Mark, there was little time. After the autumn currency storm, it looked likely to run out more quickly than anyone had anticipated.

10

Skirmishes Ahead

The cardinal question determining the fate of the currency
is the independence of the central bank.
Wilhelm Vocke, president of directorate of Bank deutscher
Länder, 1950[1]

The path to European monetary union will not be a stroll;
it will be hard and thorny.
Karl Blessing, Bundesbank president, 1963[2]

Our independence depends on our ability not to overstep
our limits.
Helmut Schlesinger, Bundesbank president, 1992[3]

On a wintry day in November 1967, an august cluster of politicians, bankers, businessmen and functionaries gathered on a building site in the north-west of Frankfurt. They were witnesses to a very special occasion: the ceremonial laying of the foundation stone of the new Bundesbank office block, which would replace the old Bank deutscher Länder building in the city centre. As the obligatory introductory overture from a Bach orchestra died away, Werner Lucht, the Bundesbank directorate member responsible for buildings and administration, welcomed the guests to what he called 'the baptism of a new citizen'.[4] Karl Blessing, the bespectacled president of the Bundesbank, strode to the podium. The ex-Reichsbanker who had participated in virtually all the monetary vicissitudes of the last thirty years solemnly outlined the central bank's creed. He chose words which were to be spelled out at his own funeral oration four years later:* 'Defending the stability of the currency is a daily struggle.'

The Bundesbank's credibility, said Blessing, was based on its virility. 'A central bank which never fights, which at times of economic tension never raises its voice, which in the age of the mass

* See chapter 2.

welfare state wants to be friends with everyone: that central bank will be viewed with mistrust.' Blessing recalled the Bundesbank's complicated pedigree, recorded on a scroll sealed inside the basalt foundation stone: 'The outcome of the Second World War led to the extinction of the old German Reichsbank. The duties of the central bank were transferred to the Bank deutscher Länder and the *Land* central banks, which were merged into the German Bundesbank on 1 August 1957.'

The primary reason for the Bundesbank's famed independence, he said, was to avoid a repetition of history: 'To make it as difficult as possible for the state to misuse the printing press, a misuse which we have seen many times in the past.' By 1967, the Bundesbank had already gained a considerable reputation for holding firm – and for toppling governments. Mindful of his own role in forcing out of office the previous year his one-time mentor, Ludwig Erhard,* Blessing added an essential touch of modesty. The Bundesbank could never be 'a state within a state'. In the final analysis, Blessing reassured his audience, government and parliament 'would always be stronger'.

Blessing rounded off the ceremony with a traditional flourish. He struck three sharp blows with a hammer on the stone. After each crack, his words rang out into the rain-washed sky: 'Stand firm! . . . Bring benefit and fortune to the German people! . . . And may all who pass in and out of here be blessed!'[5]

i. A delicate balance

In the early 1990s, the Bundesbank can look back towards its origins and reflect that it has done its job well. It has brought benefit and fortune. It has exerted a crucial stabilising influence on a country with a tortuous past. It has correctly learned the lessons of history. Stable money brings stable government, and stable government brings a stable society. German unification would never have been possible without the credibility and strength of the institution which controls the D-Mark. The corollary, however, is also true. Without stable money, prosperity can wither and die. The stresses engendered by German unification present the Bundesbank with a challenge which, if not mastered, could inflict severe harm

* See chapter 7.

on the roots of post-war German success. The damage would not be limited to Germany alone, but would ripple out across the whole of Europe.

As a central bank which exerts commanding influence on the monetary policies of the continent, the Bundesbank is a European institution. But it is above all a very German one, with a unique place in Germany's corporatist system of government. Foreign countries which have admired West Germany's low inflation record and its post-war recovery may learn from the German experience; the circumstances which allowed this development in Germany cannot, however, be transferred abroad. The Bundesbank's independence from, and lack of accountability towards, any elected organ of government is a product of German history. The Bundestag's decision in 1957 to transfer monetary powers to an institution which could not be manipulated for electoral gain was a result of Germany's bitter, unique cycle of war, defeat and inflation.

The European Community's plans for monetary union laid down that the European central bank should be a close replica of the Bundesbank, erected at a European level. A central bank established by twelve different countries would however clearly not behave like the Bundesbank; indeed, one of the prime reasons behind the move is to escape the Bundesbank's dominance. The German 'model' of central banking independence cannot be grafted on to other countries with different national traditions and experiences.

The Bundesbank is strong, but, like Germany, it is vulnerable. This most mythologised of central banks can be a victim of its own mythology. Its independence is celebrated, but – as all its presidents have been forced to recognise – it is not absolute. In the framing of German economic policy, responsibility is divided between the politicians and the central bank. If Bonn runs fiscal policies which strain monetary stability, or if the famed German consensus in pay bargaining breaks down, then the Bundesbank's capacity to improve matters is highly contracted. Its autonomy is limited to the ability to raise and lower interest rates. The notion that the Bundesbank has consistently allowed Germany to follow a 'virtuous circle', in which low inflation automatically produces sustained economic growth, is an illusion.

If a 'virtuous circle' ever existed, it was found only in the Federal Republic's first two decades, in the 1950s and 1960s, under the very special conditions which prompted the *Wirtschaftswunder*. In West Germany, periods of economic 'stop and go' have been less frequent than in Britain; but when the Bundesbank has been forced to press heavily on the monetary brakes, it has shown that monetary policy can be a blunt instrument.* At several points in its history (roughly at ten-yearly intervals between the 1950s and the early 1990s), in order to win the 'daily struggle' with inflation, the Bundesbank has engineered a recession. Sometimes, this has led to the departure of the government. In Germany, as elsewhere, beating inflation is not free of pain.

The Bundesbank's anti-inflation rectitude has been exported throughout Europe. *Stabilitätspolitik* has become part of the international consensus. Low inflation is hailed worldwide as a prime condition for improving both the quantity and the quality of economic growth. In Germany's case, the policy has been more successful than in most other countries; yet there have been important areas of failure too. The breakdown of Bretton Woods in 1973 increased the Bundesbank's ability to assert its independence; but it also ushered in a long period of below-average German growth. With the exception of the years immediately before and after reunification, West German economic performance since the beginning of the 1970s has been significantly weaker than that of most other industrialised countries.[6]

West Germany's unemployment rate rose faster during the last two decades than that of any of the country's main trading partners – partly, it is true, because a rapid rise in the labour force outweighed the number of new jobs created.[7] International comparisons show that, over lengthy periods, central banking independence is a key factor helping to produce low inflation.[8] It does not, however, pave the way to faster economic growth.

The Bundesbank has served Germany well because its results, on the whole, have conformed to the desires of the German people. The central bank stands at the fulcrum of the delicate economic balance between the political leadership and the electorate. During the last twenty years, economic stability has enjoyed a higher priority than economic growth. And stability is what the Bundesbank has delivered. The same applies to Germany's brand of political, social and management consensus. This has functioned smoothly for forty

* See chapter 7.

years because the German people have feared that the alternative would bring chaos; the German 'model' has become a shining example for other countries. Reunification, however, has weakened the foundations on which this consensus is based. In particular, the equilibrium between federalism and centralism – a balance which also crucially affects the composition of the Bundesbank's council, and the way it takes its decisions – has come under severe strain. German federalism operated well in a country of eleven relatively homogeneous *Länder*. In a nation of sixteen *Länder*, five of which are battling with the economic and social legacy of East German communism, the 'model' is looking much more fragile.

The turbulence caused by the entry of the D-Mark into East Germany, and then by the row over plans for European monetary union, revealed the limits of the consensus system, as well as the constraints on the central bank's autonomy. The prime decisions, inevitably, were made in Bonn, not Frankfurt. Because political necessities took priority over the need to maintain monetary stringency, these episodes weakened the Bundesbank's authority. In both cases, the Bundesbank under-estimated the political momentum building up for change.

Both misjudgments centred on questions of sovereignty. Over the question of German monetary union, the Bundesbank's leadership failed to realise that the desperate plight of the East German regime would force it into rapid agreement to transfer monetary powers to Frankfurt. The Bundesbank responded quickly and efficiently to the technical demands of carrying out monetary union with the east, but this did not compensate for the initial setback of being caught unawares. In the case of European monetary union, the Bundesbank did not believe that other European Community states in December 1991 at Maastricht would agree to take monetary policy out of the hands of governments and transfer it to an independent European central bank. The Bundesbank's unique ethos gives it great distinction; yet it must not be over-stretched. One of the most effective ways of harming an institution whose authority rests on its reliability and predictability is to show that it can be taken by surprise.

Since the 1950s the Bundesbank has become more closely identified than any other central bank with the aim of reducing inflation. Its sometimes exaggerated reputation is both a strength and a weakness. When, as during the mid-1980s, West Germany achieves conspicuous success in holding down price rises, the Bundesbank's credibility rises commensurately, at home and abroad; it becomes self-fuelling. When, as happened in 1991–92, German inflation rises, the Bundesbank's reputation dips, and with it, its ability to act firmly and decisively. The German central bank is Europe's dominant monetary institution, but it is highly susceptible to setbacks. If ever the Bundesbank were to experience a true crisis of confidence, precisely because of its prestige and importance, it would be hit far harder than any other central bank. The Bundesbank's resolve to defend its sanctity promises skirmishes ahead.

ii. The German path

Nicholas Ridley, the British industry minister, was at the centre of a somewhat infantile *cause célèbre* in July 1990 when he attacked the drive towards European monetary union as 'a German racket designed to take over the whole of Europe'.[9] Ridley, who resigned shortly afterwards, showed grandiose failure to analyse correctly the political and economic changes at the centre of the continent. European monetary union is not an attempt to expand Germany's dominance. Rather it is an effort, led by France and Italy, to clip Germany's wings. Germany's foreign partners know that, shorn of the D-Mark, and subordinate to a Community central bank, the Germans are likely to be less powerful than they would otherwise be. This is the basic justification for Emu; and this is why the Germans do not like the idea.

Other reasons for the reluctance are directly related to the turmoil caused by the reforging of Germany:

• The struggle to absorb East Germany is costing an annual sum in public sector transfers from west to east of at least DM150 billion a year – roughly DM10,000 for each of the 16 million inhabitants east of the Elbe. Beset by this enormous fiscal challenge, the Germans are in no mood to underwrite additional sums for less developed European regions, which EC politicians are demanding as part of the 'cohesion fund' agreed at Maastricht.

• The German electorate's suspicions about the costs of European monetary union have been greatly increased by Chancellor Kohl's subterfuge about the burdens of German monetary union. This climate of foreboding among the German population forms the worst possible environment for a policy of giving up the D-Mark.

● With unity completed, the German government has less pressing need for gestures on giving up sovereignty than it did during the twelve months before Unity Day on 3 October 1990. Foreign countries will be confronted during the 1990s with a Germany which is far more assertive in pursuing its own interests, and less enthusiastic about emphasising its Community role. This need not be uniformly negative. In one important sense, Germany is becoming like other European countries.

● Because of the wider perspectives in the rest of Europe opened up by the crumbling of communism in 1989–91, political and economic union with a limited number of western European states has lost electoral appeal. The setbacks to ratification of the Maastricht treaty following the 'No' vote in the June 1992 Danish referendum showed that these misgivings were shared, too, by other EC states. Many Germans believe the country would be better advised to strengthen monetary and economic ties with Scandinavia and central Europe than with countries like Italy, Spain, Greece or Portugal. Austria, Sweden, Switzerland and Finland – all candidates to join the EC after 1995 – are far more capable of fulfilling the Maastricht economic convergence conditions than the EC's Mediterranean states.

Ultimately, German wishes, rather than those of France or Italy, will determine the outcome of the Emu process. The march towards a single currency agreed at Maastricht was not after all irreversible. Establishment of monetary union with a single European currency seems highly unlikely to take place this century. German unification initially accelerated the move towards European union. It now seems destined to slow it down.

A central, praiseworthy tenet of German policy since the crumbling of the Berlin Wall was that German unification must be part of the union of Europe. This corresponded to the belief of Chancellor Konrad Adenauer; the dictum was also enshrined in West Germany's 1949 constitution.[10] If this doctrine proves unworkable, it may undermine the credibility of Germany's overall policies towards its Community partners. None the less, Germany's second thoughts about Maastricht since the treaty was agreed in December 1991 make this virtually inevitable.

Europe has the choice between contrasting objectives. Should it proceed radically towards a form of federally organised European government, where nations will transfer political and economic decision-making power to supranational institutions? Or should it choose to maintain the system of competing nation states which has marked – and marred – European history for centuries? Germany has always supported the former option, above all because it has been chiefly responsible this century for two world wars. Antagonisms and rivalries among European states cannot however be ruled out, whichever route is chosen. Germany's dilemma is that, for the first time since the Second World War, it sees that national and European goals impose conflicting priorities.

iii. Towards Bundesbank rule?

German politicians – as well as Bundesbank officials – have made countless statements declaring their general willingness to proceed towards Emu. Was it all insincere? In fact, Germany has wanted and not wanted monetary union at the same time. Serving a people placed in the middle of Europe, conditioned by history and geography to look both east and west, the German language itself can stretch ambiguously in several directions at once. This is the classic land of the *Doppelwahrheit*, the double truth, the high-sounding phrase which can mean everything and nothing, depending on who sounds it, and to whom it is addressed.

To serve a multitude of purposes, the Germans have, all along, been simultaneously proponents and opponents of Emu. Rather like the Reichsbank functionaries who supported and opposed Hitler at the same time, the men of the Bundesbank have always been able to see two sides of the Emu argument at once. They are content that the principles of *Stabilitätspolitik* could have been extended so widely, but they worry whether other countries really have been irrevocably won over to the Bundesbank cause. They favour monetary cooperation, but they want to remain in charge. They would like to be 'good Europeans', but they also want to hold on to the D-Mark.

This dualism finds expression in other countries too. The most telling paradox about the negotiations on European Monetary Union is the diversity of views on its consequences within the countries which are pressing for it. Emu is generally conceived as a way of curbing German dominance; indeed, that is the basic political justification for it. But it is also frequently criticised in countries like France, Italy or Britain as imposing deflationary German-style economic criteria across the whole of Europe. When German newspaper headlines thunder that Germany is abandoning its currency, while in France they proclaim that Emu is bringing 'victory for the D-Mark', observers can only conclude that the electorate is thoroughly confused.

To ask the Germans to give up a stable currency in return for a monetary system which was less secure would be a disservice, both for Germany and for Europe. Unless the proposed new European currency system can be guaranteed at least as stable as the one which the Germans have built up during forty years, the Germans are unlikely to agree to it. Yet there is a built-in impasse. Unless they live through a further currency breakdown of the sort experienced in 1923, 1948 and (in East Germany) 1990, the Germans are never likely to believe that taking away monetary sovereignty from the Bundesbank would produce a currency as stable as the D-Mark. If there is to be a single European currency, the Bundesbank's preferred solution is that this should be the D-Mark.[11]

The aftermath of unification presents the Bundesbank with an unprecedented challenge. Its stature as the guardian of Europe's quintessential hard currency has already been weakened. Yet foreign hopes that Germany's economic problems will provide the opportunity to wrest away the D-Mark are unlikely to be fulfilled. There are three basic possibilities for the outcome of Germany's unification problems, and none of them leads to Emu:

• The Bundesbank may succeed, against all the odds, in restoring Germany relatively quickly to its accustomed path of stability, prodding government finances back towards probity, and bringing inflation down to the central bank's long-term goal of 2 per cent. If the Bundesbank accomplishes this feat, the Germans, flushed by renewed success, will resist abandoning an institution which has successfully shepherded the nation through one of the greatest challenges in its history.

• Post-unity difficulties may persist for several years, until the end of the 1990s, but they will remain manageable. This is the most likely outcome. In this case, the Bundesbank will be forced to keep interest rates high for a relatively long period in order to maintain steady downwards pressure on inflation and restore the country's financial stability. High German interest rates will depress economic activity around Europe, and ensure that most Community countries fail to achieve the economic growth required to fulfil the Maastricht economic performance targets.

• Germany's problems may develop into a full-scale and persistent crisis. Germany will comprehensively fail to control its own fiscal deficits, and the D-Mark will lose its 'anchor' function in the European Monetary System, which could then pass to the French franc. German instability would be the worst possible basis on which to found monetary union. Not only would Germany itself fail to meet the Maastricht convergence targets; additionally, because of the size and importance of the German economy, financial disarray would not remain limited to Germany alone. Under this third – most dramatic, and least likely – scenario, economic and monetary union would be blocked even more comprehensively than under the first and second options. Europe would not travel at 'two speeds'; it would end up proceeding at no speed at all.

Europe has embarked towards the goal of monetary union before, and faltered along the way. This happened after the European Commission's proposals in 1962, with the Werner report of 1970, and when the European Monetary System was established in 1978–79. Renewed failure would be a setback, but not a tragedy. In view of the political capital vested in European union by the Bonn government, it would however fundamentally disturb Germany's policies towards the rest of Europe. During a period of transition and upheaval after the ending of the cold war and the break-up of the Soviet Union, reunited Germany needs to redraw its priorities towards its European partners. Yet the country is unlikely to give its full attention to this task as long as its national affairs remain depressed by the weight of its new internal responsibilities. It will be in Europe's best interests for Germany to emerge from its uncertainties as quickly as possible.

If, at the end of this period, the Bundesbank is still in charge of Europe's monetary destiny, those who sought to dethrone this most Germanic of institutions may find room for hope amid their disappointment. It will be a new Germany and a new Europe. Other governments and central banks – in both the east and the west of the continent – will have learned from the Bundesbank's successes, and from its mistakes. One notable shortcoming has been the Bundesbank's failure to shed light on, and come to terms with, its own sometimes uncomfortable history. The Bundesbank has created its own institutional mythology; the central bank itself has occasionally been too ready to believe in it.

The story of the Bundesbank underlines the central bank's successes, but also its limitations. No central bank, whatever its independence, operates in an environment free of political complications. The crucial condition for successful monetary policies is that they are understood and supported by the general public.

The better the Bundesbank's objectives are explained and debated, in a healthy and open society, the more likely they are to be accepted, in Germany and abroad. The prospect of European monetary union this century has receded. Yet the greater the support for the Bundesbank's mission, the greater the likelihood that it will eventually share its weighty responsibilities in genuinely cooperative monetary arrangements with other European countries. The Bundesbank is much too powerful to be controlled by others. But it has too much power to rule alone.

Notes

Abbreviations used in source references

BAF	Bundesarchiv, Freienwalderstrasse, Berlin.
BAK	Bundesarchiv Koblenz.
	RC Reich chancellery series
BAP	Bundesarchiv Potsdam.
	RB Reichsbank series
BB	Bundesbank archives, Frankfurt.
	Minutes Minutes of council meetings
	CF Correspondence File
	PF Personal File
	RS Rundschreiben (notices)
BDC	Berlin Document Center, Berlin
	CF Correspondence File
	PF Party File
	SS SS File
BoE	Bank of England, London.
BIS	Bank for International Settlements, Basle.
IMT	Transcripts of International Military Tribunal, Nuremberg.
LS-LZB	Lower Saxony Landeszentralbank, Hanover.
NRW-LZB	North Rhine-Westphalia Landeszentralbank, Düsseldorf.
PRO	Public Records Office, London.
St. A	Staatsbank archive, Berlin.
Uni.	Unilever archives, Hamburg.
UMT	Transcripts of US Military Tribunal, Nuremberg.
WWA/Omgus	Westfälisches Wirtschaftsarchiv, Dortmund. Omgus files.

Chapter 1: The Hub of Europe

1. Speech at savings banks association, 28.9.31.

2. Speech in Stuttgart, 24.6.66.

3. Valedictory speech at ceremony in Frankfurt, 27.8.91.

4. The letter, on 4.10.60, together with the bank's responses, is contained in BoE/OV 34/90.

5. Speech at IMF meeting in Washington, 24.9.92.

6. Interview on BBC Radio 4, 18.9.92.

7. Among the countries which at the beginning of the 1990s were seeking the Bundesbank's counsel on establishing independent central banks were Chile, Argentina, Czechoslovakia, Poland, Hungary and Romania – as well as the re-established states of Estonia, Latvia and Lithuania. In 1991, the Bundesbank signalled a more activist approach to helping foreign central banks by setting up a new department to channel technical help in this area, similar to the long-standing practice of the Bank of England and Banque de France.

8. The dollar accounted for 56 per cent, with the yen in third place with 11 per cent. Sterling accounts for just 4 per cent of currency reserves. Bundesbank annual report for 1991; speech by Helmut Schlesinger, 21.2.92.

9. Interview with Tsutomu Hata, Japanese finance minister, *Financial Times*, 2.12.91.

10. Interview with *Der Spiegel*, 17.2.92.

11. Bundesbank annual report for 1974.

12. This statement also formed the basis of the celebrated statement by British prime minister James Callaghan at the Labour party conference in 1978. Another famous conversion preceded it. Helmut Schmidt in May 1972 – during his time as finance minister – declared that 5 per cent inflation was more tolerable than 5 per cent unemployment.

13. The Bundesbank took over the building, functions, traditions and personnel of the Bank deutscher Länder. Emphasising the unbroken link between the two institutions, the Bundesbank classifies its monthly reports according to a numbering system starting in 1948, when the Bank deutscher Länder was set up.

14. Members of the directorate, members of the council, and other board members of the *Land* central banks. See chapters 5, 6 and appendix for details.

15. The word *Hüterin* was first used by Karl von Lumm, a member of the Reichsbank's directorate, in 1912. Essay on *'Diskontpolitik'* in *Schmollers Jahrbuch*. For its use during the Third Reich, see speech by Emil Puhl, vice-president of the Reichsbank, on 7.1.43, in which he described the Reichsbank as the *Hüterin der Währung*. BAP/RB 25.01/

7132. Paul Oesterrich, in his eulogistic biography of Walther Funk, described Hitler as the 'principal guardian of the currency' (*'Hüter und oberster Leiter von Deutschlands Währung'*). *Walther Funk, Ein Leben für die Wirtschaft*, 1941, p. 116.

16. Aidan Crawley, *The Rise of Western Germany 1945–72*, pp. 49, 50.

17. See, for instance, speech by Otmar Issing, Bundesbank directorate member responsible for economics, Innsbruck, 6.3.92.

18. Testimony to the Treasury and Civil Service select committee by Hermann-Joseph Dudler, November 1980.

19. Britain's money supply figures at the end of the 1970s and early 1980s gave an exaggerated impression of the true level of inflationary pressures. The statistics were artificially inflated by the growing deregulation of the financial sector, increasing competition for both loans and deposits. Ironically, a similar phenomenon appeared to be taking place in Germany in 1992, partly connected to a more sophisticated behaviour by financial investors as well as structural changes caused by unification.

20. Introduction to J. von Spindler, *Kommentar zum Bundesbankgesetz*, 1960.

21. The Bundesbank's income comes above all from lending operations with German banks, together with interest on its foreign exchange reserves. Its profits are subject to an annual valuation adjustment covering the rise or fall during the year of the value in D-Marks of the foreign exchange reserves (held mainly in dollars). During the period 1981–1991, the Bundesbank paid roughly DM120 billion in profit to the Bonn government.

Chapter 2: Safeguarding the Currency

1. Letter from Hitler to Funk on his appointment, 19.1.39.

2. Schacht, *1933 – Wie eine Demokratie stirbt*, Düsseldorf, 1967, p. 7.

3. Speech in Frankfurt, 27.8.91.

4. Law of 15.6.39. The preamble stated 'The Deutsche Reichsbank, as the German central bank, is subject to the unrestricted sovereignty of the Reich. Within the area of competence which it has been assigned, it serves the realisation of the aims of the National Socialist state leadership, in particular, to safeguard the value of the German currency.' Under Article 1, the Reichsbank was made 'directly subordinate to the Führer and Reichskanzler'.

5. Article 3 of Bundesbank Law of 26.7.57: 'The Deutsche Bundesbank regulates the quantity of money in circulation and of credit supplied to the economy, using the monetary powers conferred on it by this Act, with the aim of safeguarding the currency, and provides for the execution by banks of domestic and external payments.'

6. Article 12: 'In exercising the powers conferred on it by this Act, it is independent of instructions from the federal government.'

7. Speech to Reichsbank employees in Berlin, 11.11.41.

8. Erhard, *Wohlstand für Alle*, 1957.

9. Schiller's celebrated phrase was first used in a parliamentary debate in the mid-1960s.

10. *Einschätzung zur Stabilität der Währung der DDR*, 1989, St. A.

11. *Hitler's Table Talk*, 11.8.42.

12. The forces which made de Maizière East German premier for six dramatic months between April and October 1990 also brought his political downfall. In September 1991, less than a year after German unity, de Maizière was forced to step down from his position as deputy chairman of the reunified German CDU, following persistent reports that he had previously acted as an informer for the East German secret service.

13. The basic savings amounts for which the 1 for 1 conversion rate applied were: EM2,000 for children under 14; EM4,000 for adults up to age 60; EM6,000 for pensioners. Thereafter, a less generous rate of 2 for 1 applied for conversion into D-Marks. See chapter 8.

14. *Kunst dem Volk*, May 1940.

15. Article by Reichsbank economics and statistics department on Reichsbank building, February 1941, BAP/RB 25.01/6365.

16. The Reichsbank building was used by the East Berlin finance ministry between 1954 and 1957.

17. The scene was witnessed by the author on 1.7.90.

18. Interview with author in Bonn, 18.6.91.

19. Interview with author in Berlin, 24.11.89.

20. Interview with author in Frankfurt, 23.4.91.

21. Wilhelm Korspeter, the editor, and Gustav Schmidt-Küster, the editorial director, helped Pöhl when he started his traineeship as an 18-year-old. The newspaper financed his first three terms at the Hochschule für Arbeit, Politik und Wirtschaft at Wilhelmshaven.

22. Otmar Emminger, Pöhl's predecessor as Bundesbank president, portrayed Pöhl in his memoirs as being absent on holiday during many of the important currency events of the early 1970s. Emminger, *D-Mark, Dollar, Währungskrisen*, 1986.

23. Interview with *Wall Street Journal*, 25.1.90.

24. Bundesbank transcript of press conference on 16.5.91.

25. Letter to Reich president, 16.3.33, BAK.

26. Had it been effective, this would have prevented the Bundesbank from taking interest rate decisions without consulting the French first. The Bundesbank succeeded in watering down the provisions of the

treaty, so that the deliberations of the council, far from being binding, amounted simply to exchanges of points of view.

27. Parallel to the interest rate cuts, Stoltenberg proposed that Germany enter into firm intervention commitments with the US government to support the dollar at the end of 1987, an idea which Pöhl and the rest of the Bundesbank opposed as being potentially inflationary. There was also a bitter dispute over the government's decision in 1988 (later rescinded) to levy a withholding tax to help finance the budget deficit. This drove savings abroad and weakened the D-Mark.

28. Interview with author in Kronberg, 16.8.91.

29. Schlesinger's most active intellectual pursuit outside his professional work is focused on his chairmanship of the Freiherr von Stein association, a group of officials and managers concentrating particularly on local government matters. Schlesinger took over the chairmanship in 1990 from Manfred Rommel, the mayor of Stuttgart, part of his efforts to secure outside occupation in anticipation of his scheduled (and subsequently delayed) retirement in 1991.

30. During his time as a journalist, Pöhl had frequently criticised the Bundesbank's monetary policies. In one article written during the 1967 recession, for instance, he complained that the central bank's tight monetary policy posed a danger to 'economic growth and full employment'. *Der Volkswirt*, 28.4.67.

31. Pöhl left on a public sector pension of 75 per cent of his basic Bundesbank president's salary, giving a figure of roughly DM350,000 a year. He also took up a number of prestigious supervisory board posts – including Bertelsmann, Unilever, Shell, Zurich Versicherung, IBM World Trade and the Dutch investment group Robeco. Additionally, he became a member of the advisory board of J. P. Morgan and General Electric.

32. Pöhl came close to publicly explaining the true circumstances of his departure in a Zurich speech on 1.6.91. He complained that, during the unification process, the advice of the Bundesbank had often not been listened to, and sometimes not even sought.

33. Speech in Bonn on 2.7.91, upon award of annual Ludwig Erhard prize.

34. Memorandum of 7.1.39, signed by Schacht and seven other members of Reichsbank directorate, which led to the departure of the president and five of the others.

35. Telephone conversation with author, 12.8.91.

36. Interview with author in Frankfurt, 14.6.91.

37. The ceremony took place on 27.8.91. Because of the holiday season it was delayed until four weeks after Pöhl had relinquished his job.

38. In similar vein, Emminger declared in a speech in 1978 commemorating the 30th anniversary of the D-Mark: 'The most important experience of these 30 years has been [to learn] that maintaining monetary stability is a permanent effort, requiring a permanent defensive struggle against threats and dangers from within and outside.'

39. Joined NSDAP 1.5.37. Membership number 5226547. BDC/PF.

40. Emminger became an Assessor (graduate civil servant in the legal field) in Munich in 1938.

41. Ceremony in Frankfurt, 20.12.79.

42. Ceremony in Frankfurt, 20.12.79.

43. Speech on hand-over of Klasen's office, 1977.

44. Ceremony in Frankfurt, January 1970.

45. Vocke had been a protégé of Rudolf Havenstein (Reichsbank president between 1908 and November 1923) and Otto Georg von Glasenapp (vice-president between 1907 and 1924).

46. Vocke was dismissed at the beginning of February 1939, after failing to be sacked straight away after the directorate handed in the memorandum. In his memoirs, Vocke writes that he produced a first draft of the document in July 1938, which was then watered down later. His prime role in the affair was however not realised by the German authorities. 'Schacht, Dreyse and Hülse were immediately dismissed. And I? They had forgotten me! No one knew me in Hitler's entourage.' Vocke, *Memoiren*, 1973, pp. 103, 110. A draft by Vocke, dating from October 1938, for the eventual memorandum was published by the Bundesbank in February 1986 for an exhibition marking the 100th anniversary of Vocke's birth.

47. On his activities at the Reichsbank under Hitler, Vocke comments that he usually spent the first part of the morning horse-riding in the Tiergarten. 'I went to the bank after 10 o'clock, and would disappear again before 1 o'clock.' *op. cit.* p. 102.

48. Friedrich-Wilhelm von Schelling, a Reichsbank official who later became president of the Hamburg *Landeszentralbank*, confirmed that Vocke's general reputation at the Reichsbank was one of exceptional laziness. Interview with the author in Hamburg, 5.7.91.

49. Reichsbank report written by Vocke, 20.11.30. BAK R.43I/310.

50. Vocke claimed exceptional perspicacity in warning Schacht in 1931 of Hitler's coming downfall. Vocke, *op. cit.* p. 99.

51. He was a member of the Kuratorium of the Kaiser-Wilhelm-Gesellschaft für ausländisches und internationales Privatrecht, which carried out only very limited activities during the war. Vocke joined in 1926 at the suggestion of Hjalmar Schacht.

52. 'The ill-fortune in the end worked out favourably for my

development . . . If my father had lived a long time, it would have produced difficult tensions.' Vocke, *op. cit.* p. 19.

53. Article in *Zeitschrift für das gesamte Kreditwesen*, 1.7.71.

54. Vocke, *op. cit.* p.155.

55. Vocke, *op. cit.* p. 156.

56. Bernard was a self-effacing former Reich Economics Ministry official who had been forced out of the civil service in 1935 because his Greek-born wife was half-Jewish. He and Vocke carried out the dual leadership of the Bank deutscher Länder between 1948 and 1957.

57. Address to Bank deutscher Länder council, 1.6.48.

58. '*Schwieriger Start der neuen Zentralbank*', *Zeitschrift für das gesamte Kreditwesen*, 15.6.73.

59. Evidence of Wilhelm Vocke, 3.5.46, IMT XIII, p. 65. See also Schacht, *76 Jahre meines Lebens*, 1953, p. 621.

60. As West Germany established a run of consecutive trade surpluses which was to last until the 1990s, Vocke was able to pass on to his successor Blessing a stock of DM11 billion in gold and DM7 billion in foreign exchange holdings.

61. See speech to central bank council on 1.6.48.

62. Speech to savings banks conference in Hamburg, 12.3.50.

63. The Third Reich maintained the Reichsmark's nominal gold parity it had first acquired in December 1871. The Reichsmark retained throughout the Third Reich the notional value of RM2.50 to the dollar, established after the dollar devaluation of 1933. Taking into account the variety of different currency rates set up for foreign trade purposes, as well as subsidies to help exporters, Reichsbank officials after the war calculated that its actual value was around RM3.30 to 3.50. Similarly, in 1936, the Bank of England calculated that the Reichsmark had in fact undergone a de facto devaluation of 30 per cent from its 1933 parity level. Note on 27.5.36, BoE/OV 34/7.

64. Speech on 'Germany in the world economy', Leipzig, 4.3.35.

65. Speech at training course for Reichsbank officials, 20.6.38, BB/RS.

66. '*Die Entwicklung der Währungen und die Möglichkeiten einer Stabilisierung*.' Speech at Berlin Wirtschaftshochschule, 16.2.38, BAP/RB 25.01/3413.

67. Speech at dinner in Frankfurt on 4.12.69 in honour of Blessing and Heinrich Troeger, the Bundesbank vice-president, who was also retiring.

68. Joined NSDAP 1.5.37. Membership number 5917306. BDC/PF.

69. UMT, Case V, 18.8.47.

70. Blessing gives the date for his dismissal as 2.2.39. UMT-Flick, 18.8.47.

71. Many of the members of the circle – who met for incongruous tea parties and visits to key war establishments – were members of the Schutzstaffel or SS, Hitler's Black Guards. Blessing said in his interrogation that he saw Himmler three times in this 'circle' in 1939 and 1940, but did not meet him at all in 1941/42.

72. Vocke, *op. cit.* p. 164.

73. In a list put forward in 1943 by Carl Goerdeler, the mayor of Leipzig who became later a key figure in resistance circles, Blessing was foreseen as future Reichsbank president, with another well-known Reichsbank figure, Bodo von Wedel, foreseen as vice-president. A later list obtained by the Gestapo foresaw Blessing as economics minister, a post which would include the position of Reichsbank president. See Gerard Ritter, *Carl Goerdeler und die deutsche Widerstandsbewegung*, 1954.

74. UMT, 18.8.47.

75. *Hitler's Table Talk*, 13.10.41 (midday).

76. Letter from Blessing to Al. Ottulescu, governor of Romanian central bank, 8.10.41, BAP/RB 25.016330.

77. Letter from Funk, in which he turned down the suggestion of sending Blessing as a full-time economic adviser to Romania, 19.6.44. BAK.

78. 'Of course, the currency which we have now is completely different from the one we had before. It is kept stable with the help of an extensive system of currency controls, controls in which we Reichsbank officials can in a certain sense take pride; for such a system is possible only in a country with excellent aptitude for organisation, possessing a civil service of irreproachable integrity.' Speech during training week for Reichsbank officials, 7.5.35. BAP/RB 25.01/6514.

79. Although it was 'quite simply not possible, to damn an economy such as Germany's to a renewed period of deflation, and thus to raise again the phantom of unemployment,' Germany would not lower the value of the Reichsmark. 'We want neither to give up our policy of employment creation – although we are aware of its limits – nor to disappoint the German people's trust in their currency . . . The best safeguard for the currency is neither the composition of the central bank's reserves nor the backing of the banknotes; the best safeguard is the confidence which the people have in the state leadership and hence in the currency.' Speech to Verwaltungsakademie, Berlin, 22.1.35. BAP/RB 25.01/3414.

80. 'National Socialism has given the state priority over the economy'; and the central bank had become 'the executor of the will of the state'.

81. '*Die deutsche Handelspolitik an der Jahreswende*', article in *Die deutsche Volkswirtschaft*, January 1936.

82. Drei Jahre Neuer Plan, speech on 28.11.37, BAP/RB 25.01/3413.

83. In Schacht's speech to the employees of the Austrian National Bank on 21.3.38, the Reichsbank president introduced Blessing to the gathering as the man who would 'in future look after Austrian affairs in Berlin'. BB/RS.

84. Speech in Berlin on 20.6.38, BAP/RB 25.01/6389.

85. Blessing during his time as a civil servant had shown his usefulness to Unilever by assisting its efforts to circumvent exchange controls and repatriate funds abroad from 'blocked Mark' accounts accumulated in Germany. See for instance letter from the head of the continental side of the Unilever business, Paul Rijkens, to Blessing, 24.4.37, letter from Rijkens to Keppler 16.11.37, from Rijkens to Blessing 16.11.37, Uni. Unilever had built up large cash surpluses in Germany which could not be transferred abroad through dividend payments because of the government's 'blocked Mark' policy. During a series of meetings with Rijkens between 1935 and 1937, Blessing negotiated a complex series of financial transactions to allow these Marks to be employed for the building of ships. Under the plan put into action between 1935 and 1939, 300,000 tonnes of shipping of various kinds were constructed using the Unilever funds. Some of these were used for the concern's own operating companies within Germany, while others were exported and sold for sterling or guilders. See Charles Wilson, *The History of Unilever*, Vol. II. See also Uni. Memorandum 2.11.36, mentioning possible use of large German companies (including Siemens, Otto Wolff, AEG, Gute Hoffnungshütte etc.) to build capital goods for export with 'blocked' proceeds.

86. Hitler was fully aware of this fact when he received Francis D'Arcy Cooper, the Unilever chairman, and Paul Rijkens, the effective head of the continental business, in October 1933, and reassured them that the company's interests would be safeguarded under the Nazi state. Uni. Letter from Reich economics ministry to Margarine-Verkaufs-Union, 26.10.33, with report on meeting with Hitler on 24.10.33. The Unilever directors were particularly anxious to establish whether there would be discrimination against foreign-owned companies in National Socialist Germany. Hitler gave them the assurance that there would be no difference in treatment of foreign- and domestically-owned companies, as long as production was not transferred from Germany. See also letter from economics ministry to Unilever on 27.11.35, confirming that the state would maintain self-regulation of the margarine industry and would not discriminate against foreign-owned companies.

87. After the war, Blessing implied that joining Unilever had somehow been an act of defiance, since Unilever, he claimed, was decried in Germany as 'Jewish and capitalistic'. See UMT, 18.8.47, and internal Bundesbank document, 1965. The contributions made by Unilever to Nazi party coffers in 1939 and 1940 (RM15,000 each year) were, Blessing maintained, merely an attempt to smooth the company's relations with the Nazi state.

88. A Reichsbank memorandum in May 1940 offers a revealing insight into the basic economic reasons for the German attack on the Netherlands. 'Holland is a land which has not fought a war for 110 years, and possesses great wealth . . . Dutch industry has lately built up rich stocks of all kinds which could be useful for the German war economy and could ease its own stocks position.' The Reichsbank note drew particular attention to 'the stocks of margarine raw materials at the Unilever company' and noted the 'great importance' of the company's 'numerous margarine works and related industries.' Memorandum from Eicke, '*Was können wir von Holland erwarten?*', drawing on conversation with von Boeckh, a Netherlands expert in the Reich economics ministry, who later became Reich commissioner for occupied Netherlands. BAP/RB 25.01/7006.

89. Together with Heinrich Schicht, the chairman, and Karl Lindemann.

90. Set up under Reich commissioner for management of enemy assets.

91. Reichsanzeiger 30.6.41. Blessing claimed after the war that he had been 'thrown out' of his position at Unilever, which he left in September 1941. This was a result of disagreements with Göring caused by his opposition to the insertion of Nazi intelligence agents at Unilever. He maintained that he was 'forced' to take up a new job. UMT, 27.8.47; internal Bundesbank note from 1965; statements to Reinhard Vogelsang, in *Der Freundeskreis Himmler*, Göttingen, 1973.

92. Blessing was one of the founding members of the 28-man Kontinentale öl supervisory board. This assembled a roll-call of the German economic establishment. Other supervisory board members included Walther Funk, Göring's advisers Wilhelm Keppler and Fritz Kranefuß (the two main organisers of the Freundeskreis), Carl Krauch of I. G. Farben, Karl Rasche of the Dresdner Bank and Hermann Josef Abs of the Deutsche Bank. Document on establishment of Kontinentale Öl, BAK R.176/2.

93. Kontinentale Öl's RM80 million capital was spread among 13 shareholders, among which the Reich – represented through the Borussia holding company – owned RM30 million. Banks – led by the Deutsche and Dresdner Banks with RM7.5 million each, as well as

Commerzbank, Reichskreditgesellschaft, and Berliner Handels-Gesellschaft, owned RM30 million, while oil companies and other industrial concerns – including I. G. Farben – owned stakes of RM20 million.

94. *Staatsanzeiger*, BAK, R.176/2.

95. Production and exploration in Romania suffered severe difficulties as the war progressed, and collapsed altogether with the Soviet takeover in 1944.

96. Letter from Dr Becker of Erdöl Raffinerie Trzebinia, complaining of 'increased accommodation costs and high drop-out through illness'. 1.3.45, BAK R.176/32.

97. The German proposal was turned down by the Bank of England on the advice of the Foreign Office. Note on 29.4.58, BoE/OV 34/243.

98. Speech in Frankfurt, 7.1.58. He also gave a promise to employees: 'From my former work with the Reichsbank, I fully appreciate the devotion of which the employees of the central bank are capable because they are conscious of serving a great cause. I ask you to place your trust in me, and I promise you I shall be a just and understanding master.'

99. Speech to Bundesbank personnel representatives in Frankfurt, 18.3.58.

100. The author is indebted to Lord Roll for this reminiscence.

101. Conversation at a central bankers' meeting at the BIS in Basle, recounted to Charles Coombs, the foreign exchange chief of the Federal Reserve Bank of New York. 'Blessing wielded his enormous authority with courage and sensitive discernment of his world financial responsibilities,' wrote Coombs. 'I thought of him as a truly great man of his times.' Coombs, *The Arena of International Finance*, 1976, p. 28.

102. Funeral speech, 5.5.71.

Chapter 3: Inside the Bundesbank

1. Speech to the Federation of German Industry in Cologne, 23.5.56.

2. Interview with author in Hamburg, 4.6.91.

3. Interview with author in Frankfurt, 29.4.91.

4. Albert Speer's description of lunch with Funk at the Reichsbank in mid-September 1943. Speer, *The Slave State*, 1981, p. 69.

5. Pöhl collected his first honorary doctorate from Georgetown university in the late 1980s. He was sponsored by Ferdinand von Galen, chairman of the Frankfurt stock exchange, later disgraced in a scandal over losses at the private bank Schröder, Münchmeyer, Hengst.

6. The Bundesbank's transactions with German commercial banks

are carried out largely through the *Land* central banks, rather than through the headquarters in Frankfurt.

7. The Bundesbank is much more secretive than the Federal Reserve (which publishes minutes of its Open Market Committee with a delay of six weeks). The Bank of England, on the other hand, allows unrestricted publication of the records of its inner decision-making body, the Court, only after 100 years.

8. Helmut Schlesinger, as deputy president between 1980 and 1991, appears to have played an important role in initiating the trend towards less full recording of the Bundesbank's deliberations.

9. Interview with author in Düsseldorf, 24.4.91.

10. Interview with author in Jesteburg, 8.10.87.

11. The presidents of the *Land* central banks are nominated by the Bundesrat, on the basis of a proposal by the *Land* government, following consultation with the Bundesbank council. Several *Land* central bank presidents have been appointed in the past despite being rejected by the council.

12. The appointment of directorate members is made by the federal president, on the nomination of the chancellor.

13. At a reception in Bremen for Nemitz's 60th birthday on 10.7.85.

14. '*Das Für und Wider abzuwägen*'. Speech in Stuttgart on 24.4.92.

15. Interview with author in Kiel, 4.6.91.

16. Report of Bundesrechnungshof, 16.10.89.

17. Although the Bundesbank's statutes stipulate that the directorate may be up to 10–strong, Pöhl sought to limit the size of the body to only six. Since, in case of stalemate, the Bundesbank president has a casting vote on the directorate (unlike on the council), this meant that Pöhl needed only two other allies on the directorate to enforce his authority.

18. Storch was an adviser to the board on the state-owned Landesbank Rheinland-Pfalz between 1958 and 1969. Between 1969 and 1987 he was a board member of the bank.

19. Interview with author in London, 27.3.91.

20. An unusual guest at a council meeting was Oskar Lafontaine, prime minister of the Saarland. He took part in a meeting in June 1987 held in Saarbrücken as one of the Bundesbank's annual 'external' gatherings.

21. The meeting took place on 24.9.87, just before Pöhl departed for Washington. It set the minimum interest rate for a forthcoming securities repurchase tender at 3.6 per cent, against 3.5 per cent previously.

22. Schlesinger's desire to tighten money through the securities repurchase agreements in autumn 1987 was backed above all by Lothar Müller (Bavaria), Johann Baptist Schöllhorn (Schleswig-Holstein) and Hans Wertz (North Rhine-Westphalia).

23. All the 16 council members apart from the Bundesbank's chief interest rate 'dove', Bremen's Kurt Nemitz, were present. Two council members abstained. Had Nemitz been there to cast his vote, he would have opposed the half point increase, and the more conciliatory approach proposed by Schlesinger and Tietmeyer would almost certainly have won the day.

24. Normally an interest rate tightening will be the focal point of discreet government complaints. A rare episode where the government voiced criticism about an easing of credit policy came in February 1961. See chapter 7.

25. Interview with author in Hanover, 30.4.91.

26. Interview with author in Hamburg, 4.6.91.

27. Interview with author in Bad Homburg, 17.5.91.

28. Interview with author in Kiel, 4.6.91.

29. Interview with author in Basle, 6.3.91.

30. Whatever their normal mode of address to each other, council members at regular meetings call themselves only '*Sie*'. The president is usually addressed on such occasions as *Herr Präsident* or *Herr Vorsitzender*.

31. The only council member in the past whom Schlesinger addressed as '*Du*' was Alfred Härtl, the free-wheeling head of the Hesse central bank between 1974 and 1990. By the end of his 16 years on the council, Härtl forced the '*Du*' form on all the other council member participants.

32. Coincidentally, Karl Otto Pöhl spent several boyhood months at Clausthal-Zellerfeld during war-time evacuation from bomb-struck Hanover.

33. Against the Bank of England, the Bundesbank fields teams in football, karate, badminton, cross-country running, tennis, table tennis and swimming. It also plays against the central banks of France, Belgium, Italy, Austria, the Netherlands, Denmark, Portugal, Ireland and Hungary – and with the Bank for International Settlements.

34. Interview with author in Frankfurt, 31.5.91.

35. For instance, Vb 2201 indicates a relatively lowly functionary in a sub-section of the administration and buildings department (*Verwaltung und Bau*). A 231 denotes an official down the hierarchy in the foreign department (A for *Ausland*).

36. Among ordinary directorate members, the official in charge of the notes and coins issue (department H for *Hauptkasse*) is referred to by the Roman numeral I; the economics specialist is II – looking after statistics (S) and macroeconomic research (Vo for *Volkswirtschaft*). III is allotted to the representative for foreign monetary affairs, who is in charge of both A, the foreign department, and J, responsible for inter-

national monetary questions. The organisation chief takes number IV, while the banking man is coded as V.

37. The statistics team prides itself on exceptional resources. Unusually for a central bank, it has responsibility for collecting balance of payments figures. Before 1945, the job was handled by the Reich Statistics Office, but it was transferred to the Bank deutscher Länder with the aim of guaranteeing post-war accuracy and objectivity. The department collates information provided by 4700 German and foreign banks making monthly balance sheet returns.

38. The monthly report is about 80 pages long, with short reports on latest monetary developments, securities markets, macroeconomic developments, public finance and the balance of payments. There are three or four supplementary articles on varying subjects and a large statistical section.

39. The annual report has a circulation of 65,000, with a further 7500 copies published in an English translation. The Bundesbank prints 19,500 copies of its regular bulletin of press comment from German and foreign newspapers, which appears two or three times a week.

40. Copies in English, French and Spanish run to 5900, 1000 and 700 respectively.

41. Wolf worked at the same Berlin Institut für Konjunkturforschung as Otmar Emminger during the war. Wolf was a member of the directorate of the Bank deutscher Länder and the Bundesbank between 1951 and his death in 1964.

42. Wolf's refusal to bend rigorous standards caused sporadic discomfort for the government when the Bank deutscher Länder published assessments contradicting the Bonn view. This sparked irritated letters to Wilhelm Vocke from Fritz Schäffer, finance minister during the 1950s. See letter of complaint from Schäffer to Vocke on 23.10.54, asking the Bank deutscher Länder to restrict itself to 'objective' reporting of budgetary material supplied by Bonn. BB/PF Vocke.

43. On Wolf's death in 1964, Schlesinger was given responsibility for the monthly report at the age of 39, under the overall authority of Irmler, the board member responsible for economics.

44. Schlesinger maintained responsibility for economic publications when he joined the council in 1972, relinquishing this only in 1990.

45. Interview with author in Frankfurt, 17.5.91.

46. As part of the total, the Bundesbank, in common with the other larger European central banks, normally holds at least $3 billion on deposit with the BIS.

47. Unlike most other European central banks, which have diversified their reserves heavily out of dollars in recent years, the Bundesbank

keeps nearly all its foreign exchange reserves in the US currency.

48. Interview with author in Frankfurt, 12.7.91.

49. According to the BIS, the ratio of money in circulation to GNP in 1989 was 2.9 per cent in Canada, 3.0 per cent in Britain, 4.0 per cent in France, 4.4 per cent in the US, 5.5 per cent in Italy. Higher figures were registered in Switzerland (8.6 per cent) and Japan (10.3 per cent).

50. The Bundesbank splits its orders among two companies: the government printing works, the Bundesdruckerei, with note printing works in Berlin and Neu-Isenberg, and Giesecke und Devrient, an old-established Munich-based banknote printing firm with two plants in West Germany. Following the traditions of the old Reichsdruckerei, the imperial printing works founded in 1882, the Bundesdruckerei has concentrated on printing DM10, DM50 and DM500 notes. Giesecke und Devrient, established in 1852 in Leipzig, which moved to southern Germany after its plant was destroyed in 1943, has customarily produced DM5, DM20, DM100 and DM1000 notes.

51. The shredder, developed in partnership with a Giesecke subsidiary, has the capacity to shred 70,000 to 80,000 banknotes a day, after first sorting and analysing notes for possible forgeries. By the end of 1991, out of a total of 400 banknote handling machines in operation, 80 were fitted with the new shredder.

52. Bundesbank employees who are civil servants or *Beamten* – roughly 40 per cent of the total – receive a standard 22 per cent top-up above normal pay rates for *Beamten*. The differential was 30 per cent until 1976, but was then frozen in cash terms as part of public spending cuts. Only since 1990 has this top-up been allowed to rise slightly again.

53. In a letter to Fritz Schäffer, the finance minister, Vocke vainly resorted to an old Reichsbank argument. 'Under the Nazi system', he said, government control of salaries 'was self-evident'. He added: 'Why should the government burden itself with having to defend in parliament every salary position with the bank?'

54. Klasen was already a wealthy man after a lengthy spell as board member of the Deutsche Bank, including three years as joint chief executive.

55. The government in Bonn carried out Klasen's wishes. Later Schiller learned that, after taking over the Bundesbank presidency, Klasen continued to receive payments from the Deutsche Bank in the form of a large pension – and so suffered financially to a much smaller extent than he had earlier indicated. Similar considerations applied in 1979, when Helmut Schmidt asked Wilfried Guth of the Deutsche Bank to take over from Emminger as Bundesbank president. Guth was earning close to DM1 million a year (including supervisory board earnings), and would have taken a larger pay cut than Klasen. He turned

the job down – although claiming that the salary was merely a secondary factor. Interview with author in Frankfurt, 18.3.91.

56. Interview with author in Hamburg, 5.7.91.

57. BB Minutes/6.7.48. Klasen made the point that, in granting their most senior staff interest-bearing salary accounts, the Bundesbank was setting standards which were no different from the main commercial banks.

58. Bundesbank council members also have the right to large chauffeur-driven motor cars – often, as a mere status symbol. One thrifty *Land* central bank president, Dieter Hiss, ran into opposition from his status-conscious staff when in the late 1980s he tried to buy simply a Mercedes 200 rather than the most lavish S-class.

59. The DM370,000 figure includes an additional fixed allowance of about DM90,000. Bundesbank council members are classified not as *Beamten* (civil servants) but special-status public servants. They are none the less effectively treated as *Beamten* in that they automatically receive the annual civil servants' pay rise. The fixed annual top-up of DM90,000 is not eligible for pension. It was increased from DM40,000 at the end of the 1980s after previously remaining steady over a long period.

60. The bank makes housing loans to employees of up to DM250,000 at a low interest rate of 6 per cent. The benefit is taxable.

61. Pöhl pointed out that since 1975, the incomes of Bundesbank employees had risen by only 50 per cent, well behind the 86 per cent rise in the private banking sector.

62. Interview with author in Frankfurt, 15.4.91.

63. Interview with author in Basle, 6.3.91.

Chapter 4: Partner in Catastrophe

1. Speech to Reichstag, 20.8.15.

2. Radio address, 18.3.33. BAP/RB 25.01/7163.

3. Speech during training week for Reichsbank officials, 7.5.35. BAP RB 25.01/6514.

4. In 1871, shortly after the founding of the Reich, cash in circulation totalled M2.6 billion, of which 76 per cent were coins (63 per cent silver coins), 10 per cent state paper money and 14 per cent banknotes. The Coin Act of 1873, allowing the minting of gold coins by private interests in addition to the Reich, established the gold standard for practical purposes. Silver coins however remained legal tender until 1907.

5. Reichsbank annual report for 1919, published March 1920.

6. Hitler's dismissive remark on 12.11.41: 'One cannot establish the

solidity of a currency on the good sense of its citizens.' *Hitler's Table Talk*.

7. Between 1875 and the eve of the First World War, Germany's population increased to 65 million from 42.5 million; coal production jumped fivefold, overall economic output registered a rise of 150 per cent. Net national product (measured at constant prices of 1913) was M20.9 billion in 1876. In 1913 the figure was M52.4 billion.

8. For accounts of the monetary landscape in Germany in the mid-1800s and of the early years of the Reichsbank, see '*Währung und Wirtschaft*' by Knut Borchardt in Deutsche Bundesbank, *Währung und Wirtschaft in Deutschland 1876–1976*, 1976; Salamon Flink, *The German Reichsbank and Economic Germany*, 1930; Carl-Ludwig Holtfrerich, paper on 'monetary cooperation and the central bank question' in the German unification process during the 19th century, 1988.

9. As early as 1838, the government of Saxony, the most industrially advanced state in Germany, proposed a common coinage based on a unit one third of the value of the Prussian thaler – the solution which was eventually adopted in 1871. It put forward several names for the new coin, among them the 'Deutsche Mark', and decimal subdivision into pfennigs or cents. The idea, which was to have been based on silver rather than gold, was rejected by the other states as too radical. None the less, the German states agreed at the 1838 Dresden Coin Convention substantially to simplify the system, calling for each member state to adopt either the thaler or the gulden as a basic monetary unit.

10. In 1871, as many as 140 different sorts of money were circulating across the German states, counting foreign coins, notes issued by the cluster of German states and principalities, and old coinage dating back to the 18th century.

11. Conversion of silver coinage into the new gold-based Mark (at a rate of 1 part gold to 15.5 of silver) was carried out on a basis which ostensibly gave pre-eminence to neither the thaler nor the gulden. Significantly, however, Germans in the Prussian-dominated thaler area found it much easier to calculate the basis of the new currency – one silver thaler equalled three gold marks – than those in the gulden area, who had to use a conversion rate of M1.71 per gulden.

12. Only a small part of the reparations sums was paid over directly in gold. Roughly three quarters was paid in bills of exchange, with the rest in silver.

13. The Mark was convertible at all times into gold at M2 784 per kilo, and issued according to the formula that one-third of the notes in circulation had to be covered by the Reichsbank's gold reserves. Article 17 of Banking Act. Also accepted as substitutes for gold backing were *Reichskassenscheine* (Reich financing paper, issued in small amounts) and

foreign coins. The rest of the Reichsbank's reserves, making up the remaining two-thirds of the note issue, had to be invested in discounted bills of maximum three months' maturity, backed by at least two, normally three signatories.

14. The precursor institution was the Royal Deposit and Loan Bank in Berlin, established in 1765, which at the beginning of the 19th century was the only institution to issue banknotes in Germany. It was liquidated in 1836 and reorganised in 1846 as the Bank of Prussia.

15. 1875 Banking Act, Article 12. There was no mention of any commitment to monetary stability. Under the gold standard, this was taken for granted.

16. Article 27 of Banking Act.

17. Although money in circulation still consisted largely of coins, notes in circulation amounted to 456 million thaler in the 1872 boom, against 236 million in 1869 and only 6 million thaler in 1846. See Karl Helfferich, *Geschichte der deutschen Geldreform*, 1898.

18. Among the regulations were: Notes of under M100 were no longer permitted. The banks were obliged to redeem their notes at face value at the banks' headquarters and to accept them as settlement of debts even at their subsidiaries. Rules were also set for banks' balance sheets and for regular publication of banking statistics.

19. Dieter Lindenlaub, '*Seit 90 Jahren sind Banknoten in Deutschland gesetzliches Zahlungsmittel*', in Bundesbank house magazine, May 1989. Underlining the basic conservatism of Germany's earliest monetary arrangements, in most years up to the beginning of the First World War, the volume of banknotes in circulation remained slightly lower than that of gold coins. In 1876, out of currency in circulation of M3.05 billion, Reichsmark banknotes accounted for M747 million and private banknotes M207 million. The volume of gold coins was M985 million, against M990 million for other coins. By 1913, currency had risen to M6.55 billion, of which M2.57 billion was in Reichsmark notes, M147 million private banknotes, M2.75 billion gold coins and M928 million other coins.

20. There were no statutory limits on the state's access to Reichsbank credit (for instance, through discounting of short term Treasury certificates), but the degree of access was heavily circumscribed by the requirement of one-third gold backing for the note issue. Cash in circulation rose slightly less during the period 1876 to 1913 than economic output. Prices – which immediately after the founding of the Reichsbank had fallen as a result of the late-1870s recession – were growing in the first decade of the 20th century at around 2 per cent a year.

21. In 1914 the Reichsbank's gold stocks rose to around M2 billion as a 'Reich war reserve' of M120 million dating from the French war reparations of the 1870s, which had been kept in the so-called 'Julius tower' in Spandau, was incorporated into the reserves. The Reichsbank also benefited from transfer of a further M85 million in government gold reserves, as well as from response by individuals to the government's appeal for contributions of private gold stocks.

22. Reinhold Zilch, *Die Reichsbank und die finanzielle Kriegsvorbereitung von 1907 bis 1914*, East Berlin, 1987. Pre-1914 Reichsbank archives indicate that the first preparations for emergency war money and credit legislation were made before the turn of the century.

23. 'This simply gives formal recognition to circumstances under which the Bank Act in its original form is no longer valid.' Letter to deputy Reich chancellor, 29.4.11. Quoted in Zilch, *op. cit*. The Reichsbank's hand was forced by a run of depositors seeking to exchange bank accounts for gold at the end of July 1914, which depleted the Reichsbank's reserves of the precious metal by M100 million, or 8 per cent, in the last week of that month. The alarmed central bank responded by suspending convertibility – formalised by an alteration in the Banking Act on 4 August (Article 2 of Law on *Reichskassenscheine* and Banknotes, 4.8.14). *Reichskassenscheine*, already part of the Reichsbank's note backing, were themselves made legal tender.

24. Articles 1 & 2, Darlehnskassengesetz, 4.8.14. A limit was placed on the issue of *Darlehnskassenscheine* of M1.5 billion, but parliament was given the right to increase the limit if needed.

25. See Heinz Haller, '*Die Rolle der Staatsfinanzen für den Inflationsprozess*', Deutsche Bundesbank, *Währung und Wirtschaft*.

26. Speech to Reichstag, 10.3.15. Germany would finance the war almost entirely through floating bonds and issuing paper money, Helfferich added. He confirmed that the Reich was placing greater emphasis on issues of Treasury bills directly to the central bank, but added: 'The more that can be raised through bonds the better. Recourse to the central bank and particularly the printing press should be used, as far as possible, only to gain access to temporary resources.'

27. Speech to Reichstag, 20.8.15.

28. In particular, delays in remittances to the Treasury by subscribers of the loans meant that 'the wave of expenditure financed by short-term credit rolled ever further ahead of the "consolidation" [through long term bond issues].' Haller, Deutsche Bundesbank, *op. cit*.

29. In 1916, the government was forced to raise indirect taxes, but – in contrast to Britain – refused to countenance any thoroughgoing fiscal tightening, greatly swelling the budget deficit.

30. The figures for cash in circulation were M6.6 billion in 1913,

M8.7 billion in 1914, M10.1 billion in 1915, M12.3 billion in 1916, M18.5 billion in 1917 and M33.1 billion in 1918. The index of wholesale prices (1913=100) was 217 in 1918. The consumer price index (1913–14=100) was 310 in 1918.

31. The Reichsbank's holdings of Treasury bills, M2 billion in 1914, increased to M27 billion by the end of 1918.

32. The Reichsbank at the end of 1918 was faced with a situation which was far from hopeless: inflation during the war was not notably higher than in other combatant countries. Additionally, efforts were made in the early years of the Weimar Republic to levy additional taxes, notably under Centre party finance minister Matthias Erzberger.

33. The Reichsbank seems to have been woefully ignorant of the possibilities of large-scale inflation profits accruing to industrial borrowers which raised large sums from the Reichsbank, only to repay in hugely devalued Marks. Throughout the period of the great inflation, the Reichsbank hesitated to use interest rates to tighten monetary conditions. Discount rate was raised from 18 per cent to 30 per cent in August 1923, and then to 90 per cent in September, but was then cut again to 10 per cent in December. In view of astronomical inflation in 1922–23, these rates of interest were hardly punitive.

34. Speech in Berlin, 12.5.19.

35. Reichsbank annual report for 1918, published March 1919.

36. This, the Reichsbank said, was 'due to a not inconsiderable extent to the Reich's exaggerated recourse to Reichsbank credit, and the resultant sharp increase in issue of paper money.' Letter to Reich chancellor from Reichsbank directorate, 31.3.19, BAK/R.43 I/638.

37. Letter to Reich finance minister from Reichsbank directorate, 1.7.19, BAK/R.43 I/2391.

38. Letter of Reichsbank directorate to Reich finance ministry, 14.7.19. BAK/R.2 1894.

39. Currency in circulation rose during 1919 from M33 billion to 50 billion. Letter of Reichsbank directorate to Reich president, 6.4.20.

40. Cash in circulation rose to M81 billion by the end of 1920.

41. The Reichsbank correctly affirmed that the large volume of Treasury bills held by the public were all likely to be exchanged for banknotes in a time of crisis, which would put immense pressures on the central bank. Letter of Reichsbank directorate to Reich president, 21.5.21, BAK/R.43 I/638.

42. Currency in circulation rose to M122 billion by the end of 1921.

43. In view of the worsening gap between income and expenditure, and the government's inability to launch longer term loans, the Reichsbank wrote, 'The Reich was forced to balance its budget by issuing short-term Treasury bills ... Under these circumstances, an extra-

ordinary increase in recourse to Reichsbank credit was unavoidable.'
Treasury bills discounted at the Reichsbank more than doubled during
the year to M132 billion (Reichsbank annual report for 1921, published
March 1922). A further sign that the Reichsbank was giving way in
the fight against inflation was that the formal one-third gold cover
requirement was lifted through a change in the Reichsbank Law –
sponsored by the Reichsbank and the government – which took effect
in May 1921.

44. In a letter to Montagu Norman, the governor of the Bank of
England, at the end of 1921, Havenstein, the president of the Reichsbank, admitted that the central bank's threats to end discounting of
Treasury bills had been empty gestures: 'We saw clearly, it is true, that
we would not be able to realise this threatening [sic], for it is otherwise
impossible for the Reich to procure the means necessary for it [sic].'
Letter from Havenstein to Norman, 28.12.21, BoE/CF Norman.

45. Unless any chance of state order and economic leadership is to
be jettisoned, an end to this method of financing, which is extremely
damaging both to individuals and for the public good, can only come
about when the expenditure of the Reich, including reparations obligations, is reduced to a level commensurate with the taxation capacity
of the population.

46. Law on the Autonomy of the Reichsbank, 26.5.22. Britain and
France had pressed for the measure at a conference in Cannes in
January 1922 as a condition for a partial reparations moratorium.

47. The procedure for nominating the Reichsbank's president and
other members of the directorate was also changed. Rather than being
appointed directly by the Reich president (who had taken over the
Emperor's functions in this regard), the Reichsbank president could
be nominated by the Reichsrat (the second chamber of parliament,
representing the states) and appointed by the Reich president only after
the expert opinion of the central committee and the directorate had
been heard.

48. Letter of Havenstein to Norman, 4.3.22, BoE/CF Norman.

49. By the end of 1922, the total leapt to M1.2 trillion, and cash in
circulation soared to M1.3 trillion. Letter from Reichsbank directorate
to Reich president, 30.5.23.

50. Reichsbank annual report for 1922, published in May 1923.

51. Letter from Reichsbank directorate to Reich president, 30.5.23,
BAK.

52. Letter from Reichsbank directorate to Reich finance minister,
23.8.23, BAK/R.43 I/632.

53. Recognising that private sector wealth was either leaving the

country or was being diverted into non-monetary assets such as property, the government already put forward the idea of gold loans in 1922. But the Reichsbank turned it down on the grounds that the government itself would be encouraging a 'flight from the Mark'. See letter to the Reich finance ministry in October 1922, BAK/R.43 I/2391.

54. See Pfleiderer, *'Die Reichsbank in der Zeit der großen Inflation'*, *Wirtschaft und Währung in Deutschland.*

55. These Treasury bill issues were replaced using part of a loan of 1.2 billion Rentenmark to the state paid out by the new issuing bank, the Rentenbank.

56. Owing to the massive write-down of money and savings, the Reichsbank could proclaim that its gold cover for the note issue had never been higher. On the conversion day of 23 November 1923, Reichsbank notes in circulation amounted to only RM224 million, against gold reserves worth RM467 million.

57. Schacht was born in the Schleswig town of Tingleff, close to the Danish border. He could well have been born an American citizen, as was his elder brother William. Schacht's father had emigrated to America but his wife's ill-health forced the family's return to Germany shortly before the birth. The father's enthusiasm for the American way of life is reflected in his decision to name his son after the well-known Democratic politician Horace Greeley.

58. The title of a book by Norbert Mühlen (New York, 1939).

59. Schacht's grandson, given the name Norman Hjalmar, was baptised in early January 1939 in the presence of Norman, a fortnight before Schacht's dismissal as Reichsbank president. *Deutsche Allgemeine Zeitung*, 7.1.39.

60. In letter to Sir James Taylor, governor of the Bank of India, 22.3.39, BoE/CF Norman. An example of the intimacy on which Norman and Schacht conferred came in a letter from Norman to the Reichsbank president shortly after the Munich agreement of September 1938: 'You and I are no doubt in agreement that European prospects have improved since Godesberg and München where our Prime Minister, alongside the helpful attitude of your Führer, showed a courage of initiative which is not usual or easy in a highly democratic country. We may well be thankful to have escaped war, certainly for a short, and, I hope, for a long period.' BoE CF/Norman.

61. Vocke, *op. cit.* p. 92.

62. At lunch on 22.4.42. *Hitler's Table Talk*.

63. Before he joined the Dresdner Bank in 1903, Schacht earned M6000 a year from his job as director of the Handelsvertragsverein, and M2800 through journalism.

64. According to Schacht's own description, the nature of his quar-

ters for the job was far removed from the pompous surroundings he would later enjoy at the Reichsbank. He moved into the finance ministry on the Wilhelmstrasse in a 'semi-darkened room on the edge of a narrow courtyard'. His secretary sat in an adjacent chamber which up to then had been used by the cleaning ladies. Schacht, *Die Stabilisierung der Mark*, p. 68.

65. Letter to Reich president from Havenstein and von Glasenapp, 19.11.23.

66. Schacht later pointed out how the Reichsbank's action in allowing the Mark to fall to 4.2 trillion to the dollar considerably simplified the eventual conversion to the new Reichsmark, based on the old pre-war parity of 4.2 to the dollar. The official Mark rate was lowered from 630 billion to the dollar on 12 November to the 4.2 trillion level on 20 November. Schacht, *Stabilisierung*, pp. 72–83.

67. The president was nominated by the Reichsrat – the parliamentary chamber grouping the German *Länder*, over which the Prussian government had crucial influence.

68. Letter from Reichsbank directorate on 17.12.23, signed by von Glasenapp and von Grimm. The letter stated that the bank's rejection of Schacht represented the unanimous opinion of the directorate. BDC/PF Schacht.

69. The letter also accused Schacht of double standards. The Reichsbank directorate claimed Schacht had 'fought and tried to prevent' the Helfferich Rentenmark plan, but, as Currency Commissioner, was seeking to take the credit for the Mark stabilisation.

70. Stresemann, who had become foreign minister after the ending of his chancellorship in November, gave crucial backing to Schacht by winning the Social Democrats' support for his nomination.

71. In 1927, Schacht wrote magnanimously that the Reichsbank's preference for Helfferich was 'understandable from a human point of view'. Schacht described his own position as that of 'an outsider, whom most of the directorate had only fleetingly seen or spoken with, and who was even unknown to some of them'. Schacht, *Stabilisierung*, p. 93.

72. Schacht discussed the idea of issuing gold-backed notes through the Golddiskontbank at a meeting with Montagu Norman on New Year's Day 1924. Schacht, *op. cit.* p. 9.

73. Statement by Vocke, 2.5.46, IMT XIII, p. 60.

74. IMT XIII, p. 60.

75. Schacht, *76 Jahre meines Lebens*, p. 13.

76. Article 1 stated 'The Reichsbank is a bank independent from the Reich government.' According to Article 20, it had simply to 'report' to the government on its credit policies 'to maintain permanent contact in currency and financial matters'.

77. The general council consisting of seven German and seven foreign members (Article 14). Their nationalities were stipulated as British, French, Italian, Belgian, American, Dutch and Swiss. Foreign control over the Generalrat lasted until 1930, when another revision of the Banking Law abolished this stipulation. Article 19 set up a Commissioner for the note issue, who was required to be a foreigner. His task was to ensure that excessive increases in the banknote circulation would not lead to inflation. With this in mind, Article 25 limited the Reich government's access to Reichsbank credit to RM100 million.

78. Gold was required to make up by itself at least 30 per cent of the note cover.

79. 'The Reich finance authorities, not the Reichsbank, bore the responsibility in the first instance for this incorrect policy,' Schacht wrote in 1927. He pointed out that only 6 per cent of Germany's war costs were met by taxes, against 20 per cent in Britain. Schacht, *Stabilisierung*, p. 3.

80. Schacht's most powerful tirade against Socialist municipalities came in a speech at Bochum in November 1927. In 1931, Schacht wrote it was 'almost amusing how the unstoppable development of the borrowing economy is supported precisely by those Marxist elements in Germany whose worries for the protection of private capital are hardly at the forefront of their party programmes.' Schacht, *Das Ende der Reparationen*, p. 42.

81. Reichsbank annual report for 1928.

82. Schacht in January 1930 mutinied against his own government by declaring that the Reichsbank would not, after all, take up its stake in the BIS – a move which was successfully countermanded by the Reich government.

83. Schacht severed his connection with the Democratic party in 1926 as a result of the government's proposals for confiscating property belonging to the Hohenzollern royal family.

84. See resignation letter to Reichsbank general council, quoted in Franz Reuter, *Schacht*, p. 103.

85. Quoted in Reuter, *op. cit*. p. 111.

86. BAP/RB 25.01/7588.

87. Even the Third Reich leadership at times believed that Schacht was a party member. After Schacht was sacked as minister without portfolio in January 1941, Hitler's secretary Martin Bormann wrote to the party treasurer that, 'Various critical and disparaging remarks have caused the Führer to remove Dr Schacht from his position as Reich Minister and from the party.' Letter on 13.2.43, BDC/PF Schacht. In 1937, Schacht received the Nazi 'golden badge of honour' awarded to all members of the government. As he pointed out in his defence in

Nuremberg, this was also awarded to other prominent non-party members such as army representatives in the cabinet. He returned the badge after he left the government in 1943. Schacht encouraged the illusion that he was a party member. At a meeting at Rudolf Hess's house in November 1934, Schacht declared that he was 'a member of the movement', even though he did not wear a party lapel badge in his buttonhole. Transcript of meeting at Rudolf Hess's house, 20/11/34, BAP 25.01/6577.

88. Enmity between Schacht and the party hierarchy was evident as early as 1925, when the NSDAP informed its followers that Schacht's real name was Hajum Schachtl and that he was a Hungarian Jew exploiting poor Germans for the benefit of international Jewry. During the 1930s, the strained relations came to the surface at irregular intervals. In 1934, the party was told by an informant at the *Grüne Post* newspaper that Schacht had declared during an editorial visit that Germany would suffer inflation by July that year (24.3.34, BDC/PF Schacht). Later that year, Schacht was accused of being a 'high quality freemason and long-time associate of eastern Jewish black- marketeers of the worst sort' in a Nazi party letter to Rudolf Hess on 1.11.34, BDC/PF Schacht.

89. The SS chief once made the revealing complaint that Schacht was not only an accomplished liar, but was also given to addressing Hitler merely with the appellation of 'Herr Chancellor' rather than 'Mein Führer'. The remark, registered at the US National Archives, is recorded in Padfield, *Heinrich Himmler*, 1990, p. 207. Hitler remarked that Schacht was the only person who allowed himself such liberties in his manner of address. Ritter, p. 144. During the early 1930s, the SS appeared to be spying on Schacht through microphones hidden in his home. Gievius, p. 195. In 1936, Himmler confessed to wanting to arrest Schacht after he made a sarcastic after-dinner speech in Bremen. The speech, in which Schacht praised tradition and obliquely criticised the Nazis' love of novelty, attracted a furious note from Himmler on 1.5.36. The Reichsführer recorded that he had mentioned the matter to Hitler and 'would have preferred to arrest Schacht straight away', but had to be content simply with banning the speech from the Bremen newspapers. BDC PF/Schacht.

90. Statement at denazification trial in 1948 at Ludwigsburg. *Protokol der Berufungsverhandlung gegen Dr Hjalmar Schacht*, p. 53.

91. Before boarding the ship for New York, Schacht acquired a copy of *Mein Kampf* and read it for the first time. He later commented: 'For mass propaganda, the style was too ponderous, quite apart from the fact that one can only regard it as an assault on the German language.' Schacht, *Abrechnung*, pp. 29–32.

92. *New York Times*, 3.10.30.

93. In one hagiographic biography of the period, Schacht was termed from his return from the US in December 1930 onwards 'a conscious helper of the National Socialist movement, and one who played a valuable part in its eventual victory.' Reuter, *op. cit.* p. 12.

94. Schacht's meetings with Göring and Hitler are described in Schacht, *Abrechnung*, p. 6. For Schacht's views on reparations, see Reuter, *op. cit.* p. 5.

95. Schacht, *Ende der Reparationen*, p. 238.

96. The Harzburg rally was above all an attempt at uniting the various quarrelling right-wing opposition parties. Schacht stopped short specifically of endorsing the Nazi party. BAP/RB 25.01/6494.

97. Commiseratory letter to Hitler, 29.8.32, after the Nazis' setback at the July 1932 election. Schacht gave this advice to the Führer: 'As an economist, may I say this to you: If possible, do not announce any detailed economic plan. There is no such thing that can unite 14 million [people].' IMT 457-EC, XXXVI, p. 536.

98. Letter dated 'November 1932' reproduced in IMT 3901-PS, XXXIII, p. 531.

99. 'I have no doubt that there can be only one end to these developments: your chancellorship. It seems as though our efforts to gather a series of signatures for you from the economic world has not been entirely in vain.' Letter to Hitler, 12.11.32. IMT 456-EC, XXXVI, p. 535. Goebbels certainly formed the impression that Schacht was on Hitler's side. In his diary entry for 21 November, Goebbels wrote: 'In a conversation with Dr Schacht, I learned that he was absolutely on our side. He is one of the few who stand firmly behind the Führer.' Goebbels, *op. cit.* p. 208.

100. This took place after the ignominious two-month chancellorship of later-murdered Kurt von Schleicher.

101. Schacht helped to raise funding for the NSDAP at a meeting with industrialists on 20.2.33. Göring predicted at the meeting that the forthcoming elections on 5 March would be the last certainly for 10 years, and probably for 100 years. IMT XXXV, pp. 42–48, 203-D; XXXVI, p. 520, 439-EC.

102. *Hitler's Table Talk*, 22.4.42 (midday), p. 432.

103. Before Schacht regained his post in March 1933, Luther's annual earnings as Reichsbank president totalled RM145,000, in addition to an official residence and use of a car. Schacht's four-year contract allotted him an annual salary (including allowances) of only RM60,000.

104. In the first half of the 1930s, Schacht may have seen cooperation with Hitler as the way to power for himself. As late as October

1934, William Dodd, the US ambassador, believed that if Hitler were assassinated, Schacht would probably be called upon to head the German state. *Ambassador Dodd's Diary 1933–38*, 1941, p. 176. A close associate of Schacht, George Messersmith, who was US consul in Berlin between 1930 and 1934, testified at Nuremberg: 'There is no doubt that he nourished the ambition of becoming president of Germany.' Messersmith provided ample testimony to Schacht's ambivalence: 'Dr Schacht always tried to play both sides of the fence. He told me, and I know he told both other American representatives in Berlin and various British representatives, that he disapproved of practically everything the Nazis were doing . . . While making these protestations, he nevertheless showed by his acts that he was thoroughly an instrument of the whole Nazi programme.' IMT 451-EC, XXXVI, p. 530.

105. His formal reappointment by the Reichsbank's General Council took place on 16.3.33.

106. BAP/RB 25.01/7163.

107. Statement to Reichstag on 23.3.33. In his letter to President Hindenburg tendering his resignation on 16.3.33, Luther wrote: 'That the Reich government intends to carry out no monetary experiments is clear not only from the statements made up to now by the government, but also from express assurances given to me by the Reich chancellor.' BAK/RC.

108. Statement on elections on 12.11.33, BAP/RB 25.01/7164.

109. Schacht took over the economics ministry from Kurt Schmitt on 2.8.34.

110. Radio statement before presidential election on 19.8.34, BAP/RB 25.01/7029. Schacht's lobbying for dictatorship stood in sharp contrast to his criticism only seven years before that the German government during the First World War had been 'non-democratic' – a fact, he said, which had contributed to the financing blunders made by Helfferich. Schacht, *Stabilisierung*, p. 18.

111. Interview with *Berliner Börsen-Zeitung*, 13.8.34, BAP/RB 25.01/7029.

112. Schacht, *Abrechnung*, p. 10.

113. Schacht, *Abrechnung*, p. 13.

114. Speech to Leipzig fair, 4.3.35, reprinted in *Deutschland in der Weltwirtschaft*, 1935.

115. Unveiling ceremony on 31.7.35, BAP/RB 25.01/7167.

116. Letter to Hitler on 3.5.35. IMT 1168-PS, XXVII, p. 50.

117. The bills were designed to convert short term money market deposits into long term loans, effectively guaranteed by the state. The Mefo bills theoretically ran for 90 days, but were extended in practice for five years.

118. Transcript of meeting at Hess's house, 20.11.34, BAP/RB 25.01/6577.

119. Speech on 13.12.34, BAP/RB 25.01/7010.

120. BAP/RB 25.01/6992.

121. Memorandum, apparently for Hitler, first drafted on 14.8.35 and presented probably in September. As a sign of Germany's difficult economic position, Schacht revealed to the Führer how the Reichsbank had been forced to sell RM10 million worth of gold at the end of August (compared with total reserves of slightly more than RM100 million). This was a move 'which we cannot repeat that often'. BDC PF/Schacht.

122. For instance, in a letter to war minister Blomberg on 24.12.35, in which Schacht termed as impossible Blomberg's request for additional foreign currency needed for a doubling of the Wehrmacht's requirements of copper and lead. IMT 293-EC, XXXVI, p. 291.

123. Letter on 2.4.37, IMT 286-EC, XXXVI, p. 282.

124. Testimony of Albert Speer, IMT, 21.6.46, XVI, p. 562.

125. Letter from Hitler to Schacht, 26.11.37. Schacht's four-year mandate as Reichsbank president was renewed in March 1938. Hitler's assurance that Schacht would remain central bank chief pleased the Reichsbank staff. See speech by Rudolf Eicke, the head of the economics and statistics department, 2.12.37, BAP/RB 25.01/6360. The National Socialist press, too, tried to portray the move as cementing continuity in economic leadership. See for instance *'Schacht bleibt "im Boot"'* – 'Schacht stays on board' in *Germania*, 28.11.37.

126. Shortly before his dismissal, Schacht was carrying out negotiations in Berlin and London on financing Jewish emigration. He also intervened to help civil servants affected by racial discrimination – including Karl Bernard, the Reich economics ministry official and later president of the council of the Bank deutscher Länder, who was forced to leave the civil service on account of his Jewish wife. Schacht helped him to gain a boardroom post at the Frankfurter Hypothekenbank.

127. See Schacht memorandum on 14.8.35. 'We can, for instance, deport 700,000 Jews with a capital of well over RM1 billion only during a long period. At the moment the transfer of such large volumes of assets is totally impossible.' BDC PF/Schacht. Also BAP/RB 25.01/6444.

128. Speech on 18.8.35, BAP/RB 25.01/6992.

129. Memorandum for Schacht, 7.9.35, BAP/RB 25.01/6992. The Reichsbank was also worried that German banks' loans to non-Aryan companies – estimated to be at least RM750 million – could be at risk if these borrowers suffered losses as a result of boycott measures.

130. Letter on 1.11.35, BAP/RB 25.01/6789.

131. Letter on 24.12.35 to war minister Blomberg, IMT 293-EC,

XXXVI, p. 291.

132. BAP/RB 25.01/6789.

133. '*Die Juden im deutschen Privatbankiergewerbe.*' BAP/RB 25.01/6790.

134. BAP/RB 25.01/6790.

135. Testimony by Otto Schniewind, IMT Scha-34, XLI, p. 268.

136. Meeting at the air ministry on 12.11.38, IMT, 1816-PS. Blessing had already co-signed a Reichsbank notice on 20.6.38 prohibiting transfer of Jewish securities abroad. This followed a Reich decree on 26.4.38 calling for registration of Jewish wealth 'to secure its use for the needs of the German economy'. BB/RS IIa/14633.

137. IMT, 1.5.46, XII, p. 556.

138. See note from Dieter Lindenlaub, Deutsche Bundesbank, 30.1.90.

139. Meeting with Keppler and other government officials on 21.2.38, BAK/RFMR2/14.599.

140. BAP/RB 25.01/6675.

141. Agreement was reached that the schilling should be linked to the Reichsmark on the basis of 2 for 1. The government representatives however recommended that the schilling should remain in place as a separate currency.

142. Letter to Göring (undated), March 1938, BAP/RB 25.01/6673.

143. Joined NSDAP 1.12.39. Membership number 7312605. BDC/PF.

144. Wilhelm claimed he was alerted by Schacht in the morning on 10 March – a day before Schacht said he was informed of the *Anschluss* plans. Wilhelm, *op. cit.* 1954.

145. BAP/RB 25.01/6675.

146. The rate came into effect on 17.3.38, when the Reichsmark was declared legal currency in Austria alongside the schilling.

147. In view of the official over-valuation of the Reichsmark, the rate for the schilling may however still have been too low. A more realistic rate for the schilling-Reichsmark relationship would probably have been 1 to 1.

148. See '*Das österreichische Noteninstitut*', *Währungspolitik in der Zwischenkriegszeit*, Vienna, 1991.

149. *Österreichischer Volkswirt*, 19.3.38.

150. The legal changes were accomplished by a law of 10.2.37 which ended the Reichsbank's 'independence from the Reich government' and placed the Reichsbank president and the rest of the directorate 'directly subordinate to the Führer'.

151. The Reichsbank described the change in its 1936 annual report

as 'reestablishing unrestricted German sovereignty'.

152. Printed in *Zeitschrift der Akademie für Deutsches Recht*, 1.3.37, BAP/RB 25.01/7035.

153. Statement by Vocke, IMT 3.5.46, XIII, p. 82.

154. Schacht, *Abrechnung*, p. 21.

155. Speech in Vienna on 21.3.38, BB/RS. During his pre-Nuremberg interrogation, Schacht claimed that he had been praising Hitler for 'reestablishing the international position of the Reich', but was not giving support to Hitler's 'moral principles.' Interrogation on 9.1.46, IMT 3727-PS, XXXII, p. 586.

156. Schacht reminded employees that they were 'co-workers in the task of National Socialist construction' and warned: 'For the vanishingly small number of our compatriots who still separate themselves from the epic nature of our times, there is no room in our ranks.' BB/RS A.3749/Z.B. 12.4.38.

157. *Die Reichsbank im größeren Deutschland*, 23.4.38, BAP/RB 25.01/7037.

158. Speech on '*Finanzwunder*' and '*Neuer Plan*' to Economic Council of Deutsche Akademie, Berlin, 29.11.38.

159. Affidavit from Otto Schniewind. IMT, Schacht-34, XLI, p. 267.

160. Document from economics and statistics department, drawn up by Rudolf Eicke 3.10.38, BAP/RB 25.01/6521.

161. A magazine article bearing Schacht's name written in November 1938 concluded confidently: 'We will best serve the future goals of the Führer if we continue along the same path as before. If expenditure does not exceed savings, if management of resources is carried out with extreme care, and if capital investment is concentrated on areas of maximum use, then future monetary problems will be mastered as securely as in the past.' 'Bankpolitik im Dritten Reich', BAP/RB 25.01/6521.

162. Vocke, IMT, 3.5.46, XIII, p. 81.

163. Memorandum of 7.1.39, BAK/R 43 II/234.

164. Notes in circulation had risen during the previous 10 months by around RM2 billion – more than in the last five years (when notes had risen by RM1.7 billion).

165. Vocke statement, quoting an official ('Herr Berger') from the finance ministry. IMT, 3.5.46, XIII, p. 73.

166. A November 1938 notice had been signed by Dreyse and Hülse, while a similar message in December was authorised by Vocke and Hülse. The January notice was signed by Vocke and Blessing. BB/RS II 13691 (30.11.38), II/14800 (30.12.38), II/1202 (28.1.39). Just

over a decade later, after he took up his post as president of the directorate of the Bank deutscher Länder, Vocke suggested to the Bonn government that former members of the Nazi party should continue to pay
their monthly party membership levies. The proceeds would then be
used as compensation for the Jews. Letter to finance minister Schäffer,
20.7.50, BB/CF Vocke.

167. The letter, on 19.1.39, said, 'Your name will above all be always
associated with the first phase of national rearmament.'

168. Message to Reichsbank employees, 20.1.39, BB/RS A.822
Z.B.

Chapter 5: The March of the Reichsmark

1. Letter 26.1.39, BDC CF/Brinkmann.
2. *Bank-Archiv*, 1.10.40.
3. Radio address, 21.6.48.
4. Statement on 2.5.46, IMT XII, p. 585.
5. Schacht, *Abrechnung mit Hitler*, p. 20.
6. Karl Blessing, who declared that Hitler's 'inflationary armaments
policy' was 'dangerous', faced no apparent setback in his war-time
career. UMT, interrogation as witness in Flick trial, 18.8.47. Emil Puhl,
a co-signatory of the Reichsbank memorandum of 1939, went on to
become vice-president of the bank.
7. *Zeitschrift für das gesamte Kreditwesen*, 15.6.73.
8. Paul Oestreich, Funk's colleague on the *Berliner Börsenzeitung*,
related in his eulogistic biography how the eight year old Funk was
taken to the theatre for the first time – a performance of *The Robber
Baron* – and succeeded in playing the tune on the piano the next day, to
the natural delight of his parents. Oestreich, *Walther Funk: Ein Leben für
die Wirtschaft*, München, 1941, p. 11.
9. Funk played an important role in helping reduce the influence of
economic revolutionaries in the NSDAP such as Otto Frisch and Georg
Strasser. Funk's success in increasing the Führer's interest in conservative economic theories was shown by his authorship of a Nazi policy-
making document in 1932, which was approved by Hitler. It called for a
programme of work creation financed by public and private investment,
combined with 'productive credit creation through the Reichsbank, but
no inflation, rather the re-establishment of a healthy currency and a
healthy monetary and credit sector geared to production.' Oestreich, *op.
cit.* p. 82.
10. Underlining the dilettantish style of Third Reich personnel management, Funk took over the economics ministry post after being
offered the job by Hitler one night at the opera. The position had

already become subordinate to Hermann Göring as Plenipotentiary for the Four Year Plan.

11. 13.10.41, *Hitler's Table Talk.*

12. Douglas Kelley, in *22 Cells in Nuremberg*, London, 1953. Funk did not cut an impressive figure in jail. Kelley writes that he also made more complaints than any of the other inmates.

13. Shirer, *The Rise and Fall of the Third Reich.*

14. Telephone conversation with author, 23.7.91.

15. Abs was a particular believer in the need for effective German capital exports to the countries of south-eastern Europe to build up post-war production there. See, for instance, '*Kapitalexport als Zukunftsaufgabe*', in *Weltwirtschaft*, January 1941.

16. Funk developed ideas for a new international economic structure in a speech before right-wing students in Tübingen, 12.7.29. '*Befreiung von Kriegstributen durch wirtschaftliche und soziale Erneuerung*', published by Gesellschaft für deutsche Wirtschafts – und Sozialpolitik, Berlin, 1929. See also speech to Reichsbank central committee, 30.3.39, BAP/RB 25.01/7041.

17. Speech to Reichsbank officials, 2.2.40, BAP/25.01 7041.

18. BIS minutes of meeting on 13.3.39.

19. Speech to Reichstag, 30.1.37.

20. Bank of England memorandum on meeting between Funk and Norman at Basle, 13.3.39, states: 'Funk lays stress on Hitler's wish for good relations with Great Britain. The Governor pointed out the need for "fundamental appeasement between nations." ' BoE/OV 34/9.

21. *The Old Lady*, December 1934. Gunston's account of his three weeks with the Labour Service ended approvingly: 'The work which the Labour Service is doing is just one part of the effort which Germany is putting forth in this struggle. This seems to me a good work, and I personally should be glad to see the British people behaving equally well if we should ever be unlucky enough to find ourselves in similar circumstances.'

22. Note by Charles Gunston, 30.3.38, BoE/OV 34/7.

23. Interrogation of Schacht by Clifford Hynning, member of US Finance Division, 25.7.45. Second Report on Schacht after interrogation, 7.9.45, Economic and Financial Branch of Field Information Agency, Technical Control Commission for German BAOR. Both documents BoE/OV 34/11. In his later statements, Schacht was somewhat kinder towards his successor. 'Funk was certainly an upright man and not unintelligent, but he was slothful and possessed no overall view of the tasks which were allocated to him.' Schacht, *76 Jahre meines Lebens*, p. 577.

24. Schacht questioned whether Funk was intelligent enough to lie.

'I doubt if Funk lies. He is not in a position to lie.' BoE/OV 34/11. Another defendant at Nuremberg, Albert Speer, recorded that Funk asserted in Spandau that the one reason why he, Funk, was able to deceive his doctors about the true state of his health was because he believed in his own lies. Speer, *Inside the Third Reich*.

25. Speer recorded that the SS was rumoured to have a dossier on Funk's 'dissolute love life'. He added: 'In the celibacy of Spandau, Funk lecherously told about his erotic excursions through Casablanca, where he would go from time to time in order to experience new varieties of passion.' Speer, *The Slave State*. See also Henry Turner, *Hitler aus nächster Nähe*, 1978. Otto Wagener, Hitler's confidant and economic adviser, reported that in 1932 Funk became romantically attached to two black women in a Munich bar one night, 'ignoring all precepts of racial awareness'.

26. Schelling joined the Nazi party in 1940 after the initial flood of enthusiasm over Hitler's victories in the west. Joined NSDAP 5.9.40. Membership number 8185105. BDC/PF.

27. Interview with author in Hamburg, 5.7.91. Johannes Puhl, the son of Emil Puhl, one of the two joint Reichsbank vice-presidents during the war, confirmed leading Reichsbank officials' reputation for heavy drinking. When his father went to evening receptions he used to prepare himself by first drinking copious quantities of sardine oil. Interview with author in Cologne, 22.7.91.

28. Letter from Funk to Hitler, 25.8.39, IMT 699-PS.

29. Speech to annual general meeting of the Reichsbank, 17.3.42, BAP 25.01/7042.

30. Article on *'Wirtschaftsordnung gegen Währungsmechanismus'*, 1944, BAP/RB 25.01/6370.

31. Speech to annual meeting of Reichsbank, 9.2.44, BAP/RB 25.01/7012.

32. 'National Socialist Germany has already created a new order in Europe to form a new European economic community, a new European economic spirit and a new European economic and social order on the basis of European economic freedom.' Speech to rally of Reichsbank employees in Berlin opera house, 9.11.44.

33. The Morgenthau plan was drawn up in August/September 1944, and shelved in October.

34. In November 1948, a document from the US military government confirmed the ideas which had already crossed Funk's mind four years earlier: 'Without a healthy, prosperous Germany, there can be no effective European recovery.' Office of Military Government in Germany, 'Economic Developments since the Currency Reform', November 1948.

35. At the end of the war, total gold deposited at the Reichsbank amounted to RM655.4 million valued at the official price of RM2,784 per kilo). In February–March 1945, most of these stocks were transferred to the Merkers salt mine in Thuringia. This gold was confiscated by Eisenhower's army in April 1945. It was redistributed later to countries whose own gold stocks had been taken over by the Third Reich. See Dieter Lindenlaub, Manfred Pohl, '*Zum Verbleib des "Reichsbankgoldes" nach dem 2. Weltkrieg*', Deutsche Bundesbank, 1990.

36. 'The United Press reports sad news from Mülhausen in Thuringia. Our entire gold reserves amounting to hundreds of tons and vast art treasures, including the Nefertiti, have fallen into American hands in the salt mines there. I have always opposed the removal of gold and art treasures from Berlin but despite my objections Funk refused to take my advice. Now by criminal dereliction of duty they have allowed the German people's most treasured possessions to fall into enemy hands. On enquiry from the Reichsbahn [German railways] I learn that certain somewhat ineffectual steps were taken for the priority move of the gold and art treasures from Thuringia to Berlin; remarkably enough they were not put into effect because of an Easter holiday. One could tear one's hair out when one thinks that the Reichsbahn is having an Easter holiday while the enemy is looting our entire stock of gold.' Goebbels diary entry, 8.4.45.

37. Note from Friedrich-Wilhelm von Schelling, 25.6.57. Letter from Vocke to Funk's representative Hans Rechenberg, 27.6.57. Funk was being treated at a sanatorium in Bad Mergentheim, southern Germany. He died on 31.5.60. BB/PF.

38. *Bank-Archiv*, 1.2.39. Details of the new law were announced by Funk to the Reichsbank central committee on 30.3.39, BAP/RB 25.01/7041.

39. Speech to Reichstag on 30.1.39, commemorating six years in power.

40. The new law supplemented the law of 1937, which placed the Reichsbank under the direct authority of the Führer (Article 1), by ordaining that the bank should be 'directed and managed according to the instructions and under the supervision of the Führer and Reich chancellor' (Article 3). Foreign participation in the share capital was eliminated. Whereas granting of credit to the Reich was previously limited to RM100 million (for direct working credits) and RM400 million (for purchase of short term Treasury bills), these limits were lifted and the maximum amounts were to be set by the Führer (Article 16).

41. In an elegant subversion of Hitler's reasons for taking the Reichsbank under full control, Frede wrote that the decrees allowing

the Führer to set the maximum level for Reichsbank lending to the state was of particular importance for the aim of 'stabilising the currency'. Report on '*Die neue Reichsbank*', 20.6.39, BAP/RB 25.01/6861.

42. Joined NSDAP 1.10.40. Membership number 8182865. BDC/PF.

43. Frede was a board member of the Württemberg-Hohenzollern and Baden-Württemberg *Land* central banks between 1947-58.

44. Speech to Reichsbank training course, 11.12.39, BAP/RB 25.01/6861.

45. Award of title of *Nationalsozialistischer Musterbetrieb* on 1.5.42. BAP/RB 25.01/6367.

46. Kurt Lange joined NSDAP 1.10.30, membership number 345284; Funk 1.6.31, 551712; Paul Emde (who joined the Reichsbank directorate after Brinkmann left the Reichsbank on 5.5.39) 1.8.33, 2680559; Walther Bayrhoffer 1933, 3019575; Max Kretzschmann 1937, 3934028; Emil Puhl 1.5.37, 5852526; Friedrich Wilhelm 1.12.39, 7312605. BDC/PF. Of the Reichsbank directorate members at end-1938 only Blessing, Puhl and Kretzschmann had been NSDAP members.

47. Entered SS on 20.4.38, number 308241. Promoted to SS-Oberführer on 9.11.38. BDC/SS.

48. Article on '*Stabile Währung*', in *Völkischer Beobachter*, prepared by economics and statistics department, 10.2.39, BAP/RB 25.01/6521.

49. The Reichsbank memorandum in February 1940 said, 'Taxation [in the First World War] was avoided and was replaced by the more comfortable method of inflation. The extent of inflation was not incurable by the end of the war, and could have been suppressed through more rigorous and opportune economic measures.' In the war of 1940, the Reichsbank note concluded, 'The raising of the necessary monetary resources and the absorption of excess purchasing power will be carried out above all by means of taxation.' '*Vergleich der deutschen Kriegsfinanzierung 1914–18 und 1939*', BAP/RB 25.01/7005.

50. The Reichsbank economies and statistics department translated a *Financial Times* report on the Brinkmann speech on 21.3.39, BAP/RB 25.01/6585.

51. The story is related by Albert Speer, *Inside the Third Reich*, pp. 185–186.

52. Puhl, *op. cit*. Wilhelm, *op. cit*. Speer, *op. cit*. p. 185.

53. Letters relating to the affair in BDC/SS.

54. A memorandum for the Reichsbank directorate in November 1940 spoke, for instance, of a weakening of 'hopes of a speedy end to the war'. It recorded that 'tensions' were rising because the money supply was increasing while availability of consumer goods was falling.

'*Referat über die Währungslage*'. 29.11.40, BAP/RB 25.01/7006.

55. Article in *Die Reichsbank*, 30.1.40, BAP/RB 25.01/6365. Joined NSDAP 1.5.33. Membership number 3561949. BDC/PF. After a spell at the Landeszentralbank in Württemberg-Hohenzollern, Oechsener joined the Bavarian Landeszentralbank, serving as board member and vice-president between 1959 and 1967.

56. Windlinger was a board member between 1947 and 1952 at the Baden Landeszentralbank. He was also one of the 10 German experts consulted by the British and US military governments over the 1948 currency reform.

57. Article in *Staatsbank*, November 1940. The article appeared without the author's name. BAP/RB 25.01/7006.

58. Joined NSDAP 1.5.37. Membership number 5852526.

59. *Die deutsche Volkswirtschaft 1940*, No. 30. BAP/RB 25.01/7042.

60. Like many leading bankers, Puhl was regarded with considerable suspicion by hard-liners in the party hierarchy. A four-page memorandum (undated, but written during the war) from Nazi party headquarters records that he 'made frequent statements against National Socialism' in the Reichsbank, both before and after 1933. Puhl's children were reported as telling schoolfriends that their father had declared at home that Germany could not win the war and that Hitler 'would go the same way as Napoleon.'

61. Joined NSDAP 1.10.30. Membership number 345284. BDC/PF.

62. In the summer Puhl told Albert Thoms, an employee of the Reichsbank, that the bank was going to act as a custodian of the SS for the reception and disposition of unusual deposits which would include gold, and that the matter should be kept highly secret. Questioned in a post-war American internment camp, Puhl confirmed the arrangement to store gold and jewels for the SS in an affidavit on 3.5.46. Funk told both him and Friedrich Wilhelm that the material was confiscated property from the eastern occupied territories. Puhl said he protested but was told to go ahead and ask no questions. Oswald Pohl, chief of the economic and administration main office of the SS (WVHA), testified on 15.7.46 that he discussed the manner of delivery with Puhl and that in this conversation no doubt remained that the objects were jewellery and valuables of concentration camp inmates. See *Trials of War Criminals, October 1946–April 1949*, Vol XII, Washington, especially pp. 611–625.

63. The judgment found that 'without doubt Puhl was a consenting participant in the execution of the entire plan, although his participation was not a major one'. Puhl was found guilty on the charge of assisting in 'atrocities and offences committed against civilian populations', but was

cleared of the charge of financing enterprises employing slave labour. He was given a five-year jail sentence. But since his time in custody since May 1945 was credited against the sentence, Puhl was soon released. During the period of hardship, Puhl's family was given financial assistance by the Bank deutscher Länder. Interview with Johannes Puhl in Cologne, 22.7.91.

64. Puhl became a board member of the Hamburger Kreditbank, the institute in Hamburg formed to carry on the business of the Dresdner Bank in the British occupied zone.

65. *Bank-Archiv*, 1.10.40.

66. Benning, '*Europäische Währungsfragen*', in *Europäische Wirtschaftsgemeinschaft*, 1943. During the war, Benning's output of reports and propaganda articles was prolific. In an unpublished report on the war economy in mid-1941, he wrote: 'The impregnable lead which the German armaments industry has built up in this field over foreign economies – especially those of our opponents – is explained because the German authorities took, in good time and with foresight, the necessary measures to ensure that production would be allocated the priority demanded by public requirements. (Reichs-Kredit-Gesellschaft economic report for first half of 1941). The report showed a lack of foresight about the capabilities of the US war economy: 'In contrast to a German war economy geared to the highest performance, the economies of our opponents are in the midst of unsolved restructuring challenges. This is as true for Great Britain and the Empire as it is for the United States of America; the latter in particular offers a characteristic example of the difficulties of carrying out an over-rapid economic transformation.' See also accompanying letter from Benning to Einsiedel, 23.9.41. Both documents BAP/RB 6428.

67. Diehl was a member of the management board of the Rhineland-Palatinate *Landeszentralbank* between 1948 and 1959. He then became vice-president of the Hesse *Landeszentralbank* between 1960 and 1964.

68. Speech at rally on 30.1.41, BAP/RB 25.01/6792.

69. Document from 20.6.40, BAP/RB 25.01/7015.

70. The Reichsbank defined a *Großwirtschaftsraum* as an area where one leading country was dominant. The world would be divided up into six such 'areas of interest': German (including Belgium, Holland, Scandinavia, south east Europe); Italian (Spain, Greece, Turkey); Russian (Baltic states, Finland, Iran); Japan (China, Manchuria); Britain (undefined); US (Central and South America)

71. Raw material deliveries and debt relief were put at RM7 billion each, with a 'gold and currency fund for the Reichsbank' estimated at RM2 to 3 billion. The Reichsbank pointed out that Britain and France possessed gold reserves totalling RM10 to 12 billion, and that Germany

had managed to pay more than 68 billion gold Marks in reparations after the First World War.

72. Interrogation on 22.10.45, IMT 3544-PS, XXXII, p. 371.

73. Note from Reich economics ministry, 3.7.40, BAP/RB 25.01/6428.

74. *'Abschöpfung durch Anleihebegebung'*, *Bankwirtschaft*, 15.6.43; *'Europäische Währungsfragen'*, *Europäische Wirtschaftsgemeinschaft*, 1943.

75. 30.3.39, BAP/RB 25.01/7041.

76. Puhl's statement to Hamburg Rotary Club, 10.3.54.

77. Statement to Rotary Club, Hamburg, 10.3.54.

78. Draft prepared by economics and statistics department, May 1940, BAP/RB 25.01/6428.

79. Speech on *'Die Reichsbank im neuen Deutschland'*, Cologne, 26.2.41, BAP/RB 25.01/6365.

80. *'Deutsche Währungshilfe in den besetzten Gebieten'*. This article by Reichsbank directorate member Max Kretzschmann in *Bank-Archiv*, 1.1.41, describes how *'Goldwährungen'* were turned 'practically overnight' into *'Arbeitswährungen'*.

81. Article for *Der Vierjahresplan: 'Währungsaufbau in Serbien'*, June 1941, BAP/RB 25.01/6327.

82. Article for issue of *Weltwirtschaft*, *'Reichsbankarbeit im Dienste der europäischen Wirtschaftsgemeinschaft'*, December 1942, BAP/RB 25.01/6367.

83. Speech in Bochum on 7.1.43, BAP/RB 25.01/7132.

84. *'Die Kreditwirtschaft im Generalgouvernement'*, *Bank-Archiv*, 1941.

85. Frank letters/statements praising Paersch's capabilities – 15.3.41. 14.5.43, 7.7.44, BAF PF/Paersch.

86. Letter from Heinrich Hartlieb, member of Bundesbank directorate, to Paersch, 16.2.65, BB.

87. Memorandum from economics and statistics department, *'Gefahren der heutigen Währungslage'*, 19.1.42, BAP/RB 25.01/6428.

88. In its public pronouncements, the Reichsbank was a good deal more circumspect – just as it had been during the period of growing inflationary dangers after the First World War. Its annual report for 1941, published in March 1942, declared baldly that the bank was 'effectively handling tensions arising from opposing developments in supply of money and consumer goods.' Annual report on 3.3.42.

89. BAP/RB 25.01/7132.

90. Lecture in Budapest, 9.6.43, BAP/RB 25.01/7010.

91. Minutes of advisory board meeting, 24.6.43, BAP/RB 25.01/7133.

92. Minutes of advisory board meeting, 9.2.44, BAP/RB 25.01/7133.

93. Annual report for 1943, 31.1.44.

94. Radio address, draft from economics department, 26.10.44, BAP/RB 25.01/7010.

95. Speech at Berlin opera house, 9.11.44.

96. Schacht was incarcerated on 23.7.44 after the failed 20 July plot against the Führer. He claimed later that it was only during his imprisonment in the death camp of Flossenbürg that he learned of the atrocities against the Jews.

97. Testimony of Albert Speer, recalling Hitler's remarks in July 1944, IMT XVI, 21.6.46, p. 562.

98. He added: 'Inwardly, I was never tied to Hitler, but I worked outwardly in his cabinet because he was in control and I regarded it as my duty to use my powers for the good of my people and my country.' IMT XII, 30.4.45, p. 493. To accuse Schacht of having prepared the way for war, his defending counsel Dix declared, was like condemning a car manufacturer because a drunken taxi driver ran over a pedestrian. IMT XVIII, 25.7.46, p. 303.

99. Schacht said: 'If I had had the opportunity, I would have killed him [Hitler].' IMT XIII, 2.5.46, p. 41. Closer to the mark was Schacht's explanation that this 'half-educated man' was able through 'mass psychology and the force of his will' to win over 40 to 50 per cent of the German people.

100. Schacht's defence counsel Dix highlighted the sentence in which Schacht criticised 'people who heroically go out at night to paint slogans on windows', meaning those who perpetrated attacks on Jewish shops and businesses. See IMT XII, 30.4.46, p. 561. The US prosecuting counsel Jackson on the other hand drew attention to the passage in the same speech in which Schacht said, 'The goal that these people are following is everywhere right and good.' IMT XII, 2.5.46, p. 638.

101. Affidavit by Otto Schniewind, who said that Schacht had often told his colleagues that he needed to protect himself from attacks from the Nazi party and the SS. IMT XLI, Schacht-34, 18.3.46, p. 269. See also Vocke's statement that Schacht employed more and more 'flattery' as his opposition to Hitler intensified. IMT XIII, 3.5.46, p. 73.

102. This episode was revealed in 1987 by Harold James, 'Schacht's attempted defection from Hitler's Germany', *Historical Journal*, 30.3. Minutes of exchanges on 24.2.39 between US Treasury Secretary Morgenthau and his colleagues show how Schacht, in a conversation with Donald Heath, the first secretary of the US embassy in Berlin, put forward the idea of taking up a job with the US government. The proposal seems never however to have been taken seriously by the Americans. Minutes of meeting from F. D. Roosevelt Library, Hyde Park, N.Y.

103. Schacht, *Abrechnung*, p. 26.

104. Schacht's relations with the Bundesbank were icy. Otmar Emminger revealed that the Bank deutscher Länder and the Bundesbank during the 1950s never reprinted articles of Schacht's in the banks' regular press review (*Auszüge aus Presseartikeln*) on the grounds that he had been an 'accomplice' (*Steigbügelhalter*) of Hitler. This seems hypocritical, considering Emminger's Nazi party membership. Emminger claimed that Schacht 'took his revenge by attacking Blessing towards the end of the 1950s in an extremely unfair way as a Nazi *Mitläufer*, which deeply wounded Blessing, as it was completely unfounded.' Emminger, *D-Mark, Dollar, Währungskrisen*, p. 280 and footnote. The Bundesbank archives' copy of Schacht's polemical book *Die Politik der Deutschen Bundesbank* is heavily annotated with Emminger's angry jottings in red pencil. Emminger took particular exception to Schacht's assertion on p. 31 that 'A rising price level is the self-evident accompaniment to rising social and economic progress.'

105. In his interrogation on 25.7.45, Schacht explained occasional lapses of memory on the grounds that he never kept a diary. This elicited the sarcastic comment: 'It is going to be difficult for you to write memoirs.' Schacht's reply was, 'I never intend to.' BoE/OV 34/11 1084/31.

106. See, for instance, A. J. P. Taylor's review of the English translation of Schacht's book *My First Seventy Six Years*, published in 1955. 'His resistance has now become a little firmer, his dealings with the other conspirators more pronounced; the support which he gave to Hitler at first has become more equivocal and more obscure.' *Observer*, 31.7.55.

107. 'One of the strongest bonds forging the Reich was cast aside. It planted the seed for a lasting separation of East and West.' Hjalmar Schacht, *Die Politik der Deutschen Bundesbank*, 1970, pp. 12–13

Chapter 6: Continuity and Change

1. Article in *Neue Zeitung*, 31.12.45.

2. Memo to Gen. Clay, 21.1.48, returning Clay's note on 'need for a currency reform' of 27.12.47. WWA/Omgus.

3. Letter from Vocke to Adenauer, 31.10.49, BB CF/Vocke.

4. In a speech in Hastings, quoted in Aidan Crawley, *The Rise of Western Germany 1945–1972*, 1973, p. 61.

5. Report by the *Reichsbankleitstelle* (Head Office), January 1947. The Statistisches Zentralamt in Minden reported that industrial output was back to the level of 1880, equivalent to the figure in 1865 on a per capita basis.

6. Letter to Charles Gunston. 18.12.46, BoE/OV 34/12.

7. Well before the setting up of central government in 1949, the western Allies brought the German *Länder* or federal states into existence, delineated by either new or historical boundaries.

8. The main difference is in the size of the units. The US has 12 Federal Reserve banks for a nation of four times the population.

9. Introduction to Law setting up Bank deutscher Länder, 1948.

10. Introduction of minimum reserves in operation in the US was one of the crucial monetary innovations brought in from Washington. The German banking law in 1934 had already provided the legislative basis for introduction of minimum reserves. This part of the law was, however, never put into effect.

11. Non-interest-bearing deposits which the commercial banks had to maintain at *Land* central banks, calculated as a certain ratio of the banks' overall deposit base.

12. The central banks of the French zone were permitted to extend credit to private borrowers until 1952. The Rhineland-Palatinate central bank continued such business until 1957.

13. Law on Bank deutscher Länder, 1948.

14. The Allied Bank Commission had at first only US and British membership. The French military government acceded to it at the end of March 1948. Announcement of the Allied Bank Commission's establishment came a day after the Allies' statement on the birth of the new central bank. According to the office of the US military government, the ABC would serve 'the purpose of exercising general supervision over the policies of the Bank deutscher Länder to the end that the objectives of military government law establishing the bank shall be carried out.' Omgus statement, 15.2.48.

15. Representatives of the Allied Bank Commission had offices in the Bank deutscher Länder's Frankfurt headquarters. In the early part of the period between 1948 and 1951, when the first and most restrictive phase of Allied occupation came to an end, Commission officials sat in on the council's meetings. Many Allied representatives had only mediocre command of the German language. Their ability to influence the council's decisions was negligible.

16. The initial American proposal for the bank's name was the long-winded 'Vereinigung der Länder-Banken'. The later suggestion 'Land-Union Bank' was rejected after the Germans pointed out that a Deutsche Union Bank, owned by the Swedish match concern STB, already existed in Frankfurt. By dropping 'der' in the BdL's name, the Allies wished to avoid an affront to the Soviet Union which controlled the eastern zones. See Eckard Wandel, *Die Entstehung der Bank deutscher Länder und die deutsche Währungsreform 1948*, 1980, pp. 51–68.

17. Baden, Bavaria, Bremen, Hamburg, Hesse, Lower Saxony, North Rhine-Westphalia, Rhineland-Palatinate, Schleswig-Holstein, Württemberg-Baden, Württemberg und Hohenzollern.

18. Communiqué of US and British military governors, 14.2.48.

19. Another integral part of US aims was to curb the power of the big deposit-taking banks, led by the Deutsche and Dresdner Banks, which had abetted and taken part in financial and industrial annexation and plunder across central Europe.

20. Reports in 1946–47 by the Finance Division of Omgus recommended that the Deutsche and Dresdner Banks be liquidated, that leading officials and board members be put on trial for war crimes, and that such people should be barred from holding any important functions in Germany's future economic and political life. The reports had no force in law, and went largely unheeded.

21. Joseph Dodge memo on 'Central Banking and Bank Supervision', 8.11.45, WWA 2/169/4.

22. Memo to finance directorate, 5.4.46, BoE OV/34/11.

23. The *Reichsbankleitstelle* in Hamburg was set up in November 1945.

24. Shortly after taking up their jobs, Vocke and Hülse were suspended from their activities in Hamburg during the winter of 1945/46 pending their appearance as witnesses in Schacht's trial before the Nuremberg tribunal. Hülse in the end was not called, which Vocke described 'as a relief for me in view of Hülse's inner muddle and fearfulness' (Vocke, *op. cit.* p. 144). Hülse took up his job on 24.4.46, starting with an annual salary of a board member of RM35,000, lifted to a chairman's salary of RM40,000 from 15.6.46. Vocke's duties as vice chairman of the board started on 15.6.46 with a salary of RM37,500. NRW LZB PF/Hülse.

25. Vocke had taken part in emergency credit negotiations with the Bank of England during Luther's luckless period at the Reichsbank at the beginning of the 1930s.

26. The argument by British officials was disingenuous, since the Potsdam agreement in August 1945 was deliberately ambiguous on this point. It stated that Germany was to be treated as a 'single economic unit during occupation' but also set down that 'for the time being no central German government shall be established'.

27. Gunston was for a brief period after the war head of the banking section at the finance division in the British zone. He had been sent by the Bank of England as a trainee to the Reichsbank in 1925, and later became a key observer of the German scene for the British authorities. Some of his dispatches to the Bank in the 1930s suggest an over-closeness to his subjects. In a condescending note to Montagu Norman

on 6.1.36, Gunston pointed out that newspaper reports from the German capital from the *Times* correspondent there suggested 'that Dr Schacht is in opposition to all or part of the National Socialist party. Propagation of this idea may well be embarrassing or even dangerous to Dr Schacht, who might consider it a friendly act if we could cause the *Times* to be more discreet.' Gunston proposed that Norman should take up the matter with the Foreign Office. BoE/OV 34/7. The *Times* man was reporting speeches such as Schacht's address at Königsberg in 1935.

28. Note from Gunston, 17.1.47. 'Hülse and Vocke now have the Reichsbank head office for the British zone in Hamburg thoroughly organised as a going concern. So far the British banking branch have been able to resist the lunatic ideas of the American Dodge, who broke up the Reichsbank in the American zone into three Landeszentralbanken for the *Länder* of Bavaria, Württemberg and Hesse.' BoE/OV 34/12.

29. Statement of British position, 20.2.47, WWA. 'The British attitude towards the proposals for decentralising the banking system in Germany has been from the beginning that the drastic measures proposed in COAC/P (46) 323 are not necessary for the prevention of the excessive concentration of economic power in banks, as this latter is accomplished by prohibiting banks from owning shares or exercising voting rights in industrial undertakings. However, in the British view, the system proposed is definitely inferior from a technical point of view to that already in operation, and the greatest skill would have to be exercised if the proposed banking structure is to be able to handle the very great financial strains which will be put upon it in the coming years. If financial catastrophe is to be avoided, a strong control of the banking and financial machinery from the centre is necessary, and it would be part of Allied policy to prevent this central power from being abused.'

30. Clay cabled Washington that the lack of a bizonal central bank was 'a serious determent to the recovery of the Bizonal Area'. Cable to War Department, 16.9.47, WWA/Omgus.

31. Clay's words contained in letter from Bennett to Sir Eric Coates, 9.9.47, WWA/Omgus.

32. Letter of Albert Haynes (Kleinwort Sons & Co) to Edward Hellmuth, Finance Division, 18.7.47, PRO, Foreign Office 1046/678.

33. See Theodor Horstmann, '*Die Entstehung der Bank deutscher Länder als geldpolitische Lenkungsinstanz in der Bundesrepublik Deutschland*', in *Geldpolitik und ökonomische Entwicklung*.

34. Establishing the Reconstruction Loan Corporation was the subject of bitter controversy among US officials. According to a US memorandum on 19.2.48 on the British Finance Division's submission for a

draft law to set up the Loan Corporation: 'This draft attempts to create a new superbank . . . and build a monolithic banking bloc which could be used effectively to reduce to complete meaninglessness what we have attempted to do by way of banking reform.' Note from Adolphe J. Warner to Mr Aikin, WWA/Omgus.

35. Letter to Sir Edward Bridges, 1.6.48, BoE/OV 34/22.

36. Schniewind was previously a top civil servant (*Ministerialdirektor*) at the Reich economics ministry under Schacht. He was called into the Reichsbank directorate at the end of 1937, but departed a year later because of differences over economic policy before following a somewhat ambiguous career during the war.

37. Abs, from a staunchly Catholic Rhineland family, had enjoyed a meteoric banking career, becoming a board member of the Deutsche Bank in 1938 at the age of only 36, and representing Germany at prewar negotiations to freeze the banks' foreign debts. He was a member (like Blessing) of the war-time advisory council of the Reichsbank, and had been a close professional associate of Funk. Abs (like Funk) was regarded with considerable hostility by the more rabid sections of the Nazi party. In an investigation (undated) on Emil Puhl, the war-time Reichsbank vice-president, drawn up by the Nazi party authorities, Abs was classified among a number of 'politically unreliable' bankers; attention was also drawn to the 'strong Catholic influence' at the Deutsche Bank. BDC PF/Puhl.

38. On Goerdeler's list revealed in January 1943, Schniewind was earmarked for the post of economics minister after the war. Schniewind later fell out with Goerdeler and withdrew his readiness to serve. Ritter, *op. cit.* 1954, p. 601 (Appendix IX).

39. Abs left Berlin for Hamburg on 15.4.45 in a Karstadt department store delivery lorry loaded with Deutsche Bank files. After interrogation by the British and US authorities, in June 1945 he met Gunston of the British section of the Finance Division, who knew Abs from prewar contacts, and who appointed him as adviser to the British government in Hamburg. After an interlude of three months' imprisonment by the Americans in spring 1946, Abs was sent home to his country estate at Bentgerhof near Remagen before gradually resuming his banking career. Edward Hellmuth, a Midland Bank official who was one of the British members of the Finance Division, officially stripped Abs of his war-time directorships. Hellmuth recorded later that the warm ties he built up with the banker in Hamburg helped cement the post-war relationship between Midland and the Deutsche Bank. See Tom Bower, *Blind Eye to Murder*, 1981, p. 25.

40. Veit was an economics writer for *Industrie- und Handelszeitung* between July 1929 and January 1931, and was chief editor and section

chief at the Reichsstelle für Außenwirtschaft between February 1931 and end-March 1934. In a statement to American authorities on 18.8.45, Veit said he was dismissed 'because of my liberal economic political attitude and because of race'. His name was erased from the list of editors and Veit was unable to find a position or become accredited at a German university. He worked 'illegally' as a writer and bank adviser up to 1937 before joining the Hardy private banking house, which was taken over by Dresdner Bank in one of the numerous Aryanisation moves of the late 1930s. WWA/Omgus.

41. Minutes of 3rd meeting of Bank deutscher Länder council, 2.4.48, BB/minutes. BDL/BBK-2/1.

42. Saul Kagan, chief of the Financial Intelligence Group at the US Finance Division, had ruled out giving jobs to either Abs or Schniewind. The information was communicated to Max Grasmann, a former director of the Bavarian Industry Federation, now president of the Bavarian central bank, by Jo Fisher Freeman, the US alternate member of the Allied Bank Commission. Eugen Hinckel, the head of the Baden central bank, told the meeting that the French military government had no objections to Schniewind, but would veto Abs. Hülse, representing the North Rhine-Westphalian central bank, informed his colleagues that the British authorities had no objections to either man.

43. Kagan remarked a fortnight later that of the 30 contributions for the three top jobs (involving 15 persons) put forward on 2 April, 'At least 10 persons appear to be unobjectionable.' They were listed as Merton, Hinckel, Könneker, Hartlieb, Bernard, Blücher, Veit, Kaiser and Neubaur (a list which pointedly failed to include Abs and Schniewind). 'I am raising this point because I fear that new elections may include objectionable personalities and we may therefore find ourselves again in the unpleasant situation of vetoing such selections.' Letter on 19.4.48 to Freeman (Allied Bank Commission), WWA/Omgus.

44. Letter from Robert Fenwick, responsible for foreign exchange and banking on the UK side of the Finance Division, to Gunston at bank of England, 5.4.48, BoE/OV 34/90. BDL/BBK-2/1.

45. Letter to Bank deutscher Länder council, 9.4.48, BB/CM.

46. The two bankers pointed out that *Land* representatives on the council, who normally took decisions by simple majority voting, might be inclined to vote funds for their own *Länder* unless they could be countermanded by the BdL executive.

47. According to Abs, the *Länder* finance ministries agreed to support the Schniewind/Abs proposals. Telephone conversation with author, 23.7.91. It was nevertheless well known that the Americans were not willing to abandon their principle that power in the Bank deutscher

Länder should lie with the *Länder*, not the central bank in Frankfurt.

48. Denazification was handled by domestic German authorities. Schniewind was classified as 'absolutely non-incriminated' (*überhaupt nicht belastet*) by the Munich denazification court in on 17.5.47, confirmed by the Munich military government on 26.7.47. Abs was categorised as 'exonerated' (*entlastet*) by the Hamburg state commissioner on 19.2.48. Letter from Veit to Allied Bank Commission, 30.4.48, Minutes of council meeting on 28.4.48, BB/minutes. BDL/BBK-2/1.

49. Schniewind was also said to have refused to comply with Allied directives insisting he give up his positions as Sweish Consul General and as banker in the banking firm Seiler und Cie, in which he was a partner. The Seiler bank was also alleged to have been involved in illicit transportation of mail and parcels. Reports of investigations by Allied authorities, 9.4.47, 2.7.47 and 3.4.48. Minutes of 4th council meeting, 14.4.48, BB/minutes. BDL/BBK-2/1.

50. Abs was said to have 'cooperated hand-in-glove during the Third Reich with leading political personalities in government, industry and Party circles'. He sat on around 30 German supervisory boards (the overall figure, including foreign companies and banks, was more than 40 at its peak in 1941–42), and 'acted as a principal liaison agent of the Deutsche Bank with the economics ministry and the Reichsbank by virtue of the excellence of his relations with Minister Walter (sic) Funk, who headed both institutions.' Report on investigations by Allied Authorities, 20.2.47. Minutes of 4th council meeting, 14.4.48, BB/minutes. BDL/BBK-2/1.

51. Information from Hermann Josef Abs, in telephone conversation with author, 23.7.91.

52. Letter of Allied Bank Commission to Bank deutscher Länder council, 24.4.48. 'The Commission have given careful consideration to the foregoing proposal, but regret that they are unable to accept it.' BDL/BBK-2/1.

53. After a further interlude caused by a technical error in the way the Schniewind/Abs proposal had been communicated to the Allies. Minutes of council meeting on 5.5.48, BB/minutes. BDL/BBK-2/1.

54. 'I much regretted that Abs and Schniewind were not taken up as directors of the Bank. They are excellent men,' Adenauer told his friend Paul Silverberg in a letter on 24.5.48. Adenauer archives, Rhöndorf.

55. Bernard's civil service position became untenable in 1935 after the passage of the Nazis' anti-Jewish legislation. At the instigation of Hjalmar Schacht, Bernard was persuaded to resign voluntarily from the civil service before he was formally dismissed. Colleagues helped him to gain a comfortable job in mortgage banking. 'With the assistance of anti-Nazi friends, I became on 1.1.36 a director of the Frankfurt Hypo-

theken Bank.' Statement to Allied authorities on 17.4.45, in report by Financial Intelligence Group, 11.5.48. Bernard had been a member of the SS support association as a so-called *Förderndes Mitglied* of the SS – a 1 to 1.5 million-strong group which helped expand the organisation's economic base. As in many cases, however, Bernard's membership is unlikely to have reflected his political views. He was declared exonerated under denazification law on 30.5.47 by the Frankfurt public prosecutor. WWA/Omgus.

56. Vocke later claimed, in one of the many later examples of ill-tempered inrtrigue between the two men, that Hülse had telephoned him and advised him to reject the post, on the grounds that the British and Americans were against him. Vocke, *op. cit.* p. 147.

57. Von Wedel's name had appeared on an early cabinet list of a future German government put together by anti-Hitler conspirators associated with the 1944 assassination plot. In the list, von Wedel was earmarked, prophetically enough, as deputy head of the Reichsbank (under Blessing).

58. Another condition for acceptance of office was that the German authorities should guarantee him an adequate apartment 'with at least two rooms, separate kitchen for my exclusive use, lavatory, bath and heating.' Letter to Veit on 3.5.48, replying to Veit's message on 23.4.48.

59. Minutes of council meeting on 20.5.48, BB/minutes. BDL/BBK-2/2.

60. A post-war US memo (undated) on Vocke refuted the view that his departure from the Reichsbank was closely linked to the dismissal of Schacht. While confirming Vocke's anti-Nazi views, the memo put a slightly different interpretation on Vocke's departure than the one given by him later. 'He resigned in 1939 according to a provision which permitted leading members of the Reichsbank to retire on past pay if they disagree with policy etc. His retirement had nothing to do with the dismissal of Schacht. The reason can be found in his opposition to the Nazi party.' After 1939, his only activity was that of member of the Institute of International Law at the Kaiser Wilhelm institute. According to an inter-office memo to Kagan on 30.10.46, Vocke in 1943 was listed as 'a presiding member of the Chamber of International Law, Banking and Currency Section, Berlin. Reemployment was not considered.' Vocke himself gave his record as follows: '1939 (1 February) dismissed by Hitler for political reasons. 1939–45 No activity.' (signed statement, 12.11.46) All documents from WWA/Omgus.

61. Article on '*Schwieriger Start der neuen Zentralbank*', in *Zeitschrift für das Kreditwesen*, 15.6.73.

62. General principles for a speedy currency reform had already been put forward by German economists working at Ludwig Erhard's

'*Sonderstelle Geld und Kredit*' advisory group in the spa town of Bad Homburg during the winter and spring of 1947–48.

63. A further DM20 was paid out in August–September.

64. Liabilities were written down on the basis of DM10 = RM100.

65. Radio address on 21.6.48 on introduction of the D-Mark.

66. Documents compiled by savings banks, BB. B330/3617.

67. Allied vetting did not extend to the vice-presidents of the *Land* institutions. In several cases, the second-in-command at the *Landeszentralbanken* was either a former Reichsbank official or a Nazi member or both.

68. The French government also opposed Hülse, demanding that the British should drop their support of him as a condition for France's entry to the Bank deutscher Länder. Memo 15.3.48, PRO FO 1046/682.

69. In a letter on 6.3.48 to Coates, the British representative in the Finance Division, Bennett claimed that Hülse assumed that he would be elected president of the BdL council, and was already recruiting personnel to take to Frankfurt. Bennett drew on an affidavit from Emil Puhl, the former Reichsbank vice-president, pointing out Hülse's role in the 1930s Mefo financing, and stating that Hülse was forced out of the Reichsbank in 1939 'because he was considered a 100 per cent Schacht man'. WWA/Omgus.

70. Bennett wrote to Gen. Clay, 14.3.48: 'I think you should know about this situation. The UK has been backing this former right-hand man of Schacht in the Reichsbank for many months, in spite of our repeated references to his unsavoury past. He has carried out a one-man determined war against our efforts to liquidate the Reichsbank and create the Bank deutscher Länder. It would be catastrophic if he were chosen as the new bank president.' Bennett wrote again to Coates on 14.3.48: 'It appears to us that his [Hülse's] single interest in the Bank deutscher Länder is to obstruct that change in the German banking system which has been agreed to as joint US/UK military government policy, and in the accomplishment of which the BdL is intended to be the key instrument.' On 17.3.48, Coates responded icily to the letters of 3.3.48 and 14.3.48: 'It would take more than the allegations of a person of Puhl's dubious character to substantiate the pejorative construction which he has tried to place on Hülse's history ... I am not pushing Hülse or anyone else for the higher posts for the Bank deutscher Länder. My view is that we and you should leave this choice entirely to the Germans' unfettered judgment. If, of course, the choice were turned down by the Bipartite Vetting Party for proper reasons, that would be an entirely different matter.' All documents in WWA/Omgus.

71. Joined NSDAP 1.5.37. Membership number 4728865. BDC/PF.

72. Blessing, Emminger, von Schelling, Bröker and Fessler. Six members (Blessing, Hartlieb, Könneker, Tüngeler, von Schelling and Fessler) were formerly with the Reichsbank.

73. Blessing, Emminger, Lucht, von Schelling, Bröker, Rahmsdorf, Fessler and Dahlgrün. See appendix.

74. In 1958, eight out of fourteen vice-presidents and other board members of the *Land* central banks were former Nazis – Frede, Bernhuber, Mürdel, Gust, Krause, Braune, Wilz and Spilger. In 1968, the number had risen to 10 out of 14 – Küspert, Wießer, Gust, Schubert, Karnstädt, Thoma, Heimann, Rohland, Paduch, Hecker. See appendix.

75. Personnel continuity between the old system and the new was especially marked in the less senior echelons of the bank hierarchy, above all in the regions. In many cases, the new *Land* central banks simply took over the staff of the Reichsbank – many of them Nazi party members – who had worked there before 1945.

76. The French authorities took a favourable view of Boden. A memo to Kagan at the US Finance Division on 24.3.48 states that he 'was declared an anti-Nazi by the French'.

77. In 1946 Sentz was dismissed by the Allies from his post at the Deutsche Girozentrale. His appeal to the denazification authorities was however upheld after Sentz successfully argued that the Reichsbank advisory council effectively had no influence on the central bank's policies. See letter to Denazification Commission in Berlin-Zehlendorf, 20.3.46, LS LZB PF/Sentz.

78. Tepe was given the job after the Americans discovered that Wilhelm Schack, the first incumbent of the post, had been a Nazi party member. Letter from Tepe to Veit on 31.3.48 explaining Schack's dismissal. BB Minutes of council meeting on 2.4.48. BDL/BBK-2/1. Schack was a former *Reichsbankdirektor* who joined the NSDAP on 1.12.39, membership number 7333859. BDC PF/Schack.

79. After the Aryanisation, in which Deutsche Bank also played a leading part, Burckhardt und Cie was established in October 1938. Otto Burckhardt remained a partner after leaving the active side of the banking business. The bank was taken over by the Trinkaus bank in 1972 and was subsequently called Trinkaus und Burckhart.

80. Pfleiderer remained head of the *Land* central bank of Württemberg-Baden until the end of 1952, when he became president of the new central bank of Baden-Württemberg, produced as a merger of the three *Landeszentralbanken* in the area after the *Land* reorganisation in S.W. Germany. He remained in this post until he retired in 1972.

81. In '*Europäische Währungsfragen*', *Bank-Archiv*, 15.12.43: 'Germany itself has provided the proof that effective price stabilisation is

possible even at a time of strong credit expansion; Germany harbours however no illusions that this unique success – against which the enemy powers have nothing comparable to offer – can be achieved on any other basis than total organisation of the economy.'

82. Pfleiderer had been in 1932 the assistant of Alfred Weber, the renowned sociology professor at Heidelberg university, who lost his job when the Nazis came to power in 1933. After the war, Pfleiderer was put in charge of the Württemberg-Baden finance ministry's bank and insurance supervisory department, with the rank of *Ministerialrat*. See Leonhard Gleske in commemorative speech on first anniversary of Pfleiderer's death, Heidelberg, 6.2.90.

83. Other members of the 'conclave' who later joined the Bundesbank included Karl Bernard as well as Heinrich Hartlieb, Eduard Wolf and Victor Wrede. Wolf was nominated but did not take part in the deliberations because he failed to gain authorisation for his family to join him from Berlin. Wandel, *op. cit.* pp. 107–108.

84. See Gleske speech, Heidelberg, 6.2.90.

85. 'When the Reichsbank became acquainted with the great domestic and foreign policy tasks which the Führer had set himself and the German people, it did not hesitate for an instant to take the problems in hand, and went to the limit of its possibilities in granting bridging credits to the state,' Hülse declared in 1938. Article for German Banking Conference, *Bank-Archiv*, 15.5.38.

86. Hülse claimed that his removal in 1935 from his well-paid Basle post of assistant general manager at the Bank for International Settlements was at the instigation of the party. Hülse earned RM105,000 a year tax-free from the BIS, but his salary was reduced to RM52,000 (after tax – RM22,000) when, at the behest of Schacht, he joined the Reichsbank directorate. He continued to draw his Reichsbank salary after being dismissed from the central bank – a detail of which, he said after the war, the Hitler regime was unaware. Post-war questionnaire (undated) for Military Government of Germany; Statement to Allied authorities, 22.1.46, NRW LZB PF/Hülse.

87. Partly as a result of his strictures, the sums raised through the Mefo bills were continually refinanced through floating of large government bonds on the capital market. At the beginning of 1946, in an account of his Reichsbank career to the Allied authorities in Hamburg, Hülse put this interpretation on the events: 'When I took up my post in the Reichsbank on 1 July 1935, all the fundamental decisions concerning armaments expenditure and other kinds of employment creation (Autobahn construction, among other things) had already been taken . . . During the whole time of my activity at the Reichsbank from 1 July 1935 to 20 January 1939 I fought against the granting of Reichs-

bank credit either to or for the Reich.' Statement to British authorities, Hamburg, 22.1.46, NRW LZB/PF Hülse.

88. Statement to Allied authorities, 22.1.46. NRW LZB PF/Hülse.

89. 'Granting of credits: . . . Jews: The recent measures taken by the Reich government in respect of Jews in the economy call for the greatest caution in granting credits to Jewish companies . . .' Reichsbank notice signed by Dreyse and Hülse, 11.7.38, BB/RS 58.V. RBK-1-DRS1.

90. Notice on 5.7.38, reproducing injunctions from Goebbels and Bormann. Hülse signed this notice along with Dresye. BB/RS A. 12933 Z.B. RBK-1-DRS1.

91. Speech on 50th birthday, Wiesbaden, 29.12.48.

92. Otto Veit, *Die Zukunft des Geldes*, Berlin, 1937.

93. '*Neue Grundlagen der Krisenbekämpfung*' *Bank-Archiv*, 1.6.38.

94. '*Kapitalbereitschaft und Kriegsfinanzierung*', *Bank-Archiv*, 2.11.39.

95. Otto Veit, *Grundriss der Währungspolitik*, Frankfurt, 1961.

96. Vocke, Treue, Könneker, Wilhelm. The other two were Wrede and Zachau.

97. The horse-dealer was Heymann und Beringer. Könneker claimed that problems with the Nazis forced him to make himself available for call-up in 1942. At the time of Germany's capitulation, Könneker was a British prisoner of war. Statement to military authorities, 7.10.45. WWA/Omgus.

98. Zachau was with the central organisation of the German savings banks association, Deutscher Sparkassen- und Giroverband and Deutsche Girozentrale-Deutsche Kommunalbank, between 1927 and 1943.

99. Joined NSDAP 5.2.40. Membership number 8015808. BDC PF/Treue.

100. The council's initial choice for the banking and credit directorate job had fallen on Fritz Paersch, who failed to pass denazification procedures.

101. At the beginning of the 1990s, the Bundesbank's official register of German central bankers indicated that Friedrich Wilhelm, the former Reichsbanker, and Karl Friedrich Wilhelm, the directorate member of the post-war central bank, were two separate people.

102. Post-war biographical note (date indecipherable), BB PF/ Wilhelm.

103. Wilhelm's appointment (together with that of Bayrhoffer and Lange) was announced at the beginning of February 1939 after the departures of Vocke, Blessing and Erhard. Reichsbank notice 6.2.39, BB/RS I.2016.

104. Wilhelm maintained after the war that he joined in 1940,

whereas Nazi party records put his date of membership as 1.12.39. The application was made on 24.11.39. Membership no. 7312605. BDC PF/Wilhelm.

105. The other two motives were: 'To make sure that the influence of the party within the bank could be countered in a professional way; and finally in order not to expose myself, through a refusal to join the party, to the danger of loss of my possessions, my livelihood and my life, and to escape to the fullest extent possible from the threat of being spied upon.'

106. The idea was put forward by Alfred Rosenberg, Hitler's Reich minister for the Eastern Occupied Territories, at a meeting on 28.5.41. Wilhelm is quoted in the official German government transcript as saying that, 'on no account should the Reichsbank be exposed to the charge of counterfeiting notes.' IMT 1031-PS. In an unpublished March 1954 memoir, Wilhelm claims to have told the meeting that the action would only take place 'over my dead body'. The memoir contains an important factual error on the status of the Reichsbank. Wilhelm claims that he was promoted to a member of the directorate when the bank was still autonomous from government, whereas it had already been taken formally under Reich control in 1937. BB/PF Wilhelm.

107. Note from Redel, personnel chief of BdL, 20.7.48, BB/PF Wilhelm.

108. Wilhelm was classified as a *Mitläufer* (follower) in March 1949.

109. Bernard wrote to the Commission on 15.3.49 requesting Wilhelm's authorisation from the Allies' Vetting Committee. Bernard wrote again on 20.4.49 informing the Commission, in a polite form of ultimatum, that the bank would consider that approval had been granted unless it received a negative answer before 1.5.49. The reply was not given until 16.5.49. BB PF/Wilhelm.

110. Wrede had also participated in Ludwig Erhard's Bad Homburg '*Sonderstelle*'.

111. Letter to Hugo Scharnberg, chairman of the Bundestag's monetary and credit committee, 1.1.51. Leading politicians who were informed by letter of the BdL's version of events included Chancellor Adenauer, vice-chancellor Blücher, economics minister Erhard and finance minister Schäffer. BB PF/Wrede.

112. Questionnaire for military authorities in Hamburg, 5.7.48, BB PF/Wrede.

113. The council elected Wrede to his post on 1.6.48. After completion of vetting procedures, the Allied Bank Commission gave formal approval to his appointment on 14.7.48.

114. Wolf took pleasure in upstaging Wrede wherever he could – leading to strife within the bank. In a letter to Bernard on 4.7.49, Wrede

complained that Vocke regularly commissioned confidential reports from Wolf to prepare council meetings. Wolf also sent directly to Vocke the final versions of the BdL's monthly economic reports, without Wrede seeing them first. Wolf was regularly asked instead of Wrede to represent the BdL at outside meetings. BB PF/Wrede.

115. Off-agenda minutes of council meeting on 13.12.50. Wrede's futile search for the good life was illustrated by the fittings in the Bad Homburg home: the chrome-plated towel holders, the electric water heater, table tennis table in the cellar. Description of Wrede's house provided in report on 20.12.50 by official architect Hufnagel. BB PF/Wrede.

116. Report on the assets and income position of Dr Victor Wrede, 20.12.50. BB PF/Wrede.

117. Letter from Bernard to Wrede, 20.12.50, BB PF/Wrede.

118. 'If Dr Wrede believed that he could help explain his departure from the bank and his suicide with alleged difficulties in his position within the bank, and if he thought that, in this context, he could make certain colleagues in the bank's leadership partly responsible for this outcome, then I can only regard such ideas as a delusion.' Bernard added that, in spite of Wrede's undoubted economic expertise, he had been 'to a large extent' a failure in his work for the Bank deutscher Länder. 'He [Wrede] did not match up to the demands of his operational activities . . . The president of the directorate [Vocke] often saw no other way out but to charge the head of the economics and statistics department, Dr Eduard Wolf, with carrying out certain items of work.' Letters from Bernard to Adenauer and Scharnberg, 11.1.51, BB PF/Wrede.

119. The announcement, from the Joint Export/Import Agency, allowed German exporters to vary their Reichsmark prices, marking an important step to end the fixed price structure which had ruled since 1936. See Friedrich Jeerchow. '*Der Aussenwert der Mark 1944–1949*', in *Vierteljahrshefte für Zeitgeschichte*, 1982.

120. By coincidence, the new rate corresponded to the recommendation of the Bank deutscher Länder – but the central bank was not, in reality, involved in the decision. The setting of a relatively low devaluation figure was above all a result of the French government's wish to avoid giving German exports extra competitive edge.

121. The Bank deutscher Länder recommendation, made on 20.9.49. was made by 10 votes to 3. In the minority vote Pfleiderer and Hartlieb (representing the Bavarian central bank) both favoured a 30 per cent devaluation, declaring that the central bank should not repeat the mistakes of 1931, when the Reichsmark was not lowered in value

after sterling's devaluation. The majority recommendation for a lower devaluation was taken above all to avoid an inflationary impact of too large a decline in the D-Mark's value. BB/minutes. BDL/BBK-2/18.

122. This is confirmed in letter from Vocke to Adenauer, 31.10.49. 'The right of the Allied Bank Commission to give the bank instructions has, for practical purposes – as Sir Eric Coates [the British representative] assures me, come to an end.' Vocke added that the Commission hitherto 'has scarcely made use of it [this right].' BB CF/Vocke.

123. Compared with the 3.5 per cent Reichsmark discount rate maintained from April 1940 until the end of the war.

124. Letter from Allied Bank Commission to Bernard, 14.8.48. The letter asked for more information from the meetings. 'We should like to be in a better position to follow the course of the problems which are our common concern, and to understand intelligently the resolutions you put to us.' The Commission pointedly asked for minutes to be made available in English and French as well as German, confirming suspicions that otherwise it would have difficulty in following what was going on. 31.8.48, BB/minutes. BDL/BBK-2/4.

125. Letter from Commission on 29.10.48. Vocke's letter to Bernard on 5.11.49. BB/minutes. BDL/BBK-2/4.

126. Letter to Adenauer, 31.10.49, BB CF/Vocke. BDL/BBK-2/4.

127. Vocke disingenuously argued to the chancellor that the link with the Bank Commission represented a vital strand securing the bank's place in international monetary arrangements.

128. Letter from Vocke to Schäffer, 7.3.50, BB CF/Vocke.

129. The redrafted Article 3 required the bank 'to support, within the limits of its competence ... the general economic policy of the government'. Government representatives had the right to veto Bank measures, but could delay them only for a maximum of eight days. Change in law on Bank deutscher Länder, 10.8.51.

130. For an account of the manoeuvrings over the drawing up of the Bundesbank Law see Volker Hentschel, '*Die Entstehung des Bundesbankgesetzes 1949–57. Politische Kontroversen und Konflikte,*' in *Bankhistorisches Archiv*, December 1988.

Chapter 7: A Question of Interest

1. Letter on 5.12.21, BoE CF/Norman.
2. Remarks during Bundesbank council meeting on 3.3.61, BB/minutes.
3. Speech on 2.6.81.
4. Letter from Vocke to Schäffer, 7.3.50, BB CF/Vocke.
5. Interview with author in Kronberg, 7.2.89.
6. Pöhl repeated this remark at the press conference announcing his

resignation on 16.5.91. The term *Nebenregierung* was exactly that applied to the central bank by commentators complaining about the central bank's strong influence over government policy making. See for instance '*Die Bundesbank – Eine Nebenregierung?*' by Friedrich-Wilhelm Dörge and Ralf Mairose, in *Gegenwartskunde*, 1/1969.

7. Interview with *Der Spiegel*, 17.2.92.

8. The appellation – '*ein überständiger Kühlschrank*' – is difficult to translate. Emminger, *op. cit.* p. 463.

9. '*Ein elender Rechthaber.*' Interview with author in Frankfurt, 14.6.91.

10. Interview with author in Hamburg, 1.7.88.

11. Interview with author in Hamburg, 4.6.91.

12. When Pöhl quit the Bundesbank, Kohl pointedly did not go to the lengths of offering a ceremonial dinner for the departing president – as Helmut Schmidt had done for both Klasen (in 1977) and Emminger (in 1979).

13. Speech by Schmidt in Bonn at dinner marking Klasen's departure from the Bundesbank, 11.5.77.

14. Bundesbank annual report for 1957, p. 7.

15. The most outstanding example was the tacit understanding that the Bundesbank would postpone its December 1991 interest rate rise until after the Maastricht summit.

16. Afterwards Lahnstein joined the Bertelsmann media group with the aim, as he conceded with uncustomary frankness, of earning a great deal more money.

17. Additionally, it voted to lower banking liquidity through a 5 per cent rise in commercial banks' minimum reserve quotas. Council meeting on 18.1.79.

18. Telephone conversation with author, 12.8.91.

19. Interview with author in Bonn, 28.6.91.

20. Emminger, *op. cit.* p. 445.

21. Average unemployment rose from 889,000 in 1980 to 1.27 million in 1981 and 1.83 million in 1982.

22. Speech in Bundestag, 1.10.82.

23. Letter from Vocke to Adenauer, 4.10.50, BB/CF Vocke.

24. The council met weekly rather than fortnightly during 1950. It had convened once already in Bonn, on 1.3.50. The October 1950 meeting marked the last time that the head of government summoned the central bank council to Bonn. On more recent occasions when the chancellor has attended a Bundesbank council meeting (Schmidt in 1978, Kohl in 1988 and 1992) the session has taken place at the Bundesbank's headquarters in Frankfurt.

25. Minutes of council meeting in Bonn, 26.10.50, minutes BB/BDL/BBK-2/32.

26. Vocke, *op. cit.* p. 155.

27. The discount rate was maintained at 6 per cent until end-May 1952, when it was cut to 5 per cent. It was then reduced in four separate half point stages to 3 per cent in the following two years. Unemployment came down only slowly to 1.7 million (10.4 per cent of the workforce) in 1951 and 1.65 million (9.5 per cent) in 1952. But the trade deficit, which had been DM3.7 billion in 1949 and DM3 billion in 1950, fell to DM100 million in 1951 and switched on to a surplus of DM700 million in 1952.

28. Letter from Vocke to Adenauer, 26.2.51. Adenauer responded immediately: 'Please be convinced that I, too, judge the situation to be very serious.' BB/CF Vocke.

29. Letter from Vocke to Adenauer, 12.5.54, BB/CF Vocke.

30. Letter from Vocke to Adenauer, 20.4.56, BB CF/Vocke.

31. See Hentschel, '*Die Entstehung des Bundesbankgesetzes 1949–57. Politische Kontroversen und Konflikte*', in *Bankhistorisches Archiv*, December 1988.

32. Speech to Federation of German Industry in Cologne, 23.5.56.

33. Letter from Blessing to Vocke, 6.7.57, BB CF/Blessing.

34. According to Emminger, 'No one, really no one – apart from Vocke' believed that Vocke would be given the new job as Bundesbank president. Emminger, *op. cit.* p. 92.

35. 'I had become quite uncomfortable for him [Adenauer]. And so he gave Erhard a free hand against me with his revaluation policies, and brought in a law under which the Bundesbank president was no longer elected by the central bank council, but from the federal president, that is, practically by the federal government.' Vocke, *op. cit.* p. 151.

36. The trade surplus rose from between DM3 and DM4 billion in 1953–55 to DM5.6 billion in 1956 and DM7.3 billion in 1957.

37. Speech commemorating 100th anniversary of Vereinsbank in Hamburg, 11.8.56.

38. Irmler and Emminger both pointed in 1956–57 to the dilemma that a restrictive monetary policy could lead to revaluation pressure. Irmler first outlined his ideas in a speech on 5.11.56. Although Irmler – unlike Emminger – stopped short of proposing a revaluation, he used the same theoretical arguments to show that a higher exchange rate would lower inflation.

39. Letter of Emminger to Vocke with accompanying report, 12.11.56, BB CF/Emminger. He pointed out that flows of 'hot money' into Germany from abroad were unlikely to ebb, and noted that cuts in interest rates were unlikely to deter a further flood of international funds into the country.

40. See article by Emminger: '*Deutsche Geld- und Währungspolitik im*

Spannungsfeld zwischen innerem und äußerem Gleichgewicht 1948–1975, in Deutsche Bundesbank, *Währung und Wirtschaft*, pp. 485–555.

41. Emminger, *op. cit.* p. 81.

42. Letter from Vocke to Erhard, 2.5.57, BB CF/Vocke.

43. Speech at banking conference on 23.5.57.

44. Statement after Bundesbank council meeting in January 1958.

45. Letter from Blessing to Erhard, 6.8.59, BB CF/Blessing.

46. Memorandum of 20.1.60, BB PF/Emminger. See also Emminger, *op. cit.* pp. 104-108.

47. Emminger, *op. cit.* pp. 117–118. Blessing however couples his refusal to support a revaluation with the suggestion that a rise in the D-Mark's value could be considered if it was part of a general realignment in which weaker currencies were devalued.

48. There was also insistence that if currency parities were to be changed, the weaker currency countries should take the lead by devaluing. The German desire for the weaker currencies to devalue was similar to the basic stance over D-Mark revaluations within the EMS regularly adopted in the 1980s and 1990s.

49. Etzel told Blessing at the end of February that he and Erhard would oppose a further cut in minimum reserves, since this would create the impression in public opinion that the government and central bank were allowing the economic boom to proceed unchecked. Blessing's initial reaction to the question of revaluation was that he would 'lose face' over the matter because of his well-publicised opposition to it in the past. Etzel and Erhard however responded that a change in circumstances – above all, the continuing boom in the economy – would justify Blessing's change of mind. Etzel said: 'We will not call it a revaluation. We will say: "The purchasing power of the D-Mark must be maintained." ' Minutes of council meetings on 25.2.61 and 3.2.61, BB/minutes. B330/175/I/II.

50. This was reported by Etzel at council meeting on 3.3.61, BB/minutes.

51. Emminger records that Blessing said he would go to Adenauer and resign after he had been publicly criticised by Erhard at a meeting of CDU deputies on 20.2.61. Emminger, *op. cit.* p. 123.

52. Emminger, *op. cit.* pp. 124-25.

53. Erhard confirmed at the 3 March council meeting that, had the move not been accompanied by revaluation, the government would have opposed the 5 per cent cut in minimum reserves which the Bundesbank had decided the previous day. Minutes of council meetings on 2.3.61 and 3.3.61, BB/minutes. B330/175/II.

54. Minutes of council meeting on 3.3.61, BB/minutes. B330/175/II.

55. The 1949 D-Mark devaluation had been an exception – but the decision here was carried out essentially by the Allies with no significant involvement by the Bank deutscher Länder.

56. Press conference called to announce the revaluation in Bonn, 5.3.61.

57. Radio statement on 6.3.61.

58. After the revaluation, the rise in German exports was probably about 10 per cent less than it would otherwise have been. Emminger, *op. cit.* p. 133.

59. Memorandum to council, 28.4.49, BB/CM minutes. BDL/ BBK-2/4.

60. Letter from Blessing to Vocke, 30.12.50, BB/CF Vocke.

61. Memorandum on 23.9.55 from Dreschers of Margarine-Union reporting on meeting with Erhard: 'The minister would be prepared to permit, as a compensation, horizontal cooperation on prices as long as the overall price level could be reduced in this way.' Uni.

62. In a telex on 29.9.55 to Westrick, Erhard's key state secretary at the economics ministry, Blessing declared that Unilever would announce on the following Monday price cuts for the Palmin brand of 8 pfg per kilo and for the popular Sanella brand 4 pfg. per kilo. This was in spite of higher raw material prices which 'at present tend against a cut in prices', the telex said. 'We have shown courage and taken upon ourselves the role of ice-breaker.' Uni.

63. Letter of 29.9.55. '. . . We hope that we have fulfilled the expectations you have set in us. God knows that the decision has not been an easy one for us, and we would like to express the hope that our action will set an example and that our sacrifice will not be in vain.' Uni.

64. Blessing was aware of the opportunities for engineering his own personal advancement. It was later rumoured that he had volunteered to take over as economics minister should Erhard make good his threat to resign office. Daniel Koerfer, *Kampf ums Kanzleramt*, Stuttgart, 1988, p. 310.

65. Bundesbank annual report for 1964.

66. Speech on 15.10.65 to banking conference in Baden-Baden.

67. Speech in Mainz university on 24.2.66.

68. Interview in Leo Brawand, *Wohin steuert die deutsche Wirtschaft*, 1970, p. 56.

69. Schiller made the statement in April 1967.

70. West Germany recorded a current account deficit of DM5 billion in 1965. This swung round to surpluses of DM1.7 billion in 1966 and DM11.4 billion in 1967.

71. Emminger, *op. cit.* p. 141.

72. Emminger, *op. cit.* p. 143.

73. The conference broke all records for dilettante preparation and lack of results. Central bankers were prevented from taking part in many sessions of their finance ministers, leading the Bundesbank's Otmar Emminger to pass the time by playing table tennis with top Federal Reserve officials. See Coombs, *op. cit.* p. 183.

74. Coombs, *op. cit.* p. 183.

75. Blessing complained afterwards: 'I have a franc devaluation in the bag if we agree in parallel [to revalue]. I fought for a revaluation. But it was not possible.' Brawand, *op. cit.* p. 50.

76. Interview with *Der Spiegel*, 3.11.69.

77. One combination for the new Bundesbank leadership under discussion in political circles towards the end of 1969 was Emminger as president with Heinrich Irmler, the long-serving directorate member and ex-Reichsbanker, as vice-president. However, this was unacceptable to the new SPD-led government. Emminger became vice-president under Klasen.

78. Klasen in 1969 wrote that the increase in inflation in 1961 after the D-Mark revaluation was evidence of the limited effect of revaluations in dampening price rises. Letter to *Börsen-Zeitung*, 19.5.69, quoted in Emminger, *op. cit.* p. 170.

79. West German inflation averaged 1.7 per cent between 1967 and 1969. Between 1970 and 1972 the average was 4.7 per cent.

80. During the first five months of 1971, DM19 billion of speculative hot money poured into West Germany, following DM22 billion in 1970. The resulting increase in international banking liquidity was one of the factors behind worldwide inflationary pressures.

81. In the meantime the Americans took the historic step, announced by President Nixon on 15.8.71, of 'temporarily' ending the dollar's gold convertibility.

82. Simultaneously, the government, in agreement with the Bundesbank, brought in the so-called Bardepot capital control system to stem speculative inflows into the D-Mark. The system, introduced on 1.3.72, laid down that German companies and individuals borrowing money abroad would have to deposit 40 per cent of the proceeds with the German authorities.

83. Schiller succeeded in slightly diluting the measure, and making it applicable only to fixed interest securities rather than to shares as well.

84. One important reason for the cabinet's acceptance of Klasen's proposals was the Bundesbank president's promise that capital controls would guarantee peace on the external economic front at least until the general elections in September 1972. Emminger, *op. cit.* p. 222.

85. In a letter to Schiller after he had tendered his resignation, Brandt said the dispute concerned 'a marginal decision'. Klasen – who

The Bundesbank

took over in 1970 at the personal suggestion of Schiller – also played down the row in later public statements.

86. The final burst of speculative pressure on the D-Mark caused discord in the Bundesbank between Klasen, who favoured intervening to support the dollar, and the pro-floating faction led by Emminger. Klasen was ill in hospital for much of the crucial period, leaving Emminger (assisted by Schlesinger) to organise the Bundesbank's lobbying in favour of abandoning fixed parities.

87. Interview with author in Hamburg, 5.7.91.

88. Schiller terms as a mistake his decision to take over both the finance ministry and economics ministry portfolios after the resignation of Axel Möller in 1971. 'It was too much. I not only had to stick up for principles of stability, but I also had to control spending against the desire of the spending ministers. I had double the number of opponents in cabinet.'

89. One important factor was the large amount of forced intervention by the Bundesbank in the four weeks leading up to the final breakdown of the fixed rate system at the beginning of March 1973. In this period, the Bundesbank took in DM20 billion worth of dollars – representing a highly inflationary boost to German money supply.

90. Speech in Bonn marking Klasen's retirement, 11.5.77.

91. Annual money stock targets have remained in force continually (albeit with sporadic changes in the way the target levels are announced and defined) since the end of 1974.

92. In *'Zehn Jahre Geldpolitik mit einem Geldmengenziel'*, *Öffentliche Finanzen und monetäre Ökonomie*, Frankfurt, 1985.

93. Emminger had already told Schmidt of the outcome of the last previous participation by a federal chancellor in a central council meeting, when Adenauer's plea against an increase in interest rates by the Bank deutscher Länder was rejected in October 1950. Schmidt took the warning to heart, delaying his visit to Frankfurt until the main lines of the EMS had been agreed in order to keep controversy to a minimum. Emminger, *op cit*. pp. 13–14.

94. Kohl's exchanges with the council during his visits to the Bundesbank were much more low key than during Schmidt's 1978 visit.

95. The author is indebted to Johan Baptist Schöllhorn for his recollection of Schmidt's speech. Interview in Kiel, 4.6.91. Other participants at the meeting on 30.11.78 consulted by the author include Leonhard Gleske, Hans Hermsdorf, Kurt Nemitz, Helmut Schmidt.

96. Information from participants at meeting on 30.11.78.

97. Interview with author in Hamburg, 5.7.91.

98. In keeping with the general understated tone of Bundesbank–government encounters, the threat was distinctly low-key. Some partici-

pants at the meeting do not remember that Schmidt's statement included such a passage.

99. 'Between the lines I made them aware that I could go to parliament . . . I was very cautious in my wording. It is unusual for me to be so diplomatic . . . Emminger and Pöhl clearly understood what I was hinting at. Others [on the central bank council] who were more provincial maybe didn't understand.' Interview with author in Hamburg, 4.6.91.

100. Emminger, *op. cit.* p. 364.

Chapter 8: The Challenge of Unity

1. Article in Bonn government press bulletin, 12.9.53.

2. Speech on 10.11.67 at ceremony in Frankfurt to mark the construction of the Bundesbank building, citing a Bundesbank proclamation sealed in the foundation stone.

3. Bundesbank leaflets distributed to 8.3 million households in the weeks before 1 July.

4. Information from Wendelin Hartmann, head of Bundesbank's organisation and administrative department. Interview with author in Frankfurt, 31.5.91

5. Erhard had recognised that 'a currency reordering in the Soviet zone, that is, an inclusion in our monetary system, will be imperative.' Essay published on 12.9.53.

6. Jürgen Möllemann, Kohl's economics minister in his 1991 cabinet, told an American audience in June 1991, 'If the dollar had been revalued by 300 to 400 per cent, even economies well used to competition would have experienced considerable setbacks.' Speech in Washington, 7.6.91.

7. Interview with author in Basle, 6.3.91.

8. Bundesbank report for 1991.

9. Interview with *Süddeutsche Zeitung*, 2.6.90.

10. The government's own optimistic forecasts were supported by the research of the country's leading banks. In a typical note on the costs of unification in February 1990, for instance, Dresdner Bank said: 'Inflationary expectations of 5 per cent and demands on the capital markets of DM100 bn a year are way beyond probability.'

11. Speech in Berlin, 3.10.90.

12. In February 1991, the coalition government agreed to raise about DM50 billion in extra taxes and social security contributions over a full year – one of the biggest taxation packages in German history.

13. See '*Die ostdeutsche Wirtschaftskrise: Ursachen und Lösungsstrategien*', Kiel Institute of World Economics, Holger Schmieding, 1991.

14. In 1950, two years after the birth of the D-Mark, there were 1.9 million out of work in West Germany.

15. Helmut Schmidt forecast in 1967 that unification on the basis of unrestricted access by West German companies to the East German market would drive East German companies 'to the wall'. Schmidt, *Beiträge*, 1967, pp. 536, 543.

16. Waigel estimated in June 1990 that the public sector would be required to pay DM40 billion to DM 60 billion to East Germany in 1991. Interview with *Süddeutsche Zeitung*, 2.6.90.

17. Speech by Johann Wilhelm Gaddum in Berlin, 27.3.92.

18. This forecast made in 1991 by Kurt Biedenkopf, prime minister of Saxony, met initial scepticism, but by 1992 looked increasingly plausible.

19. Includes Treuhand, railways and German Unity Fund (Fonds der deutschen Einheit). Estimate by Ifo economics research institute, May 1992.

20. Speech at East Germany's 40th anniversary celebrations in East Berlin, 6.10.89.

21. Interview with *Der Spiegel*, No. 33, 1990.

22. Interview with author in London, 30.3.90.

23. Article '*In der DDR lebt man besser*' on 13.10.53. This was part of the East Berlin authorities' efforts to convince workers in the east – who had just launched a failed uprising over falling living standards – that the grass on the western side was not, after all, greener.

24. Letter from Vocke to Adenauer, 21.10.53, BB/PF Vocke.

25. The author is grateful to Prof. Wolfrid Stoll of the Staatsbank for access to these documents.

26. Staatsbank report for 1966, version dated 29.12.67, St. A.

27. Report on relation between state budget and credit system, 4.3.75, St. A.

28. Staatsbank report on 'stability of the currency of the GDR' on 28.7.75, St. A.

29. Report dated '1989', St. A.

30. The Staatsbank report was paralleled by a dire memorandum from five leading East German officials in September 1989 pointing out that East Germany was already 'virtually dependent on capitalistic lenders in the west'.

31. Interview with author in East Berlin, 13.5.91.

32. Interview with author in Buchholz, 13.5.91.

33. In an attempt to win time during the unification process, in early 1990 the East Berlin government put forward a plan to make the Staatsbank independent of government. As part of this scheme, the East

Mark would be turned into a convertible currency during a two-year period.

34. German TV interview, 19.4.90.

35. Just seven months before the breaching of the Berlin Wall, Pöhl stated that it might take 50 years for the border between East and West Germany to become normal 'like the one with, say, Belgium'. Interview with author in Kronberg, 6.2.89.

36. Claus Köhler plan for currency reform, 22.11.89.

37. By early February 1990, 63,000 East Germans had departed to settle in the west since the beginning of the year, compared with the total of 344,000 during the whole of 1989.

38. Interview with *Die Zeit*, 26.1.90.

39. Interview with author in Frankfurt, 29.1.90.

40. Information from Horst Kaminsky. Interview with author in East Berlin, 13.5.91.

41. De Maizière said later of the 1 for 1 suggestion: 'He [Schlesinger] was decidedly against it.' Interview with author in Bonn, 18.6.91.

42. Interview with *Der Spiegel*, 26.2.90.

43. Interview with author in Frankfurt, 20.6.90.

44. Information from Teltschik. In his book on the process of reunification *329 Tage*, Teltschik weakens the impression that Kohl radically changed his mind on 6 February. He states that the meeting on 5 February came to the conclusion that immediate currency union could 'no longer' be excluded.

45. On 5 February, Dieter Vogel, the government spokesman, issued a tough statement which reflected Kohl's thinking. He said East Germany would have to decide 'rigorous' measures in the direction of a market economy as a condition for introduction of the D-Mark. Merely implanting the West German currency into the east, without accompanying steps, 'would neither increase the competitiveness of the East German economy nor stop emigration [to the west]', Vogel said.

46. The meeting was with the East German Christian 'Alliaaz' trio who were spearheading the election campaign: Wolfgang Schnur, Lothar de Maizière, and Hans-Wilhelm Ebeling.

47. Hans Modrow, the East German prime minister, told Kohl at an international business gathering at Davos in the Swiss Alps the previous weekend that thousands were still ready to leave. He requested DM15 billion in bridging funds from Bonn to tide East Germany over its economic difficulties. The request was turned down when Modrow visited Kohl in Bonn later in February.

48. Kohl's decision had as much to do with politics as with economics. On Tuesday morning, the chancellor learned – to his irritation – that Lothar Späth, the prime minister of the Christian Democrat-

controlled state of Baden-Württemberg, was due that week to propose currency union in a government declaration in Stuttgart. The chancellor decided to pre-empt the Baden-Württemberg premier by announcing the proposal first.

49. Interview with author in Gütersloh, 24.6.91.

50. As another sign of disarray in Bonn's ranks over the plan, Kohl suggested accelerated union on 6 February at the same time as Helmut Haussmann, the economics minister, was publicly proclaiming a gradual plan for monetary union by the end of 1992.

51. Statement to Bundestag, 15.2.90.

52. Interview with author in London, 30.3.90.

53. Interview with author in London, 30.3.90.

54. German TV interview, 18.6.90.

55. According to a forecast by the Organisation for Economic Cooperation and Development in July 1990, East Germany would take at least 15 years to catch up with the west, based on growth rates of 7.5 per cent – equivalent to growth in western Germany during the 1950s. If economic growth in eastern Germany were only 5 per cent, 30 years would elapse before economic performance in the two parts of Germany equalised.

56. Interview with author in Gütersloh, 24.6.91.

57. Interview with author in Bonn, 7.5.91.

58. Interview with author in Bonn, 28.4.91.

59. Press conference in Bonn, 28.2.91.

60. Press conference in Bonn, 9.2.90.

61. The change-over – adding DM180 billion to Germany's M3 money supply of roughly DM1.2 trillion – produced a money supply increase of about 15 per cent.

62. Interview with author in Bonn, 18.6.91.

63. See for instance interview with Walter Romberg, the East German finance minister, *Die Zeit*, 11.5.90.

64. Speech in Frankfurt on 11.6.91.

65. Information from Wendelin Hartmann. Interview with author in Frankfurt, 31.5.91.

66. The main haggling took place over the use of buildings in Berlin, Neubrandenburg, Schwerin and Leipzig.

67. Interview with *Hamburger Abendblatt*, 23.5.91.

68. Lecture in Kiel, 14.5.90. Hesse's comments were not given wide publicity until they were published in an article in *Handelsblatt* on 28.5.90.

69. Minutes of Bundesbank meeting, 31.5.91.

70. Interview with author in Hanover, 30.4.91.

71. The plan drawn up by Karl Blessing and Heinrich Troeger,

president and vice-president respectively, who put forward the proposal in January 1970, one month after they had retired. The plan was contained in a report summarising the 12 years during which Blessing and Troeger had held office together. Karl Klasen, the new president, did not take the idea seriously, and it was soon shelved. The proposal was formally rejected by the Bundesbank council on 10.3.70.

72. Pöhl had been beguiled by his facility with the English language into overstating his case. Had he spoken in German, before a German audience, he would almost certainly not have used the word *Katastrophe*.

73. As an example of their capacity for periodic misunderstanding the chancellor told his aides that, when the two men had last met in Bonn on 6.3.91, Pöhl had expressed his full agreement on the introduction of the D-Mark in July 1990.

74. Letter to Kohl on 21.3.91.

75. The news of the Bonn visits leaked out in the press only in the following week.

76. In discussion with the author in Bonn on 15.5.91.

77. Von Weizsäcker, by contrast, asked Pöhl to think again when the two met in Bonn on 7.5.91.

78. Interview with *Der Spiegel*, Number 37, 1991.

79. Report by Alain Boublil, *'Les Conséquences Economiques de l'Unification de l'Allemagne'*, 20.11.90.

Chapter 9: The Quest for Europe's Money

1. Article *'Die Reichsbank im größeren Deutschland'*, in *Der Vierjahresplan*, April 1938, BAP/RB 25.01/7037.

2. Speech on 11.2.65 in Saarbrücken.

3. Press conference in Bonn, 1.7.91.

4. This point has been put with greatest clarity by André Szasz, an executive director of the Nederlandsche Bank, and one of the most experienced officials in European central banking. Giving evidence to a session of the Bundestag finance committee on 18.9.91, he said: 'With the establishment of economic and monetary union, Germany – in contrast to most other EC states – would actually give up sovereignty, in that it would renounce its dominant role in European monetary policy.'

5. For this reason, the name of the Maas river figures in the first verse (these days, no longer sung) of the *Deutschlandlied*, the German national anthem, composed in 1841.

6. The author covered the Maastricht summit meeting for the *Financial Times*.

7. Political leaders of the EC countries first announced their inten-

tion to proceed to economic and monetary union within a decade at a summit meeting in the Netherlands on 1–2.12.69.

8. The 'snake' set fluctuation bands of 2.25 per cent either way of a central rate. Members also included two Scandinavian countries which were not members of the EC, Sweden and Norway.

9. Compared with the 'snake', the EMS represented a more formal system of 'fixed but adjustable' exchange rates, backed by increased support and credit facilities. Fluctuation bands were maintained at 2.25 per cent either side of a central rate, fixed in ECUs. Upper and lower fluctuation limits were set in terms of a 'parity grid' of bilateral exchange rates against all other currencies in the system. Members with particular problems in maintaining currency stability were allowed a 6 per cent band. Italy was a member under this wider margin arrangement from 1979 onwards, before crossing to the 'narrow band' in 1990. Spain when it joined in 1989, Britain in 1990 and Portugal in 1992 all participated with wider 6 per cent bands.

10. Interview with author in Hamburg, 26.6.87. Schmidt had an extremely good relationship with James Callaghan, the British prime minister in 1979 who decided not to take sterling into the EMS. But Schmidt was constantly critical of Britain's refusal to join right up until the end of Margaret Thatcher's premiership during the 1980s. In the light of Thatcher's later rejection of the EMS, her remark in the House of Commons in 1979, commenting on Callaghan's refusal to join at the outset, was particularly ironic. Callaghan's failure to bring sterling into the system was 'a sad day for Europe', she said.

11. The EMS experienced seven changes of currency bands during its first four years in operation (between March 1979 and March 1983), mostly involving upwards moves of the D-Mark against weaker currencies led by the French franc, Danish crown and Italian lira. After the March 1983 realignment, there were just four reshapings of currency rates up to January 1987, of which only two (in April 1986 and January 1987) were major changes. Between January 1987 and September 1992, there was only one change in EMS rates – a small alteration involving the lira in January 1990. The volumes of central bank intervention – obligatory once currencies reach their permitted 'floors' – also slackened after 1987. The largest bout of intervention during the 1980s was the total DM5 billion worth of D-Mark sales carried out in early January 1987, the prelude to the following week's realignment.

12. At the time, the central role of the ECU was accepted by the Bundesbank. See, for example, Pöhl: 'That the ECU stands as the central point of the system has more than simply symbolic importance. Long term, this can lead to wide-ranging consequences . . .' in *'Neuer Anlauf für Europa'*, *Weltwoche*, 6.12.78

13. The basis for the central role of the D-Mark was laid at the Franco-German summit in Aachen in September 1978, shortly before the formal establishment of the EMS. The French and German governments agreed that currency fluctuation limits within the system would be defined in a 'parity grid' drawn up with floor and ceiling levels expressed in terms of individual currencies, rather than on the basis of percentage margins either side of central ECU rates. The Bundesbank had argued strongly in favour of the 'parity grid' system, since it would provide greater onus on weaker currency countries to take action to support their currencies. The French had argued for the ECU system for precisely the opposite reason.

14. Speech at St Paul's church in Frankfurt on 27.8.91.

15. The Bundesbank was in sporadic dispute with Chancellor Schmidt during the 1970s about Schmidt's wish to use Germany's high monetary reserves for loans to deficit countries – including, at one stage, the Soviet Union. The Bundesbank was intensely suspicious of the EMF plan for 'reserve pooling', and made a special effort to ensure that Schmidt did not have his way. Emminger, *op. cit.* p. 248.

16. The Bundesbank consented to making over 20 per cent of Germany's gold and dollar reserves to the European Monetary Cooperation Fund, to be used for settling intervention debts among the members of the system. But this was on a three-month 'swap' basis which could be revoked at the behest of the central bank, and entailed no permanent pooling of reserves.

17. As a former Banque de France official, Delors enjoyed good relations with the international central banking community.

18. The Act, setting the terms for the single market, was signed by all countries, including Britain, the only one of the 12 EC members which expressed serious misgivings about monetary union.

19. When the committee reported its findings to the EC's Madrid summit in June 1989, it firmly labelled the D-Mark the 'anchor' of the EMS arrangements: a phrase much quoted since by the Bundesbank.

20. Interview with author in Frankfurt, 29.6.89.

21. Interview with author in Frankfurt, 29.1.91.

22. Remarks to US–German economic policy group, 7.3.91.

23. Speech in Frankfurt, 11.6.91.

24. These conditions were expressed in relatively soft terms in the Maastricht treaty. The ceilings can be waived if a country's deficit is deemed 'only exceptional and temporary' or if the debt stock is approaching the 60 per cent figure 'at a satisfactory pace'.

25. The only countries allowed to participate would be those with inflation and interest rates within 1½ and 2 percentage points respectively of the three best performing EC states. Qualifying countries would

also have had to keep their currencies stable within the EMS mechanism during the previous two years.

26. When the EMS was set up in 1978, the Bundesbank welcomed the likelihood that not all Community members were likely to join the scheme: 'The absence of one or several "weaker" currencies is more likely to diminish the risks for internal and external stability,' said Pöhl in December 1978. Interview with *Welt am Sonntag*, 10.12.78.

27. Conversation with journalists in Maastricht, 9.12.91.

28. Underlining the Germans' opposition to the name of the Ecu, when the Maastricht text was printed, the government insisted that the name should be printed in capitals – ECU. This signified the acronym for the European Currency Unit, rather than the French word Ecu, and thus proved, according to Bonn, that no decision on the name of the currency had been taken.

29. *Bild*, 11.12.91.

30. *Der Spiegel*, December 1991.

31. Speech on Franco-German relations in Jouy-en-Josas, 3.12.91.

32. Statement on monetary union, September 1990.

33. Tietmeyer was pleased that he had inserted into the September 1990 statement the expression 'all for one and one for all' (in German: *auf Gedeih und Verderb*). This signified the finality of monetary union.

34. Remarks on NDR radio, 27.1.63.

35. Speech in Rotterdam, 8.11.91.

36. Apart from German monetary union in July 1990, Schlesinger cited as his other examples the unification of Germany in 1871, the *Anschluss* between Germany and Austria in 1938, and return of the Saarland to West Germany in 1957–59. In all three cases, he said, currency union came after a political union between the countries and regions.

37. Interview with author in Frankfurt, 15.4.91. The Bundesbank made its decision to 'participate constructively' in the monetary union campaign following the EC summit in Hanover in June 1988, which set up the 'Delors committee' to study the goal of Emu.

38. Speech to Ifo institute in Munich, 23.6.89.

39. Press conference in Bonn, 14.6.88.

40. Among the conditions, Kohl stated 'first and foremost' the priority towards monetary stability, followed by total independence from government, and an obligation towards convergence of economic and budgetary policies. Interview with author in London, 30.3.90.

41. The message was contained in a joint message, published on 19.4.90, to other EC leaders ahead of a special EC summit in Dublin to discuss German unity.

42. The Bundesbank, for instance, was particularly infuriated when

the chancellor agreed at an EC summit in Rome in October 1990 to establish on 1 January 1994 a new EC 'institution' which the French and Italians regarded as the forerunner of the EC central bank.

43. Speech in Paris to the Institut de l'Entreprise, 11.12.91.

44. Some members of the Bundesbank council were also irritated by a speech by Kohl on 13 December before the Bundestag, in which he added to the general confusion about the Maastricht outcome. On the one hand, he declared that realisation of monetary union depended on member states fulfilling the Maastricht conditions. On the other hand, Kohl suggested that union was already an 'irreversible' *fait accompli*. 'Europe will have, in 1997 or 1999, a common currency.'

45. Remarks at dinner in London, 17.12.91.

46. Telephone conversation with author, 28.1.92.

47. Jochimsen of the North Rhine-Westphalia central bank went so far as to produce his own draft paper on the EMU accord.

48. News of the Bundesbank statement appeared in the *Financial Times* on 29.1.92.

49. Statement published in monthly report for February 1992. It was released by the Bundesbank at a press conference on 7.2.92.

50. Article in *Der Tagesspiegel*, 14.12.91.

51. Interview with *Finanz und Wirtschaft*, 21.12.92.

52. Article in *Bayerische Staatszeitung*, 10.1.92.

53. Speech in Hamburg, 15.1.92.

54. The Republicans won representation in the state parliament in Baden-Württemberg, while the German People's Union (DVU) achieved seats in Schleswig-Holstein.

55. Both the Republicans and the DVU made considerable political capital out of the uncertainty over the future of the currency.

56. Opinion polls in previous months had already pointed in a similar direction. In December 1991, an Allensbach survey indicated that 29 per cent of West Germans, and 35 per cent of East Germans, wanted the pace of European integration to slow down.

57. Speech to American Council on Germany, New York, 15.1.92.

58. Speech in Berlin, 10.1.92.

59. Poland, Czechoslovakia and Hungary have also declared their candidature, while a variety of smaller states – from Cyprus and Malta to the remnants of Yugoslavia – are also waiting in the wings.

60. Nölling, *Abschied von der D-Mark*, Hamburg, 1992.

61. See for instance Paul de Grauwe and Daniel Gros, 'Convergence and divergence in the Community's economy on the eve of economic and monetary union', in *Setting European Community Priorities 1991–92*, Centre for European Policy Studies, 1991.

62. Article in *Bankinformation und Genossenschaftsforum*, March 1991.

63. Speech in Frankfurt, 11.6.91.

64. Interview with *Der Spiegel*, number 15, 1992.

65. Speech at foreign exchange conference in Amsterdam, 27.11.91.

66. Interview in *Financial Times*, 21.4.92. Schäuble's comments showed striking parallels with a statement in 1978 by Hans Matthöfer, the finance minister. Matthöfer put forward an overriding political motive for West Germany's support for the EMS. 'As a country which is vulnerable at various points – I need only mention Berlin – we need to be firmly embedded in the European Community and the Atlantic alliance.' Interview with *Deutsche Zeitung Christ und Welt*, 1.12.78.

67. Interview with author in Hamburg, 4.6.91.

68. Italy devalued by 7 per cent, effective 14.9.92. The subsequent British and Italian decisions to float their currencies resulted, by early October 1992, in a 16 per cent D-Mark revaluation against the lira, and one of 13 per cent against sterling. Against the peseta, the D-Mark rose by 10 per cent.

69. The Bundesbank took in DM92 billion worth of foreign exchange in September 1992.

70. On 15.9.92 – the day after the lira devaluation – Schlesinger dropped a hint in a newspaper interview about the possible need for a further realignment. Although he took care not to mention any specific threat to the pound, Schlesinger's warning, when communicated to the foreign exchange market via news agencies, was enough to trigger a heavy run on sterling.

71. In September 1990, a month before Britain's ERM entry, Karl Otto Pohl gave an indication of the difficulties likely to arise if sterling joined at too high a rate. He remarked that British membership of the system could confront the UK with 'mass unemployment and enormous payments problems.' After sterling's exit, Pöhl commented still more bluntly: 'The UK joined the ERM with the wrong rate at the wrong time.' Speech in Washington, 20.9.92.

72. Schlesinger was well aware that the need for currency adjustments would probably set back the international anti-inflation effort. At the height of the September 1992 turmoil, he recorded dispassionately: 'Countries which have, not without success, mounted domestic battles against inflation would, by devaluing, place at risk the success of these policies. They have good reason to try to avoid this solution. But that is not always possible.' Speech in Kiel, 14.9.92.

73. Speech in Hachenburg, 20.10.92.

Chapter 10: Skirmishes ahead

1. Letter to Fritz Schäffer, finance minister, 7.3.50, BB CF/Vocke.

2. Remarks in NDR radio programme, 27.1.63.

3. Press conference in Frankfurt, 7.2.92.

4. Speech on 10.11.67 at ceremony to unveil foundation stone. The stone can be seen today in the reception area on the ground floor of the main Bundesbank building.

5. '*Stehe fest! Dem deutsche Volk zum Nutzen und Glück! Zum Segen für alle, die hier ein- und ausgehen werden.*'

6. According to OECD statistics, annual economic growth between 1971 and 1990 averaged 2.4 per cent in West Germany, against 2.3 per cent in Britain, 2.8 per cent in France and the US and 4.4 per cent in Japan. Average growth across the whole of the 24 nation OECD was 3.5 per cent during this period.

7. Between 1973 and 1990, West Germany's unemployment rate rose from 0.8 per cent of the labour force to 5.1 per cent, according to the OECD's standardised unemployment data. For the US, the rise was from 4.8 per cent to 5.4 per cent; for Japan, 1.3 per cent to 2.1 per cent; for France, 2.7 per cent to 8.9 per cent; Italy, 6.2 per cent to 9.9 per cent; UK, 3.0 per cent to 6.9 per cent.

8. A number of international studies point to the link between central banking independence and success in anti-inflation efforts. See A. Alesina and L. Summers, Central Banking Independence and Macro-economic Performance: Some Comparative Evidence, Harvard University, Discussion Paper No. 1496.

9. Interview with *The Spectator*, 12.7.90. Because soon-to-be-unified Germany was growing 'uppity', Ridley also suggested that Britain should resort to its time-honoured role of playing 'the balance of power' in Europe. He indirectly compared Karl Otto Pöhl, the Bundesbank president, with Adolf Hitler.

10. The 1949 *Grundgesetz* laid down the overriding goal of reaching 'the unity and freedom of Germany' within a united Europe.

11. This point of view was put convincingly by Leonhard Gleske, the former Bundesbank director responsible for international monetary affairs, in a paper published in 1990, '*Institutionelle Aspekte einer Europäischen Wirtschafts- und Währungsunion*'. Gleske however admitted that turning the Bundesbank into the European central bank, and making the D-Mark into Europe's currency (although with a different name), would be 'politically unacceptable for most of our partners'.

Appendix

A. Personnel records

I. Members of Bank deutscher Länder/Bundesbank council & directorate and of *Land* boards who took up posts between 1948 and 1980

Key:
(R) indicates former Reichsbank official
first date after name is date of birth
N. indicates Nazi party member, with date joined and membership number
* member of central bank council
BB. Bundesbank
BdL. Bank deutscher Länder
D. directorate member
LZB. *Landeszentralbank*
MB. board member (at *Landeszentralbank*)
N(a) applied for Nazi membership, unclear if accepted
N(r) applied for Nazi membership but rejected
P. president
PC. president of council
PD. president of directorate
R. former Reichsbank official
SS. Schutzstaffel member
VP. vice-president
Z. Zentralbank (Berlin)

1. Adamski, Ernst, 13.12.18, VP.LZB Rheinland-Pfalz, 1975–82.
2. * Benning, Bernhard, 17.9.02, D.BdL/BB, 1950–72.
3. * Bernard, Karl, 8.4.90, PC.BdL, 1948–57.
4. Bernhuber, Maximilian (R), 7.8.98. N. 1940/8531823, VP.LZB Bayern, 1954–64.
5. Bertuch, Fritz, 2.10.98, MB.LZB Hamburg, 1951–54.

6. * Blessing, Karl (R), 5.2.00, N. 1937/5917306, D.R, 1937–39, P.BB, 1958–69.

7. * Boden, Wilhelm, 5.3.90, P.LZB Rheinland-Pfalz, 1947–49.

8. Böttcher, Reinhold (R), 21.1.95, MB.LZB Nordrhein-Westfalen, 1948–58.

9. Braune, Kurt (R), 29.9.91, N. 1940/7466047, MB.LZB Nordrhein-Westfalen, 1948–58.

10. * Bröker, Leopold, 5.6.06, N. 1937/3801133, P.LZB Hessen, 1958–74.

11. * Burkhardt, Otto, 3.8.94, P.LZB Schleswig-Holstein, 1948–60.

12. Cahn-Garnier, Fritz, 20.6.89, P.LZB Württemberg-Baden, 1947–48.

13. * Dahlgrün, Hans-Georg, 21.12.01, N. 1937/4575679, P.LZB Rheinland-Pfalz, 1959–69.

14. Dejon, Fridolin (R), 7.11.83, VP.LZB Schleswig-Holstein, 1948–58.

15. Diehl, Alphons (R), 18.8.99, MB.LZB Rheinland-Pfalz, 1948–59, VP.LZB Hessen, 1960–64.

16. Dietze, Helmut (R), 14.1.13, N. 1937/4301871, VP.LZB Hamburg, 1974–78.

17. * Dingwort-Nusseck, Julia, 6.10.21, P.LZB Niedersachsen, 1976–88.

18. * Duppre, Fritz, 30.1.19, P.LZB Rheinland-Pfalz, 1969–85.

19. * Emde, Hans Georg, 28.7.19, D.BB, 1973–87.

20. * Emminger, Otmar, 2.3.11, N. 1937/5226547, D.BdL/BB, 1953–69, VP.BB, 1970–77, P.BB, 1977–79.

21. Ernst, Konrad, 20.1.03, MB.LZB Niedersachsen, 1952, MB/VP.LZB Hamburg, 1954–67.

22. * Fessler, Ernst, 23.8.08, N. 1933/2132836, MB.LZB Niedersachsen, 1951–53, VP/P.LZB Nordrhein-Westfalen, 1953–76.

23. * Frede, Karl, (R) 12.3.03, N. 1940/8182865, BM/VP/P.LZB Württemberg-Hohenzollern, 1947–52, MB/VP.LZB Baden-Württemberg, 1953–58.

24. * Geiselhart, Pankraz (R), 6.7.99, N. 1941, MB/VP/P.LZB Nordrhein-Westfalen, 1949–56.

25. * Gleimius, Rudolf, 3.3.90, P.Z/LZB Berlin, 1949–59.

26. * Gleske, Leonhard, 18.9.21, P.LZB Bremen, 1964–76, D.BB, 1976–89.

27. * Gocht, Rolf, 3.7.13, D.BB, 1967–75.

28. * Grasmann, Max, 20.6.89, P.LZB Bayern, 1947–55.

29. Gulden, Walter, 13.2.26, N. 1944/10115602, BM.LZB Bayern, 1978–.

30. * Gust, Werner, 3.5.10, N. 1937/4511801, VP/P.LZB Berlin, 1958–78.

31. * Härtl, Alfred, 1925, P.LZB Hessen, 1974–90.

32. * Hartlieb, Heinrich (R), 7.7.00, VP.LZB Bayern, 1947–53, D.BdL/BB, 1954–65.

33. Hauptmann, Gerhard, 9.12.26, VP.LZB Niedersachsen, 1968–84.

34. Hecker, Wolfgang (R), 12.1.04, N. 1940/8157639, VP.LZB Schleswig-Holstein, 1964–69.

35. Heimann, Clemens, 8.9.17, N. 1937/5275229, MB.LZB Nordrhein-Westfalen, 1967–70.

36. Heinritzi, Curt (R), 13.8.02, N. 1937/4917993, BM/VP.LZB Nordrhein-Westfalen, 1963–67.

37. * Henckel, Hans, 23.1.06, N. 1933/2956359, D.BB, 1966–67.

38. * Hermsdorf, Hans, 23.12.14, P.LZB Hamburg, 1974–82.

39. Hesselbach, Walter, 20.1.15, MB.LZB Hessen, 1952–57.

40. * Hinckel, Eugen Christian, 6.2.82, P.LZB Baden, 1947–52.

41. * Hiss, Dieter, 10.7.30, P.LZB Berlin, 1978–.

42. Holzmaier, Helmut, 13.6.25, N. 1943/9404965, MB.LZB Baden-Württemberg, 1978–90.

43. * Hoose, York (R), 27.3.11, MB/P.LZB Niedersachsen, 1948–62.

44. * Hülse, Ernst (R), 29.6.81, D.R, 1935–39, P.LZB Nordrhein-Westfalen, 1948–49.

45. Hüttl, Adolf, 9.3.23, VP.LZB Hessen, 1969–85.

46. * Irmler, Heinrich (R), 27.8.11, MB/VP.LZB Niedersachsen, 1953–57, VP.LZB Nordrhein-Westfalen, 1958–62, P.LZB Niedersachsen, 1962–64, D.BB, 1964–79.

47. Jennemann, Gerhard, 21.2.24, VP.LZB Hamburg, 1978–1989.

48. * Kähler, Otto (R), 17.4.05, MB/VP/P.LZB Schleswig-Holstein, 1951–73.

49. Kaiser, Johannes (R), 19.5.80, N. 1937/4058292, VP.LZB Hamburg, 1948–51.

50. Karnstädt, Hans, 2.5.03, N. 1940/7465083, MB/VP.LZB Niedersachsen, 1959–68.

51. Kilian, Hans, 26.2.83, N(r), VP.LZB Württemberg-Baden, 1947–52.

52. * Klasen, Karl, 23.4.09, P.LZB Hamburg, 1948–52, P.BB, 1970–77.

53. * Kloten, Norbert, 12.3.26, P.LZB Baden-Württemberg, 1976–92.

54. * Köhler, Claus, 5.3.28, D.BB, 1974–90.

55. * Könneker, Wilhelm (R), 18.2.98, VP.LZB Hessen, 1947–48, VP/D.BdL, 1948–57, D.BB, 1958–66.

56. Krause, Richard (R), 3.4.98, N. 1937/5727953, MB.LZB Schleswig-Holstein, 1948–51, MB/VP.LZB Niedersachsen, 1958–62.

57. * Kriege, Walter, 15.3.91, N(r), P.LZB Nordrhein-Westfalen, 1950–52.

58. Krug, Edgar, 17.3.31, MB.LZB Nordrhein-Westfalen, 1978–.

59. Kürzel, Alfred, 25.5.01, N. 1939/7311986, MB.LZB Württemberg-Hohenzollern, 1948–52.

60. Küspert, Erich, 12.4.13, N. 1937/4335936, MB/VP.LZB Bayern, 1963–78.

61. Kulla, Walter, 24.10.28, MB/VP.LZB Hessen, 1974–.

62. Lange, Erich, 25.2.18, VP.LZB Schleswig-Holstein, 1977–81.

63. * Leist, Erich, 15.2.92, VP.LZB Nordrhein-Westfalen, 1948–51, P.LZB Niedersachsen, 1951–52, P.LZB Hamburg, 1952–57.

64. Lippert, Georg, 15.8.13, VP.LZB Saarland, 1972–78.

65. * Lucht, Werner, 7.4.10, N. 1933/2585578, MB.LZB Baden-Württemberg, 1959–66, D.BB, 1966–78.

66. Lutze, Hans Günther, 1.12.07, MB.Z Berlin, 1950–58, MB.LZB Niedersachsen, 1959–60.

67. Mees, Jürgen, 6.3.26, VP.LZB Hamburg, 1968–74.

68. Möckel, Hellmut, 21.4.93, N(r), MB.LZB Württemberg-Baden, 1947–52, VP.LZB Baden-Württemberg, 1953–57.

69. * Müller, Lothar, 27.1.27, P.LZB Bayern, 1979–.

70. * Mürdel, Karl (R), 4.8.94, N. 1937/4728865, P.LZB Württemberg-Hohenzollern, 1947–52, BM.LZB Bayern, 1952–59.

71. * Nemitz, Kurt, 10.7.25, P.LZB Bremen, 1976–92.

72. Oechsner, Friedrich (R), 29.9.02, N. 1933/3561949, MB.LZB Württemberg-Hohenzollern, 1952, MB/VP.LZB Bayern, 1959–67.

73. Offner, Walter, 11.7.12, MB.LZB Baden-Württemberg, 1968–77.

74. Paduch, Paul, 21.8.07, N. 1933/1882141, VP.LZB Saarland, 1967–72.

75. Paersch, Fritz (R), 4.3.93, VP.LZB Hessen, 1949–57.

76. * Pfleiderer, Otto, 17.1.04, P.LZB Württemberg-Baden, 1948–52, P.LZB Baden-Württemberg, 1953–72.

77. * Pöhl, Karl Otto, 1.12.29, VP.BB, 1977–79, P.BB, 1980–91.

78. Prein, Otto (R), 14.5.91, N. 1940/7403588, BM.LZB Baden, 1947–52.

79. Preiß, Ludwig, 31.12.10, N. 1933/2515299, VP.LZB Bremen, 1971–75.

80. Prieß, Friedrich, 19.10.03, N. 1937/4874013, MB/VP.LZB Hamburg, 1950–52.

81. * Rahmsdorf, Wilhelm, 18.9.08, N. 1937/5252911, VP.LZB Nordrhein-Westfalen, 1962–64, P.LZB Niedersachsen, 1964–76.

82. Röthemeier, Helmut, 24.12.26, N. 1944/9779345, VP.LZB Nordrhein-Westfalen, 1978–91.

83. Rohland, Bernhard, 23.1.12, N. 1933/34844291, VP.LZB Rheinland-Pfalz, 1966–74.

84. Rothenbücher, Heinz-Georg, 6.11.12, MB.LZB Bayern, 1947–52.

85. Ruppert, Heinz (R), 10.6.12, N(a), NP.LZB Schleswig-Holstein, 1969–77.

86. Sandler, August, 19.2.05, N. 1940/7380910, MB.LZB Baden-Württemberg, 1959.

87. Schack, Wilhelm, 23.4.86 (R), N. 1939/7333859, P.LZB Bremen, 1947–48.

88. * von Schelling, Friedrich Wilhelm (R), 3.5.06, N. 1940/8185105, P.LZB Hamburg, 1957–74.

89. * Schiettinger, Fritz, 12.8.09, N. 1933/3109855, P.LZB Baden-Württemberg, 1972–76.

90. * Schlesinger, Helmut, 4.9.24, D/VP/P.BB, 1972–.

91. Schmidt, Herwald, 25.2.24, VP.LZB Saarland, 1978–83.

92. Schmitt, Rudolf, 22.11.05, VP.LZB Bremen, 1958–70.

93. * Schöllhorn, Johann Baptist, 16.3.22, P. LZB Schleswig-Holstein, 1973–89.

94. Schubert, Werner, 7.3.04, N. 1937/4363399, VP.LZB Hessen, 1964–69.

95. Schütz, Paul, 27.6.10, P.LZB Saarland, 1961–81.

96. * Sentz, Max, 25.1.86, P.LZB Niedersachsen, 1948–50.

97. Spilger, Wilhelm (R), 11.5.99, N. 1937/4312642, VP.LZB Schleswig-Holstein, 1958–64.

98. * Stadler, Kurt, 24.4.26, N. 1944/9740657, P.LZB Bayern, 1977–79.

99. * Suchan, Franz, 19.1.11, MB/VP/P.Z/LZB Berlin, 1950–71.

100. Szagunn, Volhard, 25.3.20, MB/VP.LZB Baden-Württemberg, 1966–85.

101. * Tepe, Hermann, 17.11.93, VP/P.LZB Bremen, 1947–63.

102. Thoma, Josef, 11.2.13, N. 1937/6993430, MB/VP.LZB Nordrhein-Westfalen, 1965–78.

103. Traeger, Franz, 1.7.81, VP.LZB Niedersachsen, 1948–51.

104. Tratzsch, Werner, 10.9.20, N. 1938/7011953, VP.LZB Berlin, 1971–85.

105. Treskow, Joachim, 25.3.19, VP.LZB Bremen, 1976–83.

106. Treue, Hans (R), 19.5.98, N. 1940/8015808, D.BdL, 1948–53.

107. * Troeger, Heinrich, 4.3.01, P.LZB Hessen, 1956–57, VP.BB, 1958–69.

108. * Tüngeler, Johannes (R), 23.11.07, D.BdL/BB, 1953–76.

109. * Veit, Otto, 29.12.89, P.LZB Hessen, 1947–52.

110. * Vocke, Wilhelm, 9.2.86, D.R, 1919–39, PD.BdL, 1948–57.

111. * Wagenhöfer, Carl, 24.2.10, P.LZB Bayern, 1956–77.

112. Weidmann, Eugen, 13.3.97, N. 1940/7550688, MB.LZB Württemberg-Baden, 1948–52.

113. Werner, Reinhold (R), 2.3.02, N. 1937/5378010, VP.LZB Saarland, 1959–67.

114. * Werthmöller, Ottomar, 3.5.26, MB.LZB Nordrhein-Westfalen, 1970–78, D.BB, 1978–91.

115. * Wertz, Hans, 4.7.22, P.LZB Nordrhein-Westfalen, 1976–90.

116. Wießer, Kurt, 18.3.13, N. 1933/2196040, MB.LZB Bayern, 1967–78.

117. Wilhelm, (Karl) Friedrich (R), 22.2.89, N. 1939/7312605, D.R, 1939–45, D.BdL, 1948–53.

118. Wilz, Anton (R), 28.11.01, N. 1940/7593898, MB/VP.LZB Rheinland-Pfalz, 1947–66.

119. Winckelmann, Johannes, 29.3.00, N. 1937/4057034, MB/LZB Hessen, 1948–50.

120. Windlinger, Rudolf (R), 30.1.04, MB.LZB Baden, 1947–52.

121. Wirmer, Otto, 14.8.03, MB.LZB Hessen, 1952–57.

122. * Wolf, Eduard, 1.6.03, D.BdL/BB, 1951–64.

123. * Wolfslast, Ernst Walter, 10.1.96, VP/P.LZB Hessen, 1951–54.

124. Wrede, Victor, 30.10.06, D.BdL, 1948–50.

125. * Zachau, Erich, 1.11.02, D.BdL/BB, 1948–72.

126. Zimmer, Herbert, 2.1.27, N. 1944/9767732, MB.LZB Bayern, 1978–86.

II. Members of Bundesbank council and of *Land* boards who took up positions after 1980

1. von der Ahe, Jürgen, VP.LZB Nordrhein-Westfalen, 1991–.

2. Dauzenroth, Erhard, 16.1.30, VP.LZB Saarland, 1984–.

3. Fabritius, Hans-Georg, 21.9.45, MB.LZB Hessen, 1989–.

4. Fein, Erich, VP.LZB Bayern, 1991–.

5. Flesch, Roman, 29.3.26, N. 1944/9706529, VP.LZB Niedersachsen, 1984–90.

6. * Gaddum, Johann Wilhelm, 18.6.30, P.LZB Rheinland-Pflalz, 1985–86, D.BB, 1986–.

7. * Gliem, Hans, 6.12.23, P.LZB Saarland, 1981–91.

8. * Grobecker, P.LZB Bremen, 1992–.†

9. * Hartmann, Wendelin, D.BB, 1992–.

10. Herrman, Hans-Georg, VP.LZB Bremen, 1992–.

† Did not take up post.

11. * Hesse, Helmut, 28.6.34, P.LZB Niedersachsen, 1988–.
12. * Homp, Helmut, 28.6.23, VP.LZB Schleswig-Holstein, 1982–88.
13. * Issing, Otmar, 27.3.36, D.BB, 1990–.
14. * Jochimsen, Reimut, 8.6.33, P.LZB Nordrhein-Westfalen, 1990–.
15. * Koebnick, Hans-Jürgen, 1.6.38, P.LZB Saarland, 1991–.
16. Kremers, Johannes, 29.8.30, VP.LZB Bremen, 1984–91.
17. Langefeld, Horst, VP.LZB Niedersachsen, 1991–.
18. Leopold, Bolko, VP.LZB Rheinland-Pflalz, 1990–.
19. * Nölling, Wilhelm, 17.11.33, P.LZB Hamburg, 1982–.
20. Oberndorfer, Dietger, 17.3.32, VP.LZB Berlin, 1985–.
21. * Schieber, Helmut, 25.6.38, VP.LZB Baden-Württemberg, 1985–92, D.BB, 1992–.
22. Schmid, Günter, MB.LZB Baden-Württemberg, 1991–.
23. * Schreiner, Heinrich, 28.6.27, P.LZB Rheinland-Pfalz, 1987–.
24. * Schulz, Werner, 24.7.36, P.LZB Schleswig-Holstein, 1989–.
25. Siegmund, Hans-Jürgen, VP.LZB Hamburg, 1989–.
26. * Storch, Günther, 2.2.26, D.BB, 1987–.
27. Ströhlein, Rudolf, 1.2.26, VP.LZB Bayern, 1986–90.
28. * Thomas, Karl, 7.1.29, P.LZB Hessen, 1990–.
29. * Tietmeyer, Hans, 18.8.31, D.BB, 1990–91, VP.BB, 1991–.
30. Titzhoff, Peter, 9.10.33, VP.LZB Schleswig-Holstein, 1988–.
31. Völlgraf, Heinz-Georg, 6.12.25, N. 1943/9495609, MB.LZB Hessen, 1985–89.
32. Weiler, Eberhard, 12.12.24, VP.LZB Rheinland-Pfalz, 1983–89.

III. Reichsbank directorate members during Third Reich with no further career at Bank deutscher Länder/Bundesbank

1. Bayrhoffer, Walter, 1.2.90, N. 1933/3019575, D.R. 1939–45, N. 1933.
2. Brinkmann, Rudolf, 28.8.93, SS. 1938/308241, D.R. 1937–38, VP.R 1939.
3. Dreyse, Friedrich Wilhelm, 12.11.74, D.R. 1924–26, VP.R. 1926–39.
4. Ehrhardt, Carl, D.R. 1934–39.
5. Emde, Paul, 25.11.82, N. 1933/2680559, D.R. 1939–45.
6. Funk, Walther, 18.8.90, N. 1931/551712, P.R. 1939–45.
7. Kretzschmann, Max, 6.3.90, N. 1937/3934028, D. R. 1937–45.
8. Lange, Kurt, 8.7.95, N. 1930/345284, VP.R. 1940–45.
9. Puhl, Emil, 28.8.89, N. 1937/5852526, D.R. 1934–40, VP.R. 1940–45.
10. Schacht, Hjalmar, 22.1.77, P.R. 1923–30 & 1933–39.
11. Schniewind, Otto, 15.8.87, D.R. 1937–38.

B. Economic growth of industrialised countries

	Germany*	UK	US	OECD
1971	3.0	2.0	2.8	3.5
1972	4.3	3.5	5.0	5.4
1973	4.8	7.1	5.2	6.0
1974	0.1	−1.5	−0.5	0.8
1975	−1.3	−0.7	−1.3	−0.1
1976	5.5	2.7	4.9	4.6
1977	2.6	2.3	4.7	3.8
1978	3.4	3.6	5.3	4.3
1979	4.0	2.7	2.6	3.6
1980	1.0	−1.7	−0.2	1.3
1981	0.1	−1.0	1.9	1.7
1982	−1.1	1.5	−2.5	−0.1
1983	1.9	3.5	3.6	2.6
1984	3.1	2.1	6.8	4.6
1985	1.8	3.5	3.4	3.4
1986	2.2	3.9	2.7	2.7
1987	1.5	4.8	3.4	3.4
1988	3.7	4.3	4.5	4.5
1989	3.8	2.3	2.5	3.3
1990	4.5	0.8	1.0	2.6
1991	3.1	−2.6	−0.7	0.3

*From 1990, west Germany only
source: OECD

C. German money supply* and inflation†
performance

	Money supply target** per cent	Actual outcome** per cent	Target met	Inflation rate per cent
1975	8	10	no	5.9
1976	8	9	no	4.3
1977	8	9	no	3.7
1978	8	11	no	2.7
1979	6–9	6	yes	4.1
1980	5–8	5	yes	5.5
1981	4–7	4	yes	6.3
1982	4–7	6	yes	5.2
1983	4–7	7	yes	3.3
1984	4–6	5	yes	2.4
1985	3–5	5	yes	2.0
1986	3.5–5.5	8	no	−0.1

1987	3–6	8	no	0.2
1988	3–6	7	no	1.3
1989	about 5	5	yes	2.8
1990	4–6	6	yes	2.7
1991	3–5	5.2	no	3.5

* Money supply definition: Up to 1988, central bank money stock.
From 1988, M3.
† Annual rise in cost of living index
** Target was set on a fourth quarter to fourth quarter basis for all
years except 1975 (December-to-December basis) and for 1976–78,
when target referred to the average growth in money supply during the
year.

D. The EC and the Maastricht criteria

	Inflation per cent	Budget deficit*	Govt debt*	In EMS?	Interest rate	Ready for Emu?
Belgium	3.2	6.3	129.4	yes	9.3	NO
Denmark	2.4	1.7	67.2	yes	10.1	YES ***
France	3.1	1.5	47.2	yes	9.0	YES
Germany	3.5	3.2	46.2	yes	8.6	YES **
Greece	18.9	17.9	96.4	no	19.5	NO
Ireland	3.2	4.1	102.8	yes	9.2	NO
Italy	6.4	9.9	101.2	yes	12.9	NO
Luxembourg	3.1	2.0	6.9	yes	8.2	YES
Netherlands	3.9	4.4	78.4	yes	8.9	NO
Portugal	11.3	5.4	64.7	no	17.1	NO
Spain	5.9	3.9	45.6	no	12.4	NO
UK	5.9	1.9	43.8	no	9.9	NO

All figures for 1991.

* per cent of gnp.
** YES because budget deficit inflated for exceptional reasons (German reunification).
*** YES because projections show movement towards government debt of 60 per cent of gnp.

Criteria for membership of Emu:
1. Inflation rate must not be more than 1.5 points above the average of the three lowest inflation rates (in 1991, 2.5 per cent).
2. General government budget deficit must not be more than 3 per cent of gross national product, apart from exceptional circumstances.
3. General government debt should not exceed 60 per cent of gnp, with exception of countries showing steady progress towards that target.
4. Countries must participate in 'narrow bands' of EMS.
5. Long term interest rates must not exceed by more than 2 points those of three lowest-inflation EC states.

Sources: Bundesbank, European Commission

Bibliography

Blessing, Karl, *Im Kampf um Gutes Geld*, Frankfurt, 1966.

Bower, Tom, *Blind Eye to Murder*, London, 1981.

Brawand, Leo, *Wohin steuert die deutsche Wirtschaft*, Munich, 1971.

Brüning, Heinrich, *Memoiren 1918–1934*, Stuttgart, 1970.

Coombs, Charlie, *The Arena of International Finance*, New York, 1976.

Crawley, Aidan, *The Rise of West Germany 1945–72*, London, 1973.

Czichon, Eberhard, *Der Bankier und die Macht*, Cologne, 1970.

Deutsche Bundesbank (ed.), *Währung und Wirtschaft in Deutschland 1876–1975*, Frankfurt, 1976.

—--, *40 Jahre Deutsche Mark: Monetäre Statistiken 1948–1987*, Frankfurt, 1988.

Dodd, William, E. Jr and Dodd, Martha, *Ambassador Dodd's Diary 1933–38*, New York, 1941.

Duewendag, Dieter (ed.), *Macht und Ohnmacht der Bundesbank*, Frankfurt, 1973.

Emminger, Otmar, *Währungspolitik im Wandel der Zeit*, Frankfurt, 1966.

— —, *D-Mark, Dollar, Währungskrisen*, Stuttgart, 1986.

Erhard, Ludwig, *Wohlstand für Alle*, Düsseldorf, 1957.

— —, *Deutsche Wirtschaftspolitik*, Düsseldorf, 1962.

Fischer, Wolfram (ed.) *Währungsreform und Soziale Marktwirtschaft*, Berlin, 1989.

Flink, Salamon, *The German Reichsbank and Economic Germany*, New York, 1930.

Fürstenberg, Hans, *Carl Fürstenberg, Die Lebensgeschichte eines deutschen Bankiers*, Wiesbaden, 1961.

Gievius, Hans Bernd, *To The Bitter End*, Boston, 1947.

Gilbert, Milton, *Quest for World Monetary Order*, New York, 1980.

Goebbels, Joseph (ed. Hugh Trevor-Roper), *The Goebbels Diary – The Last Days*, London, 1978.

Helfferich, Karl, *Geschichte der deutschen Geldreform*, Leipzig, 1898.

Hitler, Adolf, *Hiter's Table Talk*, London, 1953.

Holtfrerich, Carl-Ludwig, *Die deutsche Inflation 1914–23*, Berlin, 1980.

International Military Tribunal, *Der Prozess gegen die Hauptkriegsverbrecher vor dem internationalen Militärgerichtshof*, 42 volumes, Nuremberg, 1947–49.

James, Harold, *The Reichsbank and Public Finance in Germany 1924–1933*, Frankfurt, 1985.

– –, *A German Identity*, London, 1989.

Kennedy, Ellen, *The Bundesbank: Germany's Central Bank in the International Monetary System*, London, 1991.

Koerfer, Daniel, *Kampf ums Kanzleramt*, Stuttgart, 1987.

Ludlow, Peter, *The Making of the European Monetary System*, London, 1982.

Luther, Hans, *Vor dem Abgrund 1930–33*, Berlin, 1964.

Mühlen, Norbert, *Hitler's Magician*, New York, 1939.

Müller, Helmut, *Die Zentralbank – Eine Nebenregierung: Reichsbankspräsident Hjalmar Schacht als Politiker der Weimarer Republik*, Opladen, 1973.

Nölling, Wilhelm, *Abschied von der D-Mark?*, Hamburg, 1992.

Northrop, Mildred, *Control Policies of the Reichsbank 1924–33*, New York, 1932.

Oestreich, Paul, *Walther Funk, Ein Leben für die Wirtschaft*, Munich, 1941.

Pentzlin, Heinz, *Hjalmar Schacht, Leben und Wirkung einer umstrittener Persönlichkeit*, Berlin, 1980.

Petersen, Edward Norman, *Hjalmar Schacht: For and Against Hitler*, Boston, 1954.

Pohl, Manfred, *Hermann J. Abs, Eine Bildbiographie*, Wiesbaden, 1981.

Reuter, Franz, *Schacht*, Leipzig, 1934.

Riehl, Hans, *Die Mark*, Hanover, 1978.

Riese, Hajo and Spahn, Heinz-Peter, *Geldpolitik und ökonomische Entwicklung*, Berlin.

Ritter, Gerhard, *Carl Goerdeler und die deutsche Widerstandsbewegung*, Stuttgart, 1954.

Roeper, Hans, *Die D-Mark: Besatzsungsgeld zum Weltstar*, Frankfurt, 1978.

Schacht, Hjalmar, *Die Stabilisierung der Mark*, Berlin/Leipzig, 1927.

— —, *Das Ende der Reparationen*, Oldenburg, 1931.

— —, *Abrechnung mit Hitler*, Hamburg, 1948.

— —, *1933 – Wie eine Demokratie stirbt*, Düsseldorf, 1968.

— —, *76 Jahre meines Lebens*, Bad Wörishofen, 1953.

— —, *Die Politik der Deutschen Bundesbank*, Munich, 1970.

von Schelling, Friedrich Wilhelm, *Die Bundesbank in der Inflation: Plädoyer für eine neue Geldverfassung*, Frankfurt, 1975.

Schmidt, Helmut, *Menschen und Mächte*, Berlin, 1987.

Schmidt, Paul, *Statist auf diplomatischer Bühne*, Bonn, 1949.

Shirer, William, *The Rise and Fall of the Third Reich*, New York, 1960.

Speer, Albert *Inside the Third Reich*, London, 1970.

— —, *The Slave State*, London, 1981.

von Spindler, Joachim, et al., *Die Deutsche Bundesbank*, Stuttgart, 1960.

Teltschik, Horst, *329 Tage, Innenansichten der Einigung*, Berlin, 1991.

Thyssen, Fritz, *I Paid Hitler*, New York, 1941.

Toniolo, Gianni (ed.), *Central Banks' Independence in Historical Perspective*, Berlin/New York, 1988.

US Printing Office, *Trials of War Criminals before the Nuremberg Tribunals, October 1946–April 1949*, Washington, 1949–50.

Veit, Otto, *Die Zukunft des Geldes*, Berlin, 1937.

— —, *Grundriss der Währungspolitik*, Frankfurt, 1961.

Vocke, Wilhelm, *Gesundes Geld*, Frankfurt, 1956.

— —, *Memoiren*, Stuttgart, 1973.

Vogelsang, Reinhard, *Der Freundeskreis Himmler*, Göttingen, 1973.

Wallich, Henry, *Mainsprings of the German Revival*, New Haven, 1955.

Wandel, Eckard, *Die Entstehung der Bank deutscher Länder und die Währungsreform*, Frankfurt, 1980.

Zilch, Reinhard, *Die Reichsbank und die finanzielle Kriegsvorbereitung von 1907 bis 1914*, Berlin, 1988.

Index

A Selected List of Business Titles Available from Mandarin

While every effort is made to keep prices low, it is sometimes necessary to increase prices at short notice. Mandarin Paperbacks reserves the right to show new retail prices on covers which may differ from those previously advertised in the text or elsewhere.

The prices shown below were correct at the time of going to press.

☐	7493 0840 0	**Inner Game of Selling Yourself**	James Borg £5.99
☐	7493 0217 8	**Datatheft**	Hugo Cornwall £5.99
☐	7493 0355 7	**New Realities**	Peter Drucker £4.99
☐	7493 0093 0	**Agnelli**	Alan Friedman £4.99
☐	7493 1026 X	**The Billion Dollar Battle: Merck v Glaxo**	Matthew Lynn £5.99
☐	7493 0455 3	**The Risk Takers**	Jeffrey Robinson £4.99
☐	7493 0276 3	**A-Z of Sales Management**	John Fenton £4.99
☐	7493 0253 4	**How to Double Your Profits**	John Fenton £4.99
☐	7493 0459 6	**101 Ways to Boost Your Performance**	John Fenton £4.99
☐	7493 0095 7	**So You Think You Can Cope With Customers**	Video Arts £5.99
☐	7493 1042 1	**So You Think You Can Manage**	Video Arts £5.99
☐	7493 1043 X	**So You Think You Can Sell**	Video Arts £5.99
☐	4135 8270 1	**So You Think You're in Business**	Video Arts £4.95

All these books are available at your bookshop or newsagent, or can be ordered direct from the publisher. Just tick the titles you want and fill in the form below.

Mandarin Paperbacks, Cash Sales Department, PO Box 11, Falmouth, Cornwall TR10 9EN.

Please send cheque or postal order, no currency, for purchase price quoted and allow the following for postage and packing:

UK including BFPO £1.00 for the first book, 50p for the second and 30p for each additional book ordered to a maximum charge of £3.00.

Overseas including Eire £2 for the first book, £1.00 for the second and 50p for each additional book thereafter.

NAME (Block letters) ....

ADDRESS..

....

☐ I enclose my remittance for ....

☐ I wish to pay by Access/Visa Card Number ☐☐☐☐☐☐☐☐☐☐☐☐☐☐

Expiry Date ☐☐☐☐